owac

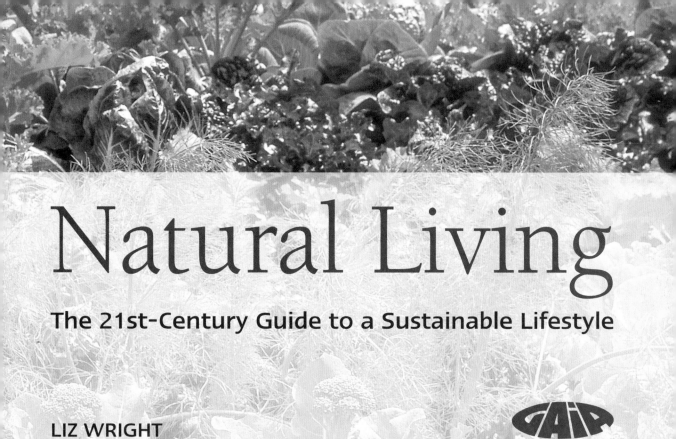

Natural Living

The 21st-Century Guide to a Sustainable Lifestyle

LIZ WRIGHT

To Mick, Buffy the cat, and my mother, Paddy Beale, a keen gardener and cook.

An Hachette UK Company
www.hachette.co.uk

First published in Great Britain in 2010 by
Endeavour House, 189 Shaftesbury Avenue, London, WC2H 8JG
www.octopusbooksusa.com

Copyright © Octopus Publishing Group Ltd 2010

Distributed in the U.S. and Canada by Octopus Books USA:
c/o Hachette Book Group, 237 Park Avenue, New York, NY 10017

ISBN 978-1-856-75320-3

A CIP catalogue record for this book is available from the British Library

Printed and bound in China

10 9 8 7 6 5 4 3 2 1

Note

The views expressed in the book are those of the Author but they are general views only and are not those held by the Publisher and you are urged to consult a relevant and qualified specialist for individual advice in particular situations.

Many wild plants are poisonous, even fatally poisonous. Foragers should always identify by all indicators before using plants obtained from the wild. Different plants might look very similar to the untrained eye. If you do collect wild plants to use at home make sure that all of the identification checks for each species are carried out in detail to avoid poisonous look-alikes. If in any doubt do not use the wild plant. Beginners should have their own identifications checked by an expert in the field.

The Publisher does not warrant or guarantee the accuracy or completeness of the advice in this book. The reader's use of the content, for whatever purpose, is at their own risk.

Cooking note

The Food and Drug Administration advises that eggs should not be consumed raw. This book contains some dishes made with raw or lightly cooked eggs. It is prudent for vulnerable people such as pregnant and nursing mothers, invalids, the elderly, babies, and young children to avoid uncooked or lightly cooked dishes made with eggs. Once prepared, these dishes should be kept refrigerated and used promptly.

This book includes dishes made with nuts and nut derivatives. It is advisable for those with known allergic reactions to nuts and nut derivatives and those who may be potentially vulnerable to these allergies, such as pregnant and nursing mothers, invalids, the elderly, babies, and children, to avoid dishes made with nuts and nut oils. It is also prudent to check the labels of preprepared ingredients for the possible inclusion of nut derivatives.

Contributors

Daniel Butler (pages 188–201) is a writer and journalist living a self-sufficient lifestyle in Wales. He leads mushroom forays and is an expert in falconry. He is the author of *Urban Dreams, Rural Realities*.

Janice Houghton-Wallace (pages 52–129, 146–147) is an agricultural journalist who writes regularly for *Smallholder* magazine. She is the author of *Not Just for Christmas: The Complete Guide to Raising Turkeys*.

Rob Jeffrey (pages 32–47, 172–177) raises organic Longhorn Beef. He also grows organic cereals and runs NewLandOwner, a consultancy designed to help newcomers to agriculture.

Donnachadh McCarthy (pages 260–281) runs the environmental consultancy 3 Acorns Eco-audits and was the founder of National Carbon Footprint Day. He is the author of *Saving the Planet without Costing the Earth* and *Easy Eco Auditing*. He works as a freelance environmental journalist.

Jane Struthers (pages 282–311) is a full-time writer with a special interest in traditional crafts. She is the author of *Red Sky at Night: The Book of Lost Country Wisdom*.

Claire Waring (pages 152–157, 182–183) is the editor of the UK beekeeping journal, *Bee Craft*, and Society Secretary of the British Alpaca Society. She writes regularly for *Smallholder* magazine and is co-author of *Teach Yourself Beekeeping*.

Natural Living

Contents

From crop to kitchen 202

Self-sufficiency in the home 260

Getting
started

Self-sufficiency for the 21ˢᵗ century

Increasing numbers of people have started to appreciate the value of growing fruit and vegetables on a small scale, or even changing their lives completely to become wholly self-sufficient.

Over the centuries in the West people have gone largely from relying on what they could produce from their own patches of land to bartering their skills in the workplace for money. They then use this money to pay for someone else's produce. There are, however, still many countries where much of the population still lives from their land.

Today more and more people are beginning to question how and where their food has been produced, and they want to take control, to a lesser or greater extent, of the food they eat. For many, the most obvious way of doing this is to grow their own fruit and vegetables and keep their own animals and poultry.

Becoming self-sufficient

Growing crops and raising animals is only part of being self-sufficient, however, which is why the principles are increasingly being applied to urban as well as rural lifestyles. Making the most of food is important, of course, and learning new skills in cooking so that all of an animal is used and rediscovering recipes from the past are part of this lifestyle. Anyone who has raised a chicken for the table will know the effort and time involved, and the value of that bird is almost beyond money. Small wonder, therefore, that people are looking for recipes that use more than just the tenderest cuts, and, of course, there are ways of cooking older birds to make the most of what is usually tougher meat.

Less obvious parts of many vegetables can be used—the flowers of zucchini and the leaves of young beet, for example—but those parts of meat and vegetables that are not wanted for the table can be made into stock.

A change in the way you regard food will go beyond the dinner table, however. Many people are thinking about sustainable household energy and building, and when they decorate they take a fresh approach to paper and paint.

"Green" issues

This is not intended to be a totally "green" book, but it is almost impossible to separate self-sufficiency from good green living principles, where nothing is wasted. It is almost by accident that, in concentrating more inwardly on your house and lifestyle, you are connecting with—and helping—a wider world to flourish because you will be reducing your carbon footprint. When you begin the journey toward self-sufficiency, whether you go all the way or just take a few steps, one of the benefits you will get is the excitement of learning new skills, of being self-reliant, and of questioning how things are done at local, national, and even international levels. It will make you much more aware of the issues surrounding food and modern life, and lead to other interests as well. You will have a lot of fun as well as hard work on your journey.

This book contains information that will provide jumping-off points along the way for you to explore further. Wherever you eventually end up, you won't be quite the same person. You will probably be wiser, and you will certainly be more content and have acquired a range of new skills.

Reasons for becoming self-sufficient

Most of the reasons for thinking about taking the first steps toward self-sufficiency have to do with food, especially the idea of food security, a phrase that was once heard only in developing countries but that is now of concern to every one of us. Self-sufficiency will enable you to:

- Make sure your food is fully traceable, allowing you to make choices about what you eat.
- Reduce the costs of the household food budget, especially if you grow some of the more unusual vegetables and salad leaves that are expensive to buy from supermarkets.
- Reduce food miles, because you can't get many fewer miles than walking from your garden to your kitchen.
- Reduce your carbon footprint by producing locally, ecologically, and effectively.
- Prepare for a future where energy will be scarce and expensive.
- Take control of the welfare of the animals involved in producing your food.
- Get the freshest taste, everyone who grows their own knows that it tastes better.
- Educate younger family members about where food really comes from.
- Enjoy healthy outdoor exercise that produces more than just a sweat.
- Reconnect with the land and with the past.
- Appreciate the effort, skill, and knowledge that goes into producing food.
- Meet like-minded people with whom you can swap ideas and experiences.

LEFT Anyone can make a start in the self-sufficient lifestyle—it can begin with the first forkful of soil.

From urban to rural

With an increasing population worldwide and the constant demand for often now-shrinking resources, it makes sense to take back some control of the basic principles of life—food, warmth, and shelter. Anyone can make a start, whether they live in an apartment or on a farm, by altering their way of life to include making time to think about food and living style. An urban dweller can walk to a market to buy fresh produce and then store seasonal treats for later in the form of pickles or jellies, for example— or even keep bees on their balcony! A rural family can go even further, producing food from their land and adopting an integrated approach where livestock waste will be used to produce vegetables and vegetable waste can help to feed livestock. It doesn't matter where you live or whether you have a high-pressured job (you could try utilizing your office windowsills if you spend little time at home) or have downshifted to the country, there are steps you can take to a longer but rewarding journey toward reaping the benefits of becoming self-reliant.

How to use this book

This book is designed to be a guide to all the things that you can do to be partly or wholly self-sufficient. The sections are designed for you to be able to take them as stand-alone advice or inspiration, or to tie together for a full cycle.

In a city area you might want to make your own sausages from meat bought from a local farmers' market, but if you have access to more land, you could use the book to find out how to keep pigs to produce the pork. Perhaps you are fed up with all the packaging on yogurt, so you decide to use this book to make your own and you could also use the grow your own section to find out how to plant fruit trees for the flavoring. If you turn to the goat or cow section, you can discover if keeping dairy animals is for you—or you could make a start on the self-sufficient lifestyle by foraging for wild food or simply growing your own herbs on your kitchen windowsill.

Some ideas in the book may be ones for you to pursue in the future, while others you might want to implement straight away, but the book is planned for you to be able to revisit as you gain confidence, master new skills and want to move on to others or if you change your lifestyle, adding a garden or buying land.

It's a book to keep on your shelf for now and for the future, to provide an insight into a full range of self-sufficiency skills and opportunities.

What is self-sufficiency?

Total self-sufficiency is a whole way of life. Being completely self-sufficient requires a full-time commitment, and you should be aware that it is not the easy option.

Many people in the world are forced to adopt self-sufficiency through economic and geographical circumstances, but there are a small number of people in developed countries who have chosen this style of living. In the West it is regarded as a "green" way of living, and for those choosing this type of lifestyle, self-sufficiency often goes hand in hand with sustainability.

Food self-sufficiency

When I first visited Africa I was humbled to find that as many as 16 people had no option but to be self-sufficient on about 19 acres of soil that I would not have thought it possible to till, let alone raise crops on. I realized that, aside from regulations such as planning and taxes, it should be possible for people in developed countries to be fully food self-sufficient.

There are, of course, varying degrees of self-sufficiency, but it's not enough just to produce the food. Most people will want to do this by sustainable methods that allow the soil and the wider environment to benefit from their efforts rather than being diminished.

Grazing animals can be of great benefit to a landscape. They allow vegetation to flourish by keeping down aggressively growing species, and some grazing animals, especially ponies and sheep, are used for "conservation grazing," where controlled movement keeps the growth at an optimum height and thickness to allow wild flowers and other plants to grow and seed.

Organic methods

Strict organic growing involves a fully traceable method that is done in conjunction with one of the certification bodies. Before you can call your produce organic, you must register and follow the requirements of that body. In reality, however, many people practice a degree of organic growing and are not certified by one of these bodies.

Whichever approach you adopt, doing it well requires knowledge. In organic systems complex management practices work with, and sometimes harness, nature to get the desired result—as in the grazing animals example noted above.

Adopting organic practices is not just a matter of not using chemicals. It is not, for example, enough to withdraw conventional veterinary treatments or wormers. The management system has to be built around a preventative ethos based on good husbandry. Pasture management becomes more of a priority than in conventional agriculture because chemical fertilizers are not permitted and herbicides are not used. Good pasture is achieved by paying attention to the quality of the soil, keeping it nutritious, well drained, and not compacted by heavy machinery. It's important to avoid overgrazing, while remembering that controlled grazing will help the sward and the manure will be good for the soil. The land can then do what it should be able to do: renew itself on a regular basis.

Integrated with this ethos of good pasture is the health of the livestock. When animals are moved regularly, not only do the grass and soil benefit but there is a far less risk of worm infestation or bacterial foot problems. Achieving this, however, means that livestock stocking rates cannot be too high, and certainly less than in conventional, more chemical-based agriculture.

Intensive production

In intensive farming large numbers are raised together, be they vegetables or animals. To achieve these levels of production, the farmer or small-scale farmer has to use drugs or pesticides to prevent or control diseases, and natural nutrients, such as good soil or grass, have to be supplemented or replaced by artificial means.

Whenever large numbers of anything are kept close together, stress is also a factor, and this can manifest itself in disease or a failure to thrive. Managing intensive farming requires not only chemical inputs but also a high standard of management. This may take the form of extreme bio-security (not allowing any form of disease into the farm) or management practices that pre-empt problems, such as routine drug control.

On the smaller scale of a small farm this means that the more animals you keep, the more proactive your management must be. You will need to identify a worming, vaccination and disease- prevention routine, and you will have to adopt high levels of hygiene, such as removing manure and having concrete where pasture has become exhausted or muddy. You may also have to overwinter livestock indoors and even consider indoor housing on a more permanent basis to preserve the pasture. This applies to poultry, too: the more there are, the more you will have to do to keep them healthy.

Mixed methods

Most self-sufficient lifestyles, although leaning toward organic systems, tend to include elements of more conventional agriculture, such as vaccinations, wormers, and routine veterinary procedures coupled with chemicals where absolutely necessary.

However, the watchwords in self-sufficiency are to work with nature, and this means developing a good knowledge of the soil, the pasture, the livestock, and, on a wider basis, the needs of the household and the acquisition of skills, such as crafts and home food preservation. There is also an element of the old-fashioned make-do-and-mend approach, making the most of everything you have and turning the throw-away culture into a "use thoroughly" philosophy.

BELOW Self-sufficiency means working with nature and livestock; putting together your understanding of good pasture with animal welfare needs.

Down to earth Cuba

In the early 1990s, due to a major supply problem in oil, Cuba had no choice but to switch from a largely intensively produced, meat-based diet to a locally grown, more vegetarian option.

The use of urban spaces was encouraged—from community gardens to balconies. People had to learn to keep small livestock again. Goats, with their generous dairy yields, became a viable option. Cities have 3 miles of land for growing around the city, while towns have 6½ feet as well as land for small farmers.

Even home life, once reliant on oil, has been considered. The scarcity of oil means that air conditioning has been replaced by building cool spaces and using shading in the form of productive fruit trees.

The cycle is closed by people learning skills in the preservation of food such as bottling or making jellies or juices.

Before you begin

The longest journey starts with the first step, as the cliché has it, and it's not always possible to know how long that journey will be. It is, however, far better to start in a small way than never to start at all.

As you begin to adjust your lifestyle, you will learn what works for you and find out what you are really good at, so you can develop your self-sufficient life in that direction. There are no hard and fast rules for how you should aim at self-sufficiency: it really is for you to take a long, hard look at your life, your family, your aspirations, and your existing talents. You do not have to give up work or even move to make a start. No matter what the size of your garden—or patio or even your balcony—there will be something that you can do, and if you already live in the country or are planning to move there, you will find there are numerous choices to make. This book will help you to make those choices, but you must first ask yourself a few questions.

What does your family think about it?

Is your partner or family totally enthusiastic, or is the dream of becoming self-sufficient yours alone? If your family is not wholly supportive you can still go ahead, but don't be surprised if you are digging your garden on your own or frantically phoning a friend to help you move your sheep on a cold, wet morning.

How much time do you have?

A lack of time rather than a shortage of money is probably the most limiting factor. Buying a few acres but still having to work on a full-time basis to pay for them is extremely frustrating. Do be realistic about the amount of time you will be able to spend. There are lots of things that you can do that don't take so much time or that require short bursts of intense effort that can be done during holidays or at weekends, but if you are thinking of keeping any kind of livestock, you must be prepared for a substantial daily commitment, especially if you are considering keeping dairy animals.

Remember, too, that you will have to make arrangements for crops and livestock to be tended to when you are away on vacation.

How much money do you have to spend?

Although your plans of being self-sufficient may be based on a desire to save money and cut down on household bills, remember that setting up something new or even moving for a new life will cost money. A few packets of seeds will cost little, but if you are thinking of something on a larger scale, you must be prepared to spend money. Chickens, for example, will need a safe run and a waterproof shed, and larger livestock will be commensurately more expensive to house. It nearly always costs more and takes more time than you have anticipated, so do your sums really well and then add a bit more to the total just to be sure. Allow for the unexpected.

Do you want to move?

One of the most significant advances in self-sufficiency in the last 50 years is the realization that we can do a lot even in the most urban of environments. Our lifestyle is important whether we live in the country or in a town, and taking on a community garden, or urban farm or renting land may allow you to achieve your dream of self-sufficiency without moving.

It may be that you cannot or do not want to move, but don't wait. Make the change now, where you live. Time goes too fast to put dreams on hold, so make them a reality now, and if you do decide to move later, you will have the huge advantage of having acquired so many new skills that the transition to a small farm will be easy.

What do you really want to achieve?

Do you want a better quality of life for your family? Will you be satisfied by being able to collect a fresh, warm egg every day? Or do you want to take the plunge and be almost totally self-supporting, if not immediately then in the future? Be honest about what is important to you.

What skills do you have?

If you are a competent mechanic, your approach to self-sufficiency may well involve more machinery than if your skills lie in another direction. If you are a talented cook, consider not only that you will be able to use your skills to preserve food but also perhaps to add value to produce that you can sell at farmers' markets.

So often we overlook the things that we are really good at because we take them for granted. What skills do you use in your job? If you are good at IT, networking, or promotion, you will be able to put those skills to good use if you decide to run a small business.

What's your personality?

If you are naturally outgoing, barter and trading will probably come easily to you, and you might enjoy having people visit your small farm. If, on the other hand, the thought of never having to see anyone again fills you with joy, you might have to do all your marketing via the internet while you talk to your chickens.

Are you squeamish?

If you are the slightest bit squeamish, don't get involved with breeding animals. If you are not certain, go on a hands-on course to see how you cope with birth, life, and death.

How do you feel about killing for food?

It can be irritating when friends ask you how you can eat animals that you have raised, even though you know that they have had a good life. However, it is no good keeping livestock if you really hate the idea of killing them. You will have to concentrate on growing vegetables and on developing crafts. Not all routes to self-sufficiency are identical, and you must adopt the approach that works for you.

How's your health?

There are significant health benefits to being outside and taking more exercise, to say nothing of eating the wonderful fresh food you produce. However, remember that self-sufficiency is hard work, so be careful about what you take on. If you have any health problems, choose less-demanding projects—deep beds will help anyone with back problems, for example, and sheep come in different sizes and temperaments, so you could choose smaller or more docile breeds for easier management.

ABOVE Don't wait to move to the country to begin your self-sufficient journey. A patio can be an ideal place to grow herbs and produce. Make a start now.

How self-sufficient can you be?

Making a move toward self-sufficiency does not necessarily mean moving house, and having access to nothing more than just a urban patio need not be an obstacle to change.

Do you have to move?

The access to land of many people living in the heart of glorious farmland will be restricted, and these restrictions may, surprisingly, make foraging in urban parks more easily achievable than in the middle of the countryside.

There are now so many ways of being self-sufficient that it is possible to incorporate them into the everyday life of living in town or country houses that have conventionally sized gardens, and it is likely that this pattern of adopting a degree of self-sufficiency in the existing family home is set to increase. You can change your life completely or you can make just a few changes. The choice is yours and yours alone.

People no longer believe that they can make a start only by moving. They are getting on with taking the initiative where they live, wherever that happens to be. Cuba is a great example of this. In 1993 supplies of oil from Russia dried up when Cuba failed to meet its export commitments. Agriculture, hitherto based on the use of oil, had to be rethought almost overnight. Food became scarce, and both urban and country people had to produce food for themselves. Natural solutions had to be found at a time when even electricity could not be relied on, and rooftops and balconies were brought into use for growing fruit and vegetables. Interestingly, the national diet, which had formerly been quite fatty and based on pork, had to change because it wasn't possible to produce pork on a small scale. People had to learn to eat vegetables and white meat, such as rabbit or chicken. Since the oil crisis Cubans have developed the ability to produce a sizeable proportion of the island's nutritional needs in areas where only small amounts of land are available. Community cohesion has become a significant aspect of food security, and there have been other lifestyle changes in housing, clothing, and travel that are part of the self-sufficiency ethos.

Unlike Cubans, you will not have to make decisions about your lifestyle overnight. Weigh up the different options and decide which of the various approaches you should adopt.

Down to earth How much space?

Before Robin Bower decided he required more space to meet his needs, his only experience of growing vegetables was experimenting with tomatoes and cucumbers on the windowsill at home.

"I like growing things and that's what spurred me on to find a plot of my own, but I had no idea how to grow things like onions and had never actually seen them in the ground. Once I had my own garden space there was much to learn, but it is so satisfying that growing my own is now a way of life."

Sixteen years later Robin has two greenhouses, a fruit cage, and an area for vegetables in his garden, and provides much of the family's needs.

"In the greenhouse there are three different grapevines, a fig, and a peach tree. I've learned a lot from my mistakes, like pruning the peach back too hard. Thinning the grapes on the vines can be time consuming, but on average I harvest around 33 pounds of grapes a year. The family eat them, I give some to friends, and with the rest I make wine."

There are raspberries and strawberries in the fruit cage and pear and apple trees in pots. All the harvesting debris from the garden goes for composting. This replenishes the soil for all kinds of vegetables and herbs as well as chrysanthemums and dahlias that are grown for cut flowers. It's not all work though.

"I also like sitting with a cup of tea and watching the wildlife by my little pond. It's a cracking place to relax."

Micro self-sufficiency

If you have no outside land available—perhaps you live in a high-rise apartment—your options might seem limited, but in reality there are plenty of things you can do. Take a long look at your space and consider the hot spots, the shady spots, and any unique features, such as a balcony or access to a roof garden. Consider indoor space as well as. Tomatoes cannot tell the difference between a sunny windowsill and a greenhouse, and even a small fruit tree will grow inside.

You could grow sprouting seeds, which have a high nutritional value and can be ready within five days. Don't overlook your kitchen, which can be used for preserving (see pages 206–7), making bread (see pages 226–31), yogurt (see pages 238), and even cheese (see pages 240-3), and you can cook cheaper cuts of meat just as well as any farmhouse kitchen. Your wormery (see page 69) and compost maker are likely to be in here as well for easy access. Indoor mushrooms are another possibility.

If you have a balcony, make the most of the vertical as well as horizontal space. Hanging baskets allow for growing trailing salad and vegetables, while other plants can be grown in beds that encourage vertical training. There are many instances of urban beehives on balconies (see pages 152–7), and if it is large enough a roof garden might be able to accommodate poultry or rabbits, as long as it is secure and provides shade and protection. It's important to look at each and every situation individually. Some covenants on buildings do not allow the keeping of poultry and other livestock, so you must check the terms of your own lease or freehold.

Your apartment itself can also become greener, with eco-friendly paints on the walls, natural fibers for soft furnishings and carpets, and, of course, the use of insulation wherever possible to minimize your use of energy. Everyone can, and should, cut down on their energy use, but you could also investigate the possibilities for saving water and using "gray" water (see pages 276–9).

Outside your apartment are city farms and community gardens (see pages 19–20), but foraging opportunities are open to all, and at the very least everyone knows where some blackberries or old apple trees grow. Will you ever have time to go to work?

ABOVE A balcony can be very productive and has advantages in that due to its height it tends not to attract the destructive pests that affect other gardeners.

ABOVE A well-planned small garden and greenhouse will provide much of a family's vegetable needs—this one is using marigolds for companion planting.

A house and small garden

If you have a house with even a small garden, all the options available to someone in an apartment are open to you, but you also have the opportunity to grow a much wider range of fruit and vegetables, and you might even have space for a small greenhouse and a house for a couple of chickens or a breed of fowl that will do well in a limited space. Quail, for example, are particularly suitable for small areas.

Look at the sunny areas and the cold areas and site things appropriately. Remember, too, to think of your neighbors—quail are noisy birds. If you are planning to keep any form of livestock, such as poultry or rabbits, they will have to be kept scrupulously clean so that they do not attract vermin (especially rats and mice), and you will have to protect them from urban foxes, which are now as widespread as they are in the country. You will have to store feed and dispose of soiled bedding, and although composting may be the obvious solution, you must take care that you do not attract vermin to your garden.

In a limited space you can successfully grow a range of crops in containers. Find out if crops are deep or shallow rooted and accommodate them accordingly, and remember that even in the most urban of environments you will need to protect your crops from birds with netting or something similar. Raised beds—really containers on a large scale—enable you to control the soil fertility and pH, and because you do not walk on the soil there is no danger of compaction. They are ideal for anyone who finds it difficult to get down on their hands and knees to plant and weed and for "no dig" gardeners, who build up a fertile soil without turning it over every year. Herbs do well in well-drained compost on sunny, outdoor windowsills, and you can grow fruit trees on an appropriate rootstock (see pages 58–9) in large containers.

Remember to grow some plants that will attract bees and other beneficial insects to your garden for pollination and pest control (see pages 92–3). Artificial and natural habitats for overwintering insects in strategically placed areas will also encourage beneficial insects and, as a bonus, benefit urban bird life.

Carry out an energy audit of your house to see what is currently being used and how you can save (see pages 266–7). Something as simple as better insulation in the form of thick curtains can be surprisingly effective. You might be able to install a wood-burning stove, for heating and hot water, but if the fuel is not available locally, you might end up spending more money and energy collecting it. Solar panels might be an option.

Look at reducing water use. Can you introduce a system for using "gray" water on your garden? Think about collecting rain water from gutters (but make sure rain barrels are safe so that small animals and birds do not drown in them).

Community gardens

In America community gardens, sometimes known as Victory Gardens, have existed since the 1890s, and they include the still-existing School Garden Movement, the War Garden Campaign and Victory Gardens, and the National Urban Garden Campaigns and Garden Progams of the 1930s Depression in their history.

If you are interested in getting involved in a community garden, the first step is to contact your local city or town council, which is normally involved with such projects to a lesser or greater degree. There is often a waiting list, so it's best to get your name down sooner rather than later. As the demand for community growing continues to increase, other groups, including privately organized "landshare" schemes, have emerged. In some areas, for example, it's possible for people with land they would like to cultivate, but can't, to lease it to people who are able to use it for food production. This simple model translates to any country, and it promotes not only community growing but also encourages people to work together to keep food local and traceable.

If none of the more formal schemes provides you with a plot, you might consider an approach to a neighbor to work their land in return for a share of the crops. Remember to formalize any such arrangement to the benefit and protection of both sides before the first fork goes in.

Although community gardens might contain individual plots, they are more focused on a community working together to produce food, flowers, fruit, a green area, or a combination of all of these. They make provision for disabled participants and tend to be in more urban areas.

Keeping an allotment— self-sufficiency in the UK

In Britain a series of Acts of Parliament recognized that the rural poor, many of whom had moved to towns and cities from the country in search of employment, needed to be able to feed themselves. In 1845 an Act required that those who were without land should have "field gardens," and as people increasingly moved to towns a movement to provide plots of land for urban dwellers gathered force, and by the early 19th century local authorities were required to provide sufficient "allotments" to meet demand.

Despite a dip in their popularity in the late 20th century, the demand for allotments has never been higher in Britain, with waiting lists in many areas and some allotments being offered privately.

BELOW A well-stocked garden will provide successive crops throughout the year's seasons.

Joining a community garden

Before you decide to join a community garden, you should ask yourself the following questions:

- How much time can you realistically spend on the plot?

- Given the time you have available, what size do you want to work on? How many people will be working together?

- How far is the plot from your house and will you be able to walk or cycle there, or will you have to drive or take public transport? How will you transport tools and equipment to the garden?

- Are there safe and secure sheds at the garden or will you have to transport everything you need each time you go to do some work?

- What are the rules and regulations? Some keep livestock, whereas others focus on food, flowers and fruit. Some have a strong "green" policy about the use of pesticides and fungicides. Some have rules about the presence of dogs and children.

- What do you want to grow? Will the regulations allow you to grow what you want?

- Are there any regulations about water useage?

- Are there fees to pay for the upkeep of the garden and how much will they be?

Farm vacations

If you cannot get to a community garden, you might want to consider the city farm movement. This worldwide movement allows city dwellers to gain hands-on experience with a range of livestock and growing opportunities. Shared knowledge is important—immigrants, for example, can grow crops that are native to their own countries but are new to where they have settled. These farms show children and young people how their food is produced and where it comes from, and visiting a city farm can be an entertaining and educational day out for a family.

A farm vacation can provide opportunities for raising livestock that you might not be able to do at home through lack of space, and it will also give you the chance to learn skills that will be invaluable even if you make the move to the country to become wholly self-sufficient. These skills could include handling livestock, milking, foot trimming, ear tagging, and even assisting at a birth. There are also opportunities for marketing and perhaps even attending farmers' markets. Volunteers are usually welcomed, and it is up to you to decide how many hours you can give.

Look on the internet for farms in your area and make yourself known to the farm manager, offering whatever help or time you have. You do not have to be skilled yourself although you may have things to offer that you don't realize. For example, you might not know much about growing or livestock care but your job may mean that you are good at sales, marketing, people skills, or accountancy—all of which are very much valued by an urban farm. It's so much better to get on and get involved with a farm vacation before you make a move to the country as it will increase your skill base. It also means that if you are not planning to go rural, you still have access to the joy of small farm.

Large gardens

If you are fortunate enough to have a large garden with no near neighbors, you will be in a position to take several quite major steps toward self-sufficiency without having to move house. Rural properties tend to have larger gardens than houses in towns and cities, and they offer many opportunities for self-sufficiency and some potential for a small business as well.

If there is room, top of your list for growing more fruit and vegetables may be a polytunnel. Before you erect one, however, check that you do not need planning permission. Although some regulations seem designed to deter the big commercial growers in picturesque areas, you should never take for granted that no one will object to your proposal. If you can erect one, a polytunnel will allow you to produce a wide range of crops for your family, and you will have surplus to sell. You will also be able to consider specialty enterprises, such as bedding plants, hanging baskets, and cut flowers. Carefully planned (and maintained), the polytunnel will provide some income as well as produce.

Even a large greenhouse will give you sufficient capacity to sow a variety of crops earlier and get a good start with planting out, and you can also grow on fruit and vegetables (see pages 74–5). A large garden might also include a small orchard of top fruits and a bed of soft fruit, which you can eat yourself as well as selling as fresh or in the form of preserves.

The extra space will enable you to expand your vegetable garden to produce on a larger scale—asparagus is a good cash crop for the spring, with strawberries providing some income in the summer. A larger herb bed offers possibilities of drying the surplus.

Because you will be operating on a larger scale, you will be able to make more compost from a wider range of materials than you would in a small garden, and you will be able to collect rainwater more effectively and expand your use of "gray" water (see pages 280–1).

Depending on the size of your garden and proximity of your neighbors, you will be able to keep more livestock. You will have space for a proper run for more than a couple of chickens, and you might even be able to think about ducks and geese (which will be a real help in the orchard eating fallen fruits). Turkeys not only produce meat for Thanksgiving but there is also a market for their eggs. Quality rare breeds can achieve a good price as breeding stock, and if space permits you might keep a couple of pigs, for bacon or pork, or goats, for milk and meat. An apiary will help pollinate the fruit trees.

In the house think about a log burner and consider alternative energy ideas, including a wind turbine (see pages 272–3).

LEFT A larger garden will enable you to produce on a bigger scale, using mini polytunnels for protection to increase your seasonal produce and to use rotation more effectively.

Moving to the country

The dream of moving to the country often goes hand in hand with leaving the rat race behind. But you are moving to another type of work, and you now have to decide if you are going to go into that new life on a full-time or part-time basis.

It's quite possible that, if you are going to realize your dream, you—and your family—will also need some kind of paid income. It's a decision you need to think about early on, and it will undoubtedly influence what you decide to do with your land and how you live your life. It's quite possible to work and run a small farm if you choose enterprises that fit in with your working life or—and many people do choose this way round—work that fits in with your new small farm life, such as part-time, shift, or contract work. There are real advantages to both approaches.

Full-time or part-time self-sufficiency?

The advantages of adopting a full-time approach to self-sufficiency include:

- You have plenty of time to develop new ideas and to get the small farm established.
- There is no need to leave the farm so you are on hand for day-to-day tasks, such as milking, seasonal tasks, such as lambing, and the inevitable emergency.
- You can concentrate all your energies on your small farm.
- You will enjoy a reduction in costs in terms of transport to and from work and in clothes for work.

Part-time self-sufficiency, on the other hand, offers:

- A reliable income, which will especially welcome during the inevitable set-up costs and might allow for faster development of some ideas.
- A potential market for goods and services, such as eggs, within the office.
- A good introduction to people in the area, especially in jobs such as retailing.
- A reduction in heating and lighting costs at home when you are out at work.
- Keeping a fresh outlook on life, which will not be totally spent on the farm.

Managing the money

The dilemma about whether to go for a full- or part-time commitment to being self-sufficient often comes down to whether you have the time or money available. It can be simplified by not overstretching your finances in the initial purchase so that you do have a broader choice. If you have to make a considerable investment in the property or have a mortgage, working as well as running the farm may not be an option but a necessity. On the other hand, getting a business up and running—and producing a large proportion of your own food is a business—takes time.

Many small-scale farmers get into difficulty through not fully evaluating this choice early on and overreaching themselves, either through the amount of work they think they can do on the farm or by totally underestimating how much money they will need and what start-up costs there will be. When you are planning the move and estimating your costs (see page 28), remember that you should also factor in a percentage for learning. For example, the first lambing season will require more veterinary advice and intervention than future lambings. You cannot sacrifice animal welfare for money. You will inevitably make mistakes that lead to the loss of crops, and although this book will help you to avoid many of them, some will still occur and most will be costly.

Some couples find that it works well if one person brings in an income from an outside job, although who this is can vary over the years. To begin with it might be the less practical person who goes out to work, while the heavy work of fencing, building, and clearing is done, but that might change to the more marketing-minded person staying on the farm once the physical business has been properly established.

Flexibility has to be the watchword in all self-sufficiency, especially in the range of skills needed (see page 31). If it is a partnership of any kind, you do need to be able to work together as well, not only in direct tasks but also when apart so that someone is always able to undertake the work required on your small farm.

The hobby farm

If you are working, you can still practice self-sufficiency at quite a high level. Structure your land to be productive but not to put pressure on you. Concentrate on things that will wait for you to look after them without coming to harm—an orchard or a garden where crops, like root vegetables, are slow to mature, for example.

Livestock can fit round your work. Poultry, as long as they are kept safe from dogs and predators and provided they have a run, water, and feed, will be fine while you are away from them, although you must still find a small amount of time to care for them every day. There are also things that will need time that can be provided at weekends and during holidays. Bees need attention every week or fortnight in summer, when you have to remove honey and repair the hive (see pages 156–7). Sheep require some daily attention, but you can, with thought, arrange your schedule to coincide with the times they need more intensive care, such as lambing and shearing.

What you can't plan for with livestock are emergencies, so if your work can't accommodate you having the occasional unplanned day off, then avoid all forms of livestock, except for perhaps poultry.

An ideal out-at-work small farm could be a small orchard with geese, ducks, or chickens, as long as they are well fenced to protect them from predators. They will still need shutting in the house at night and letting out in the morning, but the fencing will stop daytime problems. There could be a productive vegetable garden, which is designed to be managed at weekends so that only picking is done during the week, and a couple of hives of bees. You will have to plan your holidays to cope with busy times, like fruit picking and the honey harvest, but otherwise your weekends and evenings in the summer may be enough time to keep on top of the work. It will be productive, but you won't have to be at home all day, every day.

BELOW Having a productive vegetable garden and hives of bees could easily be managed around a full-time job.

Small farms and truck farms

Although there is no real legal definition, a small farm is generally an area of land of 1–10 acres that is worked by the owner and their family. Soil type, drainage, and position will all affect what and how much you will be able to produce (see pages 29–33).

If you have a truck farm, you must be near a market (such as a large town or thriving village shop) to sell the produce, which will be mostly fresh fruit and vegetables, cut flowers, poultry and eggs, and perhaps honey. Small farms, on the other hand, tend to include farm livestock, and although they might incorporate all the aspects

BELOW A truck farm means you can make enough for the household and sell the surplus locally from your farm gate or at a market.

of a truck farm, they will be based on grassland, which in itself requires good management to "grow" livestock.

On a small farm of 1 acre, depending on the quality of the grass, the drainage, and the situation, you could do everything already described for someone with a large garden, but you can also keep breeding livestock, which requires a high level of livestock management skill and a knowledge of the livestock breeds. If you are rearing for meat, it is far more effective to buy in a young animal and rear it on. Small-scale farmers can make a virtue of their limited size by developing a real knowledge of specific breeds and by breeding the best animals they can, so that they capitalize on the market for quality breeding animals as well as the meat market. This takes time to learn and to develop, but it's worth having this thought in mind when you are initially selecting your breeds. Consider breeding rare breeds and take the time to research their unique points. There's also a market for rare breed meat if it is properly presented, and you will, of course, have meat for your own freezer.

Cattle require good grass, and you do not want to have too many in a small area, although a house cow or a couple of calves for fattening is a possibility. In addition to dairy goats, you could keep a number for meat and fiber. Camelids produce quality fiber and llamas can be used as pack animals, perhaps for a trekking business.

Livestock need fodder in winter in the form of hay, haylage, or silage (see page 35), and you must have enough land available per animal for both grazing and fodder conservation and sufficient space to be able to keep livestock off the hay field throughout the nongrowing period. You will need to grow fodder, such as mangels, fodder turnips, and beet, not to replace a concentrate ration but to bulk out the animals' diet.

On your small farm you will be able to grow vegetables on a greater scale, allowing you to offer onions or potatoes for sale by the net or sack, and you will also have space to grow cereal for making bread (see pages 128–9).

Keeping a horse to help on the small farm requires considerable skill, but if you have experience of working with horses, this is an obvious step toward sustainability. You might be able to find a suitable semiretired children's pony or a ride/drive buggy.

Taking on a small farm

Moving to a small farm is a major step on the road to self-sufficiency, but it will require a major change in your life. Before moving, think about the following questions:

- What machinery will you need? How much do you know about tractors? Most tractors are woefully underused and are capable of doing a great many more tasks than their owners realize.

- What livestock are you 'carrying'? Many small farms contain animals that have other uses, such as companionship or riding, as well as

the productive livestock, but you need to make sure that you allow space for both kinds.

- What are your family's needs and wants? How much food will you need in the course of the year? Planning your farm requires you to have some idea of the market requirements—in this case your family.

The small farm

There is no hard and fast definition of a small farm, but in general a small farm would be one with up to around 100 acres, although self-sufficiency should be achievable with up to about 25 acres.

Such a self-sufficient farm would be mixed and integrated, with livestock managed to benefit the soil, manure used to maintain the soil, and where conservation in the form of management of hedges, woods, ponds, and other natural resources is a priority. It might also provide something toward the household, such as heating (from sustainable forestry) or foraging for food, but also provide income in the form of leisure activities, such as fishing or opening up woodland to off-road cyclists or horse riders.

What you cannot do with a small farm is to have 20 acres of mono-culture such as wheat, which will neither provide sufficient income nor food for your table. Some people make a living out of a few hectares by having a number of different enterprises, such as a truck farm, organic livestock, poultry, and an additional source of income, such as bed and breakfast or renting out buildings to small businesses. The list is varied and will depend on the area, your skills, what you feel you want to do, and, of course, the land and buildings on the farm.

Consider your expectations. If you are content to live frugally and use your own produce in the house, adopt an energy-efficient approach, and run modest vehicles, you will not need the amount of money that someone who has more consumerist aspirations will do. The small family farm, though now much reduced in numbers, was successful largely because members of the family in some part lived from the farm produce and were there to act as labor when necessary.

If you are hoping to become wholly self-sufficient, a small farm will offer many possibilities, and if you retain the principles from the micro farms through all the other degrees of self-sufficiency, you have a good chance of making it truly productive, not just in the sense of crop yield but in sustainability at a low financial and carbon cost.

Before you take the plunge, however, ask yourself some questions. Will you be able to manage the extra acreage? How do you plan to manage it? Can you make enough money or be self-supporting enough to justify this?

Once you get over a few acres machinery becomes essential. What will you need? Should you buy new or used? How much mechanical knowledge will you need? Can you rent in specialized machinery, use contractors, or share with neighbors to keep down costs?

BELOW A small farm needs to be well integrated and be able to produce fodder for its livestock as well as cash crops for sale. It needs to have a range of enterprises.

The road to self-sufficiency

First steps

You've decided to make the move to the country to become more self-sufficient, but how do you decide on the area and the type of property that you need? This is one of the most important landmarks on your journey to a new lifestyle.

Considerations

Even if you are planning to stay in your current location, you will need to consider the financial aspects of the lifestyle change you are planning to make as well as the type of land you already have or want to purchase.

Money

The amount of money that you will have to spend when you move to the country is the single most important factor to get right and the one that many people miscalculate. It isn't the math that's at fault; it's that enthusiasm quite naturally overtakes reality. But this is an area that has to be thoroughly thought through from the start, or you will never catch up and may even be forced to move again a few years down the line.

Everyone's circumstances are different but it is vital to do some serious calculations if you are planning to give up work. Remember that you will have no income from the property or produce for at least the first year. You might be fortunate and be able to set up your business or produce food within the first 12 months, but it is much better to be cautious. Allow for the setup costs, which include the obvious renovations, repair and building work, and also the really quite high costs of equipping a small farm. Items like hurdles, electric fencing, first aid kits, and so on all add up. Don't rely on being able to buy cheap, second-hand machinery—around the world there is an increasingly active market for collectible old machinery, which is pushing up prices. Estimate that everything you need will cost more rather than less, and then, if you get something more cheaply, it will be a bonus.

Draw up a proper business plan, even if you are not intending to sell much surplus. You will find it a useful discipline to work out how much food you can produce, how much your energy needs will be, and how much transport will cost, and then see if you can live from the residue of the money. Be brutal about these calculations, and allow for more costs rather than fewer. We've all done it and been overoptimistic about costs and then had to struggle to make ends meet, resulting in perhaps having to borrow and take on additional costs. Be honest with yourself and avoid this at the start. If you think you will need to get a mortgage or loan, be sure to factor that in and allow for an increase in rates as well.

Don't forget to include the costs of moving—the move itself, stamp duty or local taxes, if applicable, legal fees, agents' fees, and other incidentals will eat into your budget.

Zoning permission

Never assume that you will get zoning permission unless you have it in writing. "Believed to be able to get zoning permission," is a belief, not a fact. If a property has outline permission, check carefully and make sure that it hasn't expired.

Zoning permission is generally thought of only in terms of buildings—this can include structures like polytunnels and greenhouses—but it can be needed for a range of other things, such as a change of land use—to or from agricultural, to or from business use, for example—the establishment of small businesses, camping, caravanning, and even running a bed and breakfast. Even if you are aiming to provide your household with an alternative energy source, you might need to apply for zoning permission. Always take advice—and that means before you buy a property or business, let alone before you move and lay the first brick.

Even within countries or areas, some districts are more amenable to self-supporters than others. There are no hard and fast rules, but getting in touch with the local cooperative extension services is likely to tell you what kind of planning authority you are moving into.

Remember that you must abide by existing planning law and rights of way. If your property has a right of way across it, you must maintain it and allow access. You cannot just decide that you will build across it or cultivate the land. But remember that rights of way can be an asset as well as a responsibility—they bring walkers or riders to your property who might want to buy produce or even refreshments. Are you the sort of person who will welcome strangers on your land? Think about your reaction before you buy.

The land

Is the land flat, undulating, or mountainous? The terrain will affect what you can do with the property and what livestock you can keep. Steep ground may look lovely in summer, but in winter, with winds blowing and rain lashing down, it will be much more of a challenge for both you and your stock. If the land is waterlogged, there will be months of each year when you can't get access

to it, although it might produce a good hay crop if the summer is not too wet.

Look at the land carefully. If the particulars state that there are about 4 acres, check that the entire area is suitable. It may well be that a quarter is too steep for anything but sheep, another quarter is too wet for all-round use, and another quarter is poor soil that needs scrub clearing. The price will reflect this, so be aware that a cheap small farm may be more expensive in the long run, because you can't use all the land. It then becomes a small farm with whatever area you can use as opposed to the area that actually goes with it.

You should also think about the climatic conditions. If you erect a polytunnel, will you have to make sure it isn't blown away in frequent winds? Will the ground dry up in the summer sun, reducing the amount you can produce? It is often difficult to tell when you are viewing a property on a fine day what it will be like in the depths of winter or height of summer.

Buildings

Does the property have all the buildings you will need? If not, are you absolutely sure that you can afford to erect them and that zoning permission

ABOVE Check your planning permission before you invest in a new enterprise or buildings.

ABOVE Solidly built farm buildings are an asset on any small farm.

the work. For instance, it is vital that the electricity is safe and that you have some form of heating as winter approaches. It is also important that it is secure and not easy to break into. Look at the structural features, not at the décor, which can easily be changed if necessary.

Although it will depend on your family and situation, if you think that you could actually live in the property, despite the wallpaper, and if it has a useable kitchen, bathroom, hot water, and safe electricity, this will make life much easier as you set up your small farm, especially if another member of the family is going out to work or working from home. Broadband internet access could be important as well, so check availability. Other alternatives are to rent a trailer or mobile home while the house is being renovated— remember to put this down as another cost on your business plan. It's much better to live on site while the work is done if you can.

will be granted? There might not be any buildings because previous owners have been unable to get permission for them. There are, for example, conservation areas, such as the National Parks in Britain, where not only is permission difficult to obtain but the buildings have to be built to specific and possibly more expensive criteria.

If possible, buy somewhere that has a range of useful and solidly built buildings. Try to imagine what use you would put them to and how much you would need to spend to get them to the standard you want. It's always better to have too many buildings than too few.

Look at the interior. Are the buildings too dark for livestock and will they need some conversion? Are the ceilings too low for all but small livestock—and will you have to bend double yourself, which is back-breaking over a long period? What are the floor surfaces? How good are the roofs? If there is electricity, does it look safe or will rewiring be necessary? You will also need a safe, lockable area for your machinery, such as a tractor, as well as a workshop.

The house

True enthusiasts will put the house further down the scale than the outside factors, but don't let your enthusiasm for the rest of the property lead you to overlook the living accommodation.

Whatever you think a house is going to cost to repair or alter, it will, in fact, cost more and take longer than you originally estimate. Be honest with yourself about what it needs and prioritize

Location

Where you really want to live and where you actually live will be a complex equation, involving such factors as money, local schools, family commitments, and practicality.

Properties in some areas are less expensive than in other apparently similar or equally desirable areas. The reasons for variations in price may not be immediately obvious, but they may be due to a lack of employment opportunities. Although this may not initially be important to you, if you find that you need to supplement your self-sufficiency and there is no income and no market to sell your produce, you might be forced either to travel many miles to work or to move.

It's impossible to be dogmatic about location, but if you are choosing an isolated property you must be secure in your financial situation, your relationships, and your business plan. Living closer to "civilization" gives you a greater degree of flexibility and is a safety net if things don't go according to plan.

If your plans for your new self-sufficient life include selling produce, you must live near a market, such as a village or town, or in an area with farmers' markets within traveling distance. Other goods could be sold via the internet.

Take note, too, of local interests. If you dislike shooting, be careful not to locate into the middle of a sporting area, for example.

The skill base

What skills will you need to be successful in your new venture? Before you take the plunge into a new life, be certain that you've got the requisite skills. You never stop adding to the skills you have, and many take a lifetime to learn properly, but you must, at the very least, have a basic understanding of what you are going to be doing.

- **Business**—to plan proper budgets and stick to the plan you have drawn up.
- **Building**—from minor repairs, which will be a necessity, to possibly major works.
- **Mechanical**—maintaining your vehicles, tractors, and equipment.
- **Horsemanship**—if you will be using horses, you will need a high level of skill.
- **Gardening**—a knowledge of all aspects of growing, from sowing seeds to harvesting; you will also need to be able to keep your soil functioning well in structure and nutrients.
- **Keeping stock**—a thorough knowledge of the livestock you keep, including preventative measures, and stock skills, such as handling, restraining, traveling, veterinary tasks, foot trimming, shearing, and, of course, birthing.
- **Secretarial**—to keep the necessary records efficiently from all of the above and send in the appropriate forms.
- **Marketing**—from selling surplus to setting up a small business; never forget that you need to be able to sell.
- **Conservation**—making your land sustainable for all forms of life and recognizing them.
- **Arable farming**—a knowledge of hay, silage, or haylage making.
- **Cooking**—being able to preserve surplus crops by making preserves, chutneys, and jellies.
- **Brewing**—ability to make cider, wine, or beer.
- **Foraging**—from edible fungi to shooting rabbits, this covers a range of varied skills.
- **Crafts**—the ability to use the wool your sheep produce for spinning and weaving.
- **Forestry**—pruning, logging, and replanting.

This list is by no means exhaustive, and as you go through this book and further on your journey, you will find that there will be many more to add. You have to be a jack-of-all-trades and a master of most of them, especially if you are planning to keep livestock, whose lives depend on you.

Down to earth 3-year plan

A couple with a young family have bought a 4-acre small farm on flat, well-drained land within 2 miles of a sizeable village and 4 miles of a market town.

They are keen to produce organic veg and interested in goat dairying. He has a background in sales; she has a PR business and works from home.

Year one—He will carry on with his job until they have the structure of the small farm in place. She will carry on her job but with a smaller number of clients. They will enroll on a course at the local agricultural/ horticultural center part time and use exisiting sales and PR skills to begin creating a market.

Year two—He will give up his job and begin growing the market he has identified in conjunction with a realistic financial business plan. They will take day courses in practical small farm skills while expanding their stock.

Year three—If income is not as great as planned, then she can increase her part-time work. A small portion of their business should be up and running, providing a small cash flow. They will check their financial plan to see if they are on target to continue.

Gaining skills

There are several ways you can acquire the basic skills you will need for your new life, and a few useful examples are:

- Practical courses are an excellent way of finding out if you are not only keen but capable of various practical aspects of self-sufficiency.
- Practical help, on a farm or small farm or WWOOFing (a worldwide organization for placements on organic farms), will give you hands-on experience. Look for volunteer organizations, such as the Department of Agriculture's "Earth Team", on the internet.
- Research through books such as this one will give you an insight into the possibilities in self-sufficiency, allowing you to pick the ones that you think will work for you.
- Research on-line and on like-minded forums is a useful starting point for advice on livestock, though it can never take the place of hands-on experience.
- Join a small farmers' organization, where skills and knowledge are shared.
- Specialty magazines usually also have their own websites, which will often put you in touch with local groups.
- Join a breed society for your livestock or a skill-based organization, such as machinery clubs.

Look to the land

How you treat your land will directly affect how it repays you in productivity. Your first task, therefore, is to undertake a careful analysis of the land, including the soil, drainage and water, to allow you to plan your management.

The soil

The soil, whatever its quality, is the most valuable asset on any farm, and it comes in a range of textures, from sand to clay.

Clay soil requires expertise to manage it, and crop failures are frequent for the inexperienced. Sandy soils dry out quickly and require expensive water and fertilizer to grow good crops. Something in the middle, called loam, is ideal. Loam is a dark, friable material, is easily cultivated, has water-retaining characteristics, and is very forgiving of a newcomer's mistakes.

You may be surprised to learn that the above comments apply to grassland as much as to land cultivated for growing crops. The feet of grazing animals can destroy good pasture in a day or two if too many animals graze on soil that is too wet to carry them, and this problem arises with water-retentive clay much more quickly than with free-draining sand or gravel, which allows the rain to drain straight away into the subsoil.

When you are looking at land, therefore, look at the soil first. It will dictate your life, your cropping, and the livestock you keep. Avoid heavy clay, be wary of light, sandy soil, and aim for something in between.

Looking for the signs

The signs indicating the quality of the soil are all around you and are visible from the car, even before you arrive at the farm. Some of the more obvious ones are:

- The size and health of the trees or hedges—big trees signify good land
- Unkempt fields and boundaries can indicate cash-strapped farmers, where the land has not been bountiful, possibly because of poor soil
- Rushes in fields indicate unduly wet areas, which are rarely productive
- Black soil is often more productive than lighter-colored ground

When you can get to the land, pick up some soil and rub it between your fingers to evaluate the clay and sand content. This takes practice, so try it whenever you can. Clay soils feel soapy and smooth, frequently staining your fingers. It comes in a variety of colors, but is rarely black.

Sandy soils feel gritty, and stones of all sizes are often, but not always, evident. The colors range from yellow to dark brown.

Loam, the best soil, will contain a bit of both clay and sand, and the color ranges from gray when dry to chocolate brown when moist.

Soils that contain a lot of peat, which are the very best when drained, are quite rare. They contain a great deal of fiber from the decomposed vegetable matter from which they have been formed over the centuries. They are most common in areas that were once very wet and have been drained or that are still wet, when they will be unsuitable for crops or productive grass.

Soil productivity

The capacity of different soils to produce grass or crops varies with the topography, the geography, and the weather, so it is impossible to predict how many animals a half-acre of good grassland will feed. However, some of the factors that help increase production are:

- Dark-colored, loamy soil
- Low altitude
- A temperate climate, with medium rainfall and medium sunshine

- A field sloping toward the midday sun, which will be much warmer than one nearby that faces away from the sun
- Some protection from strong, persistent winds
- Adequate drainage for the local rainfall
- Protection from uncontrolled flooding

Drainage

Moisture in the soil is essential for plant growth, but too much can be detrimental, and you can often increase production and livestock-carrying capacity through some simple intervention. Ditches, to intercept and divert surface water, are relatively cheap and can be very effective. Under drainage, using plastic or clay pipes buried deep in the soil, is expensive to install and appropriate only where high-value crops are regularly grown.

Water supply

A plentiful supply of clean drinking water is essential for all livestock and adequate moisture is needed to grow crops and grass. Look for the water supply, whether it is from a stream or a pipe, before you purchase: land without water is of little use for agriculture. Check that the supply is sustainable in the quantities you will require for your planned operation throughout the year. Irrigation can be demanding and needs a great deal of water, often at a time of year when the natural supply is at its lowest.

Grazing animals will stay close to the water supply, moving only as far as they need to stave off hunger, so numerous drinking places—every 325–550 yards—will often increase growth rates.

Soil management

The soil is a great deal more than just a growing medium, supplied by the farmer with water and nutrients that are appropriate to the current crop. It is a delicate environment, home for countless living things, many of which have yet to be understood or possibly even discovered.

It is said that there is a greater weight of living creatures in the first foot of topsoil than there is walking about on the surface of the Earth. Each of these creatures has a purpose, and many need to move about in the soil to fulfill that purpose, so anything that you do to deny them that movement will prove detrimental to the fertility of that soil. From worms to microscopic organisms, we need to provide them with every opportunity to thrive and do their invaluable work, for these creatures interact with everything around them to create the natural fertility that becomes available to plants.

Compaction

If you ill-treat your soil by compacting or smearing it, you will restrict the movement of air and water, which soil-dwelling creatures need for their survival, and you will curtail the movement of the creatures themselves.

Compaction usually results when you work the soil when it is too wet and the tiny soil particles are pressed together and then stick, forming a solid block or lump of soil through which air or water cannot pass. The compaction may not be obvious to the untrained eye, but it can seriously reduce the fertility of the soil.

Walking on soil can be sufficient to start compaction, which is why raised beds are useful in gardens. Machinery will cause compaction, as will grazing livestock, so it is almost unavoidable on a farm, but it can be minimized with thought and care. Many tools—the plow in particular—smear wet soils, creating an impermeable barrier to movement, especially when the soil is wet.

Clay soils are more easily compacted than sandy ones, and water increases the tendency for soil particles to stick together, so keep off wet soils, particularly if they are clay.

BELOW If this land had flooded, rushes would be seen within the grassland. The livestock will need a safe water source rather than the river.

In grassland a strong mat of plant roots will help the soil to carry livestock and these conditions can be encouraged through the use of old-fashioned grasses, carefully managed over a number of years.

Fertility

A soil's natural fertility can be affected, for good and ill, in many ways.

Mechanical cultivation, which can be often necessary to bury weeds and rubbish or to create a seedbed, is basically unsustainable and damages the structure of the soil to the detriment of its fertility. Unless you practice permaculture (see pages 36–7), however, some form of cultivation is largely unavoidable where crops are to be grown. Grassland soils should be left well alone, except where the drainage requires improvement.

Nutrients can be added to the soil in the form of a petroleum-based chemical fertilizer or, preferably, through the use of animal manure.

The plants grown in the soil will also affect its fertility. Cereals and many root crops deplete the soil, but legumes, such as clover and peas or beans, will capture nitrogen from the air and deposit it in the soil where other plants can use it.

Some deep-rooted plants, such as chicory (*Cichorium intybus*), bring trace elements and minerals up into their leaves, where they become available to the grazing animal and are returned to the soil in the manure.

Continual mowing, with the removal of the crop for hay or silage, will rapidly deplete soil fertility, but grazing and topping leave the nutrients in the field.

Grassland management

Looking after grassland is more complex than simply growing vegetable or fruit crops in a field.

Stocking rates

Grassland is something more than an area in which animals exercise—it is the most valuable source of cheap food there is. Do not destroy it through overstocking—that is, keeping too many animals to an acre. Be aware that there is a limit to the capacity of any field or farm, no matter how well managed.

It is all too easy to start with a few breeding livestock, all of which are dearly loved, so none is sold, and which multiply rapidly until they begin to starve as a result of overstocking. Sometimes this can become a welfare issue, but because it happens slowly the owners don't realize or notice their animals' deteriorating health.

Topping

Topping is the cutting, at a height of 4–6 inches, of surplus grass and weeds.

The most delightful feature of grass is that it thrives on being cut or grazed and puts additional effort into growing more aggressively. Grassland weeds, such as docks (*Rumex* spp.), thistles (*Carduus* spp.), and nettles (*Urtica* spp.), can be weakened if they are cut when the seedheads are forming, which means that topping pastures can greatly assist their management, encouraging the grass while weakening the weeds.

Remember never to top poisonous weeds, such as ragwort (*Senecio jacobaea*). Animals tend to avoid these plants when they are living but will eat them when the plants are dead, even though they are still poisonous.

Reseeding

Establishing grass seeds successfully is one of the most difficult farming activities you can attempt. You will need an intimate knowledge of the soil and how to cultivate it correctly and at the right time of year, together with an understanding of, and ability to predict, the weather to achieve a successful reseed, which is more productive than the grass that was there before. The exercise is rarely worth the cost, the risk, and the loss of production during the process. It is always better to try and improve the grass you have.

A pasture full of weeds can rarely be improved by reseeding because the soil will be full of weed seeds, which, being in their natural environment, will take total advantage of the cultivation and germinate and grow, swamping the carefully selected and sown grass, clover, and herb seeds, which may be alien to that environment.

Conserving grass

Ideally, you need to have enough grass to be able to conserve it for feeding during the cold months, when it does not grow. This can be in the form of hay, silage, or haylage.

Think about how long the winter is likely to last and calculate your forage needs accurately, bearing in mind that all animals will need supplementary fodder at this time. Good hay is

the single most important feed for all livestock and should not be skimped on. For both haylage and silage you will need plastic sheeting and special wrapping machines, but hay can be made comparatively cheaply.

Hay The traditional and possibly the safest method for anyone getting started is to make hay. The grass is cut at any time in the summer when a week of fine, dry weather is forecast. The grass lies for a day or so to dry and is then turned so that it lies in a different position, sometimes described as being "made," to get it dry with the help of the prevailing wind and sun. If it rains during this time the grass may be saved by further turning (but with the feed value decreased) or it may be lost.

Deciding to bale requires skill, and it can be a stressful time, sometimes determined by a looming storm, but if you bale too soon with too much moisture still in the dried grass, the hay will go moldy and dusty in the bale. There are scientific methods to determine the correct time, but they are rarely employed and haymakers normally apply a common-sense assessment of the dryness of the grass. Ask advice the first year or so from more experienced haymakers if you are not sure.

Grass can be baled into small or large bales. Small bales should be collected before it rains, but big bales can stand longer on the field and, due to their density, will take longer to spoil. If you are good with machinery, it is possible to make 6–20 acres with an elderly tractor and mower. The art comes in taking time to do the turning with another implement.

Balers are the most expensive and complex piece of equipment, so you might choose to rely on a contractor to do the work for you. The downside of this, of course, is being sure that the contractor is available to come and do the job when your hay is ready to be baled.

As you cut, turn, and bale, look out for toxic weeds—you should have eliminated these by pulling them or by chemical methods, but a second check is always a good idea.

Silage Silage needs less dry weather than hay, but it is not suitable for horses. It is cut, turned only once (if at all), and then baled when it is green and damp by being wrapped very tightly in plastic or stored in an airtight silo. The moisture causes the grass to begin to ferment, which is stopped by preventing additional air from entering. As the oxygen in the sealed grass is used, the fermentation halts.

Because they are wet silage bales are heavier than those of grass, and where any fermentation processes are involved there is a greater risk both in nutrition and in feeding fermented fodder.

Haylage A cross between the hay and silage, haylage is left to dry longer than silage, but fermentation still takes place. It must also be packed tightly and all air excluded.

Be very careful because molds such as lysteria, which form in badly made haylage, can be lethal to horses.

Making good haylage is not a job for a beginner, and it is a good idea to get it tested before feeding to horses, ponies, or donkeys.

Working the land

In the 21st century we need to consider how to work with the land, rather than just force production from it. There are many ways to manage land, but it is important to always think about leaving the land in a healthy condition.

What type of land use should you choose?

There are many ways of managing your land, and the type of soil, the position (on a hill, in a valley), location (near a town, in the open), dry or wet, and your time and expertise will largely determine what you choose. Whichever method you adopt, the land needs to be managed to get the best growing potential from the soil, but there are different ways of approaching this, and never forget that all management is more successful if the land is not expected to overproduce or overstock grazing animals.

Organic farming

Organic farming is something more than farming without chemicals. It embraces a whole ethos of working with nature to produce fertility in the soil and control pests and diseases in both plants and animals.

Organics is a huge step toward sustainable agriculture, away from the intensive, petroleum-based, chemically managed farming that has become today's "conventional farming." Organic farmers are expected to have respect for their livestock and the countryside and to abuse neither, providing farm animals with a lifestyle as close to their wild, natural habitat as possible.

It is a sad fact that even the best organic farms, ones using no chemical fertilizers, sprays, or antibiotics, still have a negative energy balance—that is, they consume more energy in the form of fuel than they produce in the form of food.

For most small farms the cost of registering with one of the organic bodies so that they can use their logo and officially describe the produce as "organic" renders the process unviable. It is fortunate, therefore, that a small enterprise,

retailing all its produce, is able to meet the end-user face to face and explain how the food is produced, and this is a marketing method that can be far more effective than qualifying for an "organic" logo on food in a supermarket.

This type of face-to-face retailing provides 100 percent traceability, something that increasing numbers of discerning customers demand, alongside fresh and local provenance.

There is now plenty of information on how to farm organically, and much research has been done, so if you are going down this route, you should join an organic organization. Organic farming does not deny welfare treatments to sick animals, nor deny worming—the idea of organic farming is to prevent such situations arising with non-intensive management.

Permaculture

This method of food production is based on the premise that we cannot continue to use up raw materials and create pollution at our present rate and expect to survive on this planet forever.

Permaculture attempts to model its methods on ecosystems, which are natural communities of wild plants and animals, such as forests, meadows, and marshes. Mechanization and oil-based fuels have no part to play in permaculture. While still in the initial stages of development and dismissed as "cranky" by conventional agriculture, it is possibly the only way in which we can hope to feed the world as oil supplies dry up. The more people who can turn to permaculture, the more quickly it will develop into an acceptable and necessary form of agriculture, just as organic farming is doing at the moment.

The example used by those who promote permaculture is the abundance of growth in forest and woodland, with far greater production per acre than is possible with arable or grassland farming—and all without any cultivation, weeding, fertilizer, or work by man. If the fertility in the forest floor can be used to grow crops and if trees that grow fruits and nuts were encouraged, it would seem that there is a chance of saving the world and feeding the population. We have to create edible ecosystems, similar to traditional woodland, to replace the existing agriculture we all know and love, but which operates within such a thin layer of cropping, so close to the surface (see also pages 54–5).

Conventional farming

Conventional farmers can use all approved chemicals within a country for both crops and livestock. Many smallholders will use some chemicals, especially as they learn how to produce food, but most will not indiscriminately use chemicals as preventatives or for "fire fighting" overstocking and stressed livestock and crops, but as sensible aids when needed.

Most smallholders who keep livestock will usually include a chemical worming program, sprays and pour-ons to prevent welfare problems with flies and maggots, and vaccinations, but they do not routinely use antibiotics, except for a specific problem or for a particular disease. In the same way they sometimes use chemicals to deal with crop problems, but they do not habitually spray for pests that could be controlled in another way or for plant diseases that have been caused by poor or nonexistent rotations.

The thought of enhancing the soil is the first principle for any self-sufficient smallholder, and healthy soil will in itself prevent many plant and even livestock problems.

Woodland

Permaculture values woodland for more than timber, and it is altering the traditional view of woodland. Do not think of woodland as being unproductive of food, offering limited yields of wood for fuel and as little more than a habitat for wildlife. It has an important role in helping

BELOW A permaculture garden, based on the principles of creating an edible ecosystem, may look a little different to the usual veg plot.

Permaculture is
bringing a change in
the way woodland is
viewed—now it
need not be simply
about fuel but can
also produce food
too.

to reduce the world's carbon dioxide emissions and is also a great potential source of foraging and food as well.

In earlier times a "smallholder's hedge" produced berries and nuts and supported wildlife for the pot, such as rabbits. Woodland can become a wonderful habitat for pigs and poultry and provide shelter for cattle, while creating a renewable source of fuel for the house. It is usually cheaper than farmland, and it can be much more pleasant to live and work in than a large, open field. Do not dismiss it, but adapt to it and be creative in its use.

Energy

Farming's demand for energy in the form of fuel is voracious and unsustainable in the long run. All forms of fuel are going to become more expensive as supplies diminish, so if you are starting from fresh, now is the time to consider your demand and supply. You can manage woodland to provide heating for the house, and it might be worth making charcoal.

Sun, wind, and water

Alternative sources of energy, in the form of wind, water, and sunlight, are being developed and refined, and the location of your land and natural resources will determine what you can harness. Take a good look at your land because it is often easier to get energy-saving or -producing devices in place at the beginning—new buildings fitted with solar panels, or a good-size windmill or watermill. Research is racing ahead, and many innovative efficiencies are being incorporated into the generating machinery appropriate to small farms. It's now possible to buy updated, more efficient versions of equipment used years ago and also to get pony and horse implements that were virtually obsolete.

Be aware that alternative systems, particularly if they have wearing parts, will have running costs and depreciation, even though the electricity they provide appears to be "free," so choose carefully, because the electricity from a worn-out wind generator, purchased only a few years earlier, may turn out to be far from cheap.

Generators

The cost of connecting to the public supply can be unbelievably expensive, even when a supply is nearby, so many new small farms rely on diesel generators while they wait for "alternatives" to develop. This seems to be the best option—as, sadly, it has been for several years.

As far as diesel or petrol generators are concerned, the small and cheap ones will not stand up to daily use, and it may be cost effective to buy a more expensive generator designed specifically for the job.

It is, perhaps, more important to restrict your demand for heating and electricity by careful planning of everything you do and how you live. An old, traditional farmhouse will require large quantities of heat to make it comfortable in winter compared to a modern building with insulated walls and roof, double-glazing, and draft-proofing. In the long term the cost of insulating an old house can be cost effective, even though it will be expensive at the time.

Working with the seasons

It always costs more if you work against the seasons, keeping things cool in summer or warm in winter, so plan your enterprises to work with the most appropriate time. Produce in season may not sell for as much money as out-of-season produce, but you have to balance the expense of extra energy combined with the long-term viability of pushing crops or livestock to produce out of their natural time. Early lambs may make a premium, but the extra feed needed because the grass is not ready can soon take that back.

If you are producing solely for yourself or your family, then the most cost-effective method, as well as the most environmentally friendly way, is to work in harmony with the seasons.

LEFT New: a windpowered generator and solar panel bring renewable energy into the 21st century.

LEFT Old: the traditional water mill is still capable of providing power and new ways of harnessing water are being developed.

Storage, machinery, and tools

You will need plenty of outbuildings, both to keep stock in bad weather and to store your produce, tools, and machinery. Make sure your buildings suit all of your needs.

Storage

If you are starting out on the road to self-sufficiency, on any scale, be it a few square yards or a small farm of several acres, you will need some form of storage. If you like to plan ahead and be prepared for whatever comes in the way of weather, you might think of using a little-used room in the house or a huge farm building, but the principles will be the same.

Produce

Produce for human consumption will for the most part be consumed or sold fresh, but some might profitably be manufactured into a product with added value and longer shelflife, in which case you will need the facilities to do this work within your home or building.

For milk production, you will need a milking facility and dairy, and their design and construction will fall within the remit of a regulatory body concerned with consumer welfare, unless you are going to consume all the produce at home. The same will apply to meat products and many of the added-value products, which involve cooking. Seek their advice before you begin any construction work. You'll find that it helps to get them on your side from the start.

Tools and machinery

You will have to acquire at least some tools and machinery to work your new small farm, and it's only sensible to have somewhere safe to keep them, particularly those machines with engines. A well-constructed store will be essential, but a steel, lockable "container" of the type that travel the world on ships and trucks can be an inexpensive, temporary, or even permanent, alternative to a building.

Livestock food

Food for your livestock must be protected from the rain and damp. Hay, for example, becomes inedible once it has been rained on, and cereal-based (concentrated) feeds deteriorate when wet.

All feeds are expensive, and the cost of protecting them from the weather will be quickly repaid. Damp rising from an earth or a concrete floor will spoil dry food almost as quickly as rain from above, so stand it on a pallet. If vermin are present it will be necessary to store concentrated feeds in plastic or metal, vermin-proof containers. Dustbins and garbage bins often fit the bill.

Housing livestock

When livestock are damaging the grassland as a result of poaching (treading with their feet in wet conditions), it can sometimes be worth housing them during the wettest time of the year, and all animals require shade from prolonged hot sun. Cattle and sheep thrive out of doors in conditions that seem intolerable to humans, but the grass they walk on frequently doesn't, and as a result it can pay to provide some indoor housing.

The welfare of housed livestock should always be a priority, and pigs and poultry in particular must have a shelter, especially in cold or wet conditions. Small, specialized huts and arks, which can be moved to give access to fresh pasture, are useful.

Other considerations

In addition to the above, ask yourself how long the storage will be needed. If, for example, you buy livestock feed in small quantities at frequent intervals you will probably pay more, but in the short term it may be cheaper than paying for a storage facility. You must have a shelter with a fixed roof to store homemade hay, and if you haven't got a suitable building, don't make hay.

Work out how valuable the item is in relation to the cost of the store. Is it economical to construct a building to store something that can be replaced cheaply if it deteriorates due to the weather? Is there a more cost-effective alternative to providing your own storage?

Machinery is expensive to own and to run, let alone store, and it might be more economical to use a contractor or rent the machinery as and when you need it, thus obviating the need for costly storage facilities.

Never store anything of value under a plastic sheet or tarpaulin for more than a few days. The first strong wind will remove the sheet, no matter how securely you fastened it down, exposing the equipment to the rain.

Try to work out how your storage needs might develop later in the future. Circumstances and finances change, and your requirements might alter with them. Specialized buildings frequently fall out of favor for one reason or another, and flexibility of use is always a bonus.

Consider if any nonstorage activities could take place within the building. Machinery maintenance, food preparation, and livestock isolation or treatment are all possibilities.

Costs of storage

All storage has a cost, some much greater than others, so give the matter some thought before spending money on permanent specialized storage. Look for alternative and cost-effective solutions before spending your money.

Where the weather is unpleasantly cold or wet for long periods, creating a multipurpose store and workplace in one large building, with temporary partitions, will be the most cost-effective solution in the long run. Although such a building might appear initially expensive, the cost per square yard covered will be low, as will the maintenance and depreciation over the years. It will be more appealing to the eye and far more efficient and pleasant to work in than a group of small, specialized buildings, particularly if they are just thrown up as the need arises without any forward planning.

Modern steel-framed buildings and homemade pole barns can be extended as the need and finance dictate, provided that they are designed accordingly and positioned correctly.

BELOW A well-constructed, secure from predators and weather, poultry house is essential —moveable is even better.

Building a barn

Agricultural barns look such simple buildings, and wooden alternatives—pole barns—appear to be cheap and easy to construct. However, unless you really have lots of time on your hands, when you cannot be doing anything constructive elsewhere, and you are particularly skilled in woodwork and construction, leave barn building to the professionals. Learn from all the pole barns that can be seen leaning at crazy angles after a big storm.

Recycled steel buildings can be excellent if they are erected by an experienced builder, with adequate assistance and equipment, on well-prepared footings. It can be dangerous work, particularly for the amateur, however.

Location and design

Deciding on the location for any farm building, the way it faces, the materials to be used, and the design of the roof and side cladding can dramatically improve its value to the farm and the way it fits into the landscape. Think about it carefully before rushing ahead.

Livestock buildings

All housed livestock require carefully designed buildings, ones which maintain air flow and temperature at levels they find comfortable. This is not always what a human would require, and it takes skill and understanding to construct a satisfactory livestock building.

Ventilation and air flow in livestock buildings are critical to the health of the animals, which love slow, constantly moving fresh air but hate drafts. A ventilated roof ridge and space boarding on three sides, with one side open, is normal for housing cattle over winter, allowing cool, fresh air to enter slowly through the walls, while warm, moist, stale air exits through the ridge. Strong walls of horizontal concrete beams to a height of 5 feet are ideal when cattle are housed for any length of time.

All farm animals are descended from wild species, and it is all too easy to overprotect them

BELOW Barns look like simple buidings but take skill and money to erect. It might be more cost effective to hire a professional if you are short of time.

from the cold, as if they were humans. If cattle and sheep have dry coats they can withstand considerable cold. Perversely, however, when they are in the field they always seek protection from the wind, although not always from rain. A field shelter is always appreciated, but sheep and cattle without a shelter do thrive in most outdoor conditions.

The rare breeds that are indigenous to an area are much more comfortable out of doors than breeds that have been developed for intensive farming or those that have moved from their native country into a colder climate.

Pigs, which have little hair, do feel the cold more readily and require shelter from wind and rain. They also burn and become very distressed in harsh direct sunlight.

Hens need a house for secure protection from predators at night and for perches and nestboxes, although the nestboxes are mainly for the owners' convenience in locating eggs. They also suffer from cold when their feathers are not dry.

Concrete makes an excellent floor, but is expensive, so keep it to a minimum.

Workshop

The size and contents of any workshop will depend entirely on your interests, skills, and depth of pocket. If you are not enthusiastic about using spanners, leave it to those who are while you get on with something you enjoy and are good at. It will pay in the end.

Machinery

Machinery is expensive, both to buy and to own. Unless you are going to use something regularly or can afford it merely for the pleasure it provides, it is usually best to avoid buying machinery that is used for only a short period each year and instead beg, borrow, or rent it.

If you can find a contractor, remember that you are also hiring an experienced operator, who will probably make a much better job than you could and in half the time.

Remember, too, that no matter how shiny and attractive a machine is when it is in the showroom, the minute you put it to work it will have depreciated in value and will continue to depreciate every day. In fact, it will be costing you money even when it is standing idle. A machine has only one eventual destination—the scrap

Tool kit

Even the most disinterested mechanic or maintenance person should have some basic tools ready to hand before they start keeping any livestock:

• Pocket knife and something to sharpen it with
• First-aid kit
• Powerful torch
• Battery charger and jump leads
• Tire pump

You will also need some basic tools for general use:

Pliers, a hammer, assorted screwdrivers, assorted adjustable spanners, a hacksaw and wood saw and pipe grips.

To repair fences you will also need fencing pliers, a claw hammer, a very large hammer (maul) for knocking posts into the ground, a heavy metal spike for making a hole to start the post before knocking it into the ground, a wire-tightening device, a bag of staples, assorted nails from 2¾ inches through to 6 inches long, safety glasses and thick leather fencing gloves for handling barbed wire.

To repair machinery you will need a socket set with ½ inch drive.

For day-to-day work with livestock you will need a long-handled, two-tined fork for hay and straw, a short four-tined fork (with round tines) for farmyard manure, a steel shovel, a yard brush and a sturdy wheelbarrow.

For garden work you will need a spade, a four-tined fork (with flat tines), a steel rake, a long-handled hoe and a hand trowel and fork. The truly self-sufficient will no doubt be coppicing and will require an axe, or a chainsaw, in addition to the above.

yard. Spend the same money on livestock, and, given food and good treatment, they will grow and multiply, creating food and making money.

Farm transport

You will need some form of transport to haul goods in and produce out. The type of vehicle you will need will depend on your circumstances, but it is always more cost effective to try to manage with one multipurpose vehicle rather than two specialized ones. The tax, insurance, and depreciation will be doubled with two vehicles, making the second one an expensive luxury.

A van can be useful, as long as it can take all the family. A twin cab 4x4 truck may be expensive but can accommodate five people as well as a respectable load and can get round the farm, too. In these circumstances a 4x4 can be "greener" than a van, a car, and a tractor to do the same job.

Boundaries

Boundaries are essential for anyone who keeps livestock of any kind, particularly for security reasons. Well-maintained boundaries will also enhance the appearance of your property.

Stock-proof boundaries

Even if you do not intend to keep livestock but just produce fruit and vegetables, you will have to erect a perimeter fence. Rabbits will quickly consume young vegetable plants, usually long before you have realized that the plants have emerged. Birds will do the same, and it is often a race between the pests to get there first. Even a windowbox may need protection from birds—no plot is too small to attract wildlife, whether it is welcome or not (see pages 92–3).

Boundary barriers vary in construction, from hedges to brand-new fences and walls, and they are much more than just a marker between one piece of land and another. They should keep your livestock in and your neighbor's stock out, of course, but they can also be specifically designed to keep out unwanted pests and to provide a variety of habitats for untold hordes of wildlife,

large, small, and microscopic, most of which we never see but are nevertheless important to the local ecology. Most boundaries are multipurpose, having developed over a number of years.

Responsibility

If you keep livestock, it is your responsibility to contain them and stop them escaping, regardless of who owns the boundary. It is the responsibility of the owner to maintain a boundary, but only to their standard—if you have no stock, your boundaries need not be stock proof.

The importance of stock-proof boundaries cannot be over stressed. Many new smallholders unthinkingly purchase livestock and turn them into a field, only to discover the following morning that they are nowhere to be seen. If they can escape, they will. It is one of the unwritten laws of farming.

RIGHT Cattle do rub on fences so they need to be strongly constructed—this one contains a small stile for easy access.

Nothing upsets neighbors more than straying stock, and the consequences can be both expensive and result in a difficult relationship for years to come, which is the last thing a newcomer to an area wants. It is also surprising just how valuable your neighbor's crop becomes on the day your animals get in, even if they were bemoaning a lost crop due to the weather only the night before. Make sure you have insurance to cover straying animals before you buy them.

Priorities

Securing the perimeter of the farm should be a priority when you acquire any land on which livestock are to be kept. Insurance should be the first, fencing the second, and water the third.

Boundary ownership

Few people consider who owns the boundaries when they buy property, and many ignore their condition, often to their cost. Making poor boundaries stock proof can add considerably to the cost of the property.

It is rarely possible to be precise about the line of a hedge or fence, and each locality and country has its own rules on the matter, so find out before purchasing, because it will pay you to know your responsibilities in the event of a dispute.

From a purely economic point of view it is usually better if the neighbor owns the boundary and you have no responsibility for its maintenance. Fencing, hedging, walling, and ditching are all expensive operations, and a field with stock-proof boundaries is worth so much more than one requiring lots of renovation. Look into the cost of fencing in the area so that you can calculate what it is going to cost to make your land secure. It can add up to a lot of money, which will come as a shock if you are unprepared for the expense.

Protective fencing

It's not just about keeping livestock in—you need to keep animals out. To fence for this, first understand the pest: can it climb or jump?

Rabbits

Keeping rabbits out of a vegetable plot can prove to be a long and continuous battle and will require small-mesh rabbit netting, buried up to 12 inches into the ground to prevent them

burrowing and at least 3 feet high to prevent them jumping over.

Foxes

Foxes are a problem for poultry keepers. They can be very determined, particularly in spring when they have young cubs to feed. They have been seen burrowing under, jumping over, and climbing up wire-netting fences. Electric fencing wires, combined with poultry or sheep netting, can be effective, but nothing is 100 percent effective against them.

Erect sheep netting, to keep your birds in, then add three electric wires, one 8 inches above the top of the netting, to increase the height and discourage jumping, one 10 inches above ground and 10 inches out from the fence, to prevent burrowing, and a third halfway up the netting, on the outside of the posts, to discourage foxes from climbing. These wires should be connected if possible to a powerful, mains-powered, electric fencing unit.

Remember to think about the design of gateways to keep foxes out.

Deer

Like rabbits, deer will destroy your vegetable garden in a night. Unlike rabbits, the larger breeds can easily jump a 5-foot fence. Deer netting for the large red deer should be at least 6 feet high and is expensive to erect and maintain. Again, electric fencing will add to its effectiveness.

ABOVE If keeping out deer, the fence will have to be higher than they can jump. Foxes can climb fences and they can dig as well.

Rivers and streams

Lowland sheep will not cross water, but many larger animals love to wade through water up to their bellies, when it is not too cold, so a fence may be required.

Fences

Each type of fence has its merits and is suited to particular applications. These are the most common, but local variations can be seen.

Post and rail Possibly the smartest and the most expensive form of fence, post-and-rail fences that are made of good-quality timber have a long life, if well maintained. Poor-quality posts will rot in the ground and rails will break and warp.

Post and netting Sheep netting is one of the most popular and versatile fencing materials available. It is suitable for cattle, sheep, pigs, and, in some cases, poultry. It is made of galvanized wire and has a life of 10–15 years, depending on the air quality, which affects the corrosion speed.

The life of the fence can be dramatically extended by the skill with which it is erected and by the addition of a barbed, or better still, electric wire (hot wire) positioned about 6 inches above the netting to prevent cattle and horses rubbing on the wire.

Post and wire The use of two or three strands of plain or barbed wire, suspended tightly between wooden posts, provides a cheap and effective fence. The wires must be taut and carefully positioned for specific animals. While in place it is usually safe but isn't always recommended in some countries for fencing animals. Once it breaks and is loose, livestock may become entangled in it and be injured in the process.

Electric fencing The advent of fence energizers has transformed the electric fence into a useful, temporary or semipermanent form of barrier for most farm livestock, from poultry to cattle. It is quick and easy to erect and dismantle and can be reused many times.

The system is based on an energizer, which transforms potentially lethal domestic power into a perfectly safe current that pulses along the wire every second or so. The shock is painful, but causes no damage to the recipient, be it

Traditional field boundaries

Even these will need maintenance. An extra fence might also be needed, although natural boundaries are wonderful for wildlife.

Walls

Traditional dry stone walls, using pieces of stone that can be picked from the nearby land, are built in many areas where the stone is readily available. The walls are effective for sheep, but cattle often rub against them until the stones are dislodged and the wall is breached.

Maintenance consists of skillfully replacing the fallen stones so that the shapes interlock, without the use of any fixing agent like cement.

Hedges

Hedges are still very popular in ancient lowland farming areas in some parts of the world, although maintaining them can be expensive, which explains why so many have fallen into disrepair or have disappeared altogether. Twice yearly trimming is cheap, but maintaining them as stock proof requires an expensive operation known as layering every 15–20 years.

Because restoring a neglected hedge is expensive, a post-and-wire or netting secondary fence is usually a cheaper and more effective option than the traditional layering.

Hedges do provide superb wildlife corridors and habitat, frequently housing rabbits among their roots.

livestock or human. Many miles of electric fence can be powered by just one energizer to power one or more electric wires, stretched tightly between corner posts and suspended from plastic intermediate posts.

It is possible to contain massive cattle with just one wire, while poultry may need up to nine wires, on posts about 6 feet high.

A degree of training is advisable to educate the animals to respect this innocuous-looking, plastic-based wire.

Erecting fences

Although it looks quite easy to erect a fence, it can be more cost effective to use a professional contractor, because the resulting fence will last for years and years. Farmers themselves often lack the skills required, so don't assume your neighbor can do the job satisfactorily.

Gateways and gates

Giving a little thought to the siting of gateways can dramatically ease livestock movement.

It is almost impossible to drive a reluctant animal, flock, or herd through a gateway in the middle of a straight hedge or fence, but they will easily walk through one in the corner of the field.

Simple rules of fencing

When you are erecting a wire fence, even electric fences, you must observe a few simple rules:

- The wire must be stretched tightly between two strong tension posts.
- Intermediate posts can be placed in a straight line to support the wire at the correct height from the ground; undulating land requires more posts than flat land.
- Each time the fence changes direction, even slightly, another strong post is required, often with a prop or guy wire to prevent it from leaning.
- On runs of 300 feet and more of galvanized wire, tremendous tension must be applied, and you should use a special machine or even a tractor to secure the wire to the second straining post, which must be robustly supported with a strategically placed prop at an angle of no more than 30 degrees to the ground.

The direction in which the gate swings can also make a huge difference, either by assisting or hampering livestock movements when it is open.

Metal gates, while not attractive, are cheap and because they are light do not pull the hanging post over so quickly.

LEFT Be careful a stream does not become too shallow so that animals accidentally cross it. It will need proper drinking places otherwise they will fall in and drown.

Working with wildlife

Whether you have an urban micro-farm or you have moved your family to the country to have a small farm, all self-sufficient lifestyles will want to harness nature to help them rather than work in opposition to it.

Organic and permaculture small farms in particular rely on a management system that is linked to natural processes in order to work efficiently. So much is written about learning the skills needed to work with domestic livestock and to grow crops, but working with wildlife is also a skill that needs to be honed. The rewards are great: a more productive plot plus the sheer enjoyment of being at one with nature.

Do nothing

The first step is to do nothing at all. Put your plans on hold while you find out what is actually living on your land. It's too easy to bring in diggers, prune trees, and drain the land and accidentally remove wildlife forever that may be beneficial or simply unique to your farm.

Carry out your own survey, looking in every nook and cranny, writing down species of trees and hedges, noting nests and burrows, and not forgetting that most important of creatures—the insects. Bees of all species are in decline, so make a particular note of which plants are attracting bees and other pollinating insects. The role of insects in pollination, breaking down matter, keeping the soil healthy, and as a food for mammals and birds is only just being recognized as a truly vital part of the food chain. What species do you have on your land? Can you work with them and not destroy their habitat?

Then get some professional advice. Most districts and countries have state-subsidized agricultural conservationists or you can contact a wildlife charity for help. Features to treat with especial care are:

• **Meadows**—how old are they and should you be "improving" them with drainage and

RIGHT Don't rush to remove dead trees as they provide food for a whole new ecosystem and are home to many essential insects, birds, and even some mammals.

fertilizer, or should you leave well alone and manage them as conservation meadows?

- **Woodland**—the age can usually be told by the species and age of trees. What habitat is it providing and what opportunities for foraging for food during the seasons does it offer?
- **Dead trees**—they provide food as they rot for an important army of insects and a variety of fungi, some edible, and offer shelter for birds and mammals, so don't rush to remove them.
- **Ponds**—never drain ponds unless they are truly stagnant; instead, go "pond-dipping" to find out what species are colonizing the pond and surrounding area, and be wary of changing the ecology by allowing domestic livestock, such as ducks, to foul the water and consume the surrounding vegetation.
- **Plants**—make a note of what plants are growing in your pastures and woodlands. Some poisonous weeds must be removed for the

safety of livestock, but be careful not to remove all the wild flowers while you are doing this.

Maintaining wildlife

When you have found out what is on your land, continue to provide habitat and food by careful management. Allow some rough grass to flourish, don't overtrim hedges, and minimize the use of chemical fertilizers, pesticides, and herbicides. If you have to use any of these, always consider the organic option first and assess the implications to wildlife before applying. If you have no option but to use a chemical treatment, leave escape routes so that the wildlife has somewhere to go while the treatment is in process. Grazing and cutting are the most sustainable options for grassland, but beware of overgrazing, which will remove habitat for insects, small mammals, and ground-nesting birds and also, of course, have a detrimental effect on the soil.

ABOVE A wild flower meadow is not only beautiful but also provides much needed food for bees and butterflies.

Attracting wildlife

Some land will come with its own ecologically friendly features, but what should you do if you buy bare land or overgrazed, wire-fenced paddocks? The first step is to bring the soil back to good health by, in the worst cases, cultivating and reseeding, using an organic fertilizer or manure and leaving the land to rest. You should also carry out a soil test to assess the level of nutrients in it (see page 65). At the same time, planting a hedge and some trees will attract future generations of wildlife to your land.

Plant a hedge with native species to encourage bees and other pollinating insects—early sources of nectar and pollen are useful—and also species that will provide you with some foraging. Good plants include wild cherries (*Prunus avium*), quick-growing willows (*Salix* spp.), blackthorn (*Prunus spinosa*), hawthorn (*Crataegus* spp.), and *Rosa rugosa*. Brambles (*Rubus fruticosus*) provide fruit, and their prickles discourage anyone walking through them. At intervals along the hedge plant trees such as crab apple (*Malus* spp.).

For a small woodland the choice of species is up to you, but again look at native trees where possible and those that provide some benefit, be it timber, coppicing, or fruit or nuts. You will need to protect all newly planted trees from domestic wildlife until they are well established, and even then most trees will benefit from protection because livestock will strip the bark. Tree guards protect against rabbits and other wild livestock, and you can also use mats in order to suppress weeds around new hedging plants and trees.

A pond will attract a range of wildlife, whether you have nothing more than a depression dug out by spade with a butyl liner and plants around the edge to a much larger project excavated with a mechanical digger. Choose a naturally wet part of the land and don't allow access by livestock. Remember that small children can drown in just a couple of inches of water, so take appropriate precautions to keep them away.

Too much wildlife

What makes an animal an unwanted pest or vermin? Often the answer is that there are too many of them. A pest is something in direct competition for your resources, your crops, or your livestock, and these range from insects to larger mammals. In a well-balanced ecology many of these will be kept under control by natural processes—they will be lunch for the larger predator—but if you get overrun, before you turn to shooting or poison, consider other methods:

- **Protection**—a fox has a territory, and as soon as you wipe out one fox, another will move in. It may be more effective to protect your poultry by secure fencing, such as special electric fencing or strong wire mesh designed to be fox proof, and a secure hen house.
- **Non-toxic but seriously unpleasant substances**—it's sometimes possible to deter individual species. Lion dung, which is

BELOW Land can be managed to allow optimum conditions for wild flowers—some you may need to sow, but others will reappear given the right conditions.

Wildlife pond

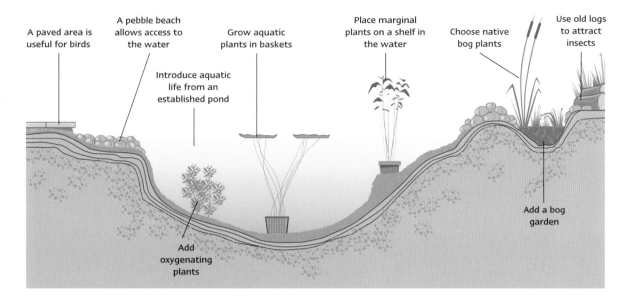

A paved area is useful for birds

A pebble beach allows access to the water

Introduce aquatic life from an established pond

Grow aquatic plants in baskets

Place marginal plants on a shelf in the water

Choose native bog plants

Use old logs to attract insects

Add a bog garden

Add oxygenating plants

available from some zoos, is a favorite way of frightening away mammal predators.

- **Ultra-sonic devices**—a high-frequency noise may be effective in deterring a number of species, including moles.
- **Scarecrows and bird-frightening devices**— crow scarers mimic the sound of shooting without the accompanying slaughter and can be effective deterrents.
- **Discouraging vermin**—the best way to keep vermin away is to keep all animal feed in sealed, vermin-proof containers. Make sure you do not leave waste lying around and manage your compost bins correctly.

If you do have to eliminate any wildlife visitors to your land, make sure you are not infringing any regulations. Check with your local state or council for advice, and you might find that there is a pest-control service.

Make sure that you do not kill breeding animals and therefore starve the young. Finally, the method must be humane and not kill other species—some slug pellets fall into this category by poisoning rodents. All must be used correctly so that they target only the species for which they are intended and don't kill either directly or indirectly by other animals consuming the poisoned carcasses. Always ask yourself:

do I really need to do this or is there another method available?

Finally, surplus rabbits and pigeons can be a useful addition to your diet. Make sure you are a competent shot and adhere to all gun legislation. Slaughter must always be quick and humane.

Hints for wildlife

Working with the wild and encouraging a wide range of biodiversity to your land is not a luxury but an absolute necessity. Only by working with nature and allowing natural systems to enhance your land can you produce a quantity of quality food from healthy livestock and plants.

Artificial fertilizers and pesticides are expensive—you can reduce costs and increase the value of the environment by really understanding the wildlife in your area from the ground up. It's challenging to think of a species that is annoying to humans and then consider its part in the whole ecosystem. Although they might be considered unpleasant, it's often possible to see the part that nature intended for them in the greater pattern.

Wildlife are great indicators and a lack of a species can point to an ecological problem either on the way or already here. Rivers without fish spell pollution, woods without birds indicate a lack of insects, and a barren soil indicates an exhausted and unproductive soil.

ABOVE A wildlife pond will attract everything from amphibians to birds and from insects to small mammals.

Growing your own

Why grow your own

The benefits of growing your own food become clear once you realize that you can save money and that there is nothing to beat the flavor, aroma, and texture of vegetables and fruit that are harvested and eaten on the same day.

Growing your own food will be hard work but fun. It will enrich your lifestyle and probably change your whole attitude to modern living. You will learn new skills, work with the seasons, and gather crops that will undoubtedly improve your standard of living, for nothing can compete with tasting those first fresh asparagus spears or gathering wheat from which you can make flour for your own bread. More importantly, the whole family can participate in growing your own, whether you have 5 acres, a large garden, or a patio garden. Another important advantage is the fitness that gardening brings and the healthy eating regime that you will become used to. Fresh produce contains more vitamins, minerals, and other nutrients than food that has had to travel miles to reach the store shelves and taken time to do so.

First steps

How you go about growing your own fruit and vegetables will depend on whether you want to garden using the convenience and effectiveness of pesticides and chemical fertilizers or being as environmentally friendly as possible.

There are several approaches to gardening. You could choose to adopt organic principles, gardening with natural materials that work alongside one another. Permaculture involves growing sustainably for the good of the surrounding environment, while biodynamics involves gardening in conjunction with an understanding of nature and growing crops according to the astronomical calendar.

Organic gardening

Adopting the principles of organic gardening means that you should avoid the use of all chemical fertilizers and pesticides in order to produce wholesome food, maintain soil fertility, and naturally control pests and diseases. An important feature of this approach is the use of natural manures and fertilizers that are derived from plant or animal remains. Other elements include conserving the world's natural resources, avoiding pollution, and rejuvenating the land to improve fertility.

Commercial food production requires high yields and consistency, and constantly delivering produce that meets supermarkets' stringent requirements means that inorganic fertilizers, herbicides, fungicides, and pesticides have to be used. These artificial elements have been shown to have harmful effects on soil structure, they can pollute essential water resources and they are harmful to wildlife. Although relying on nature's way of combating pests and diseases and nourishing the soil regularly may mean that the home grower cannot grow huge quantities of produce, careful planning makes it possible to provide for a family while still being kind to the environment.

If you are to meet the challenges of growing food without inorganic help, you will need to understand the life cycles of friends and foes in the garden or farm, so that you can use every aspect of organic gardening to advantage.

Permaculture

Working to meet the needs of the land introduces us to permaculture, a word that means permanent agriculture, and this is achieved by working with nature to look after the land in such a way that it is able to sustain small, permanent, high-yielding ecosystems. Permaculture is much more than simply growing fruit and vegetables for yourself:

it involves planning ahead to cut down on waste and unnecessary traveling and even working with others to combine what each can or cannot grow so that communities can benefit.

If you adopt permaculture you will need to observe which parts of the garden have the sunniest spots, are sheltered from wind, contain a damp area, or are visited by wildlife. You then site plants according to their needs while taking into account the efficient use of time, energy, and resources. A good example of this is planting herbs, often used every day, as close to the kitchen door as possible.

In practice permaculture does not mean that every household is totally self-sufficient in growing their own food. Instead, it is about working together with nature and those around you to share resources and knowledge to the benefit of all.

Biodynamics

Gardening based on natural systems and working in conjunction with the environment goes one step further if you grow biodynamically. Since humans first began to farm they have observed the natural sequences of the night sky and the effects that the moon, planets, and stars have on Earth. These patterns were used to determine the best times to plant and harvest crops and look after farm animals, and this knowledge was passed down from generation to generation, becoming outdated only when artificial means of controlling growth were discovered with the development of chemical fertilizers in the 19th century. However, Rudolf Steiner (1861–1925), philosopher and scientist, sought to revive some of the lunar gardening traditions by developing biodynamic techniques.

The biodynamic production of food, which is one of the most sustainable forms there is, is founded on a holistic and spiritual understanding of nature and humans. The aim is for total self-sufficiency in compost, manures, and animal feeds with as little external input as possible. Compost is treated with special herb-based preparations, crop quality is improved through the application of natural manure and quartz-based preparations, and crops are balanced so that the ecosystem thrives.

An astronomical calendar is used to determine the best planting, cultivating, and harvesting

times. For instance, it has been found that during an ascending moon sap rises and fills the upper part of the plant with vitality, so it is a good time for harvesting fruit, grafting, and gathering herbs. Sap flow slows and there is greater vitality in the roots when the moon is descending, which is good for pruning, pricking out, transplanting, repotting, and applying compost.

ABOVE By working with the seasons you will learn new skills and undoubtedly improve your standard of living.

Growing produce in small spaces

A surprising amount of vegetables and fruit can be grown in the smallest of gardens, and even a patio can be productive. There are few plants that cannot be grown in containers.

Raised beds

A raised bed raises the level at which plants can be grown, and as well as enabling plants to be grown in situations that would normally be impossible—for instance, in soil-less areas—they are also an ideal solution for anyone who is less mobile or elderly people who find it difficult to bend down.

You can construct a raised bed from wood, brick, stone, or plastic. If you are using wood, make sure you get rot-resistant (tannalized) lumber that won't rot and that is sufficiently thick not to warp. You can use ordinary soft wood, which is less expensive, but you will have to paint it with a specially formulated preservative that is not harmful to plants. Some preservatives are toxic to plants and leach from the wood over time. For the same reason avoid any wood that has been treated with creosote.

An ideal width for a raised bed is 3–5 feet so that you can reach the complete working area from either side. It can be as long as you like and have room for. If the structure is made of wood and is more than 6–7 feet long, stakes the height

of the sides should be fixed along the center of the raised sides at 3-foot intervals to prevent the wood from bowing and twisting with the weight of the soil. If there is room for more than one raised bed leave about 20 inches between them to allow for easy access.

The height can be whatever is easiest to manage without stooping too much, but bear in mind that the soil needs to be only about 9 inches deep to accommodate most vegetables.

Use a spirit level to make sure the raised bed is level. If it is not the soil will find its own level, and as well as looking untidy, space for soil will be wasted. When the walls are level, add stones or rubble for drainage, then mix plenty of well-rotted manure with compost and some natural fertilizer and fill the bed. Water thoroughly and allow to settle for a few days. Spread some more soil over the top because the level will have sunk.

One of the main benefits for soil in raised beds is that it will not become impacted because it is not walked on, so the soil will "breathe" and be able to drain freely. Soil compaction can reduce a crop's harvest by up to 50 percent, which is worth remembering if you work in the garden when the soil is wet and sticky.

Salad vegetables are ideal for growing in raised beds, and although you can grow almost any other vegetables you like, be selective. With space at a premium it is worth growing plants that don't take up too much room.

Container gardening

All kinds of herbs, vegetables, and fruit can be grown in containers, from ordinary flowerpots to windowboxes, hanging baskets, barrels, wooden boxes, and buckets. Indeed, you can use almost anything that holds soil or compost and has holes

Advantages of growing in a raised bed

- You can grow vegetables on a paved area.
- The soil will warm up more quickly in spring.
- You do not have to dig.
- It is easier to keep the soil weed free and this can be done by hand.
- Pests are easier to spot and can be dealt with immediately.
- Vegetables can be grown closer together
- Frames or cloches are easy to use to extend the growing period.

LEFT A raised bed can be constructed of wood, but make sure the timber has been pressure treated and it is thick enough not to warp.

BELOW Herbs are ideal for growing in pots and it is the best way to keep those that are invasive, such as mint, under control.

in the bottom for drainage. Herbs are ideal for growing in pots, and it is the best way to keep invasive plants, such as mint, under control. Root vegetables, such as carrots and parsnips, will need deep pots, and plants that grow tall and become top heavy, such as tomatoes, will need deep pots as well as canes or string to prevent them from falling over.

Choose containers that will be large enough for the mature plants. Most plants will grow in pots ranging from 8–18 inches across, while vigorous plants will need larger, deeper pots to give them room to spread.

Before reusing containers, make sure that they are completely clean, removing all particles of soil or compost from previous plantings and washing them with a horticultural disinfectant. Place a layer of small stones or gravel in the bottom before filling the container with compost, and check the soil requirements of the plants because some species dislike acidic (ericaceous) compost. Mix a handful of water-retaining crystals or granules into the compost to keep the plants moist without the roots becoming waterlogged. You can use ordinary garden soil in containers, but a multipurpose compost is usually better, especially as it won't contain weed seeds or pests and diseases. Do not reuse compost from last year's containers because the nutrients will have been taken up by the previous crop.

Mix in a natural organic fertilizer before planting up, and this should last for the growing season.

Fill the container to about 1 inch from the top with compost and gently firm it down with your fingers. Remove some compost from the center so that you can position the plant. Firm it in carefully and add a little more compost if necessary. Position large containers before adding the compost because they will be difficult to move when full.

Check vegetables in containers twice daily, especially during the summer months, to make sure that the compost never dries out. Do not site containers in full sun, especially if your patio area gets hot when the sun is high in the sky. You might have to find a way of shading them to prevent scorching if your patio is exposed to full sun all day. Remember, too, that dark-colored containers will absorb heat, which could cause damage to a plant's roots.

If you are growing from seed, sow in small pots or seedtrays and then transplant the number of seedlings you need to the container. Alternatively, grow ready-grown plants, which will allow you to harvest more quickly.

Almost all vegetables can be grown in containers, but lettuce, sweet (bell) peppers, eggplants, trailing varieties of tomato (which are ideal for hanging baskets), and chili peppers will all flourish in containers if maintained well. The important thing is to look for varieties that are labeled as bushy or low growing, or even described as suitable for growing in a container.

Fruit trees

Fruit trees are decorative as well as productive, and almost all can be grown in large containers. It is becoming possible to grow in temperate areas species such as peaches, nectarines, apricots, and figs that used to be restricted to warmer regions. Even citrus fruits and olives can be grown in pots as long as they are moved to the greenhouse or conservatory during the coldest months.

Plant bare-rooted or container-grown fruit trees or bushes in pots 3 inches larger than the diameter of the root area. Before planting trim back thick or damaged roots of bare-rooted plants. Tease out the roots on the outside of the rootball of container-grown plants to prevent the plant from becoming pot bound.

Position the plant in the center of the pot 1–2 inches below the rim so that water does not run off. A loam-based compost is best for fruit trees and bushes, but do not use garden soil, which does not drain quickly enough for pot-grown fruit trees. Ericaceous plants, such as blueberries, need an acidic compost or a mixture of peat and sand.

Pot on the plants each autumn until they are in 15–18 inch diameter containers. You can do this by leaning the pot on its side, tapping the rim, then turning it upside down, taking care to support the plant so that it doesn't get damaged. Take the opportunity to trim back any thick roots by about one-tenth and, if necessary, to tease and trim the secondary roots. Remove any loose soil from the rootball and repot into fresh compost. Apply a high-potash liquid feed every seven to ten days in spring and summer. When the plant has reached its final size, replant it in the same container with fresh compost and a slow-release fertilizer in the fall.

Looking after container-grown plants

Plants that are in containers are dependent on you far more than are plants growing in the open garden, especially when it comes to watering and feeding. The only moisture and nutrients that are available are those that are already in the container or that are routinely provided by you. Most plants will struggle on without sufficient food—they may look straggly and cease bearing fruit—but without water they will quickly die.

Watering

Never rely on rainfall to provide sufficient water for plants in containers. A downpour will scarcely penetrate the compost, because the foliage will largely shelter the surface. Use a watering can without a rose so that you can apply water to the compost under the foliage. Allow it to seep in before applying more. If you water too quickly, it will flood the surface and run off down the sides.

Plants need water at their roots, and a good way of supplying this is to sink a length of plastic pipe with holes drilled down its length into the container when you are adding the compost so that water can reach all levels in the pot.

Expect to use 2–3 gallons of water at a time for large pots, although this will depend on the crop. Tomatoes and cucumbers, for example, are thirsty plants and need plenty of water. In general, the larger the pot, the more slowly it will dry out and will need watering less frequently. Smaller pots can be stood in water-filled saucers, and the water will be drawn through the bottom of the pot into the compost.

If you have allowed a container to dry out completely, put it in a bucket or butt of water. When air bubbles stop rising to the surface, the compost has been soaked throughout.

Remove the pot from the bucket and allow excess moisture to drain away.

Plants in containers may well need watering twice a day in summer, depending on the species, the size and type of container, where it is sited, how sunny it is, and the ambient temperature. If you know that you will not have time to water frequently, remember to mix water-retaining crystals or granules into the compost at planting time. Alternatively, install an irrigation system.

ABOVE A narrow pipe inserted into the soil alongside the plant will take water straight to the roots where it is required.

One of the simplest systems is a length of hose with spouts at intervals, inserted into a container. When the water is turned on at the tap, the drip system releases water slowly to the base of the spout. Some systems can be used with timers, which are invaluable if you are away on vacation.

Do not allow the compost in containers to become waterlogged. Too much water will have a similar effect on your plants as drought: stunted growth and yellowing or curled-up leaves that eventually drop. Every container must have at least one hole in the base so that excess water can drain away, and always add a layer of rubble, crocks, or gravel before adding compost. Stand the containers on pot feet or small bricks to allow water to drain away easily, and always feel the compost before adding more water.

Self-watering containers have a reservoir of water under the base of the pot that contains the plant. The water seeps up into the compost via wicks of capillary matting through holes in the base of the pot. Another system allows a small area of compost to come into direct contact with the reservoir. You must remember to top up the reservoir regularly.

Feeding

Most proprietary composts will contain sufficient fertilizer to sustain your plants for up to six weeks, after which you will have to feed the plants yourself. Slow-maturing crops, such as tomatoes, need an intense feeding routine, whereas fast-growing crops like cut-and-come-again salad leaves usually require none. There are many different kinds of fertilizers available, some general and others for more specific application. Controlled- or slow-release fertilizers come in the form of plugs, which gradually release nutrients into the compost, or as granules, which are mixed with the compost at planting time.

General maintenance

Keep plants in containers tidy by gathering up fallen leaves or debris. Your plants will be more productive if they are compact and bushy, achieved by pinching out and pruning.

Encourage bush tomatoes to produce more fruiting spurs by pinching out the leading shoots. Pinch out the sideshoots of cordon tomatoes. Dwarf fruit trees in containers need careful pruning to produce a good crop. Apples, pears, and bush fruits are pruned in the winter while the plant is dormant. Top fruit, such as plums, cherries, nectarines, and peaches, should be pruned in late spring. A little summer pruning may also be necessary to keep container-grown trees in a neat and manageable shape.

Pests and diseases

Plants in containers are as susceptible to pests and diseases as they would be if they were growing in the open garden (see pages 86–91). Check for signs of infection every day and deal with any problems immediately, because the sooner they are eradicated, the better chance there is of the plant surviving and cropping. Foliage and stems that show signs of pests or disease should be binned or burned and not put on the compost heap, which might spread the problem around the garden. Disinfect tools, such as secateurs, that you use to cut back diseased material, and it is also a good idea to wash your hands after handling diseased foliage—not because of a threat to human health but because it is all too easy to pass on spores to healthy plants.

Lightly trim evergreen herbs when necessary so that they remain tidy and are kept in proportion to the container. Topiary specimens of plants like sweet bay (*Laurus nobilis*) that are trained into a particular shape should be trimmed with hand shears every few months in order to maintain their shape.

Trailing edible flowers, such as nasturtiums, grow well in hanging baskets, and they should be picked or deadheaded regularly, if they are allowed to go to seed the plant will stop flowering and concentrate on feeding the seeds. Other trailing or climbing plants need to be supported so that they are not buffeted about or blown over in windy weather. Climbing beans and gourds, for instance, should be trained onto an obelisk or wigwam of bamboo canes. You can lightly tie in the stems to allow air and light to penetrate to the center of the plant, but provide sufficient support to prevent wind rock. Less rangy plants, such as bush tomatoes and dwarf beans, will also benefit from the support of bamboo canes or twiggy prunings. The branches of bush or soft fruits such as red currants may need some support if they are heavily laden with fruit.

LEFT Encourage bush tomatoes to produce more fruiting spurs by pinching out the leading shoots.

BELOW Plants in containers should be checked every day for any signs of pests and diseases and also dead foliage removed.

Planning your plot

When you are planning a vegetable plot there are several things to take into consideration: how much space you have, how much time you have available, the growing space that different crops require, and what you like to eat.

Why you should plan

Making a plan is essential. Even if you have 5 acres, the area that may be available for growing food will depend on what else is grown or reared there. A smaller garden or share of a larger community garden can be the perfect space to grow your own vegetables, fruit and herbs, and a plot of about 2,700 square feet can provide enough space to grow food to keep a family of four for a year. Even if you have only a small garden or patio, you will be surprised at just what you can achieve in containers if you make sure that you plan carefully first.

Take into consideration the type of soil and the climate. Don't waste time, space, and energy trying to grow crops that are not suited to your area. Ask your neighbors what grows well in their soil. Begin with those crops and experiment with more exotic crops later on.

BELOW Peas, potatoes, and carrots are all excellent choices for your vegetable garden. Peas are highly nutritious, potatoes are a good source of energy and can be readily stored, while carrots are rich in vitamin A.

Crop rotation

For healthy soil and high yields, practice crop rotation, which is the process of moving crops of the same family group around the plot annually so that they are not grown in the same place each year. Every species of plant draws from the soil nourishment peculiar to itself. Heavy feeders, such as broccoli and tomatoes, deplete more of the soil's minerals than light feeders, such as carrots and onions. Some plants, such as peas and beans, actually improve the soil. Alternating the types of crop in the plot will help maintain the soil. Crop rotation also prevents soil-borne pests and diseases peculiar to a particular crop from building up, as their host has been removed and replaced with a plant from another family that is not usually susceptible to the same problems. Perennial crops, such as fruit bushes, herbs, asparagus, and rhubarb, do not need to be rotated.

Making a plan

Start your plan by listing all the vegetables you want to grow and then dividing them into their specific botanical families: Alliaceae (onions), Apiaceae (parsnips), Asteraceae (endive), Brassicaceae (brassicas), Chenopodiaceae (spinach, chard), Cucurbitaceae (squashes, pumpkins), Papilonaceae (peas), Poaceae (corn) and Solanaceae (potatoes, tomatoes).

Divide the area that you want to use into sections of roughly the same size. If you have only a small area available you should use a three-course rotation, for which the vegetable plot would be divided into three areas for:

• **Root crops**—carrots, parsnips, beet
• **Brassicas**—cabbage, cauliflower, broccoli, sprouts, turnips
• **Other crops**—potatoes, leeks, peas

This arrangement would give root crops in plot 1 in the first year, brassicas in the second year, and everything else in the third year, returning to root crops in the fourth year.

If a lack of space leaves you wondering where to site plants, the following principles will enable you to plan your own rotation:

• Leave the largest gap between potatoes and brassicas occupying the same piece of ground.
• Brassicas like limey soil, so if part of the plot has been treated, plant brassicas there.
• Lime causes scab in potatoes, so plant those away from any soil that has had lime applied.
• Keep plants of the same family together.
• Do not plant root crops, such as carrots and parsnips, in ground to which manure was applied the previous autumn because the extra nutrients will cause them to fork and split.

Vegetable plots in large gardens and community gardens should have space for a four- or even five-course crop rotation. An area of about 2,700 square feet, which is the average size of an allotment in Britain, should provide year-round cropping if carefully planned.

Crop rotation is not such a concern if you are growing vegetables in containers, a very effective form of vegetable gardening, but you must take care to wash and disinfect the pots after each use and refill them with suitable fresh compost.

The area you devote to individual crops will depend on how much of the vegetable you require (or your family likes!). When you are working out how many plants you need, the planting space required between them should be a guide. For example, parsnips and dwarf green beans should be 12 inches apart; climbing beans and turnips 9 inches apart; fava beans 6 inches apart; onions 6–12 inches apart, depending on type; and beet 12–18 inches apart.

The hungry gap

In late winter and early summer fresh vegetables and fruit are less readily available. However, there are ways in which you can overcome this gap.

Grow hardy vegetables that can overwinter in the ground, such as leeks or parsnips. Sow crops that mature quickly from an early-spring sowing under cover, such as radishes or cut-and-come-again lettuces. It is also important to store and freeze produce when it is abundant. Beans and peas can be dried and stored in the fall, while late-ripening varieties of apples and pears can be stored in a dark, well-ventilated place.

Down to earth Vegetable patch

David and Janette have had a vegetable patch for the past 10 years and are now self-sufficient in fruit and vegetables. They both stopped eating meat 30 years ago, so vegetables are a staple part of their diet.

"You need to concentrate on the things that are going to feed you, and planning where and when to grow them is essential," says Janette. "As well as eating fresh vegetables and fruit, we store plenty. Brussels sprouts, Swiss chard, and leeks are excellent for winter, and we enjoy stored parsnips, potatoes, onions, and garlic.

Throughout the winter and spring we also have zucchini, cauliflowers, all the beans, Brussels sprouts, and corn and soft fruits from the freezer. We wouldn't want to go back to having to buy fruit and vegetables—the taste is so different."

David and Janette enjoy planning meals that use what is in season, and they have saved money by no longer having to rely on their local supermarket. They also know that they are benefiting the environment by cutting down on food miles and eliminating the over-packaging of much supermarket produce.

Preparing a new vegetable plot

Before you begin to plant anything in a new plot you must prepare the ground thoroughly or your plants will struggle to compete with weed growth and your harvest will be affected.

Clearing by hand

If the ground is overgrown, use hand pruners or shears to cut down tall growth and brambles. Remember to wear a pair of gloves to protect your hands from briers and thorns. The easiest way of clearing an area of grass and weeds is to apply a nonselective herbicide. After application the entire plant will die, including the roots.

If you prefer to avoid chemicals, try covering the ground with thick black plastic for at least six months, it is best to work on a small area at a time. If you are clearing a community garden, check first: some have specific rules about the use of heavy-duty plastic or even carpet.

Using animals for clearing

Grazing animals will save you a lot of hard work. Goats prefer young growth but will eat most weeds if they are kept in the same area, and sheep eat most vegetation and chop weeds off close to the ground. They would need to be confined, but could be fenced in to strip graze—where one area of the land is allowed to be grazed at a time.

You might be able to borrow goats or sheep for a few weeks, because many owners will be grateful for additional grazing. Small farm clubs will be able to put you in contact with an owner willing to help out. Before the animals are allowed on your land, their owner will check that there are no poisonous plants there, and you will have to dig these up and burn them.

The pig is the most efficient animal for clearing ground because of their habit of searching for edible roots, and as well as clearing weeds from an area, they will also loosen and fertilize the soil. You could keep a couple of weaner piglets in even a relatively small area—they would require some conventional feed—and by the time they are large enough to be slaughtered the land would be ready for you to work on. An electric fence will keep them in.

Chickens and ducks are also good at clearing land because they scratch and dabble around to find insects and grubs. They do need to be confined, and you could use either a mobile poultry housing unit or electric poultry netting.

BELOW The most effective animal for clearing ground is the pig and a couple of weaner pigs can be kept in a relatively small area.

Knowing your soil

Soils are classified according to the amount of sand or clay particles they contain. They are also described as acidic or alkaline. It is useful to dig a few holes in different parts of the land to be cultivated, taking up the top spit (the depth of your spade's blade) and getting into the subsoil. Leave the holes open for a few days, and if it has not rained but water has gathered in the base, the subsoil in those areas is waterlogged.

Clay

It is difficult to garden on clay, which is heavy in texture, retains water, slow to drain, and goes hard when it is dry. Clay is quite high in nutrients, however, and the texture can be improved by adding plenty of well-rotted garden compost.

Sand

Sandy soil drains well, but consequently does not retain moisture and dries out rapidly. Nutrients quickly leach out, so you need to apply plenty of organic matter to improve it. Well-rotted garden compost or farm manure will help to retain moisture and enhance the nutrient levels.

Silt

Silty soil has particles that are between those of sand and clay. It is sticky and heavy, but can be improved greatly by adding lots of organic matter.

Loam

A loam soil is what most gardeners would love to have. It contains a mixture of clay, sand, and silt, plus organic matter and plant nutrients. It is easy to work, retains moisture yet drains well.

Peat

Formed mainly of partially decomposed organic matter, peaty soils are dark in color, usually acidic, and poorly drained. To improve a peat soil you will need to add lime, nutrients, coarse sand, grit, or weathered ashes. In extreme cases extra drainage may be needed.

Digging

In the first season you should dig the soil to improve the texture, incorporate any manures, composts, and fertilizers that are necessary, and remove all perennial weed roots. There are two ways of turning over the soil, single digging and double digging. It is best to dig over heavy soils in the fall so that frost can penetrate the clods of earth. However, never work on soil that is frozen or waterlogged because this will compact the soil and damage its structure.

Although digging can be hard work, you can make it easier by using the correct tools. Use a spade that is the right size for you so that you don't have to bend. Make sure that the blade is clean, not rusty and penetrates 12 inches into the ground. Good digging consists of driving the spade almost vertically into the ground and completely turning over the spit of soil.

Single digging

If your soil is a reasonable depth and does not cover a heavy, clay subsoil, single digging should be sufficient to prepare the area. This means that you turn the soil to the depth of one spit. Never try to dig too large an area at a time. Divide it up into strips about 3 feet wide and work on a strip at a time. When you are digging, try to keep your back straight and don't lift too much soil at a time so that you don't strain yourself. Turning lighter, smaller spadefuls will be quicker and more efficient than struggling with large spadefuls. Remember not to tread on the soil you have just dug over so that you do not compact it.

Double digging

If you have ground that has never been cultivated before or if you want to improve the drainage, you could double dig it. This will also give you an opportunity to improve the subsoil by adding plenty of well-rotted compost or manure. This is hard work because you have to make sure that you keep the top- and subsoil separate, moving the first batch of topsoil from one end of your trench to the other.

Soil pH

The amount of lime in soil determines its acidity. If it is rich in lime or chalk, the soil is alkaline. Soil that lacks lime is acidic. The degree of acidity or alkalinity is measured on the pH scale. Soil with a pH of 7 and above is called alkaline; below 6.5 the soil is acidic. Test the pH level of your soil with a simple soil-testing kit, taking samples from several areas. Acid soil turns the solution deep yellow and alkaline will turn it green.

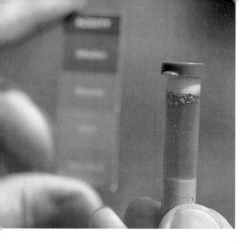

Improving your soil

Whenever anything grows it takes nutrients from the soil. In nature these are returned as plants rot down naturally. When you remove old growth nutrients are not replenished, and you have to intervene to keep the soil in good condition.

Adjusting the pH

When you have found the pH level of your soil (see page 65) it is possible to adjust it to enable you to grow plants that prefer another type of soil. If your soil is acidic, increase the alkaline balance by adding hydrated lime, chalk (calcium carbonate), or ground limestone. Follow the instructions on the bag, but only carry out the work on a still day, as any breeze will produce a dust cloud and blow the lime everywhere except where you want it. Spent mushroom compost, which is sometimes available, is also alkaline.

To lower the pH level and make it more acidic, enrich the soil with a peat substitute or plenty of acidic organic matter, such as leaf mold made from pine needles. Then apply flowers of sulfur. Test the soil on a monthly basis and reapply the treatment as necessary.

Do bear in mind that any changes to the soil will be only temporary because you cannot alter the underlying geology of your land. It is far easier to concentrate on growing plants that will thrive in the soil you have. If you really want to grow vegetables or fruit that need a different soil type, grow them in containers or a raised bed filled with the appropriate compost.

Using fertilizers

Fertilizers are concentrated plant foods that contain the main nutrients that plants need to grow: nitrogen (N), phosphorus (P), and potassium (K). The packaging will indicate the levels of each of these, set out as N:P:K—4:4:6, for example. When you buy fertilizers, remember that a high level of nitrogen will produce leafy growth, one high in phosphates will promote root growth, and one high in potassium will encourage fruit and flowers (see also page 77).

There are two basic kinds of fertilizer: organic and inorganic. Organic fertilizers contain carbon and come from natural sources—plants, animals and rocks. They are slow to break down and need the help of soil bacteria to make them available to plants. Inorganic fertilizers do not contain carbon, do not improve the texture of the soil, and do not add humus, but they are often quick-acting and richer in nutrients.

To improve the texture and structure of the soil you need to add plenty of organic matter, and most plants will thrive in soil that has been dressed with well-rotted manure, garden compost, or leaf mold before planting.

Animal manure

Such manure is valuable in the garden because it improves the soil's structure and provides nutrients. You should always let any animal manure rot before applying it to the ground because in its fresh state it gives off harmful ammonia. In addition to this, until bacteria have had time to work on the manure, the nitrogen is not available to plants. Rotted manure is pleasant to use and does not have an odor.

Garden compost

A valuable alternative to animal manure, garden compost consists of a range of garden and kitchen waste that has been left to rot over a long period. It is quite rich in nutrients and is an excellent soil conditioner (see pages 68–9).

Leaf mold

Although it is a good soil conditioner, leaf mold provides few nutrients. It turns the soil slightly acidic and makes a very good mulch. You should never take leaf mold from the wild.

Peat

Used by generations of gardeners to grow seeds and plants, peat cannot be extracted from natural areas in ecologically sustainable ways, and gardeners are now being urged not to use it. There are alternatives, such as coir and bark. Avoid bagged peat-based proprietary composts.

Coir

Coir (coconut fiber) is a soil conditioner and a potting compost. It does increase the acidity, so is appropriate only for ericaceous plants.

Seaweed

A good source of plant nutrients, particularly potash, seaweed decomposes very quickly. It can be dug straight into the ground while it is wet or composted with garden waste. You can buy dried seaweed meal from garden suppliers.

Spent mushroom compost

If you have a local source this is well worth using to boost the organic matter in your soil. It usually contains a combination of animal manure, loam, and chalk and can be used in all soils except those that are growing ericaceous plants.

Worm compost

A beneficial plant food and soil conditioner, worm compost (see page 69) can be applied wherever feeding is needed.

Green manures and other soil improvers

Some plants, known as green manures, are grown to be deliberately dug into the soil to improve the humus content. After the land has been dug in the fall, sow the seed thickly in spring or early summer and rake it in. Rape, annual lupins, vetches, mustard, and perennial rye grass are often used. These grow quite quickly and the whole plants are dug into the soil just before they flower. This is a useful way of dealing with a vacant part of the vegetable plot that is being left fallow as part of crop rotation.

Other natural fertilizers that can be used include decomposing green crops, such as the haulm of potatoes, peas, and beans, and the stumps and leaves of cabbages, Brussels sprouts, and cauliflowers. Pond mud, burned wood ashes, and soot will also supply useful plant food.

In addition to deterring slugs, soot is effective as a manure. In liquid form it can be applied to the roots of plants. Place soot that has been kept for three to four months in a bag and suspend it in a bucket of water from a stick held across the top of the bucket. Let it hang for a few days and then squeeze the bag until the water turns light brown. This process can be repeated several times before the soot bag needs refilling. In its dry state soot should be left for a fortnight before use, as it is too caustic straight from the chimney. You can then spread it over the onion plot, as a fertilizer and help to ward off onion fly (see page 104).

BELOW Some plants are deliberately dug into the soil to improve the humus content.

Composting

No matter how small it is, any garden will benefit from having a compost heap, which, if managed correctly, will turn both garden and kitchen waste into a soil-enriching material—an eco-friendly and money-saving process.

To make good compost you must make sure that all the organic material decomposes rapidly and does not either dry out, thus preserving the material in its original form, or turn into a pile of rotting slime. Air, moisture, and nitrogen must be present so that bacteria and fungi can break down the raw materials. It is certainly not a case of piling up garden rubbish and leaving it for a year.

When it is ready for use compost takes on a crumbly texture, turns a deep brown in color, is slightly moist, and has a pleasant, sweet smell.

Compost bins

There are many compost bins on the market, but a homemade one can be just as efficient, and wooden pallets are ideal for constructing a simple cube. Alternatively, erect four stout corner posts and screw or nail timber planks, at least 3 feet long, to the two sides and the back. Secure another two posts at the front, fixing to each side but allowing a plank width gap between the two upright posts. Planks can then be slid through the side posts to cover the front as the compost increases. They can be removed when you empty the heap. A timber frame with wire netting panels would make an equally suitable heap.

It's generally better to have two compost bins, because if the previous season's compost is not quite ready to use, it can be left to mature further while fresh material is gathered in the second bin.

Place a layer of brushwood on the base or wooden planks supported by bricks so that air can penetrate the compost. Once the heap is full, place an old carpet or piece of plastic on the top, held down, to keep in the moisture. Another way of getting more air into the heap is to place three stakes in the compost heap as it is being built. Remove these when the heap is full, allowing air into the holes that are left.

Materials for composting

Most green garden waste can be turned into compost. Lawn clippings are excellent, but you must layer them with other raw material or the clippings will ferment quickly and produce a slimy mess. Soft hedge clippings, leaves, and fresh vegetable waste can also be added. Kitchen waste, including vegetable peelings, crushed egg shells, and tea leaves, can be used, and you can add newspapers, torn cardboard, and natural wool, which will combine well with soiled livestock litter and animal and poultry manure to provide plenty of material to encourage decomposition.

When it is ready for use, the compost will be dark and crumbly. Well-made compost does not smell unpleasant. It can be incorporated into the bottom of trenches if you are digging a plot or, if it is really well-rotted, used as a mulch. Return any pieces of stems or roots that have not rotted down to the new compost heap.

Leaf mold

Most deciduous leaves break down more slowly than grass clippings and green garden waste, so

Don't compost

Do not include lawn clippings that have been treated with weedkiller, hard woody stems, perennial weeds, annual plants that have set seed and diseased plants. Do not add cat litter, dog feces, disposable diapers or coal and coke ash, and never add meat, fish or fat. They will attract vermin, which can be a problem with poorly constructed heaps.

keep gathered autumn leaves separate to make leaf mold, which is an excellent soil improver. Place the leaves in a simple container made of wire mesh supported by four corner posts or pack them in a plastic sack with the top tied. Make holes in the sides of the bag with your garden fork and leave the bag in a secluded corner until spring.

Wormery

Vermiculture—using worms to make compost—is a way of turning kitchen waste into a plant feed and soil conditioner. The worms used, brandlings (tiger worms), are small red worms found in manure and compost heaps and you can also buy them in angling shops. A bought wormery usually resembles a plastic refuse bin, but you can construct your own with sections, similar to a beehive with a lid. Remember to add holes along the bottom and top to allow air to enter and make a drainage hole for liquid.

Put some sand in the bottom and cover it with damp newspaper. Put a small heap of garden compost or leaf mold on the paper and place about 100 worms on the compost. Add a thin layer of kitchen waste. Leave the lid off for a while so that the light encourages the worms to bury into the material. Leave the wormery for a week before adding more kitchen waste and after two to three weeks a small amount can be added daily.

You can overfeed worms, and if the material begins to get too wet, add some brown cardboard and newspaper. The liquid is full of nutrients, but dilute it before using. The compost made will be at the bottom of the wormery, because the worms work upward. You can remove this and place the empty section of the wormery at the top, under the lid, to keep the process going.

Building up the heap

Arrange the raw material in alternate layers and firm it down with the head of a rake. As you are building up the heap, you can add a proprietary compost activator, although young nettles do the job just as well. Continue layering material until the heap is full, water it thoroughly, and cover the top. You can spread a layer of soil about 2 inches deep over the top instead of a cover and then insert some zucchini or squash seeds into the soil. The rotting materials will provide feed for the plants, which will not take too much goodness from the compost.

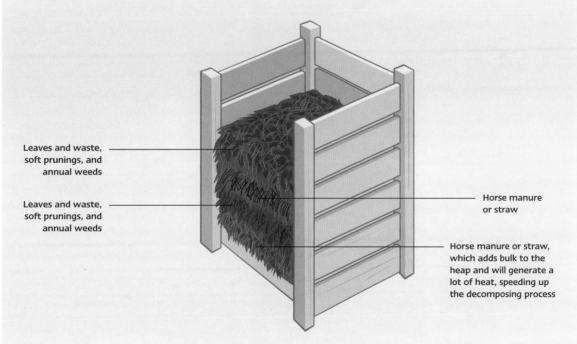

Leaves and waste, soft prunings, and annual weeds

Leaves and waste, soft prunings, and annual weeds

Horse manure or straw

Horse manure or straw, which adds bulk to the heap and will generate a lot of heat, speeding up the decomposing process

Sowing and propagating

Being able to produce strong, healthy new plants is vital if you are going to be successful at growing your own vegetables. Start with easy to grow veg before expanding your selection.

Sowing

The most economical way of producing vegetables is to grow them from seed. There is an enormous range to choose from, including different varieties of the same vegetable. When you are buying seeds, always check that the variety is for sowing when you want to, because some are best sown in spring and others in late summer, while salad crops can be sown at regular intervals throughout spring and summer to produce a succession of plants over several weeks.

BELOW Vegetables for early crops should be sown in a greenhouse using a proprietary compost for seedlings or a mild loam.

Always use fresh seeds from a reputable seed company, whether you are buying over the counter or from a mail order catalog. Although old seeds may still grow, germination is likely to be erratic. As you grow your own crops you will be able to save your own seed.

Types of seed

Improvements in seed technology mean that there are now several different types of seed available, including:

F1 hybrids The seeds are bred for improved quality; they produce excellent, uniform crops, but are more expensive than ordinary seeds, and after flowering the seeds cannot be saved because they will not necessarily breed true again.

Disease resistant Some vegetables have been bred to be resistant to specific diseases, although they might be more susceptible to others. For example, some lettuces have been developed to be resistant to mosaic virus, but not to other diseases. In addition, disease-resistant varieties are not always as well flavored as other varieties.

Treated and dressed seed Some seeds are treated by the seedsman either to kill diseases that are carried on the seed by certain vegetables or to combat soil-borne diseases likely to attack the seed after sowing.

Pelleted seed Some seeds are made into small balls with a protective covering of clay, which breaks down in the soil. Because they are larger than many seeds, they are easier to handle and to space accurately, so thinning is not required (see page 73).

Foil packaging Seeds sold in air-sealed foil packs will keep longer than seeds in ordinary paper packets. Once the packets are opened, the seeds will deteriorate as normal, of course.

Containers

The ideal place to sow seeds will depend on the type of seed and the crop. Pots and seed boxes give improved control over germination, so extremely small or expensive seeds are best sown in these under cover. Cloches and frames (see page 75) provide shelter and warmth to seeds sown directly into beds outdoors.

The depth for sowing will depend on the seed size, but a guide is to cover seeds to a depth equal to twice their diameter for indoor sowing and three times for outdoors. Do not cover dust-fine seeds with compost. Seeds germinate faster in warm conditions, but too much heat can delay germination or even kill the seed.

Sowing indoors

Vegetables that need a quick start or vegetables for early crops should be sown indoors in seed boxes, pots, cell trays, or compost blocks. Plastic containers are readily available from gardening outlets, but always wash old ones thoroughly before using them, again to avoid contaminating the new seedlings.

You can buy proprietary composts that are specifically formulated for seedlings, but a mild loam that is not too rich in nutrients is fine for most vegetable seeds. Dampen the compost before sowing. Large seeds, such as fava beans or pelleted seeds, are best sown individually, but smaller seed can be scattered in seedtrays. After sowing, cover all seed, except the smallest dust-like seeds, with sieved compost. Make sure there are no clumps and make sure you do not bury seeds too deeply. Lightly spray the surface with water and cover with a sheet of glass and then a sheet of paper, which will aid germination.

Propagators

A heated propagator is useful for germinating seeds that need a warmer temperature. Where artificial heat is used, it is essential that the compost does not dry out. Ordinary propagators, which are essentially seedtrays with raised, transparent plastic covers with some air holes, also provide a germination-friendly environment.

Newspaper pots

A simple and cheap way of sowing seeds is to make paper pots from old newspapers. Don't use colored paper, because the ink might be toxic to plants.

Lay a double-page sheet of newspaper flat and fold it in half lengthwise twice to form a long, narrow strip. Place a glass tumbler or empty food can on its side and on the end of the strip of paper. Roll the newspaper around the glass or can so that about half of the strip of paper overlaps the open end. Push the ends of the paper into the open end of the glass. Pull the tumbler out of the newspaper pocket, and the newspaper pot is ready to use. Fill with compost and stand the pots side by side so that they support each other. Plant the seeds, and when two sets of leaves appear, tear off the bottom of the pot and plant it into the ground. The pot will decompose once it is in the soil. You can make almost any size of newspaper pot, but large ones will need to be of thicker newspaper to support the compost.

You can also use plastic ice cream and margarine tubs as seedtrays, but they must be clean, and you must make a hole in the base for adequate drainage.

Take great care with positioning propagators because intense sunlight at certain times of the day can radically raise the temperature inside the propagator and may scorch the seedlings. Similarly, do not leave a propagator on a cool windowsill without extra protection in case the temperature dips sharply overnight.

LEFT Small seeds can be sown in cell trays and covered with the lightest amount of fine compost. These can be easily thinned or the complete cell planted out.

Sowing outdoors

Before you sow outdoors, prepare the seedbed. Dig the ground to at least a spade deep, adding plenty of well-rotted manure at a rate of a bucketful to each square yard. Add a similar amount of sand to clay soils to improve the texture. Fork over the soil to break up any lumps and then rake it over to remove any stones or hard clumps of earth. Firm the soil by treading heel-and-toe and then continue to rake backwards and forwards to form a fine tilth.

Many vegetable seeds are sown in shallow furrows or V trenches up to 1 inch deep. Draw the corner of a hoe across the ground to make a slit in the soil. Use a garden line as a guide, so that the rows are straight and the plants are easy to weed around as they grow. A garden line is a long piece of string tied to a short stake at each end. The string is pulled across the seedbed and the stakes are pushed into the ground at the other side of the bed.

Drills of up to 2 inches and over can be made for sowing larger vegetable seeds, such as dwarf green beans. Use a spade to make flat-bottomed drills, 6–8 inches wide and 2 inches deep for peas.

Avoid the temptation to sow seeds too thickly, which is a waste of seed, for when they germinate and start to grow, the seedlings will need to be thinned (see opposite). Sow large seeds, such as beans, peas, corn, cucumbers, and squash, in individual holes made by a piece of doweling or the tip of a trowel. Always label rows of seeds after sowing because the memory can play tricks.

Transplanting and hardening

When seedlings have developed two seed leaves (cotyledons), you should transplant them into larger pots or seedtrays—spacing them 1–2 inches apart—so that they have more room to develop into sturdy plants. Any move temporarily sets them back, so make sure they are well watered in and shaded from strong sunshine until they become established. They must, however, have plenty of light so that they do not become too tall and straggly.

Before you can transplant seedlings to their positions outside, you have to harden them off so that they are acclimatized to the natural weather conditions. Put the plants outside in mild weather and bring them inside again in the late afternoon before the temperature begins to fall.

BELOW Vegetable seeds are sown in shallow furrows in a prepared seedbed.

Do this every day, gradually extending the length of time they spend outside until, after seven to ten days, they can remain out overnight, but this must be only when there is no frost forecast.

Thinning and transplanting

Even if you sow only a small amount of seed, some groups of seedlings will need to be thinned until they are at the required distance apart. However, not all thinnings are wasted. With care, crops such as lettuces can be thinned and the seedlings transplanted elsewhere. When you are transplanting seedlings, always hold them gently by the leaves and not the stem, which can damage the tissue and kill the plant.

Thinning and transplanting allows individual plants more room for growth and reduces competition for food, light, and air. The process also helps to keep plants healthy and reduces the chances of attack by pests and diseases.

Thin crops grown outdoors or transplant those that have been hardened off during a mild, calm day. Do not attempt this task if there is strong sunshine or a wind blowing.

Keeping straight against a garden line, use a trowel to make a hole large enough to take the roots of the plant at the same depth as it was originally. Gently firm the soil around the roots with your fingers and water it in.

Propagating fruit

You can increase your stocks of soft fruit by layering, dividing, or by cuttings.

Layering

Strawberry plants can be increased by layering the runners, which develop plantlets. Peg down a runner into moist compost and roots will form in just a few weeks. Once the roots have been given time to develop further, the runner can be severed to give you a new strawberry plant.

Loganberries also reproduce easily if the tip of a stem is pegged down and layered in the soil.

Division

Raspberry canes spread by underground suckers. Dig these up in the fall, divide, and replant them. Use only strong, healthy suckers and destroy any stunted plants with yellowing leaves, because raspberry suckers get raspberry mosaic virus (see page 121) and quickly deteriorate.

LEFT With care, some crops, such as lettuces, can be thinned and transplanted elsewhere.

LEFT Strawberry plants can be easily propagated by pegging down the runners into moist compost.

Cuttings

You can propagate gooseberries from cuttings taken in mid- to late fall. Select any well-ripened shoots that are roughly 12–15 inches long. Cut horizontally through the bottom of the shoot just below a joint, then cut off the unripe top and remove all the buds except for the five at the top. Insert the cutting into a V-shaped trench about 9 inches deep so that the first of the buds is just above the ground, then fill in with soil and tread down firmly. Plant the cuttings 6 inches apart. The following fall they will have formed sufficient roots to be lifted and planted in their permanent positions.

Red, white and black currants are best propagated by cuttings in the same way as gooseberries, but you do not have to remove the buds from black currant cuttings.

Sowing and propagating   **73**

Growing under cover

Growing your plants in a protected environment will enable you to get them off to a flying start at the beginning of the growing season and also allow you to grow plants that might otherwise be too tender to thrive outdoors.

Whether you have a small greenhouse or a large polytunnel, this additional protection will offer scope to widen the range of plants you grow.

Greenhouse

Although you do not have to have a greenhouse to grow your own food, if there is room for one you will be able to extend the growing season by germinating seeds and getting plants into growth earlier. It's also a good working area because tasks such as transplanting and potting on can be done when the weather prevents you from working in the garden.

The size of your greenhouse will depend on space and cost, but even a small one will help

BELOW A greenhouse enables you to grow plants that will benefit from extra warmth.

tender plants thrive. If you don't mind the work of dismantling and re-erecting, buying a second-hand one may be the answer. At least with a new one there is only the erecting to do. Building your own is another option, and viewing different styles of greenhouse will give you some ideas. You can get small polythene greenhouses, but these need to be well secured to withstand severe winds. Remember that all greenhouses need ventilation of some kind.

Inside the greenhouse you will need staging, which is like a trestle table with slats instead of a solid top. You can stand seedtrays and potted plants on the staging, but it can also double as a work bench. Keep compost in a large plastic tray on the staging to make potting up easy. The staging also needs to be removable so that it can make room for growbags that stand on the ground to enable you to grow crops such as indoor tomatoes in summer.

Having water available in the greenhouse will save a lot of time and effort. If there is room, run some guttering along the under rim of the outside, with a downpipe coming into a rain barrel through a wooden panel in the place of glass. This will provide rainwater that is at the same temperature as the greenhouse.

A cool greenhouse has no artificial heating. It will be warm when the sun falls on it from spring through to fall and may get very hot in midsummer, when ventilation will be needed, but it will not be frost free during the winter months.

There are several ways of heating: electricity, oil, a paraffin lamp, or even a wood-burning stove. An environmentally friendly way to provide power and heat is to install a roof-top wind generator or a solar panel, which need not be mounted on the greenhouse itself as long as it is nearby. Whichever system you use will depend on the area to be kept warm and your budget. Even with heating, the greenhouse will also benefit from insulation in the form of plastic sheeting around the inside in winter. Make sure the air vents are kept clear for ventilation.

Polytunnel

A polytunnel is a single-span structure made from hoops supporting a polythene film. This creates a bubble of still air, which is warmed by solar energy. Compared to a greenhouse it is more difficult to keep frost free in winter and needs insulating if it is to be heated. Polytunnels are becoming increasingly popular, including in community gardens, but check any local planning regulations. When they are installed correctly they are very stable and hard wearing, but they must be sited where there is some protection from strong prevailing winds. Do not site a polytunnel near overhanging branches, which will compromise light levels inside the tunnel, and there is also a risk of debris falling on the film or wind damage from falling branches.

Polytunnels are suitable for a wide range of exotic plants, including guavas, loquats, nectarines, peaches, figs, and pomegranates. Growing citrus fruits, such as grapefruit and oranges, is possible as long as the temperature does not fall below 41°F.

Hotbed

A hotbed provides bottom heat. Dig a shallow rectangular area in well-drained land and build a clamp. Add fresh manure mixed with soiled straw to a depth of 2–3 feet. Tread it in well. The manure will begin to ferment, which generates the heat. Test the heat with a thermometer after a few days—the optimum is 75°F or plants will be scorched—and if it is too hot turn the material over with a fork and spray it with water. Place a layer of compost 8–12 inches deep on top of the bed and cover it with a frame. Allow to stand for a day or so and then test the temperature again.

Salad plants and radishes can be sown directly into the soil in midwinter. In late winter you can add trays of peas, beans, turnips, and cauliflowers to bring the plants on. In mid- to late spring zucchini or melons can be planted. The hotbed will last for two or three months.

Cold frames

A cold frame is basically four walls with a pane of glass laid on top. The glass should be set in wood—an old window is ideal—so that it can be opened up one end to ventilate the frame. If you put compost in the cold frame you can put plants straight in the compost. Alternatively, stand potted plants in the frame.

Cold frames are ideal for plants that need to be cold in winter but that also need to be protected from wind and excessive rain.

Cloche

A cloche is a small, portable covering. There are various styles, made from hard or corrugated plastic, glass barn types, soft plastic tunnels, and glass tents. If you place a cloche over a seedbed before sowing, you can warm up the soil and then grow on the plants in a protected environment.

Glass bells were traditionally used to provide individual plants with cover and warmth, but a less expensive way of achieving something similar is to cut off the bottom of a large, clear plastic drinks bottle and place this over a plant.

You can lay plastic sheeting or garden cloth on the ground to protect seeds until they germinate, and once the seedlings appear place cloches or a plastic tunnel over them.

ABOVE Glass bells were traditionally used to protect growing plants, but plastic bottles with the bottoms removed will do the same job.

Watering and feeding

Water is vital for plants to survive and thrive. They draw it from the soil through their roots, and it then passes through all parts of the plant, eventually being released onto the surface of the leaves where it evaporates.

This is a continuous cycle that provides the plant with the moisture it needs, and watering plants regularly is more important than feeding them.

Watering crops

In hot weather water evaporates more quickly from the leaves, and if the supply of water to the roots does not keep up with the water loss, pores on the leaves that release the water are closed and the plant's system closes down. The plant then stops growing, having become severely stressed. Once the temperature has dropped or the plant

BELOW Guttering from a greenhouse, garage, or shed roof with a downpipe into a rain barrel will provide you with essential rainwater.

receives moisture to its roots, the system starts up again. However, if water isn't provided and the roots remain dry, the plant will wilt and die.

The flow of water through a plant will be effective only if the roots can absorb moisture. This is why newly planted plants should be regularly watered because they need new roots to grow and seek moisture from a wider area.

Fruit and vegetables are thirstier than ornamental plants, especially when the fruit is forming. Any period of drought will curtail growth and seriously affect the harvest.

How you water is just as important as when you water. The temperature of the water should be similar to the air temperature so that plants are not shocked. Avoid directing a hosepipe of icy cold water straight at a plant on a hot day, as the plants could collapse in a few days because of the chilling effect of the cold water. Once this happens it is unlikely that the plant will recover. If you use a hosepipe, direct the flow onto the soil around the plants and not at the plants themselves. Applying a mulch to well-watered ground will help keep the water in the soil and prevent surface evaporation (see pages 78–9).

A sprinkler is useful on a vegetable patch, but switch it on in the cool of the evening so that your plants are less likely to be shocked and less evaporation takes place.

The simplest way of applying water is with a watering can. Put a rose on the spout so that you can gently water seeds and seedlings, but remove the rose when you are watering around the base of a plant. A simple way of directing water to the roots is to insert a plastic flowerpot in the ground—not so close to the plant that the roots are damaged—and then you can water into the pot. You may not have to water the vegetable plot every day, but once you start, water thoroughly. If you apply too little water, it will not penetrate the soil sufficiently to benefit the roots.

Storing water

Water is an increasingly scarce resource, and even in areas that enjoy sufficient rainfall climate change may mean that it is not always available. The use of hosepipes, for example, is sometimes banned in certain areas, or you may have environmental concerns over using a hosepipe.

If your house does not have a rain barrel, you can easily connect a downpipe from the guttering into one. Guttering could also collect rainwater from the greenhouse, garage, or shed roof, and with a downpipe into a rain barrel there will be plenty of water at a suitable temperature.

Feeding

Water helps plants draw nutrients from the soil to help them grow. Although plants need around 30 different nutrients, the main ones are nitrogen (N) for leaves, phosphorus (P) for roots, and potassium (K) for flowers and fruits. In lesser quantities plants also require magnesium, calcium, sulfur, carbon, hydrogen, oxygen, iron, manganese, boron, molybdenum, zinc, and copper. Although these nutrients are found naturally in soil, you will have to replace them as plants use them up. Plants lacking in any of these nutrients will look distressed and develop discolored foliage or they simply will not grow.

To grow bountiful vegetables and fruit you need to feed the soil before planting, watch for any nutrient deficiencies, and then feed the plants accordingly. There are many different types

Foliar feeds

A quick way to apply nutrients to a plant is through a foliar feed. Spraying a liquid fertilizer directly onto the foliage will boost a plant that is suffering from any deficiency. Spray the underside of the leaves as well as the upper surface until the liquid drips off. This type of feed should be regarded as supplementary feeding only, because feeding the soil, and therefore the roots, is of prime importance.

of fertilizer, but all fall into two categories, organic or inorganic. Organic fertilizers can be of animal, plant, or mineral origin, and the nutrients they contain are released slowly by being broken down by micro-organisms in the soil. Some fertilizers, such as pelleted chicken manure or seaweed meal, contain a range of nutrients, while others, such as rock phosphate, are more specific. Inorganic fertilizers are made from chemicals.

Some of the fertilizers most readily used are:

Bonemeal is high in phosphates to stimulate root growth.

Dolomitic limestone contains calcium and magnesium, but is used to raise the pH of the soil.

Potash is a soluble potassium suitable for a deficiency of potash in tomatoes and fruit.

Rock potash is an alternative to bonemeal when a shortage of potash turns leaves bluish-green.

Seaweed meal is a slow-acting soil conditioner that is rich in trace elements.

Whenever you use fertilizers made from animal derivatives, such as bonemeal, you should always wear gloves, apply them on a still day, wear goggles, wash your hands after use, and keep animals and children away.

Apply slow-release fertilizers to the soil several days before sowing or planting so that they will be in the soil when the plants need them.

If your plants are growing well the soil is already being cared for. Do not be tempted to overfeed plants because in doing so you may upset the balance of the nutrients in the soil, in addition to being rather wasteful.

LEFT Organic fertilizers release their nutrients slowly by being broken down by micro-organisms in the soil.

Mulching and weeding

Weeds that develop in the garden compete with your crops for light, moisture, and nutrients. Regular weeding is essential, but mulching the ground prevents weed growth in the first place.

Mulching

A mulch is a layer of material that is laid over the surface of the soil to reduce moisture loss and also to prevent weed seeds from germinating. Depending on the material used, it can also provide nutrients for plant growth.

A mulch is usually put on the soil around plants in spring, while the soil is still moist from winter rain but has begun to warm up a little. You can mulch later in the summer, but make sure the soil has had a good soaking beforehand—a mulch can keep moisture out just as efficiently as it can keep moisture in. Any mulch still remaining on the soil come fall can be dug or forked in.

Mulching materials

The following are among the most often used mulches in the garden.

BELOW Keep the vegetable patch free of weeds and mulch the area to help with weed control and to retain the soil's moisture.

Biodegradable materials Burlap and hemp sacking can be kept in place with pegs or bricks.

Black plastic Although it looks unsightly, this is one of the most efficient ways of eradicating weeds. When it is laid on the soil it eliminates all light, so weeds cannot germinate and survive. Anchor the plastic by burying the edges in the soil or use a few bricks to hold it down, especially if you live in an area that experiences high winds. Cut X-shaped slits through the plastic wherever you want to plant, but remember that you will have to water the plants individually because rainfall will not be able to penetrate to the ground.

Paper Tough brown paper, the sort used for parcels, can be bought in a roll, which can be unrolled and anchored, either by burying the edges in the soil or securing it with bricks. Cover it with grass clippings to stop it tearing when wet.

Newspaper This is one of the cheapest and most widely available mulches, although you should use pages with black ink only, because colored ink can be toxic to plants. You will need six to eight layers of paper, and remember to soak them first so that they do not blow away. Cover the newspaper with grass clippings, leaf mold, or straw, which may also need to be dampened so that it doesn't blow across the vegetable plot in windy weather.

Cardboard So many businesses throw away brown cardboard boxes that these should be readily available for free. Do not use cardboard that has colorful printing on it or a glossy finish. Secure it and then cover with grass clippings or compost to improve the look. Vigorous crops, such as pumpkins, can be planted through cardboard.

Shredded prunings You can buy or hire shredders, and they are immensely useful for chopping up most woody prunings. They are not suitable for mulching vegetable crops, but they can help to keep weeds down in an area of fruit by making useful pathways between the crops.

Grass clippings As long as you have not treated your lawn with any chemicals, grass clippings have many good uses in the garden. You can spread them, to a depth of about 2 inches, directly over an area you want to keep weed free, or you place them over other materials, such as newspaper or cardboard, to improve their appearance, and, of course, you can add them to your compost heap.

Chipped bark Chipped bark is often spread over plastic to improve the appearance. Remember that fungal spores can grow on bark that is constantly moist, so check it regularly and replace it as necessary.

Weeding

Weeds are plants that are not wanted among your vegetables and fruit. They compete with crops for light, water, and nutrients and can have a debilitating effect on the growth of the plants that you do want to grow.

There are two types of weed, annuals and perennials. Annual weeds have a short life cycle but are prolific seed producers, so throughout the growing season they reappear. In the fall and winter, digging annual weeds into the bottom of each trench will kill them, and, with every cultivation, the number of seedlings will be reduced. Perennial weeds are difficult to eradicate as they overwinter in the soil, and many have long roots, which are hard to dig out and the smallest piece of root is capable of growing.

If your intended vegetable plot is infested with weeds, you must remove both the topgrowth and roots before it is worth sowing any crops. Double dig the area (see page 65) and remove every piece of root and rhizome that you find. Gather the waste together and burn it or dispose of it, but do not put it on the compost heap.

Once you have cleared an area, stay in control by weeding regularly. It's easier to remove weeds when they are still small. Weeds are survivors and will take over again if you allow them.

Hand-weeding In raised beds and containers hand-weeding is recommended. Use a hand fork to loosen the roots.

Hoeing The traditional way of weeding in the vegetable plot is to slice the topgrowth of weeds with a Dutch hoe. Keep the hoe on the surface of the soil so that further weed seeds are not disturbed and brought into growth.

Heat A thermal weeder powered by kerosene or gas eradicates seedling weeds. The heat will cause them to wilt then die. Take great care and direct the flame only at the weeds you want to eradicate.

Digging This is a labor-intensive but efficient way of dealing with weeds if every piece of root is meticulously removed.

Mulching Covering an area with a mulch or black plastic will help with weed control. Bury the edges of the plastic so that it cannot blow away and to prevent small birds and animals getting trapped underneath.

Inorganic chemicals Weedkillers kill vegetation and root growth. Some become inactive when they come into contact with the soil. If you decide to apply weedkillers, use them only on a dry, still day when there is no danger of drift.

Annual and perennial weeds

Some of the most persistent annual weeds are:

Scarlet pimpernel (*Anagallis arvensis*), shepherd's purse (*Capsella bursa-pastoris*), white deadnettle (*Lamium album*), groundsel (*Senecio vulgaris*), charlock (*Sinapis arvensis*), chickweed (*Stellaria media*), and speedwell (*Veronica filiformis*).

Common perennial weeds include:

Ground elder (*Aegopodium podagraria*), creeping thistle (*Cirsium arvensis*), field bindweed (*Convolvulus arvense*), couch grass (*Elymus repens*), creeping buttercup (*Ranunculus repens*), blackberry or bramble (*Rubus fruticosus*), dock (*Rumex* spp.), dandelion (*Taraxacum officinale*), and stinging nettle (*Urtica dioica*).

Pruning and training

You will have to prune fruit trees and bushes to keep them cropping well, to keep them in shape, and to remove dead and damaged branches. If you are growing plants against a wall, you will have to train new growth.

Pruning tools

Well-maintained pruning tools are essential if they are to cut through branches cleanly and not damage the plant. They must be sharp, so wash and wipe them after use and do not leave them where they can rust. Oil metal parts if they are not often used.

Hand pruners Good hand pruners are vital for pruning. Find a pair that feels comfortable in your hand and that is the right size for you, and spend as much as you can afford, because good-quality pruners will last far longer than less expensive ones.

Loppers Long-handled pruners, loppers are used with both hands to cut branches up to 1½ inches thick.

Tree loppers These long-handled pruners are used to cut shoots in tall fruit trees. They cut branches to 1 inch thick that are up to 10 feet high and are operated by a rope and pulley or metal rod and handle. They are ideal for pruning standard trees that have been neglected.

Saws An average folding pruning saw is about 7 inches long, extending to 16 inches for use. The teeth cut on both push and pull strokes and will cut wood to 1½ inches thick. Straight-bladed, fixed-handled saws will cut branches up to 5 inches thick. Grecian saws, which have a tapered and pointed blade, cut on the pull stroke and are suitable for using in narrow spaces.

Knives Pruning knives are used for paring cut surfaces smooth, bark-ringing trunks, or notching and nicking buds.

Pruning techniques

When you are pruning, always make cuts just above a healthy vegetative bud, not a blossom bud. The ideal cut starts opposite the base of the bud and slants up toward the top of the bud. A cut that is too slanting exposes too much hardwood, and you should avoid making a cut that leaves a long stub beyond the bud as the stub may die back. If the cut is made too close to the bud, there may be no growth from that bud.

Support long or heavy branches while you are using a pruning saw so that the branch doesn't accidentally fall and tear the tissue. It is often helpful to reduce some of the weight by removing the branch in sections. The first of the final cuts should be about 12 inches from the trunk. This will be an undercut until the saw binds. The second cut is made 1–2 inches beyond the first sawing but from above the branch to remove it. This will leave a stump that can be sawn off close to the main stem. This procedure avoids splitting the wood or stripping the bark, which would create an ugly gash and probably injure the tree.

Apple and pear Apple and pear trees are pruned in winter to restore the basic framework and encourage fruiting. Start by removing all shoots from below the point where the main branches grow out. Prune out any upright branches and branches that grow across the center of the tree. Cut back any dead, damaged, or diseased wood to healthy tissue. Remove any shoots in the center of the tree to open it up, leaving main branches free of sideshoots between the branch and 24 inches along the main branches. Work along each of the remaining branches, shortening sideshoots and thinning the fruiting spurs.

Plum and cherry Plum trees are pruned in a similar way to apples and pears, but not so severely. Cherry trees are seldom pruned. Plums and cherries should not be cut in winter, which encourages silver leaf disease; wait until mid- to late summer.

Raspberries Cut out old fruiting canes of summer-fruiting raspberries after you harvest the crop. Autumn-fruiting raspberries produce fruit on the current year's growth, so they are best pruned by midwinter when all the canes should be cut down to ground level.

Red and white currants To create a free-standing bush from a new plant, prune all the main stems by about one-third immediately after planting. Subsequent pruning consists of cutting back sideshoots to five leaves from their point of growth in late summer, then cutting back again by about one-third to one or two buds in winter. Open bushes by cutting out any crossing shoots.

Black currants Prune after leaf drop by cutting back a few of the older shoots to the ground every year. Cut out any crossing shoots. The aim is to remove about one-third of the bush each year.

Training

Some fruit trees and bushes are trained to grow along walls or fences with the aid of a framework of wires.

Espalier An espalier consists of a vertical main trunk from which side branches are trained along horizontal wires to right and left about 15 inches apart. Espalier trees are useful for growing

alongside pathways, and a single-tier espalier is called a stepover. Apples and pears grown on semi-dwarfing rootstocks are suitable.

Cordon A cordon consists of a single fruiting stem 8–15 feet long, which is grown diagonally at an angle of 45 degrees. It may also be grown vertically or with two parallel stems, when the arrangement is known as a double cordon.

Bamboo canes are fixed to the wire fence, and the cordons are tied to these. The flowers and fruits are produced on short spurs along the trunk, and these are built up over the years. Apples, plums, and pears make good cordons.

Pyramid A pyramid form has a central trunk with branches trained in increasing length from the top of the tree to the bottom, producing a cone shape. It is suitable for apples, pears, plums, and damsons.

ABOVE Some fruit trees can be trained to grow along walls or fences with the aid of a framework of wire.

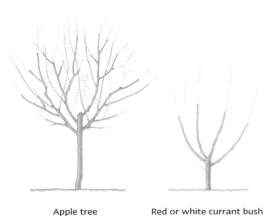

Apple tree   Red or white currant bush

Plum tree

Black currant bush

Supporting and protecting plants

Some plants need support to keep them in their trained form. Others need protection to prevent wind damage, or need a framework to climb over or to be trained over a support.

Staking fruit

Fruit trees grown on dwarfing rootstocks will require staking from the moment they are planted, and even standard fruit trees must be staked until they are well established and the stake is no longer a support.

When you are planting bare-rooted fruit trees, put the stake in once you have dug the hole so that you don't damage the plant's roots when you hammer the stake into the ground. The stake should be a length of 2 x 2 inch environmentally friendly preservative-treated lumber, one-third of which will be buried in the ground. When you are planting container-grown trees, the stake should go in at an angle of 45 degrees, and the tree is secured where it meets the stake. Place stakes on the windward side of trees so that they are blown away from the stake in blustery conditions.

Use plastic tree ties to secure the plant to the stake, and check them throughout the year to make sure the tie is not pinching the trunk or has worn loose. Alternatively, cut ties from pairs of tights—the material is strong and slightly elastic.

Trees trained as cordons or espaliers need stout posts and strong supporting wires, and to make a permanent, stable framework the posts should be set in concrete. If you prefer, use post holders, long metal spikes that you hammer into the ground. Whichever method you prefer, it is essential that the wires and posts are strong enough to bear the weight of the plant, which will be even heavier when it is bearing fruit. Raspberries, blackberries, loganberries and grapes need similar support. The more substantial the posts and wires, the longer they will last.

Staking vegetables

Climbing beans The simplest way of supporting green or climbing beans is to make a wigwam support of five or six bamboo canes. Arrange them in a circle, spacing them evenly, and hold the tops with string or in a special rubber top. For a row of climbing beans you can use pairs of bamboo canes, spaced apart and then drawn together at the top, with another cane running the length of the tops. A wooden frame with netting secured to it will also provide climbing support, but make sure that the netting is tight and strong or the weight of the plants will make it sag.

Peas Garden peas can be supported with twigs and sticks, so that the tendrils have something to cling to. If you do not support them, the peas will trail over the soil and become easy meals for slugs and snails. Twigs and branches from prunings can be used to support pea plants.

RIGHT Tomatoes will need supporting—here a bamboo cane is being used.

Fava beans A row of broad beans can be supported by setting a couple of bamboo canes at either end of a row, with two more on each side of the row, and winding strings around the canes and along the row, through and around the plants. As the plants grow the foliage will disguise the string, but it will still be sufficient support to prevent the plants from falling over and the pods from rotting on the ground in wet weather.

Tall-growing vegetables Tall-growing crops such as Brussels sprouts should be staked individually if you live in an area that suffers from strong winds. Tie the plant to the stake with garden twine and check it regularly to make sure that it is not chaffing the stem.

Tomatoes Tomatoes grown outdoors or in the greenhouse will need supporting, because the plants grow quite tall and have a considerable weight to support when fruiting. A post and wire support system similar to that used for raspberries will be ideal outdoors. In the greenhouse wires or thick string supports can be fixed to the greenhouse, or to canes placed in the ground or tomato containers.

Flowers You might decide to grow some flowers to use in the house or to sell, and flowers in season could provide a welcome income. Sweet peas (Lathyrus odoratus) are always popular, and the more often the blooms are cut, the more flowers will be produced. They are climbing plants and need cane supports just like climbing beans. Dahlias and chrysanthemums, which also make cut flowers but later in the year than sweet peas, grow into quite large plants and should be individually staked.

Protecting plants

Staking plants helps to protect them against wind as well as offering them support. Wind can do lots of damage, blowing over plants and desiccating leaves, which then wilt and die. Erecting screens or planting low hedges will provide some shelter in areas where wind is a problem.

You will have to protect cherries and soft fruit against birds. Once the fruits begin to ripen, the birds will be up at dawn feasting on your labors if you do not prevent them. A standard cherry tree is difficult to cover, but colorful strips of glittering foil tied on branches so that they move in the breeze will frighten some birds away.

Erecting a fruit cage around soft fruit is certainly one way of dealing with the problem. These come in all sizes and are quite straightforward to construct, but you should remember to take down the netting on the roof in autumn when all fruiting has finished to prevent broken branches getting tangled in the netting during winter storms. In addition, a heavy fall of snow could cause the netting to collapse.

Saving seed

Saving seeds from your own vegetables is the best way of preparing for next harvest, and it's certainly the cheapest. It's also one of the best ways of being self-sufficient and having a sustainable vegetable plot.

Because most plants produce more seeds than you will need, you might be able to exchange your seeds with your neighbors who have grown other plants.

Remember, don't save seeds from F1, F2, or other hybrids, which are unlikely to come true to the parent plant.

Use plants that set good seeds with their own pollen, but even these self-pollinating plants can be cross-pollinated by insects, so take care if you grow different varieties of the same vegetable. If other varieties are being grown nearby, plant tall crops on either side of the vegetables you want to save seed from. Leave seeds and fruits to ripen on the plant and save seed from the strongest plants. Take the first seeds that are formed. Thoroughly dry them before storing in burlap bags or paper envelopes in a cool, dry, dark place. Remember to label all the seeds so that they are clearly identified.

Beans

Fava beans Let the seeds mature on the stalks. When the pods are dark brown and wrinkled, pick and shell them. The seeds should be hard and brittle when they are ready to store.

Green beans Allow quality pods to ripen on the plant and start to dry out. Place them in a dry place until they are brittle, then store in a shallow, paper-lined tray.

Italian flat beans These beans need to be pollinated by insects or the wind. A sprinkling of water on the flowers also helps to set them. If you are growing on a community garden, it would be useful if everyone grew the same variety. Collect and store as French beans.

Beet, Swiss chard, and leaf beet

Cover the flowerheads with a cloth bag and shake occasionally to distribute the pollen. As the seeds mature they turn brown and dry out. Rub them into a bucket and then dry.

Brassicas

All brassicas will produce a flower stalk with yellow flowers and seed pods. Cut the stalks as soon as the pods look dry. Place the stalks on newspaper indoors and leave them to mature fully, when the pods will shatter and release the seeds. Place another sheet of newspaper over the top once the pods start popping so that you do not lose seed.

Carrots

Overwinter carrots in the ground or dig them up and store and replant them in spring. When they flower, cut off the flowers when they begin to turn brown. Dry the seedheads and rub them between your hands to retrieve the bearded seeds.

Chilies and sweet (bell) peppers

Take well-ripened sweet peppers, cut them open and rub the seeds off the core onto a plate and dry. Do the same with chilies, but wear rubber gloves because chili oil is difficult to wash off. Dry the seeds in a warm place until they snap rather than bend.

Cucumbers

Pick cucumbers when they are very ripe and turned yellow. Keep for another week, then cut open and scoop out the pulp and seeds. Spread the good-quality seeds out on a plate to dry.

Eggplants

The skin color of most ripe eggplants is a dirty purple-brown. Cut the ripe eggplant into quarters and put in tepid water to rub the seeds out. Good seeds will sink. Retrieve and allow them to dry.

Herbs

Identify the plants you want to provide seeds, and when the flowers start to wither and turn brown, the seeds will be ripening. Cut the flower spikes and place them on paper indoors, and rub the heads together to release the seeds.

Lettuce

Do not collect seed from lettuce that has bolted early. About two weeks after the lettuce has flowered, cut it and place it, head down, in a clean bucket. The seeds will ripen further and fall over several days. Retrieve the seeds and put them on a flat surface to dry.

Melons

Grow the plants under a cloth and pollinate them with a paintbrush, making sure you take pollen from one plant and insert it into a flower on a separate plant. Pick the melons when they are ripe and after a few days open the fruit, scoop the seed into a sieve, and wash under running water. Lay the seeds out on a plate to dry.

Peas

Let peas mature until the pods are brown and the seeds begin to rattle. Once they start to wither, pull them up. When the pods are really dry, shell the peas and leave them on paper to dry.

Pumpkins, zucchini, and squashes

Male pumpkin flowers have a straight stem, the females have an immature fruit beneath the flower. When the flower buds turn yellow, put a rubber band over the petals so that they cannot open. Next day pick a male flower, remove the protection and petals. Uncover a female flower and gently brush the pollen from the male flower onto the stigma in the female. Cover the female flower and put identification on the stem. Pick when ripe and keep in a cool, dry place for a month to ripen further. Cut open the pumpkin, scoop out the seeds, and spread them out to dry. Treat zucchini and squashes the same.

Tomatoes

Allow tomatoes to ripen fully, then collect the fruits and slice them in half before squeezing the juice and seeds into a sieve. Wash under running water, then place the seeds in a well-ventilated place away from direct sunlight to dry.

Turnips and oriental brassicas

Grow the seed crop in late summer where they can overwinter protected from harsh weather. In spring they will flower and produce seed pods. When the pods are dry and brittle, cut the stalks and lay them on paper indoors to finish drying. Crush the pods to release the seeds.

LEFT Let fava beans mature on the stalk, then when dark brown and wrinkled pick and shell them.

Pests and diseases

It may be tempting to reach for an insecticide or fungicide if your crop that you've spent months tending has succumbed to a pest or disease. However, there are plenty of other ways to protect your plants that don't involve chemicals.

One of the best ways of avoiding pests and diseases is to keep your plants healthily in fertile, well-drained, well-watered soil. If plants are under stress for whatever reason, they are much more likely to succumb to attacks from insects and soil-borne diseases, which will certainly affect their cropping potential. Be vigilant and immediately remove and destroy any diseased plants so that the problem does not spread.

Practice crop rotation (see page 62) so that you are not planting the same type of crop in ground that might be harboring a particular problem. Intersperse your vegetables with companion plants, such as marigolds (*Tagetes* spp.), which help deter some insect pests. Monoculture—vast areas of a single crop—tends to attract specific diseases or pests, so planting small areas of different crops will help in two ways: first, any infestation or outbreak of disease will be confined to a small area, and second, insect pests, looking for a particular host plant, may be confused by the neighboring plants and move on to another garden.

There are several biological controls, which can be especially useful in greenhouses and polytunnels, and you can water nematodes into warm soil to kill soil-dwelling slugs. Remember that you will have to tolerate a low level of pests for the biological controls to survive. In addition, if you encourage plenty of wildlife into your garden (see pages 92–3), you will eventually build up a natural balance of pests and their predators.

You might decide, as a last resort, to use chemical deterrents and solutions if a problem becomes more serious. Always follow the manufacturer's instructions about timing and quantities, and remember to wash the produce particularly carefully. Wherever possible, select pesticides that do not harm beneficial insects. Do bear in mind, though, that although the following lists of pests and diseases look formidable, there are few gardeners who encounter more than one or two problems in a lifetime of gardening.

Biological controls

Among the most widely used biological controls are:

Control	Pest
Amblyseus cucumeris (predatory mite)	thrips
Aphidoletes aphidimyza (predatory midge larva)	aphids
Cryptolaemus montrouzieri (predatory beetle)	mealybug
Encarsia formosa (parasitic wasp)	glasshouse whitefly
Heterorhabditis megidis (parasitic nematode)	vine weevil and chafer grubs
Metaphycus helvolus (parasitic wasp)	soft scale
Phasmarhabditis hermaphrodita (parasitic nematode)	slugs
Phytoseiulus persimilis (predatory mite)	red spider mite
Steinernema feltiae (parasitic nematode)	leatherjackets

Pests

The pests you are most likely to encounter are described below, along with a note of the best way of controlling them in an organic garden. Companion plants are suggested where they are appropriate.

Ants

Infestations are more of a nuisance than a threat to plant life, although they can disturb the soil, especially in containers, and encourage aphids.

Control Boiling water or a solution of equal parts of borax and confectioners' sugar will kill them.

Companion Lavender (*Lavandula*), peppermint (*Mentha x piperita*), spearmint (*Mentha spicata*), and tansy (*Tanacetum*).

Aphids (*Aphidius* spp.)

These are small, soft-bodied insects, and the most common are greenfly and blackfly, although they can be other colors. They feed on sap, weaken plants,

Blackfly weaken plants by feeding on sap.

and spread diseases, but they also excrete a sticky, sugary honeydew as they feed, and this turns into a sooty mold and the leaves turn black. They reproduce rapidly because females can give birth from a week old without needing to mate.

Control Ladybugs, lacewings, and hoverflies are natural predators. For an initial infestation, pick off the aphids with your fingers. Dried pyrethrum (*Tanacetum cinerariifolium*) flowers, pulverized to a powder and mixed with water, make an effective spray against both aphids and flea beetles.

Companion French marigold (*Tagetes*), nasturtium (*Tropaeolum*), pyrethrum (*Tanacetum Linerariifolium*), spearmint (*Mentha spicata*), and stinging nettle (*Urtica dioica*).

Apple woolly aphids (*Erosoma lanigerum*)

These pinkish-brown aphids are covered in a waxy coating that looks like cotton batting. Severe infestations can devastate apple and pear trees.

Control Spray affected areas with a jet wash, then scrub with soapy water.

Companion Nasturtium (*Tropaeolum*).

Birds

Many birds pull out onion sets and eat emerging pea and brassica leaves and bush and top fruit. Flocks of pigeons can devastate some crops.
Control Cover vulnerable crops with netting or cloth. Growing raspberries, strawberries, and currants in a fruit cage is effective. Shiny ribbons and old CDs that twist in the wind can help deter birds.

Cabbage root fly (*Delia radicum*)

Eggs are laid at the base of plants that have been transplanted, and the larvae attack the roots, causing the plant to wilt and die.

Control Water plants and earth up well. Place collars of card or carpet underlay around the plant or cover them with cloth.

Small white butterfly (*Pieris rapae*)

The larval stage of this butterfly is a voracious caterpillar that devours the leaves of brassicas.

Control Pick the caterpillars off by hand and either squash them or put them in a bucket of soapy water. Cover the plants with netting to prevent butterflies from laying their eggs.

Companion Peppermint (*Mentha x piperita*).

Capsid bugs (*Lygocoris pabulinus, Lygus rugulipennis*)

Smaller than, but similar to, aphids, capsid bugs cause brown patches on leaves, which then fall. They affect apples, bush fruit, potatoes, and beans. Vegetables can withstand capsid bug attack, but they greatly damage fruit trees and bushes.

Control Spray apple trees after flowering with an appropriate pesticide. Winter tar washes are also helpful.

Companion Garlic (*Allium sativum*).

Carrot fly (*Psila rosae*)

These small black flies lay eggs in the soil around carrots, parsnips, and parsley in late spring, with a second generation laying eggs in late summer. The white larvae tunnel into the root flesh, and the damage can ruin the crop.

Control Sow carrot seeds in early summer to miss the first infestation. Make cardboard collars and place them on the soil around individual carrots or parsnips. Cover seeds with weed cloth after sowing.

Companion Onion and leek (*Allium*), rosemary (*Rosmarinus*), wormwood, sage, and black salsify repel carrot fly.

June beetle (*Melolontha melolontha*)

The adult beetle eats leaves and flowers, but the white grubs feed on plant roots, damaging strawberries, raspberries, lettuce, grasses, and cereals.

Control Kill grubs whenever found. Parasitic nematodes are available.

Companion Petunias deter beetles, and legumes planted in rotation will protect grain crops.

Codling moth (*Cydia pomonella*)

The codling moth lays eggs on growing apples and pears from early to midsummer. The brown-headed, white caterpillar larvae hatch out in 2 weeks and tunnel into the fruit.

Control Pheromone traps hung in the trees will attract male moths and prevent them from mating.

Companion Garlic (*Allium sativum*).

Currant blister aphid (*Crytomyzus ribis*)

Also known as American blight. Pale yellow aphids are found on the underside of mainly red and white currant plant leaves in early summer, but black currants and gooseberries are also susceptible. Damage is seen as blisters.

Control Infected leaves should be detached and destroyed.

Companion Encourage aphid predators by planting flowers that attract hoverflies and other insects.

Cutworms (*Noctua pronuba*)

The larvae of certain nocturnal moths feed on the stems of young plants and kill them.

Control A cardboard collar around young plants will foil cutworms.

Companion Oak leaf mulch will repel them.

Deer

Deer populations are increasing and proving a nuisance to growers. They eat young trees and trample other crops.

Control Fencing is the most effective protection, but it must be made of strong wire and be at least 7 feet high. A thick hedge may discourage deer, but it would be worth planting some lavender bushes (*Lavandula*) around the fruit and vegetable area because deer dislike the scent of lavender.

Earwigs (*Forficula auricularia*)

Earwigs accumulate in large numbers and feed on plants overnight, causing a great deal of damage.

Control Trap earwigs by placing flowerpots filled with straw, dry grass, or crumpled newspaper upside down on the tops of canes. These should be placed in the soil around susceptible plants, checked daily and any earwigs destroyed.

Flea beetle (*Phyllotreta* spp.)

The small black, jumping beetles live in plant debris and attack brassicas, radishes, turnips, arugula, and Chinese cabbage. Grubs tunnel into stems and eat roots; adult beetles eat holes in the leaves.

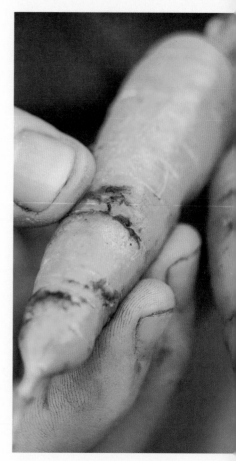

Wireworms damage the flesh of carrots.

Control Keep the ground clear of debris. Encourage seedlings to grow quickly and make sure they are always well watered. Cover with cloth after sowing. A piece of wood smeared with grease and brushed over the plants will entice the beetles to jump up, and they will stick to the grease.

Companion Catnip (*Nepeta*).

Leatherjackets (*Tipula paludosa*)

The larvae of the crane fly, leatherjackets feed on the roots of plants from summer through the winter and into spring.

Control Water the soil well in early fall and cover with black plastic overnight when the larvae will come to the surface. Lift the plastic next day to expose the larvae to birds. There is a biological control in the form of a pathogenic nematode, which can be watered into warm soil. Turkeys and chickens love eating leatherjackets.

Potato cyst nematode
(*Heterodera rostochiensis, H. pallida*)

An infestation can be identified when potato leaves turn yellow before dying. Where there are eelworm infestations the potato tubers will be exceedingly small. This pest is a threat if potatoes are grown on the same area as the previous year.

Control Practice crop rotation. Burn affected plants, and do not grow potatoes in the same area for at least 6 years.

Companion Deadnettle (*Lamium*) and horseradish (*Armoracia rusticana*), which should be planted at the corners of the plot.

Rabbits

These prolific mammals can destroy green crops overnight.

Control Wire netting at least 3 feet high and 12 inches below ground level with small mesh specifically to repel rabbits is widely available.

Red spider mites
(*Tetranychus urticae*)

Primarily a problem in the greenhouse, these minuscule, yellow green mites with two dark spots on their backs feed under leaves and suck sap from the plant. They can produce a mass of webbing over the tops of plants. In autumn the mites develop the red female forms, which mate and overwinter in covered areas.

Control Red spider mites do not like damp areas, so misting plants helps to keep them at bay. They have become resistant to most

pesticides, but the predatory mite *Phytoseiulus persimilis* is a way of controlling the pest biologically.

Companion Garlic (*Allium sativum*) and pyrethrum (*Tanacetum cinerariifolium*).

Sciarid fly (*Sciara fucata*)

The fly lays its eggs in organic compost. The larvae are colorless with a black head and feed on organic matter. Larvae will succeed in killing plants through attacking the roots and burrowing up into the stems.

Control The adult flies will fly up during watering, so hang sticky yellow plastic traps to catch them. Compost heaps can be watered with the nematode *Heterorhabditis megidis* or introduce the predatory mite *Hypoaspis miles*.

Companion Basil (*Ocimum basilicum*).

Slugs and snails

These common pests eat the foliage of many plants. Slugs especially accumulate under wooden planks.

Control Keep the garden tidy. Place jars of beer into the soil around plants to attract and drown them. Use a flashlight so that you can gather them by hand on warm nights. Sprinkle wood ashes, diatomaceous earth, sharp sand, or broken egg shells around plants to deter cutworms, slugs, and snails. Calcified seaweed on the soil will also help. Water parasitic nematodes into warm soil to control soil-borne slugs.

Vine weevils (*Otiorhynchus sulcatus*)

These insects are serious pests. The larvae especially damage plants in pots, feeding on roots and tubers, and the adult weevils eat the foliage. Weevil beetles also attack apple blossom, peas, beans, and turnips.

Control Treat the soil around affected plants with parasitic nematodes (*Heterorhabditis megidis* and *Steinemema carpocapsae*). Weevils that attack top fruit can be controlled by placing bands of sacking around the tree trunks in early summer, removing and burning them later.

Companion Garlic (*Allium sativum*).

Whitefly (*Trialeurodes vaporariorum*)

Most commonly found on greenhouse plants. The pest sucks the plant sap and excretes honeydew, which eventually kills the plant. The adults lay numerous eggs on the leaves, and several generations can build up during the period from spring to fall.

Control Sticky yellow plastic traps can help to reduce the numbers of whitefly. The parasitic wasp *Encarsia formosa* can be introduced from early summer onward; it will only survive in warm conditions.

Companion French marigold (*Tagetes*) and nasturtium (*Tropaeolum*).

Wireworms (*Agriotes* spp.)

Brown larvae of the click beetle attack the roots of brassicas, beans, beet, and onions as well as the flesh of carrots and potatoes.

Control Dig the land in winter to expose the larvae to birds. A green manure dug into the soil can help.

Diseases

Keep a close watch on your plants and immediately remove and destroy any that appear to be infected so that the disease cannot spread. Plants that are growing strongly are less likely to be infected, so water and feed your plants regularly to keep them in good condition.

Black currant reversion (Cecidophyopsis ribis)

This is a viral disease of black currants thought to be spread by the big bud mite. Diseased leaves are darker in color as well as narrower than normal and also have fewer indentations. The crop of fruit is reduced. Mainly a problem in Europe and uncommon on other continents.

Control Remove any distortions on the plant throughout the year and destroy heavily infected bushes. Buy only plant bushes that are certified disease free.

Chocolate spot (Botrytis fabae), fava bean rust (Uromyces viciae-fabae)

Fava beans are attacked by two fungal diseases, chocolate spot and rust. Chocolate spot causes small brown spots of dead tissue to form on the leaves. In wet conditions the fungus thrives and the spots rapidly enlarge and the leaf collapses. The spores of rust are seen as brown, dusty spores produced in pustules on the under and upper sides of the leaves during summer. The disease also attacks the stems and pods of fava beans and can affect peas.

Control Destroy all infected debris by burning or composting. Avoid overfeeding and overcrowding plants.

Club root (Plasmodiophora brassicae)

This soil-borne fungus is probably the most serious disease for plants in the brassica and other cabbage family plants. Root tissue swells up and in severe cases the plant dies. The fungus can persist in the soil for more than 20 years and spores infect the roots via moisture. The disease occurs more often on acidic soil and can be spread on boots, tools, manure, and even flood water.

Control Crop rotation is vital, and it's important to lime the soil where brassicas are to be planted. Raise seedlings in pots of proprietary compost to give a healthy root system before planting out. Dip the roots of young transplants in a fungicide solution to reduce the severity of attack on those plants. After harvesting remove all roots and other debris from the plot.

Cucumber mosaic virus (CMV)

One of the most common plant viruses, this causes yellow mottling on leaves and flesh, distortion, and stunting. Cucumbers, zucchini, spinach, lettuce, celery, tomato, sweet peppers, melon, squash, beets, and carrots are all susceptible to attack from this disease, which is spread by sap-sucking aphids and via tools and hands that come into contact with diseased plants.

Control Wash tools and hands in soapy water if disease is suspected. Destroy infected plants. Keep the plot weed free, because groundsel and chickweed can harbor CMV. Some cultivars are resistant to the disease.

Damping off (Pythium, Rhizoctonia and Phytophthora spp.)

These fungi attack seedlings and young plants that are overcrowded or have been overwatered and that do not have sufficient air circulating around them. The stems turn black and rot.

Control Always use new compost in clean seedtrays or pots when you are sowing seeds or planting up. Avoid overcrowding, very wet compost, and overhumid conditions. You can add a copper fungicide to the water once a week to prevent the fungus establishing. When transplanting seedlings, always hold them by the seed leaves only.

Gray mold (Botrytis cinerea)

This is a fungus that lives on dead and dying material and thrives in warm and humid conditions. The spores are spread by wind and rain, and infection usually occurs where a plant has been damaged. Gray mold can devastate strawberry crops, especially during a damp summer.

Control Remove all diseased parts of the plant and any surrounding debris. Make sure that the plants have plenty of air circulating around them. Place a layer of straw or other material under and around strawberries so that fruit do not sit on wet soil.

Rust (Puccinia allii)

Fungal rusts are spread by spores that live on crop debris primarily on nitrogen-rich soils. Leeks, garlic, chives, and onions can be infected. The orange pustules appear on leaves and stems over the summer, and badly infected plants will turn yellow and die.

Control Burn any infected plant material and make sure that there is good air circulation around the plants. Crop rotation is vital, and check the potassium level of the soil. Grow leeks where nitrogen levels are lowest on the plot.

Onion white rot
(*Sclerotium cepivorum*)

This soil-borne fungus affects all members of the onion family and can survive in the soil for around 15 years. Fall-planted sets are most vulnerable, and the disease manifests itself in late spring when the soil begins to warm. Roots become stunted and rot, leaves turn yellow, and white fungal growths appear at the base of the plants.

Control Remove and burn all infected material and debris around the plants. Onions should not be grown in the same place for at least 8 years.

Potato blight
(*Phytophthora infestans*)

This is a fungal disease that affects both potato tubers and tomato plants, and it spreads rapidly in warm, damp conditions. Spores first attack the foliage and then descend to the tubers, which soon become a putrid mess. The first symptoms are dark blotches on the leaves and stems, and tomato fruits begin to rot.

Control Choose cultivars that are resistant. Remove any foliage showing signs of infection and destroy potatoes that have grown after being left in the ground following harvest. Spray potatoes with an appropriate fungicide when weather conditions favor the spread of spores. Spray tomato plants at the same time.

Potato scab (*Streptomyces scabies*)

Potato scab is an infection on the skin, and the flesh is not usually affected. Potatoes with scab can be cooked and eaten, although they look unsightly. The disease is often found in sandy soil with a high lime content and is encouraged when too much manure is added to the soil or not properly mixed with it. Areas where brassicas have been grown recently are more prone to scab.

Control To reduce scab on new potatoes, add a few handfuls of grass clippings when planting. This increases the acidity in the soil as the clippings decompose.

Powdery mildew
(*Erysiphe, Sphaerotheca,* and *Podosphaera* spp.)

There are many species of powdery mildew, each with its own host range. One of the most common in vegetables is pea mildew, which can completely coat a pea vine with white spores; the leaves turn brown and the plant shrivels up and dies.

Control Water plants well and mulch around the roots to keep moisture in the soil. Do not apply nitrogen fertilizers or organic matter. Remove badly affected growth and place in a covered bag before burning.

Silver leaf (*Chondrostereum purpureum*)

The fungus causes a silvery sheen on leaves. It mostly affects plum and cherry trees but can also infect peaches, nectarines, almonds, apples, and pears. The silvered leaves are not sources of infection, but the affected branches will begin to die back and produce purplish fungal bodies on the surface. These contain the spores that spread the infection.

Control Cut out and burn all infected wood. Fruit trees susceptible to silver leaf should be pruned between early and late summer if required when the danger of infection is at a minimum.

Tomato blight

See potato blight.

Fungal rust on leeks is spread by spores.

Attracting wildlife

If you take the native wildlife into consideration when you are growing vegetables and fruit, you will be closer to caring for the environment, but you will also be encouraging nature to help you as well, thereby creating a self-sustaining environment.

Pesticides and poisons are known to have had devastating effects on wildlife populations, so if you do decide for any reason to use chemicals on your plants, make sure that you use them responsibly and always follow the manufacturer's instructions. If you want wildlife to thrive in your garden, growing organically is the best and safest approach, but you can also encourage wildlife to visit your garden in the first place by including certain plants, providing a suitable habitat, and making sure that there are nesting sites as well as food and water. In return, the wildlife will repay you by devouring pests and giving you pleasure.

Once you have assessed what naturally grows around your garden area and which animals, birds, and insects already visit, you will have a better idea of what is needed to encourage other wildlife. The area that you are enhancing does not need to be wild or overgrown, and even the smallest patio can provide something for nature.

BELOW Plan an area of flowering plants that bloom from early spring to fall to provide nectar throughout the season.

Beneficial insects

Bees, along with many other insects, will come to feed on nectar and pollen in flowers, and not only do honeybees collect pollen and produce honey, but in collecting pollen to feed their young all bee species pollinate the flowers that will develop into fruit and vegetables.

Make an effort to attract beneficial insects by sowing flowers to provide them with food. Some of the most valuable plants are those of the pea family, deadnettles, mints, scented herbs, aubretia, budleia, honeysuckle, nicotiana, pyracantha, calendula, and sedum. Plan an area of flowering plants and shrubs that bloom successively from early spring through to fall to provide nectar throughout the season. Single-petaled annuals and biennials (double-petaled forms generally have less pollen) will not only attract insects but might also provide you with an alternative source of income, selling bunches of cut flowers for the home.

Hawthorn (*Crataegus*) and birch (*Betula*) provide food for insects and birds, but a dwarf fruit tree will provide food and shelter for some species. Help the bee population by erecting earth banks, fences, walls, and bee boxes, which are all important nesting habitats for honeybees.

The ladybug is one of the most efficient predators of aphids, with both adults and larvae feeding off them, and some ladybugs are mass reared for use as biological control against infestations of mealybugs and whitefly in greenhouses. They do have predators themselves, being vulnerable to parasitic wasps and some other insect eaters. The adults hibernate in winter among dense vegetation, under tree bark, and inside sheds. Leave them or move with care to another hibernating spot if necessary.

Syrphid flies are an asset to the garden. They look like tiny wasps but do not sting, and their larvae devour aphids. Daisies and mints (*Mentha*) will attract both syrphid flies and predatory wasps. The wasps will catch caterpillars and grubs. Fennel (*Foeniculum*), angelica, and cilantro (*Coriandrum*) are good for parasitoid wasps. Large, nectar-filled blooms can drown these small insects, so tiny flowers in large quantities are more valuable. Clovers (*Trifolium*), yarrow (*Achillea millefolium*), and rue (*Ruta*) also attract predatory insects, including the lacewing. To encourage these insects provide shady, protected areas in which they can lay their eggs.

Ground beetles eat insect pests, including the root fly larvae. They require the cover of low-growing plants, especially those in which they can overwinter. Be kind to centipedes, which move very quickly and have fewer legs than the millipede, for these live on mites, bugs, and slugs.

Water

Adding a water feature, such as a man-made garden pond or even a small birdbath, will attract birds and other garden-friendly wildlife. Even an upturned garbage can lid is sufficient to provide drinking and bathing for some species.

When you are making a pond, remember to include plenty of oxygenating plants to help keep the water clear and free of algae.

Frogs and toads

Frogs and toads were once extremely common but are now under threat. They are hugely beneficial in gardens, eating large numbers of insects. You can provide a suitable habitat by leaving some areas of long grass in which they can hide and rest. They also require water in which to breed, so a pond will draw them into the garden. Make sure that your pool has a small ramp or pile of stones so that the amphibians can climb out—they will drown if they cannot reach dry land. They are more likely to do well in organic gardens because both species are sensitive to pesticides and fungicides of all kinds, and be careful if you are using wood ash to raise the pH level of your soil as it is toxic to toads.

Birds

Songbirds and insect-eating birds are useful. Blackbirds, robins, tits, and thrushes eat insects,

Taking care of wildlife

If you go to the trouble of attracting wildlife to your garden, the last thing you will want to do is to harm it in any way. Take care, therefore, to:

- Check long grass before strimming, whcih mutilates hedgehogs, frogs, toads, and the like.
- Provide an escape route from ponds for frogs and toads.
- Keep drains covered.
- Take care when forking over compost heaps, which are ideal nesting sites for hedgehogs.
- Keep potentially harmful chemicals, oils, and so on out of reach of wildlife, pets, and children.
- Tidy away netting, barbed wire, and plastic that is not serving an immediate purpose.
- Pick up slugs and snails killed by metaldehyde slug pellets so that hedgehogs do not eat them.
- Check bonfires before lighting because hedgehogs and other wildlife are likely to make their homes in such places.

LEFT Frogs and toads are hugely beneficial in gardens, eating large numbers of insects.

caterpillars, slugs, and snails. Putting up feeding stations in the winter and water throughout the year will encourage birds into the garden. Visiting birds, such as swallows, will gather insects, so providing nesting places and a muddy patch will encourage them to stay for the summer. A log pile will provide insects for birds, as will an area of unmown grass. Leave wild flowers, such as teasels, for finches to feed on. If you are growing fruit, make sure that it is protected in a fruit cage or by properly supported netting in which birds cannot be accidentally trapped.

Timetable of planting and harvesting

Establishing a routine of sowing, transplanting, pruning and harvesting can be daunting, especially if you also have a greenhouse that you want to use to the greatest advantage.

The following calendar of tasks to be done throughout the seasons will help you plan your work, and for the first few seasons at least it might be worth pinning up a copy in your shed or greenhouse as a guide.

Early spring

Vegetables

Sowing Fava beans, beet, Brussels sprouts, cabbages, calabrese, carrots, endive, leeks, kohl rabi, lettuce, onions and scallions, peas, radishes, salsify, spinach, Swiss chard, turnips, and salad crops outside. Beet, radishes, cabbages, carrots, turnips, lettuce, green beans, cauliflowers, and salad crops in cold frames. Cucumbers in a frame over a hotbed (see page 75). Transplant autumn-sown onions.

Greenhouse Prick out tomato seedlings and pot on. Sow tomatoes, eggplants, celery, celeriac, cucumbers, and peppers.

Planting Early potatoes in sheltered borders; maincrop potatoes 2 weeks later. Jerusalem, globe, and Chinese artichokes, onion sets, autumn-sown onions, shallots, garlic, seakale, horseradish, asparagus, and leeks. Transplant cauliflowers, peas, and spinach from greenhouse.

Harvesting GROUND Savoy cabbages, collard greens, sprouting broccoli, spinach, Chinese and Jerusalem artichokes, Brussels sprouts, winter cabbages, calabrese, cauliflowers, kale, celeriac, chicory, endive, leeks, lettuce, scallions, parsley, parsnips, radishes, rhubarb, salsify, seakale, spinach, and Swiss chard.

FORCING Endive and seakale.

Ground work Finish all digging and manuring in vegetable plot. Clean asparagus bed and topdress with well-rotted manure; make new asparagus bed. Apply nitrogen to early cabbages. Apply general fertilizer to all open ground. Hoe to remove weed seedlings. Place cloches over soil to warm before seed sowing. Sow green manure on vacant ground.

General Pinch out tops of flowering fava beans to reduce blackfly. Check seed potatoes.

Fruit

Pruning Complete pruning of cobnuts and filberts. Cut out older wood on acid cherries.

Planting Finish planting trees and bushes. Plant perpetual strawberries and remove all blossoms until end of June.

Ground work Add potash to cane fruits. Complete mulching of young trees, bushes, and canes. Apply nitrogen to black currants. Give second application of nitrogen to pears in grass. Cover blossom and young fruitlets to protect from frost damage. Spray peaches and nectarines against peach leaf curl. Apply sticky bands to apple trees.

General Inspect tree stakes and ties and check for wind damage. Remove weeds from around bushes and trees.

Mid-spring

Vegetables

Sowing Fava beans, carrots, peas, sprouting broccoli, Brussels sprouts, cabbages, calabrese, kale, red chicory, kohl rabi, leeks, lettuce, onions and scallions, parsnips, maincrop peas, radishes, beet, salsify, spinach, Swiss chard, turnips, and salad crops. Green beans in sheltered border. Eggplants, celery, endive, peppers, corn, green beans, outdoor cucumbers, zucchini, squashes, pumpkins, and outdoor tomatoes in cool greenhouse or under cloches.

Greenhouse Sow green beans and cauliflowers in heated greenhouse.

Planting Early and maincrop potatoes, Chinese, globe, and Jerusalem artichokes, asparagus, and onions. Plant out lettuce raised under frames. Plant out cabbages. Plant out squashes on prepared bed with manure at base.

Harvesting GROUND Jerusalem artichokes, asparagus, sprouting broccoli, spring cabbages, cauliflowers, celeriac, chicory, endive, leeks, scallions, parsley, radishes, rhubarb, salsify, seakale, spinach, Swiss chard, and salad crops.

Ground work Scatter lime and soot under gooseberry and currant bushes and dig in lightly to check caterpillars and sawfly. Cover strawberry beds with netting. Protect lettuce, potatoes, and tomatoes with weed cloth.

General Clear old brassica stumps. Earth up early potatoes. Prepare trenches for celery. Prepare pumpkin and squash beds. Hoe weeds from among crops.

Fruit

Pruning Prune gooseberries, red and white currants, and figs where necessary.

Planting Complete strawberry planting.

Ground work Apply nitrogen to strawberries if growth poor. Protect early-flowering fruits with weed cloth if frost is forecast; uncover afterward for pollination. Spray against pests and diseases where required. Check netting for bird protection. Spray peaches and nectarines against peach leaf curl.

General Water all newly planted trees, bushes, and canes when necessary. Untie and retrain branches of wall-trained figs. Hand-pollinate peach and nectarine flowers. Control weeds around fruit trees, bushes, and canes.

Late spring

Vegetables

Sowing Fava and Italian flat beans in well-manured trenches (3 weeks apart); cabbages, calabrese, cauliflowers, sprouting broccoli, kale, carrots, chicory, endive, Sweet fennel, kohl rabi, leeks, lettuce, zucchini, squashes, turnips, gourds, pumpkins, green beans, scallions, parsnips, peas, radishes, salsify, seakale, spinach, rutabaga, turnips, and salad crops.

Greenhouse Feed tomatoes showing fruit. Spray plants night and morning and watch ventilation. Sow green beans, peppers, eggplants, corn, tomatoes, ridge cucumbers, and squashes in greenhouse or under cloches.

Planting Outdoor tomatoes, Jerusalem artichokes, eggplants, celeriac, celery, chicory, lettuce, parsley, peppers, potatoes, and seakale. Transplant Brussels sprouts, cabbages, and cauliflowers.

Harvesting GROUND Asparagus, fava beans, sprouting broccoli, cabbages, cauliflowers, carrots, celeriac, chicory, endive, kohl rabi, lettuce, scallions, peas, radishes, rhubarb, salsify, spinach, Swiss chard, turnips, and salad plants.

Ground work Earth up early potatoes. Sprinkle onion beds with soot to prevent onion fly. Thin out vegetable seedlings and weed by hoeing between rows. Stake peas. Divide and replant mint. Earth up potatoes. Mulch where necessary. Have cloth available to protect against frost when necessary.

General Stake peas. Pinch out tops of fava beans and early peas. Spray against pests. Apply diluted liquid manure to cauliflowers and celery.

Fruit

Pruning Thin gooseberries.

Planting Set out companion plants around all trees and bushes.

Harvesting Gooseberries and strawberries under cloches.

Ground work Apply nitrogen to strawberries if growth poor.

General Place straw around strawberry plants to keep fruit clean. Spray wall-trained fruit trees to keep down insect pests and aid foliage condition. Protect blossoms against frost. Net soft fruits against birds. Put out codling moth traps. Shorten leaders of restricted mature trees. Water all plants. De-blossom newly planted trees. De-shoot wall-trained peaches, nectarines, plums, and damsons. De-blossom spring-planted strawberry runners. Remove weeds from around trees, bushes, and vines. Check all plants for pests and diseases and dieback. Remove tied-on greasebands.

Early summer

Vegetables

Sowing Salad crops, radishes, parsley, winter turnips, green beans, beet, calabrese, cabbages, chicory, endive, Sweet fennel, kohl rabi, zucchini, squashes, pumpkins, scallions, peas, rutabaga, and turnips.

Greenhouse Corn, eggplants, and tomatoes in greenhouse or under cloches.

Planting Mustard and collard greens, celery, gourds, Brussels sprouts, and tomatoes. Transplant sprouting broccoli, Brussels sprouts, cabbages, cauliflowers, and leeks.

Harvesting GROUND Asparagus, fava beans, green beans, beet, cabbages, calabrese, cauliflower, carrots, chicory, endive, kohl rabi, lettuce, onions and scallions, parsley, peas, potatoes, radishes, rhubarb, spinach, Swiss chard, turnips, and salad crops.

Ground work Finish earthing up potatoes. Water, mulch, hoe, and weed all crops. Stake peas and climbing beans. Draw soil away from onions.

General Pinch out tops of fava beans if blackfly present. Check for pests and diseases. Remove sideshoots from tomatoes and water well; when fruits form apply liquid manure. Tie up cos (romaine) lettuce. Thin carrots and turnips. Keep weeding. Feed asparagus bed with liquid manure.

Fruit

Pruning Gooseberries, currants, and raspberries. Train new blackberry shoots. Remove any fruits of fan-trained cherries and plums growing toward wall; pinch back other laterals and tie in; thin fruits. Pinch out top buds on young shoots of figs at 5 leaves.

Ground work Apply nitrogen to strawberries. Remove weeds from around all trees, bushes, and canes.

Harvest beet from golf-ball size upward.

General Begin layering strawberries when picking finished; pinch out unwanted runners; remove cloches when picking has finished; peg down runners for new plants. Thin out grapes when size of small peas. Continue to net soft fruits. Water and spray foliage in evening during hot weather. Tie in new growth of climbing fruit plants.

Midsummer

Vegetables

Sowing Dwarf beans.

Greenhouse Sow beet, spring cabbages, calabrese, chicory, endive, Sweet fennel, kohl rabi, lettuce, parsley, peas, radishes, Swiss chard, turnips, and salad crops in greenhouse or under cloches.

Planting Kale. Transplant sprouting broccoli, cabbages, cauliflowers, kale, and leeks.

Harvesting Globe artichokes, green beans, beet, cabbages, calabrese, cauliflowers, carrots, celery, chicory, cucumbers, endive, Sweet fennel, kohl rabi, lettuce, zucchini, squashes, pumpkins, onions, parsley, peas, potatoes, radishes, rhubarb, spinach, shallots, Swiss chard, corn, turnips, and salad crops.

Ground work Thin out beets and hoe between rows. Earth up celery and potatoes. Earth up brassicas on exposed sites.

General Pinch out tops of climbing beans when they reach top of sticks. Bend over tops of scallions near neck of bulb. Apply foliar feed to all crops. Spray potatoes for blight. Check for pests and disease. Spray water on flowers of Italian flat beans in the evening. Tie in and remove sideshoots and tops of outdoor tomatoes after 4–5 trusses formed. Hand-pollinate gourds and zucchini if not setting. Dry shallots ready for storing.

Fruit

Pruning Summer prune wall-trained fruit trees. Thin raspberry canes after fruiting. Thin apples. Train fan-shaped plums and cherries. Complete pruning of cherry trees. Train new blackberry canes; top layer for new plants. Cut out old raspberry canes and tie in new ones. Remove unwanted suckers and control weeds. When strawberries stop fruiting, cut off all old leaves and remove straw; remove surplus runners and weeds; burn all debris.

Harvesting Strawberries, raspberries, gooseberries, blueberries, blackberries, loganberries, currants, cherries, and peaches.

Ground work Apply nitrogen to strawberries.

General Check trees for constriction by ties and stakes. Protect all fruits from birds. Water thoroughly and spray foliage in evening in hot weather. Support heavily laden branches.

Late summer

Vegetables

Sowing Cabbages, oriental greens, chicory, endive, Sweet fennel, kohl rabi, lettuce, onions and winter-hardy scallions, radishes, Swiss chard, turnips, and salad crops.

Greenhouse Repeat sowings of salad crops and spring cabbage. Water and feed crops that are under glass. Provide ventilation and shade when the temperature is high.

Planting Mustard greens between rows of potatoes. Transplant leeks and Sweet fennel.

Harvesting Globe artichokes, eggplants, fava and green beans, beet, cabbages, cauliflowers, oriental greens, carrots, celery (self-blanching), chicory, endive, Sweet fennel, garlic, kohl rabi, lettuce, leeks, zucchini, squashes, pumpkins, onions, parsley, potatoes, radishes, spinach, shallots, Swiss chard, corn, tomatoes (outdoor), turnips, and salad crops.

Ground work Make mushroom beds. Weed and mulch around all crops.

General Apply foliar feed to all crops where necessary. Pull onions and leave in sun to dry. Spray potatoes for blight. Check for pests and diseases. Thoroughly water beans, celery, celeriac, lettuce, and peas. Stake outdoor tomatoes and stop when 4–5 trusses have set. Earth up brassicas. Cut off and burn any potato haulms with blight.

Hold the carrot stem firmly when lifting.

Fruit

Pruning Plums, damsons, apples, pears, wall-trained peaches, fan-trained plums and raspberries. Cut out old canes of blackberries and loganberries.

Planting Prepare new strawberry beds and plant well-rooted runners.

Harvesting Apples, pears, plums, peaches, apricots, blackberries, raspberries, loganberries, and perpetual (remontant) strawberries.

Ground work Prepare vacant ground by removing all weeds, digging and working in well-rotted manure.

General Transfer strawberries layered in pots into large pots for forcing. Apply plenty of liquid manure to celery and continue to earth up rows in dry weather. Protect all fruits against birds. Spray foliage of plants in evening during hot weather. Support heavily laden fruit trees.

Early autumn

Vegetables

Sowing Lettuce, radishes, spinach, calabrese, salad crops, and cauliflowers (for transplanting later). In greenhouse sow bok choy, chicory, radishes, and salad crops.

Planting Onion sets. Transplant oriental greens, calabrese, chicory, endive, Swiss chard and lettuce.

Harvesting Eggplants, potatoes, green beans, beet, Brussels sprouts, cabbages, calabrese, cauliflowers, oriental greens, carrots, celery (self-blanching), chicory, cucumbers (outdoor), endive, Sweet fennel, garlic, kohl rabi, leeks, lettuce, zucchini, squashes, pumpkins, onions, parsley, parsnips, peas, radishes, spinach, Swiss chard, corn, tomatoes (outdoor), turnips, and salad crops.

Ground work Dress land that is infested with wireworms with lime and leave for 2 months before digging in. Sow green manures on vacant plots. Earth up celery, brassicas, and leeks; pull soil up around celeriac roots.

Harvest plums from late summer.

General Wash off any shading on the greenhouse. Heat greenhouse when frost threatens. Pull up tomato plants with green fruits and hang in greenhouse to ripen.

Fruit

Pruning Apples, pears, plums, damsons, wall-trained peaches, nectarines, gooseberries, black currants and blackberries. Tidy wall-trained cherries.

Planting Strawberries.

Harvesting Apples, pears, plums, damsons, figs, grapes, raspberries, blackberries, blueberries, cobnuts, and filberts.

Ground work Prepare ground for planting hardy fruit trees. Apply nitrogen to strawberries if growth is poor.

General Protect all fruit from birds with netting or cover strawberries with cloches. Spray against apple and pear scab.

Mid-autumn

Vegetables

Sowing Cauliflowers, carrots, lettuce, peas, radishes, and salad crops in greenhouse. Fava beans and spinach outside.

Planting Garlic, onions, and winter lettuce; spring cabbages in shallow drills. Transplant cabbages, lettuce, and Swiss chard.

Harvesting Chinese artichokes, green beans, beet, Brussels sprouts, cabbages, cauliflowers, oriental greens, carrots, celeriac, celery (self-blanching), chicory, endive, Sweet fennel, kohl rabi, leeks, lettuce, onions, parsley, parsnips, peas, peppers, potatoes, radishes, salsify, spinach, rutabaga, Swiss chard, corn, tomatoes (outdoor), turnips, and salad crops.

Ground work Lift and store carrots, garlic, onions, potatoes, shallots, winter endive, and turnips. Clear ground of late potatoes. Dig vacant ground in dry weather and leave surface in ridges. Cut down old asparagus growth and remove weeds. Lift some roots of mint, pot up and grow in greenhouse for winter supply. Make new compost heap. Mulch rhubarb.

General Sweep up leaves and use for leaf mold. Cover cauliflower curds with bent-over leaf. Cover parsley, herbs, and salad crops with cloches. Clear away pea and bean supports.

Fruit

Pruning Root prune fruit trees that bear a lot of foliage and little fruit. Prune top fruits, black currants, gooseberries, red and white currants, and blackberries where necessary.

Planting Top fruit trees, soft fruit bushes and soft fruit canes toward end of the month. Complete strawberry planting.

Harvesting Strawberries, raspberries, blackberries, plums, apples, and pears.

Ground work Prepare ground for planting fruit trees.

General Cover strawberries with cloches to extend season. Place greasebands around apple and pear trees. Remove fallen leaves from around fruit trees. Order new trees and bushes and plant after leaf fall.

Late autumn

Vegetables

Sowing Peas in greenhouse. Fava beans and spring cabbages outdoors.

Planting Horseradish, garlic, onion sets, and rhubarb. Plant new vines; lift and replant poor specimens.

Harvesting Jerusalem and Chinese artichokes, Brussels sprouts, cabbages, cauliflowers, carrots, celeriac, chicory, endive, kohl rabi, leeks, lettuce, parsley, spinach, ruta-baga, Swiss chard, turnips, and salad crops.

Ground work Prepare asparagus beds. Continue digging and manuring when weather favorable. Earth up celery for the last time. Heel over broccoli with their heads away from the midday sun.

General Draw plan for next year's cropping in vegetable plot. Place mushroom spawn in prepared beds. Lift and store beet, carrots, turnips, and rutabaga. Protect celeriac and globe artichokes with straw or weed cloth. Cover overwintering root crops with straw. Heel cauliflowers against frost. Clear fallen leaves for leaf mold. Prepare new compost heap and cover when full. Remove decaying stems from brassicas. Cover endive with pots to blanch it. Cut and remove all dead asparagus fern and cover beds with well-rotted manure.

Fruit

Pruning Established fruit trees and wall-trained and pyramid fruit trees, blackberries, currants, gooseberries, and raspberries.

Planting Start planting fruit trees, raspberries, gooseberries and red and white currants if weather favorable.

Harvesting Mid-season apples and pears.

Ground work Mulch newly planted fruit trees with well-rotted manure, spreading it out to cover root area.

General Take cuttings of gooseberries and currants. Remove all garden rubbish. Check netting on fruit cage and close gate. Give figs winter protection and mulch root area. Gather together blackberry canes and tie to wire for winter protection.

Cut a cabbage above the base leaves.

Early winter

Vegetables

Sowing Sow first batch of tomato seeds in a heated greenhouse. Fava beans outdoors.

Planting Lettuce. Plant seakale roots in large pots and place under greenhouse staging for forcing; exclude light but keep moist. Plant shallots in greenhouse.

Harvesting Chinese and Jerusalem artichokes, Brussels sprouts, cabbages, cauliflowers, oriental greens, carrots, celeriac, chicory, endive, kohl rabi, leeks, lettuce, parsley, parsnips, radishes, salsify, spinach, rutabaga, Swiss chard, turnips, and salad crops.

Ground work In cold weather distribute well-rotted manure over vacant plots. Continue digging if weather favorable.

General Carry out improvement works around vegetable plot, build new shed or repair path. Look out stakes, bamboo canes, and sticks for next year, tie in bundles and store. Ventilate cold frames on mild days.

Protect globe artichokes with straw or bark and celery tops with straw. Tidy the vegetable plot. Lift and store carrots, rutabaga, beet, garlic, onions, potatoes, shallots, and winter squashes.

Fruit

Pruning Vines under glass. Finish pruning fruit trees except in frosty weather. Destroy all prunings.

Planting Lift rhubarb roots, plant in deep boxes and place under greenhouse staging for forcing; exclude light but keep moist. Propagate vines by cuttings. Plant all fruits if soil conditions suitable. If too wet, loosen bundles and heel in plants in temporary trench. In frost keep the plants in cool, frost-proof place. Plant as soon as possible, soaking the roots first.

Harvesting Complete picking of late apples.

Ground work Continue digging vegetable plot in favorable weather. Spray dormant trees with winter wash to control pests.

General Check trees for wind rock; replace stakes, supports, and ties if necessary. Check greasebands. Tie fig shoots and protect with sacking or cloth. Remove any unwanted or rotten fruit from trees. Cover fan-trained peaches and nectarines to protect against peach leaf curl. Inspect stored fruits and discard rotten ones.

Midwinter

Vegetables

Sowing Fava beans and peas in cool greenhouse or under cloches. Early peas in a warm border on light soil.

Greenhouse Sow seeds of leeks, onions, carrots, radishes, and early varieties of cauliflowers in boxes in heated greenhouse. Sow seeds of mustard and cress in shallow boxes and grow on in heated greenhouse.

Planting Horseradish, shallots, and rhubarb. Divide and replant long-established rhubarb. Dig up some dormant mint roots and plant in boxes for forcing in heated greenhouse.

Harvesting GROUND Kale, leeks, cabbages, parsnips, Brussels sprouts, celery, cauliflowers, Chinese and Jerusalem artichokes, celeriac, chicory, endive, parsley, radishes, salsify, spinach, and Swiss chard.

STORE Root vegetables, Jerusalem artichokes, potatoes, beet, carrots, shallots, rutabaga, turnips and salsify.

FORCING Rhubarb, salsify, seakale, and endive.

Ground work Trench, dig, and manure the vegetable plot. Protect broccoli hearts by snapping a leaf and bending it over. Build hotbed (see page 75) for raising early vegetables. Prepare onion bed.

General Plan vegetable plot on paper. Make out seed order for early vegetables. Thoroughly clean glass of greenhouse inside and out; fumigate if there are any signs of pests. Burn woody rubbish (if allowed) or take to refuse tip. Check and maintain all tools. Prepare seed potatoes by placing them close together in shallow boxes and putting in frost-free place to sprout.

Fruit

Pruning Prune vines under glass. Finish pruning and securing all fruit trees on walls. Collect all prunings and shred.

Planting Plant fruit trees, bushes, and canes if conditions allow and there is no frost.

Harvesting Check fruit in store for any deterioration.

Ground work Apply potash to strawberries and bush fruit and general fertilizer to cobnuts and filberts.

General Check all fruit tree stakes and ties. Cover wall-trained peach trees to prevent peach leaf curl. On a still day spray fruit trees, canes, and bushes with winter wash.

Late winter

Vegetables

Sowing Brussels sprouts, fava beans, peas, carrots, turnips, lettuce, and radishes in a cool greenhouse or under cloches. Spinach, lettuce, radishes, early dwarf beans, and parsley in sheltered areas. Parsnips if conditions are dry.

Greenhouse Disbud vines under glass. Sow tomatoes, cauliflowers, celery, green beans, and eggplants in a heated greenhouse. Watch temperature in greenhouse during day and ventilate as necessary.

Planting Jerusalem artichokes, rhubarb, garlic, shallots, seakale, and onion sets.

Harvesting GROUND Chinese and Jerusalem artichokes, sprouting broccoli, brassicas, Brussels sprouts, winter cabbages, calabrese, winter cauliflowers, celery, kale, oriental greens, celeriac, chicory, endive, leeks, parsley, parsnips, radishes, rhubarb, salad greens, salsify, seakale, winter spinach, and Swiss chard.

HEATED GREENHOUSE Lettuce, mustard and cress, bean shoots, and mushrooms.

STORE Jerusalem artichokes, beet, carrots, garlic, onions, potatoes, shallots, rutabaga, turnips, radishes, and salsify.

FORCING Rhubarb, salsify, and seakale.

Ground work Complete digging, liming, and manuring vegetable plot. Incorporate compost into seedbeds. Test soil. Dress asparagus bed with general fertilizer. Feed spring cabbages. Remove dead leaves from strawberries and topdress soil with well-rotted manure.

General Place further seed potatoes in trays to chit. Gather sticks together for bean and pea supports.

Fruit

Planting Fruit trees, strawberries, raspberries, and young vines.

Pruning Cut down autumn-fruiting raspberries to ground level and newly planted canes to 9–12 inches. Prune trees of top fruit. Prune cobnuts and filberts if catkins releasing pollen.

Ground work Apply potash if necessary to all trees and bushes. Apply nitrogen to trees in grass and then (3 weeks later) to trees in cultivation. Apply compost around all trees and bushes as a mulch.

General Watch for birds attacking fruit buds on currants and the like and protect with netting. Protect wall-trained trees from frost with draped burlap or weed cloth. Cover strawberries with cloches. Spray peaches and nectarines against peach leaf curl. Apply sticky bands to apple trees.

Vegetable directory

The vegetables described on the following pages are examples of what can be easily obtained and grown, and as long as you pay attention to their needs, they will provide you with a good harvest of succulent crops.

Grow what you like to eat, what will do well in your soil, and what you have space for. The first seedlings to appear will give you immense satisfaction, and as you build in confidence and experience, even the most exotic plants will become attainable.

Vegetables are grouped according to family, which often require similar growing conditions.

Beet family (Chenopodiaceae)

Beet (Beta vulgaris)

Round or cylindrical vegetables, of which the swollen root is eaten. The flesh is usually deep red, but some cultivars have yellow or creamy-white flesh.

Sowing to harvest 7–13 weeks.

Site and soil Plant in an open, sunny site in fertile soil over a long period from spring to autumn. Beet will not tolerate acidic soil.

Cultivation The seed can be slow to germinate, so soak overnight before planting. For an early crop, sow seeds in modules on the windowsill in late winter or early spring under cloches or frames. Beet does not germinate below 45°F. When sowing outside, allow a thumb's width between seeds, in short rows 9 inches apart, every 10–14 days.

Thin seedlings to 3 inches apart, harvest every other one.

Care Water well in hot, dry spells.

Problems Take care when weeding, as the root will "bleed" if damaged.

Harvesting Harvest roots from golf-ball size upward by twisting rather than cutting off the tops. The young leaves can be eaten as greens. Store the roots in a cool, dark, frost-free place over winter.

Spinach beet (Beta vulgaris subsp. cicla var. cicla)

Also known as perpetual spinach, this is easier to grow than spinach. Although it is a biennial and does not go to seed as quickly as ordinary spinach, it is best treated as an annual.

Sowing to harvest 8–12 weeks.

Site and soil Will tolerate coastal conditions and some shade. A good winter crop, but it will benefit from protection with cloches. Needs lots of nutrients, so apply a nitrogen-rich fertilizer or well-rotted manure before sowing.

Cultivation Sow one seed per module and place on a windowsill in early spring. Harden off seedlings before planting outside. Sow outside in spring every 10–14 days in rows 15 inches apart, then thin or plant out at 9 inches in the rows.

Care Water in dry weather and mulch to retain moisture.

Problems Downy mildew and beet leaf miner, which causes brown blotches on the leaves.

Harvesting Harvest leaves from the outside of the plants first. Can be frozen raw or cooked.

Spinach leaves are eaten raw or cooked.

Swiss chard (*Beta vulgaris subsp. cicla var. flavescens*)

This vegetable is similar to spinach, but has a slightly different flavor. It is highly ornamental, with large leaves and broad stems in shades of white, red, pink, orange, or yellow.

Sowing to harvest 8–12 weeks.

Site and soil Grow in an open site. Apply a nitrogen-rich fertilizer or well-rotted manure to the soil before planting. Swiss chard is good in coastal areas and will tolerate a little shade.

Cultivation Sow one seed per module in a plastic cell tray in late winter on the windowsill and harden off before planting outside in mid- to late spring. Unthinned seedlings can be used for a cut-and-come-again crop. Plants should be spaced 9 inches apart in rows that are 18 inches apart.

Care Water plants in dry weather and mulch to retain moisture. Cover with cloches in winter.

Problems Slugs and powdery mildew. Older leaves are more prone to pests and diseases.

Harvesting Harvest large leaves as needed. The whole plant can be cut, but leave 2 inch stems for regrowth.

Spinach (*Spinacia oleracea*)

This fast-growing plant is grown for its highly nutritious leaves, which are flat or wrinkled depending on the cultivar. The leaves can be eaten cooked or raw. It is an acquired taste, but spinach is full of iron and folic acid.

Sowing to harvest 5–10 weeks.

Site and soil Prefers slight shade in hot weather. Spinach needs plenty of moisture and lots of nutrients.

Cultivation Sow seeds every 10–14 days from early spring until early autumn. Late sowings will overwinter if covered with cloches. Space rows 12 inches apart and thin seedlings to 6 inches apart.

Care Water well in dry weather.

Sweet potatoes have red skins and yellow flesh.

Problems The plants go to seed at an early stage in warm weather. They are vulnerable to downy mildew, but resistant cultivars are available.

Harvesting Start picking individual leaves when 2 inches tall. When 6–8 inches tall pull out the whole plant. Use fresh or freeze. Particularly good raw. When picking, place into a plastic bag and store in the refrigerator. To cook, steam or stir-fry.

Potato family (*Solanaceae*)

Peppers (*Capsicum annuum*)

Sweet peppers are tropical annuals with fruits that are usually oblong and green, red, or yellow. Eat raw or cooked.

Sowing to harvest 20–28 weeks.

Site and soil A sunny site with fertile soil, along with a minimum temperature of 70°F.

Cultivation Sweet and chili peppers are best grown in a polytunnel, greenhouse, large frame, or cloth tent. Grow in pots of multi-purpose compost or growbags.

Care Pinch out growing tips after transplanting. Keep plants well watered.

Problems Aphids and blossom end rot (through lack of moisture).

Harvesting Pick when green or leave to color and sweeten. When frost is forecast, lift the plants and hang them in a frost-free place for the fruits to ripen. Sweet peppers can be stored for up to 14 days in a cool place. Chilies should be left to ripen on the plants. Use fresh or hang to dry, then store in an airtight jar in a dark place.

Sweet potatoes (*Ipomoea batatas*)

Sweet potatoes are tropical tubers similar to elongated rutabagas, often with a red skin and yellow, sweetish flesh. The tubers are cooked, and the leaves can be used in the same way as spinach.

Sowing to harvest 13–20 weeks.

Site and soil An open, sunny, warm, and sheltered location. Ample potash in the soil is essential. They are difficult to grow in temperate areas, which are rarely warm enough, but can be grown in southern Europe, the southeastern United States, and the warmer parts of New Zealand.

Cultivation Buy plants from a specialty grower. Ideally plant under cover on ridges of soil around 10 inches high with 12 inches between ridges and plants 12 inches apart.

Care Keep soil weeded until the growth meets between rows. Do not overwater.

Problems Slugs, wireworms, and aphids.

Harvesting Lift the crop when leaves begin to turn yellow. Leave in the sun for 10 days or place in a warm room for 10 days. Store in a dry, warm place.

Tomatoes (*Lycopersicon esculentum*)

The tomato originated from Peru, so likes to be protected in a warm greenhouse. There are many cultivars in shades of red, orange, and yellow, and varying sizes. The tiny cherry tomatoes have become very popular.

Sowing to harvest 9–20 weeks.

Site and soil Grow tomatoes under glass unless they are an outdoor cultivar. There are also tomatoes suitable for hanging baskets and windowboxes. Fertile soil is essential, and tomatoes do well in growbags or containers of fresh compost, especially if grown in the greenhouse. For plants in the ground add plenty of well-rotted manure.

Cultivation Tomatoes germinate easily, but need a temperature of 61°F to thrive. Sow in a heated propagator on a windowsill. Prick out seedlings into 3-inch pots to grow on. Plant in growbags or pots under cover or outside when all risk of frost has passed. Protect with cloth if the weather is cold. Tomato plants should normally be grown in rows 18 inches apart. Bush, trailing, and other types will vary.

Care With cordon plants, pinch out sideshoots and train the growth against canes. Pinch out the growing tips when 4 trusses of fruits have set. Water well at the base after the first fruits form, but keep water off the fruits. Mulch with straw or plastic to keep fruits off the soil.

Problems Tomato blight and blossom end rot.

Harvesting Pick fruits as they ripen. At the end of the season pick the remaining unripe fruit and leave on a sunny windowsill or place in a drawer with 2 ripe apples or bananas, which give off the ripening gas ethylene. Store in the refrigerator until required or use to make sauces, pickles, or chutneys.

Eggplants (*Solanum melongena*)

These tender Mediterranean vegetables are also known as aubergines. They can be round, oval, or pear-shaped and are available in white, mauve, green, and striped cultivars. They are often used in Asian and Indian cookery.

Sowing to harvest 16–24 weeks.

Site and soil Well-drained, fertile soil. The temperature needs to be 77–86°F for a good crop.

Cultivation Sow seeds under cover in 70°F from late winter or early spring. Sow in seedtrays and move to individual pots when seedlings are large enough. Grow on at 61–64°F and harden off before planting 2–3 in a growbag, one in a 12 inch pot or 24 inches apart in rows outside.

Care Pinch out the growing tips once plants reach 12 inches. Water well in dry spells. Regularly apply high-potash liquid feed.

Problems Aphids.

Harvesting Harvest in sun. Can be stored in the refrigerator for a few days.

Home-grown tomatoes have lots of flavour.

Potatoes (Solanum tuberosum)

A mainstay vegetable, of which there are many cultivars. Early varieties are best when young and sweet, and are ideal for small plots, as they can be planted close together. Maincrops occupy the ground for longer.

Sowing to harvest 13–20 weeks.

Site and soil An open, sunny site in humus-rich soil. Avoid waterlogged, low-lying spots.

Cultivation Seed potatoes (certified against viruses) are sprouted (chitted) before planting. Place the tubers with the "eyes" uppermost on seedtrays or in shallow boxes in a well-lit, cool room. Green shoots will develop. Plant 6 inches deep, 12 inches apart, with 24 inches between rows for earlies and 16–30 inches for maincrop, taking care not to damage the shoots.

Care Earth up the soil around the plants as they grow to stop tubers going green; this also kills weeds and helps prevent blight. Water well when the flowers develop.

Problems Slugs, potato blight, and scab.

Harvesting Harvest early potatoes when the plants begin to flower and maincrop when the topgrowth has died. Harvest on a dry day and place undamaged tubers in paper sacks in a cool, frost-free, dark place.

Carrot family (Apiaceae)

Celery (Apium graveolens)

Celery can be blanched or self-blanching. The stalks can be eaten raw or cooked, and the attractive leaves are often used as a garnish.

Sowing to harvest Self-blanching 16–24 weeks; blanching 9 months.

Site and soil Celery needs a fertile, moisture-retentive soil. It benefits from well-rotted manure dug into the soil or nitrogen-rich fertilizer.

Cultivation For trench (blanching) celery, dig a trench 15–18 inches wide and 12 inches deep in early spring. Mix organic matter into the soil, then fill in the trench to a depth of 4 inches. Plant trench celery 12–18 inches apart and allow 4 feet between trenches. Self-blanching celery should be 6–12 inches apart.

Care Water frequently. Blanch trench celery when it is 12 inches high by earthing up soil around plants. Tie newspaper around the plants first to prevent the soil from rotting the crown.

Problems Slug, celery leaf spot (caused when conditions are damp), and calcium deficiency (caused by irregular watering).

Harvesting Harvest trench celery in autumn and self-blanching cultivars from midsummer. Eat when fresh.

Celeriac (Apium graveolens var. rapaceum)

A swollen root similar to turnip, but used like celery. The roots are ugly but they are nutritious.

Sowing to harvest 26 weeks.

Site and soil Full sun or semi-shade in fertile, moisture-retentive soil.

Cultivation Seeds germinate at a temperature of 50–66°F. Sow in late winter in heat or early spring if no heat, in trays. Prick out when large enough and harden off before planting outside. Space plants 12–15 inches apart in rows with the same space between them.

Care Water well and mulch to retain moisture. Remove some leaves to expose the crown.

Problems Slugs and celery leaf spot.

Harvesting Harvest when the bulbs are 3–5 inches across. Store in the ground, covering with straw or cloth in severe weather, or store in boxes in a frost-free place.

Carrots (Daucus carota)

Although traditionally a long, orange tapered root vegetable, there are now stumpy and rounded cultivars with white, purple, and yellow flesh.

Sowing to harvest 9–20 weeks.

Site and soil Grow in an open, sunny site in loam or sandy, stone-free soil. Crops grown under cloches will extend the season of cropping. Incorporate plenty of well-rotted manure into a bed intended for carrots a year later.

Cultivation Sow under cover in late winter or outdoors from early spring. Warm the soil outside by covering with plastic. Sow thinly in rows 6 inches apart and thin to 3 inches apart.

Care Weed the rows and water the plants well in dry weather.

Problems Carrot fly. Onions help keep this pest at bay, so sow 4 rows of onions to each row of carrots.

Harvesting Pull the roots while still young. Maincrop carrots can be left in the ground and used as required or lifted and stored in boxes of moist sand.

Sweet fennel (Foeniculum vulgare var. dulce)

This is grown as an annual and is different from the perennial herb fennel (see page 125). It has a unique aniseed flavor, and you can eat the swollen stem of the plant raw or cooked. The bulbs are rich in potassium and folic acid. The fine foliage can be used as a mild flavoring or garnish.

Sowing to harvest 10–15 weeks.

Site and soil A warm, sunny position with moisture-retentive soil. Does not like heavy, clay soils. Grow in soil that has been manured for a previous crop.

Cultivation Sow seeds in a minimum temperature of 59°F in biodegradable pots because the roots dislike disturbance. Put 2–3 seeds in 3 inch pots from spring to midsummer and thin to leave the strongest.

Plant out 12 inches apart after hardening when the threat of frost has passed in rows also spaced at 12 inches.

Care Early- and late-sown plants may need cloche protection. Water plants regularly. When bulbs are egg size earth up to blanch.

Problems Plants can run to seed (bolt) if watered irregularly and slugs.

Harvesting Cut bulbs when they are the size of a tennis ball. Store in the refrigerator for up to 2 weeks. The raw root can be shredded for salads or cooked and is superb with fish.

Parsnips (*Pastinaca sativa*)

A white-fleshed winter vegetable.

Sowing to harvest 16 weeks.

Site and soil A sunny, open position in well-drained, sandy, stone-free soil. Grow in soil that has had well-rotted manure added the previous year, then add a general fertilizer before sowing. Do not add organic matter in the same season as sowing. Prepare a fine, crumbly seedbed.

Cultivation Parsnip seed is slow to germinate. Sow in mid-spring, thinly in shallow drills or 3 seeds every 6 inches, the drills being 12 inches apart. Cover seeds lightly with fine soil.

Care Keep seedlings weed free.

Problems Carrot fly also attacks parsnips. Parsnip canker can be a problem, so buy a resistant cultivar.

Harvesting The flavor of parsnips improves after a frost. They can be left in the ground over winter, but may be lifted in autumn. Store in boxes of sand so that they are not touching and keep in a dry shed. Cut into "fingers," removing any woody parts, before roasting. Can be fried with garlic to bring out their flavor.

Onion family
(*Alliaceae*)

Onions (*Allium cepa*)

A popular vegetable that seasons all manner of dishes, from casseroles to soups and sauces.

Sowing to harvest Spring-sown seeds 20–24 weeks; autumn-sown seeds 42 weeks; spring-planted sets 18–20 weeks; autumn-planted sets 36–38 weeks.

Site and soil A sunny, sheltered site that is moisture retentive but with good drainage. Plant in an area that had well-rotted manure added for a previous crop. If this was not done, apply a general fertilizer, depending on the soil condition. Do not plant onions on freshly manured ground because of rotting.

Cultivation The quickest way to raise onions is by planting sets from early to mid-spring. Push the sets into the soil so that the tips are just visible. Plant 3–4 inches apart in rows 10–12 inches apart.

In spring sow seed thinly in rows 12 inches apart and thin to the above spacings. Plant Japanese sets in autumn where the ground does not get waterlogged.

Care Hand-weed with care because onions are shallow rooted. In spring apply nitrogen fertilizer to overwintered onions.

Problems Birds or frost can lift bulbs out of the soil, so replace them and cover with cloth. Onion fly, powdery mildew, onion white rot, and bolting are the main problems.

Harvesting Harvest when bulbs are large enough to use. Dig up and spread them out on a raised bench for the skins to ripen in the open. Once they are dry, hang them up in a cool, frost-free place.

Scallions (*Allium cepa*)

Scallions are smaller and milder than other onions and are best eaten fresh. They are traditionally used in salads and for flavoring other dishes.

Sowing to harvest 8 weeks.

Site and soil An open site is preferred, but they will accept a little shade.

Cultivation Will grow well on a site that was well manured for a previous crop. If not, apply a general fertilizer. However, they will tolerate poorer soil than other onions. Sow 5–6 seeds in modules indoors in early spring and plant out when 4 inches tall. Don't thin out. Outside sow from spring to summer every 3 weeks for a continuous crop. Sow in late summer for a spring crop.

Care Water well in dry conditions. Protect winter crops with cloches.

Problems Scallions are susceptible to the same problems as other onions.

Harvesting Harvest by pulling from the soil when about 6 inches high. Will keep in the refrigerator for a few days, but are best eaten fresh.

Shallots (*Allium cepa Aggregatum* Group)

Shallots are basically small onions but with a sweeter flavor. There are yellow- and red-skinned cultivars, and you can eat them raw or cooked. The leaves can be used in the same way as scallions.

Sowing to harvest From seed 20 weeks; from sets 20–24 weeks.

Site and soil Shallots require the same growing conditions as onions in an open, sunny site, but they will tolerate some shade.

Cultivation Shallots are mostly sown from sets planted from late winter to mid-spring. Plant sets by making a hole with a trowel or take out a drill. The tip of the set should be at soil level. Sow seeds in spring in drills and thin out. Plant or thin so that they are 6 inches apart in rows 12 inches apart.

Care Water well in dry weather.

Problems Shallots are affected by the same problems as onions.

Harvesting Lift shallots when the leaves die back. Leave lying on the surface of the soil to dry. Once the skins are dry, store in nets or in single layers on trays in a cool, dry place.

Thinly slice shallots with a sharp knife because if they get bruised they will lose some flavor.

Leeks *(Allium porrum)*

A superb winter vegetable grown for its stem-like, rolled leaves. The edible part is the white stem, which is usually blanched by earthing up the soil.

Sowing to harvest 16–20 weeks.

Site and soil Leeks prefer a sunny site in moisture-retentive, fertile soil.

Cultivation Dig the site in autumn or winter and add plenty of well-rotted manure. Leave the ground in rough clods and rake over before planting, incorporating a general fertilizer. Seeds can be sown in early spring in pots on the windowsill. If sowing outside, place the seeds in shallow drills 1 inches deep, then transplant seedlings to their final site. Transplant all seedlings when they are 8 inches tall or pencil thick. Water thoroughly the day before transplanting. Make a wide hole and place a single seedling in it, filling it with water, which will wash some soil into the hole to settle around the roots. Plant leeks in rows 6–9 inches apart each way.

Care Weed regularly and soak the plants every 10 days or so. For longer white shafts, earth up the soil around the stems while they are growing.

Problems Leek rust may occur in damp weather. Burn any affected leaves (those with orange pustules) and choose a resistant cultivar in future.

Harvesting Lift leeks when they are large enough and as required. They can be left in the ground over winter. Slice lengthwise and wash thoroughly under running water before cooking.

Garlic *(Allium sativum)*

A vegetable that is easy to grow and widely used as a flavoring in recipes. It is grown from cloves (individual portions of the bulb) and never from seed.

Sowing to harvest 16–36 weeks.

Site and soil Needs to be grown in a sunny

Once garlic is dry, hang it up.

site, in rich soil that is moisture retentive but with good drainage. Soil that has been improved for a previous crop is ideal, but do not plant in freshly manured soil.

Cultivation Plant in autumn for best results. On heavy ground make a raised ridge of soil and start off cloves in trays in the greenhouse before transplanting outside in late winter. Divide the garlic into individual cloves before planting. The pointed end should be uppermost, with the tip 1–4 inches below soil level. Plant 3–4 inches apart in rows that are 10–12 inches apart.

Care Check regularly for bird or animal damage, pushing back any uprooted bulbs before they dry out. In spring and summer an occasional thorough watering will improve the yield, but do not water once the bulbs are large. Keep the area weed free.

Problems Downy mildew or rust may occur during long, wet spells. Badly affected bulbs should be destroyed. The foliage turns yellow and wilts if infected with onion white rot, with white growths on the bulbs. Discard infected bulbs and avoid planting garlic or onions in the site for 8 years.

Harvesting Harvest in the summer once leaves turn yellow and bend over (as opposed to wilting). Leave the bulbs to dry in the sun. Keep them dry. Once dried, tie into bunches or place in a net bag and keep in a cool, dry place. Garlic will keep for up to 10 months. Do not let garlic burn in hot oil, as it becomes bitter.

Corn is ripe when the tassel browns.

Corn family
(Poaceae)

Corn *(Zea mays)*

Home-grown corn, cooked and eaten as soon as it is cut, tastes far better than anything you can buy. As soon as it is picked the sugars begin to turn to starch and it quickly loses its tenderness and flavor.

Sowing to harvest 10–15 weeks.

Site and soil A warm, sheltered, sunny spot in well-drained soil is preferred. Avoid very dry or heavy clay soil. Grows best in soil that has been well manured for a previous crop. If not, apply a general fertilizer.

Cultivation Corn needs a minimum temperature of 50°F to germinate. Sow seeds indoors in individual biodegradable pots and harden off before planting out when all threat of frost has gone. Planting through black plastic, which warms the soil, will speed up growth. Plant in blocks with 14 inches between the plants each way, because it is a wind-pollinated crop. Grow at least 26 feet from other cultivars to prevent cross-pollination.

Care Earth up the soil around the base of plants for extra support on exposed sites. Water well when the corn starts to swell, hand-weed or mulch to keep weeds down and retain moisture.

Problems Slugs, mice, and birds.

Harvesting The corn is ripe when the tassel at the top of each ear turns brown. A milky juice should appear when a kernel is pricked. Corn freezes well.

Baby corn

This is normal corn planted in rows at distances of 8 inches. Plant slightly deeper than corn to prevent wind rock. Baby corn is harvested before the ears are mature, when it is about 3 inches long. Eat raw or lightly cooked. Put in a pan of boiling water for a few minutes, drain, and serve with butter, salt, and pepper.

Squash family
(Cucurbitaceae)

Melons *(Cucumis melo)*

The sweet melon is a tender annual vine with a climbing habit. There are 4 main groups: honeydews (yellow flesh), cantaloupe (orange flesh), ogen (green flesh), and musk (green to orange flesh, worthwhile only under glass).

Sowing to harvest 12–20 weeks.

Site and soil Melons require a warm, sunny spot in rich, well-drained soil and high humidity. They are most successful in a greenhouse or on a sunny, sheltered wall with the help of cloches or frames. If planting outside, dig in plenty of well-rotted manure.

Cultivation Sow seeds individually in 3-inch pots in a heated propagator at 68–77°F in plenty of light. Keep compost moist. When the first true leaves appear, remove from the propagator and grow at 64–68°F. If these conditions cannnot be met, buy plants later

in the season. Harden off before planting outside under cloches in early summer, spacing 24 inches apart. In a greenhouse plant 2 in a growbag or single plants in 12-inch pots. Water the compost the day before to allow it to warm before planting.

Care Shade indoor crops with whitewash on the glass. Keep well fed and watered and apply a high-potash liquid feed. Pinch out growing tips to encourage shoots and flowers. Open up the greenhouse or remove cloches on warm days to allow insects to pollinate flowers. Thin fruits to 3–4 on each plant. Net and support fruits as they grow. Water frequently to prevent splitting.

Problems Aphids and powdery mildew.

Harvesting Pick melons when they smell sweet. Can be stored in the refrigerator for a few days, but they are best eaten when warm and fresh, especially with prosciutto and cheeses.

Cucumbers *(Cucumis sativus)*

No salad is complete without the fresh taste and crunchy texture of a home-grown cucumber. It used to be a vegetable that needed to be grown under cover, but new introductions have made it possible to grow them outside as well.

Sowing to harvest 12 weeks.

Site and soil Grow in the greenhouse or outside in a warm, sheltered site in moisture-retentive soil. Cucumbers grow best in a minimum temperature of 64°F. They thrive in large pots, growbags, or in the ground as long as they are in rich potting compost or the soil has been treated with plenty of well-rotted manure.

Cultivation Sow the seeds on their edge, individually in biodegradable pots in a heated propagator at around 68°F. When fully rooted, plant in final positions in containers in the greenhouse or outside when all threat of frost is passed. Young plants will benefit from cloche protection until established. Space the plants in rows 18–39 inches apart.

Care Erect canes or netting to support trailing cucumbers. Pinch out the growing tips when they reach the top of the supports and pinch out lateral shoots when there are two leaves. Ridge cucumbers can trail on the flat, but pinch out the growing tips when they have produced 5–6 leaves. Place black plastic or straw underneath ridge cucumbers to protect the crop. Water well throughout the season and feed them weekly with a tomato fertilizer.

Problems Slugs and aphids.

Harvesting Cut with a sharp knife once the cucumbers are large enough. Do not leave mature cucumbers on the plant. Use them fresh or keep in a refrigerator for a few days.

Pumpkins and squashes
(Cucurbita maxima, C. moschata, C. pepo)

These are novelty vegetables, especially the large pumpkins that children like to grow for Halloween. Winter squashes come in all shapes and sizes, and the skin colors can be blue, orange, yellow and dark green.

Sowing to harvest Pumpkins 10–12 weeks; squashes 22–24 weeks.

Site and soil A sheltered site in full sun and fertile, moist soil. Pumpkins do well on a well-rotted compost heap. If they are growing in the ground, add a general-purpose fertilizer before cultivating.

Cultivation Sow individual seeds in 3-inch pots in a temperature of 55°F. Choose cultivars that ripen early because they need a long growing season. Harden off before planting outside when all threat of frost is passed. Sow seeds outside in early summer. Cover plants with cloches if the weather is chilly. Plant bush cultivars 2–3 x 3–4 feet apart, and trailing cultivars 4–6 x 6 feet apart.

Care As the fruit swells, support it off the ground and water and feed with tomato fertilizer every 2 weeks.

Problems Slugs and powdery mildew.

Harvesting Cut off fruits as required when they are large enough. Leave the fruit on the plant for as long as possible so that it is fully ripened if you want to store. Will keep for up to 12 months in a cool, frost-free place.

Zucchini and vegetable marrows *(Cucurbita pepo)*

Zucchini fruits can be green, yellow, or striped. The flowers and leaves can also be eaten raw or cooked. Vegetable marrows are grown in the same way.

Sowing to harvest Zucchini 8–10 weeks; vegetable marrows 9–11 weeks.

Site and soil Sunny position in fertile soil.

Cultivation Sow 1 seed in each 3 inch pot in a warm place. Harden off before planting out. Zucchini and vegetable marrows do well on a well-rotted compost heap. There will be plenty of fruit from 3 zucchini plants. Plant bushy cultivars 2–3 x 3–4 feet apart, and trailing cultivars 4–6 x 6 feet apart. Although gourds are mature zucchini, if you want gourds it is better to select a gourd cultivar because the fruits will be easier to use.

Care Weed the area and water well because zucchini are thirsty. Trailing cultivars can be trained up supports.

Problems Slugs and powdery mildew; poultry like them.

Harvesting Pick zucchini when they are 4–6 inches long. Keep picking and more will grow. Will keep in a refrigerator for up to 3 weeks. Pick gourds when they are hard and sound hollow if tapped. Will keep in a cool, frost-free place for many months.

Keep picking zucchini and more will grow.

Harvest fava beans before they get tough.

Pea and bean family
(Papilionaceae)

Italian flat beans
(Phaseolus coccineus)

This summer vegetable is a heavy cropper, and the tall wigwams of green leaves with vivid red flowers are attractive enough for ornamental borders, too. A good row will provide sufficient beans for a long period, either eaten fresh or for storing in the freezer for winter.

Sowing to harvest 12–16 weeks.

Site and soil A sunny, sheltered position with moisture-retentive soil. In autumn dig a trench with plenty of well-rotted manure in the bottom where you intend to grow the beans. Plain newspaper, cardboard, grass clippings, and other organic matter can be dug in and left over winter. Before sowing add a general fertilizer to the soil as well.

Cultivation Seeds can be sown in shallow wooden boxes or pots indoors in mid-spring to be planted out when all fear of frost is passed. Sow directly outside from late spring to early summer. Plant 6 x 24 inches apart in double rows, 6–12 inches apart in wigwams.

Care Plants need good support, so wigwams and canes for rows should be strong and around 8 feet high. Water and mulch well to retain moisture. Lightly spray the whole plants in the evening when in flower to encourage pollination.

Problems Slugs. A poor pod set can be as a result of cold weather or a shortage of moisture in the soil.

Harvesting Pick pods when they are about 6 inches long and still young. Old pods become stringy, but you can leave on the plant to dry, then save the seed.

Green beans (Phaseolus vulgaris)

There are two types of green bean, dwarf and climbing, and both are ideal for the small garden. Green beans crop over a long period and can be very attractive, with cultivars bearing green, yellow, purple, or red beans.

Sowing to harvest 7–18 weeks, depending on the cultivar.

Site and soil Green beans need a warm, sunny site with fertile, moisture-retentive soil. Dig well-rotted manure into the site where the beans are to be planted.

Cultivation Can be started in early to mid-spring in pots under cover and planted out when all fear of frost has passed. They are tender plants, so cover the soil outside with plastic or cloches to warm the soil before sowing. Sow outside in early to late summer, 2 inches deep. Plant dwarf cultivars in rows 2 x 18 inches apart and climbing cultivars up wigwams 24 inches apart with 6 inches between supports.

Care Train climbing beans to grow up small wigwam canes or netting. Pinch out the growing tips when at the top of their supports. Watering thoroughly when pods begin helps to increase the crop.

Problems Mice, aphids, and viruses.

Harvesting Pick when pods are about 4 inches long and snap crisply. For dried beans, leave them on the plant until they turn brown.

Peas (Pisum sativum)

Peas picked fresh from the plant can scarcely be bettered for flavor. Different cultivars will provide you with peas right through the summer. The complete pod of snow peas and sugar snap peas can be eaten.

Sowing to harvest Early cultivars 11–12 weeks; maincrop 13–14 weeks.

Site and soil Peas are good vegetables for small gardens because they grow upwards, but they do need plenty of strong support, which their tendrils will hook around. They like a soil that has plenty of well-rotted manure added and does not dry out. Watering and mulching is needed in hot weather, as they do not like the heat.

Cultivation Start early crops in pots or shallow boxes under cover from early spring. Harden off and transplant when plants are 4 inches tall, under cloches if needed. Sow outside at regular intervals from mid-spring onward in 4–6 inch wide drills. Place seeds 2 inches apart and leave 2–3 feet between drills, depending on the height of the cultivar.

Care Insert bamboo canes, place 6-foot chicken wire attached to stakes or netting along rows for tall cultivars and pruning offcuts or sticks and twigs for the dwarf varieties. Water the crop thoroughly twice a week if necessary. The pods will not fill if moisture is denied.

Problems Mice love pea seeds, and pigeons like to eat the young growth. The caterpillars of the pea moth can devastate crops. Peas are also susceptible to powdery mildew.

Harvesting Harvest peas when the pods are plump and the peas have formed fully but are not large and old. Snow peas and sugar snap peas are picked once the pods are large enough to eat but before the peas inside have formed.

Fava beans (Vicia faba)

This easy-to-grow bean is quite prolific. It is also a useful green manure crop, returning nitrogen to the soil.

Sowing to harvest Spring-sown seed up to 16 weeks; autumn-sown seed 35 weeks.

Site and soil A sunny, sheltered site. Will benefit from well-rotted manure dug into the ground before planting. Does not like either dry or waterlogged soil.

Cultivation Sow seeds individually in biodegradable pots indoors from late winter to early spring. Plant outside under cloches when 3–4 true leaves have formed. Sow outside from early to late spring or in autumn for a crop the following year. Seeds are sown in double rows, with 6–8 inches between the seeds and 2 feet between each double row, and seeds 2 inches deep. Three sowings will produce a good harvest. Sow the second crop when the first beans are 6 inches high.

Care Fava beans are susceptible to wind damage, so provide some twiggy supports. Insert these into the ground while the plants are small. Pinch out tips when flowers begin to open to deter black bean aphids and encourage fruiting.

Problems Aphids, pea and bean weevils, chocolate spot, and rust.

Harvesting Harvest when the beans can be felt through the pods but before they get large and tough. Fava beans are delicious fresh, but also freeze well. Briefly blanch in boiling water before freezing.

Daisy family
(*Asteraceae*)

Endive (*Cichorium intybus*)

Endive looks a bit like lettuce and can be harvested in spring, summer, and autumn. There are two different types, one that needs blanching and is a good winter vegetable, and the other that does not.

Sowing to harvest From 8–10 weeks, depending on the cultivar.

Site and soil Endive grows best on a light soil that has been well manured, which helps to keep it moist. It will tolerate some shade. If necessary, apply a general fertilizer before planting.

Cultivation Sow the seeds from mid-spring to summer either in seedtrays in the greenhouse or in the ground outside. Germination can be difficult, so sowing in warmth is preferable. Handle the seedlings carefully during transplanting because they do not like root disturbance. Space plants 14 inches apart. Those for forcing should be sown in late summer. Cut the plants down to 2 inches and cover with soil. Within a few weeks the blanched chicons will form. They can also be forced indoors and similarly treated having been lifted and planted, 3–4 roots in 9-inch pots of moist compost, then left in a warm, dark place.

Care Water well until established. Cover with cloth or cloches if frost is forecast.

Problems Slugs, snails, and sometimes caterpillars. The plants will bolt if watering is not consistent.

Harvesting Pick individual leaves of the salad cultivars or the whole plant, or leave a stump that will grow again. The leaves will store longer than lettuce if in a cool place. Blanched endive can be cut when chicons are 4–5 inches tall. Blanching removes the bitterness, but the plants will revert to their dark green color and bitter taste once the cover has been removed or the plant is introduced to light.

Even frilly-leaved lettuce cultivars are available.

Lettuce (*Latuca sativa*)

No salad is complete without some form of lettuce in it, and there are many cultivars available. There are frilly-leaved ones, loose-leaf ones, hearted or cut-and-come-again cultivars, and in an array of different colors as well.

Sowing to harvest 4–14 weeks.

Site and soil Needs a sunny site with fertile, moisture-retentive soil. Crops grow well on land that has previously grown a nitrogen-fixing green manure or had well-rotted manure applied in the autumn. Dig in a general fertilizer if necessary.

Cultivation For an early crop, sow seeds indoors under heat in late winter and transplant after hardening off. Depending on the cultivar, space the plants 6–12 inches apart. Sow seeds directly into shallow drills and thin seedlings when they are large enough.

Care Water plants well and keep weed free.

Problems Slugs, aphids, botrytis,n and powdery mildew. Hot, dry weather encourages bolting.

Harvesting Pick when leaves are large enough or when hearts are firm, as required.

Cabbage family
(*Brassicaceae*)

Rutabaga (*Brassica napus Napobrassica* Group)

Rutabagas are a valuable winter crop, mainly used in casseroles, roasts, and soups.

Sowing to harvest 26 weeks.

Site and soil An open site in well-drained, moisture-retentive soil. Grow on soil that has had well-rotted manure added the previous autumn. Rutabagas like alkaline conditions, so check the pH and add lime to the soil before sowing if required. Prepare and firm the soil before sowing.

Cultivation Sow the seed outside in late spring in warmer areas and early summer in cold regions, thinly in drills ½ inch deep and rows 15 inches apart. Thin gradually until all plants are 23 cm (9 inches) apart. Rutabaga can also be grown in pots like other brassicas.

Care Once sown cover with cloth or small-mesh netting to protect from flea beetles, cabbage root fly, and pigeons. Water every week to avoid root splitting and to prevent powdery mildew. Keep weeds down.

Problems Flea beetles, cabbage root fly, whitefly, powdery mildew, and club root.

Harvesting Harvest the roots as required over the autumn and winter, as soon as they are large enough to use. Lift before the worst of the winter because they can become woody if left in the ground. Store them in boxes of sand and keep in a frost-free place.

Kale (*Brassica oleracea Acephala* Group)

Also called borecole, kale is an ancient vegetable, which is a good source of iron and vitamins A, C, and E. There is curly-leaved kale, plain-leaved, rape kale, and the leaf and spear types.

Sowing to harvest 7 weeks.

Site and soil Kale will tolerate any soils, and also shade and frost. Digging in well-rotted manure in the autumn before sowing will help to improve the crop, and following a green manure will also boost the plants' growth. Rake the surface to produce a crumbly tilth before sowing or planting.

Cultivation Sow seeds in trays indoors in late winter or outside in drills in early spring. Transplant seedlings grown indoors when they have true leaves and have been hardened off. Sow seeds in drills outside in mid- to late spring and transplant after 6–8 weeks to their final positions, spacing them 18 inches apart. Some dwarf cultivars can be planted closer together. Puddle in the plants with water, making sure they are as deep as the first true leaves.

Care Keep plants well watered. Support stems if necessary and remove any yellowing leaves. Keep weed free.

Problems Cabbage white butterfly, aphids, whitefly, club root, and pigeons.

Harvesting Harvest young leaves as required from autumn until mid-spring. Cut with a knife from the crown outward and more shoots will grow.

Cabbage (*Brassica oleracea Capitata* Group)

There are cabbages for harvesting in spring, summer, and autumn to winter, so it is a vegetable that can provide an all year round crop. Spring cabbages are grown over winter and are small, pointed vegetables; summer and autumn cabbages include the red cultivars that are excellent for pickling; and there is a good range of winter cabbages from the tight, globular drumheads to the crinkly leaved Savoy types.

Sowing to harvest Around 20 weeks.

Site and soil An open, sunny site and firm soil. Dig in well-rotted manure in the autumn, and before planting rake it over and shuffle up and down the rows, digging your heels into the soil. Apply a general fertilizer before planting.

Cultivation Sow summer and autumn cultivars from late winter indoors. Transplant the seedlings when large enough and hardened off, but protect under cloches. Sow outside in early to late spring. Sow autumn and winter cultivars outside in late spring, and spring cabbages outside in the autumn. Successive sowings will provide a gradual harvest of each. When sowing outside, rake over the soil so that it is crumbly, and using a length of string as a guide, make a ½ inch drill with a hoe. Lightly water and sprinkle the seeds thinly before covering with soil. Cover seedbeds with cloth to keep insects at bay. Transplant when large enough, allowing 12–18 inches between the plants, depending on the cultivars. Spring cabbages will need less room and can be set 4 inches apart. Puddle them into the hole with water and then fill with soil.

Care Place collars around the plants when transplanting. Water well throughout development. Remove any dead leaves as they appear.

Problems Cabbage root fly, caterpillars, flea beatles, club root, and pigeons.

Harvesting Cut as needed. They are best eaten freshly harvested, but some cabbages can be lifted in the autumn and stored in a straw-lined box in a cool, frost-free area or left in the ground.

Brussels sprouts (*Brassica olerarea Gemmifera* Group)

These vegetables resemble miniature cabbages, and they have quite a strong flavor and are an important winter crop.

Sowing to harvest Around 20 weeks.

Site and soil A sunny, open site with protection from wind. Grow in soil that has had plenty of well-rotted manure incorporated into it in autumn or has had a nitrogen-fixing green manure grown on it. Apply a nitrogen-rich fertilizer in midsummer if plants are not thriving. Avoid any digging before planting.

Cultivation Grow from seed in trays indoors, then harden off before planting outside when the roots begin to show through the tray, or sow outside in a seedbed in mid-spring. Transplant the seedlings to their permanent position from late spring to early summer. Allow 30 inches between the plants and rows.

Care Some taller cultivars may need staking to support them when fruiting. Water well until established. Weed between plants and remove any yellowing leaves.

Problems Cabbage root fly, cabbage white butterfly, flea beetle, whitefly, and pigeons.

Harvesting Sprouts have more flavor after being frosted. Leave on the plant and pick as required, harvesting the mature sprouts from the bottom of each plant and working up the stems. Sprouts freeze well.

Kohl rabi (*Brassica oleracea Gongylodes* Group)

This rather odd-looking vegetable is a member of the cabbage family, but you eat the swollen stem, which forms an edible corm, instead of the leaves.

Sowing to harvest 5–9 weeks.

Site and soil A sunny, open site is preferable for kohl rabi.

Cultivation For an early crop, sow indoors in modules from late winter, harden off, and plant out when no higher than 2 inches. Otherwise, sow outside in drills. Seedlings can be transplanted 10 inches apart before they are 2 inches high in rows 12 inches apart. Sow every 10–14 days from summer to autumn for continuous cropping. The purple cultivars are hardier than the white or pale green ones and can be sown later for harvesting in autumn and winter.

Care Water during dry periods. A mulch will help conserve moisture. Weed regularly.

Problems Flea beetles, cabbage root fly, and club root.

Harvesting Harvest the corms when young and about the size of a tennis ball. Peel before cooking. Later crops can be left in the ground or lifted and stored in boxes of sand in a frost-free place.

Broccoli (*Brassica oleracea Italica* Group)

Grown for the florets, which resemble miniature cauliflowers. Calabrese or broccoli are summer vegetables, whereas sprouting broccoli, with more, smaller flowerheads, is harvested in late winter and spring. There are purple and white cultivars.

Sowing to harvest 8–12 months.

Site and soil Likes full sun and needs to be protected against cold winds. Needs plenty of well-rotted manure in the soil or plant after a nitrogen-fixing green manure has been grown in the site.

Cultivation Young plants of calabrese and sprouting broccoli can be bought in late spring, but they are easy to grow from seed. Sow indoors in modules or trays in early spring or outside in shallow drills, ¾–1 inch deep, from mid- to late spring. Harden off indoor-grown seedlings before planting outside. Transplant seedlings in early to midsummer after they have made 2–3 true

Brussels sprouts are an important winter vegetable.

leaves, not the seed leaves. Space calabrese plants 12 inches apart, and sprouting broccoli in rows, 30 inches between the rows.

Care Water well until established and give some protection from birds with netting or cloth.

Problems Cabbage root fly, cabbage white butterflies, aphids, flea beetles, and pigeons.

Harvesting Cut off the florets before they open. With regular harvesting the florets will continue to grow for up to 8 weeks.

Oriental brassicas (types of *Brassica rapa*)

Oriental brassicas are grown mainly for the leaves, and in the right conditions they crop well. There are several cultivars in this group, including Chinese cabbage, tight-headed Chinese cabbage, bok choy, oriental mustards, Chinese broccoli, and mizuna greens.

Sowing to harvest 8–10 weeks.

Site and soil They like plenty of sunshine, warm temperatures, ample water, and a rich soil. Dig plenty of well-rotted manure into the soil in autumn, and if necessary apply a general fertilizer before planting.

Cultivation For an early crop, sow individually in pots on a windowsill and transplant when large enough and hardened off. Best sown outside in midsummer for harvesting in late summer and autumn. Sow thinly in drills and then thin further to 12 inches apart and the same distance in rows.

Care Water regularly and mulch. Flea beetles are attracted to them, so cover with cloth.

Problems Flea beetles, aphids, caterpillars, powdery mildew, and slugs.

Harvesting Can be picked at any stage of growth, and mature plants will regrow if part of the main stem is left. Oriental brassicas are best used fresh, either raw in salads or cooked.

Turnips (*Brassica rapa Rapifera* Group)

One of the easiest root vegetables to grow, turnips should be eaten when small. The flesh is pink or white, and the young leaves can be eaten as well.

Sowing to harvest 8–12 weeks, depending on whether early or maincrop.

Site and soil An open site. Turnips do well with plenty of rainfall.

Cultivation They do best where plenty of well-rotted manure has been added to the soil. If this hasn't been done, add a general fertilizer before sowing. Turnips do not transplant well, so sow directly into the ground from late winter onward at fortnightly intervals. Sow thinly in ½-inch drills and thin out when 1 inch high to 6 inches apart.

Care Weed between the crops and keep well watered to prevent bolting. If you have a flea beetle problem, cover the crop with cloth or fine-mesh netting, making sure the edges are secured. A bad infestation can be dusted with an appropriate powder treatment.

Problems Flea beetles, cabbage root fly, club root, and powdery mildew.

Harvesting Pull turnips when they are the size of an apricot; do not let them grow much larger before harvesting because they become woody and have less flavor. They need to be lifted before the frosts, but can be stored in a frost-free place.

Radishes (*Raphanus sativus, R. sativus Longipinnatus* Group)

One of the easiest vegetables to grow and a staple colorful ingredient of summer salads.

Sowing to harvest Summer radishes 4 weeks; mooli cultivars 7–8 weeks; some autumn and winter cultivars around 20 weeks.

Site and soil Open ground in fertile, moisture-retentive soil. Dig in well-rotted manure in autumn or add a general fertilizer before planting.

Cultivation Sow seeds outside from early spring onward, sowing at fortnightly intervals until the autumn. Mooli cultivars are sown in late summer, and winter ones from mid- to late summer. Seeds can be sown fairly thickly and then thinned to 1 inch apart in rows, or in vacant spaces between other crops. Radishes do not transplant successfully.

Care Water regularly. Both irregular watering and overwatering can lead to the fruits splitting or lush growth. When the seedlings begin to show, cover with small-mesh wire netting to prevent bird damage.

Problems Flea beetles, cabbage root fly, slugs, and snails. Birds attack seedlings.

Harvesting Pull radishes as soon as they are large enough. Wash, wipe dry, and store in a plastic bag in the refrigerator for a few days. Use sliced or grated in salads.

Miscellaneous salad leaves

Land cress, salad arugula, mustard, garden cress, and corn salad

These green crops, which provide a range, different flavors, are ideal for inclusion in salads.

Sowing to harvest 4–12 weeks.

Site and soil Tolerant of shade, but they like moisture-retentive soil. These crops grow well if the soil has had well-rotted manure incorporated for a previous crop.

Cultivation These plants grow quite quickly and will run to seed, so make successive sowings through spring until late summer. Corn salad can be sown in late summer or early autumn for a winter crop. Sow seeds in shallow drills 4–6 inches apart.

Care Keep plants well watered and remove any that are about to flower and seed.

Problems Flea beetles and slugs.

Harvesting Cut some leaves when 3 inches high. Leave some growth, because it will sprout out again. Use these crops as cut-and-come-again vegetables and use while fresh.

Miscellaneous tender vegetables

Okra *(Hibiscus esculentus)*

The fleshy seedpods of this ornamental plant are widely used in African and Indian cookery.

Sowing to harvest Around 12 weeks.

Site and soil Okra needs full sun and a well-drained site with a temperature of 72–86°F to thrive. Best grown in a greenhouse or polytunnel.

Cultivation Seed needs to be bought fresh or save your own. Start in a heated propagator at 77°F in early spring. Sow individual seeds in 3½-inch pots and keep well watered. Remove pots from the propagator when seedlings emerge, but continue growing at 72–86°F and water with tepid water. When 12 inches tall, plant in growbags or 12-inch pots with multipurpose compost. Plants need a humid atmosphere to self-pollinate.

Care Support with canes, because plants can reach 4 feet high. Water well and feed with a high-potash liquid feed.

Problems Aphids, red spider mite, whitefly, and wilt.

Harvesting Pods take 3–5 days to develop after flowering; pick with a sharp knife when 2–3 inches long. They should be bright green and firm. Pods bruise easily, so handle with

care and eat as soon as harvested. Young pods can be eaten raw, and mature pods can be boiled, fried, or added to casseroles.

Perennial vegetables

Asparagus *(Asparagus officinalis)*

An increasingly popular late-spring or early-summer vegetable, which is expensive to buy in the shops. It is a perennial, and although it can be 3 years before the first crop, the plants will continue to be productive for up to 20 years.

Sowing to harvest 2–3 years.

Site and soil A sunny, well-drained, and sheltered site because wind can snap off the tall, mature stem that produces food for the crown. Add plenty of well-rotted manure before planting.

Cultivation Asparagus can be raised from seed, but it will take several seasons before cropping. Soak the seed overnight, then sow ½ inch deep in individual 3-inch pots of seed compost and raise in heat. Harden off and plant out in early summer at a depth of 4 inches. Crowns are readily available to buy and are planted in spring. Dig a trench 6 inches deep and 12 inches wide and make a ridge of soil along the bottom onto which the crowns should be carefully placed. Cover the trench with 3 inches of soil and water well. Do not cut any spears the first summer and level the trench with more soil in the autumn.

Care Keep the asparagus bed well watered and mulched. Hand-weed throughout the growing season to prevent the crowns from getting damaged.

Problems Asparagus beetle (pick off the larvae and adults by hand and burn old foliage), slugs, and root rot.

Harvesting Harvest a few spears in the second or third year once the plants are

Okra seedpods develop just days after flowering.

Globe artichokes are a delicious edible perennial.

established. Harvest when around 6 inches high, using a sharp knife to cut the spear about 1 inch below the soil. In the fourth year cut all spears, even those that are not quality ones. This will stimulate the crowns. Stop cutting in midsummer to allow shoots to grow and the fern-like foliage to feed the crowns.

Seakale (*Crambe maritima*)

An old vegetable that is easy to grow. Young leaf stalks are cooked like asparagus and eaten with melted butter. It is a perennial plant, and grows wild on shingle beaches in different parts of the world.

Sowing to harvest Up to 2 years.

Site and soil An open, sunny site in well-drained soil. Seakale can be placed with other perennial crops. The plants like an alkaline soil, so if it is acidic, apply lime.

Cultivation Best grown from seed, which is available from specialty seed suppliers. It can be slow to germinate, but this can be hastened by rubbing the seeds with sandpaper. To grow as an annual, sow in pots in early spring and transplant the seedlings when they have 3–4 leaves. Sow directly outside from early to mid-spring. Sow in drills 1 inch deep in rows 12–15 inches apart, and thin the plants so that they are eventually 12 inches apart. Dig the plants up in the autumn and trim the roots for cuttings for the next year. The main root is then kept in a pot of damp sand and placed in the dark to blanch. Plants grown as perennials are blanched in early spring by being covered by a tall pot. Seakale plants in permanent beds should be replaced after 5 years.

Care Seaweed fertilizer is an appropriate summer feed and encourages growth for the following season. Remove any yellowing foliage and flowers so that the plant's energy goes into the root system.

Problems Club root, slugs, and botrytis. However, these problems are not suffered on windy seashores.

Harvesting Seakale needs to be at least 1 year old before blanching. The plants can have 2–3 cuts taken off when shoots are about 8 inches long, then be allowed to grow in full light over the summer. Seakale needs to be eaten fresh; it does not keep well.

Globe artichokes (*Cynara scolymus*)

This truly architectural perennial plant is also delicious to eat. The green and purple flower buds are edible and can be cooked or pickled. Once in flower, they are inedible but are great for attracting pollinating insects to the garden.

Sowing to harvest Approximately 28 weeks from planting in the first season; late spring and early summer thereafter.

Site and soil A sheltered, sunny site with well-drained, moisture-retentive soil to which plenty of well-rotted manure has been added. They do not like shade, heavy clay soil, or waterlogged ground.

Cultivation Sow seeds in late winter or early spring, individually in 3-inch pots in a temperature of 59°F. Harden off and plant outside when fear of frost is over. Buying in a named cutlivar of a pot-grown plant is more reliable, because seeds can be of variable quality. Allow at least 3–5 feet between each plant. In deep beds allow 18 inches each way and grow as annuals.

Care Water well in the first year and especially when flower buds are forming in subsequent years. Keep the plants weed free. Take offsets from plants every 2–3 years, as they crop best up to 3–4 years old.

Problems Aphids.

Harvesting Cut the artichoke heads while the buds are still tight from late summer to early autumn and eat fresh.

Jerusalem artichokes
(Helianthus tuberosus)

A root vegetable similar in flavor to the globe artichoke but easier to grow.

Sowing to harvest 16–20 weeks.

Site and soil Jerusalem artichokes prefer a sunny site, but will also grow in part shade. They like a moisture-retentive but well-drained soil. Prepare the soil with well-rotted manure or a general fertilizer.

Cultivation Tubers are planted in late winter or early spring 6 inches deep and 24 inches apart. Rows should be spaced 3 feet apart. Jerusalem artichokes grow to 10 feet tall, therefore site them so that they don't cast shade over other plants.

Care Earth up around the roots once plants are 12 inches tall. Stake plants, especially on windy sites. Water in dry spells. Cut away topgrowth once it has turned brown. When frosted, cut back stems to 6 inches from the ground. Provide a protective mulch of straw in winter.

Problems Slugs and wireworms. If you decide against growing Jersulem artichokes for a second year, clear every piece of tuber from the ground because they are invasive.

Harvesting Harvest when needed and use fresh. They will keep in the ground, but if the weather is likely to be harsh, lift and store them in moist sand in a frost-free place.

Rhubarb *(Rheum cultorum)*

Rhubarb is often thought of as a fruit, but it is a vegetable. It is a useful plant and once it is growing you have it for many years. Rhubarb is eaten stewed and in pies, and can be made into chutneys and preserves.

Sowing to harvest Seeds from 2–3 years; crowns from 1–2 years.

Site and soil It prefers a sunny, moisture-retentive but well-drained soil. The crowns will rot in heavy, waterlogged soils. Prepare the area well the previous autumn by digging in lots of organic matter, especially well-rotted manure.

Cultivation Sow seeds, dormant rhubarb crowns, or pot-grown plants. Sow seeds under cover in late winter, harden off, and plant outside after the threat of frost has passed. Sow outside in spring in drills 1 inch deep and transplant in autumn. Crowns are planted in late autumn with the dormant buds just above the soil. Two crowns will probably provide sufficient rhubarb for a family of 4. Plant crowns 3 feet apart.

Care Water regularly. If plants begin to bolt, remove the flower spikes. Clear all debris in winter and mulch with an organic compost.

Problems Honey fungus; dig up and burn an affected plant. Buy virus-free stock from a reputable grower. Slugs and snails.

Harvesting Harvest in the second year, taking a few stems only. Do not pick after midsummer. Once established rhubarb can be forced to provide an earlier crop. Place a tall pot over a crown in midwinter and surround it with fresh manure to keep it warm. Once shoots appear they will be ready to cut 2–4 weeks later. Alternatively, lift crowns,

leaving them exposed for a week, and then plant them in pots of compost and move to a cool, dark room with a temperature of around 61°F, no warmer. Ventilation will be needed, and this is best done at night. Do not force the same crown for consecutive years. To store, wash and dry the stems and place in a clear plastic bag in the refrigerator for up to 2 weeks. Rhubarb freezes well.

Rhubarb is eaten in desserts and preserves.

Fruit directory

Eating fruit straight from a tree or bush growing in your own garden is immensely rewarding. In addition, if you are able to store some of your crop, freeze it or make it into preserves that you will be able to enjoy during the winter months.

Lemons and oranges
(*Citrus spp.*)

Lemons and oranges need warmth to survive and fruit well. In cooler regions grow under glass in frost-free conditions. In warmer climates plant as apples in well-drained, sandy loam with a pH between 5.5 and 6.00. Water well and mulch with compost away from the trunk. Harvest in winter when required, as the fruit keeps well on tree.

Cobnuts and filberts
(*Corylus avellana, C. maxima*)

Popular nuts for winter eating, cobnuts and filberts are related to hazelnuts. They produce male and female flowers on the same tree, but 2 cultivars planted next to each other are needed to give good cross-pollination.

Site and soil A sheltered site on well-drained soil. Cobnuts are tolerant of soil with a pH of around 8.0. Too rich a soil could lead to excessive growth and too much foliage at the expense of nuts.

Cultivation Cobnuts can be grown as open-centered bushes with a 12-15 inch stem or as trees 6-8 feet high and 15 feet apart. Newly planted trees should be staked and cut back by half to an outward-facing bud. Remove other branches to 3-4 buds. Pruning is carried out in late winter, but weak laterals are not pruned because they carry the female flowers.

Care Manure well in midwinter or add a general fertilizer.

Problems Squirrels, nut gall mites, nut weevils, and winter moth larvae.

Harvesting Harvest in early autumn when the husks turn yellow. Spread out in a warm place to dry, turning them every few days. De-husk when dry and store in jars in a cool, airy room away from mice and squirrels.

Quince (*Cydonia oblonga*)

An attractive tree with flowers that are like those of the dog rose (*Rosa canina*) and large, golden fruits.

Site and soil Any soil with well-rotted manure added.

Cultivation Plant as for apple. Quinces have lax growth and are best grown as bushes to 12-15 feet in height and spread.

Care Prune between late autumn and early spring. Initial pruning is similar to an apple or pear, and a mature tree only needs the removal of dead, crossing, or broken branches. Feed and mulch in early spring.

Problems Aphids, codling moth, caterpillars, brown rot, powdery mildew, and also quince leaf blight.

Harvesting Leave the fruit on the tree until it is golden and has a powdery bloom. Pick in mid-autumn but before frosts. They are hard and acid, so rarely eaten raw, but they make excellent jellies and flavor apple pies.

Figs (*Ficus carica*)

Figs picked on a sunny day and eaten fresh for dessert or at breakfast are simply superb.

Site and soil This Mediterranean fruit likes warmth, but will fruit in cooler areas, including many parts of the northern USA. A sandy loam is preferred, but trees also crop well on poor soil.

Cultivation Grow against a south-facing wall and contain the roots otherwise plants will put on too much growth at the expense of the fruit. Dig a large, square hole and insert 4 paving slabs, each 2 x 2 feet, along the sides. These should stand about 1 inch above soil level. Place 9 inches of brick rubble in the base of the hole and fill with a loam-based compost. A pot 18 inches diameter in could be inserted into the ground. Figs can also be grown in large pots on a sunny patio. Fruit is formed in the axils of the leaves in late summer and over winter, producing a crop the following year. They do not require

Pick figs when soft and hanging down.

pollination. A fig tree needs about 20 feet, but fan-trained plants on a wall can be pruned and restricted.

Care In early spring after planting, prune back the single stem to 15 inches and any sideshoots by one-third. In summer tie in sideshoots to wires. Once established, prune growing shoots back to 4–5 leaves before early summer and tie in 6–12 inches apart. Remove surplus shoots and any diseased or old wood. Mulch with well-rotted manure in early spring. Give a high-potash liquid feed every 2 weeks in summer until the fruit ripens. Protect figs from frost with cloth or place pot-grown plants in a frost-free place over winter.

Problems Frost. Ripe figs soon rot on tree.

Harvesting Pick when soft and hanging downward. Eat fresh or dry and store for winter in jars.

Walnuts (*Juglans regia*)

Walnuts are a favorite dessert nut.

Site and soil A well-drained loamy soil in a light and airy site. Walnut trees grow large and need plenty of space.

Cultivation Walnuts are best planted in autumn or spring. Dig a deep hole, remove all perennial weed and incorporate well-rotted manure into the soil before planting.

Care Lightly prune after the threat of any frost, but as the tree matures little pruning is required. Trim off straggling growth, crossing branches, and dead wood as required just before the leaves fall.

Problems Caterpillars of some moths and walnut wilt.

Harvesting Walnuts will fall when ripe. Do not thrash the tree to release the fruit. After gathering, the nuts should be spread out to dry and regularly turned until they part with their husk. Pack in jars and store in a cool, dry place. For pickling, walnuts should be gathered while the shell is soft. Fresh walnuts will stain your hands brown, so wear gloves.

Apples (*Malus domestica*)

Apples are one of the most popular fruits, and there are now numerous

Fresh walnuts will stain your hands brown.

cultivars on a range of rootstocks, making it possible to grow them as small trees in pots, as fan-trained plants against a wall, as espaliers and cordons or, when there is space, as large specimens. The tree's ultimate size will depend on the rootstock the cultivar has been grafted onto, so always check when you are buying a new plant, because rootstocks range from extremely dwarfing, dwarfing, semi-dwarfing, semi-vigorous to standard.

Some apples are self-pollinating, but most will need another apple in the same pollination group to pollinate them. Apples within the same group will cross-pollinate one another because they flower at the same time, and those in different groups may pollinate one another if there is an overlap in the flowering period. Different fruits, such as pears, will not cross-pollinate apples.

Site and soil Preferably a sunny, open site. Where wind is a problem, apples will benefit from some protection or cropping could be reduced. They will tolerate most soils if well drained. Clear grass and perennial weeds before planting.

Cultivation Bare-rooted trees and bushes should be planted from autumn to spring; pot-grown trees can be planted at any time, but must be watered well. Dig a hole 3 feet across and 12 inches deep, forking the subsoil at the bottom to loosen it to allow for root penetration. Incorporate well-rotted manure into the subsoil. Mix more manure with some of the soil removed from the hole. Insert a stake 3–5 feet long into the hole, just off the center. Place the apple tree into the hole by the stake, making sure it will not be deeper than when it was previously planted. Backfill with some soil if you need to adjust the depth. Insert the tree, fill the hole with soil, and firm thoroughly. Water well and use a plastic tree tie or a section of nylon tights to make a figure-of-eight around the tree trunk and the stake, and then tie. This will prevent wind from rocking the tree and damaging the roots.

Space standard, bush, and espalier trees 8–10 feet apart, depending on the type of rootstock used. Cordons are planted 30 inches apart.

Care Water well until established and keep weeds at bay. Mulches of well-rotted manure, coconut fiber or compost can be placed around the trees to suppress weeds and retain moisture in the ground.

There are two groups of apples and pears for pruning purposes: tip bearing and spur bearing. Tip bearers produce fruit on the tips of the previous year's growth; spur bearers produce fruit on spurs on older wood.

Problems Codling moth, aphids, and powdery mildew.

Harvesting There are dessert, cooking, or dual-purpose apples, which ripen from late summer to late autumn. If an apple is ripe it will come off the tree into your hand when you cup the fruit and gently twist it. Do not bruise fruit when picking. Late cultivars can be stored in a cool, dark, and frost-free place. Throughout winter check that none of the fruits have gone rotten; remove any rotten fruit immediately.

Apricots (*Prunus armeniaca*)

Fresh apricots are a great addition to any fruit collection, and as the climate changes they can increasingly be grown in areas that were, until recently, too cold to ripen the fruit.

Site and soil Give apricots a sheltered site on a south-facing wall or grow under glass. They need cold in winter to go dormant, but warmth and sunshine in summer to produce fruit. A light, loamy soil prepared with well-rotted manure before planting is ideal.

Cultivation Plant as apple trees.

Care Mulch with well-rotted manure in late winter. Thin to remove small, misshapen, or overcrowded fruits and leave them 3–4 inches apart.

Problems Aphids, red spider mite, apricot die-back, bacterial canker, brown rot, and silver leaf.

Harvesting The fruits are ripe when the skin turns yellow and they part easily from the spur. Take care that you do not bruise when picking. Eat fresh because they will not keep long, or use for jelly, cooking, or bottling.

Plums (*Prunus domestica*)

Plums are a favorite fruit because they are so tasty when picked and eaten straight from the tree, but they can also be used in pies, crumbles, fruit compotes, made into chutney or jelly, and kept by stewing, bottling, and freezing. Some cultivars are self-fertile, but all plums will pollinate more effectively if there are other plum trees in the vicinity that are flowering at the same time. Plum blossom appears earlier than apple and pear blossom and is particularly susceptible to late frosts. Frost damage will ruin a crop, so protect with cloth if frost is forecast and the tree is not too large to cover.

Site and soil Plums like an open, well-drained site that is sheltered from strong, gusting winds.

Cultivation Plum trees should be planted in the same way as apple trees.

Care Water well and keep the base of trees weed free. Do not prune plum trees for the first 3 years, and then lightly prune as apples between spring and autumn. Plums are not pruned in winter because they are susceptible to silver leaf (see page 91). If there is a heavy crop, some natural thinning will take place in early summer, when small or diseased fruit drop off. Further thinning may be necessary to leave the remaining fruits around 2–4 inches apart to develop fully.

Problems Aphids, caterpillars, plum fruit moth, red spider mite, sawfly, silver leaf, bacterial canker, brown rot, frost damage, birds, and wasps.

Harvesting Plums are ripe once they are fully colored and the fruit readily leaves the spur. Picking will need to be done over a period because not all fruits ripen at the same time. Most plums will not keep long, so are best dealt with as soon as they have been picked. Eat fresh, cook or stew slightly, and remove the pits before placing in suitable containers and freezing.

Almonds (*Prunus dulcis*)

Almonds are similar to peaches (see below) in growth, form, flower, and requirements. They are harvested in mid-autumn. Pick when they begin to fall, and place them on wire mesh outside on a sunny day to dry completely. Remove the husks and store in a cool, dry place. Beware of squirrels during the harvesting period.

Damsons (*Prunus spp.*)

Treat as plums (see left).

Peaches and nectarines (*Prunus spp.*)

Peaches (*Prunus persica*) are one of the juiciest fruits; nectarines (*P. persica* var. *nectarina*) are like peaches, but the skin is smooth and the flesh is harder.

Site and soil They have similar requirements to apricots.

Cultivation Only cultivars that ripen earlier will be successful outdoors in cooler regions. Later-fruiting varieties will need warmth under glass.

Care Pruning in the first 3 years is the same as for apples and should be carried out in early spring. Peaches produce fruit on the previous year's wood. In early to mid-spring cut out some 2- and 3-year-old wood back to replacement shoots and remove dead, crossing or overcrowded branches. Protect all cuts with wound paint. Thin small fruits to 4 inches apart, and when they are the size of a walnut, thin to 8 inches apart. Mulch well with well-rotted manure in late winter.

Problems Aphids, plum fruit moth, red spider mite, bacterial canker, brown rot, powdery mildew, peach leaf curl, silver leaf and split pit.

Harvesting Harvest as apricots.

Cherries (*Prunus spp.*)

Prunus avium is the sweet species of cherry, and *P. cerasus* is the sour or acid cherry used in cooking.

Site and soil Sweet cherries favor a loamy soil; sour cherries prefer clay soil with plenty of moisture. Roots can go down to 6 feet.

Cultivation Treat as plums (see left). Cherries are usually grown as standard trees, but if they are trained against a wall, it is easier to protect the blossom from late frosts and the fruit from birds by covering with cloth or net. The Morello cherry, which is a sour cherry, can be grown as a fan on a north-facing wall.

Care Mulch well in late winter. Prune and burn any branches that have die-back and any dead wood.

Problems Aphids, caterpillars, bacterial canker, brown rot, silver leaf, and birds.

Harvesting The longer the fruit is left on the tree, the riper it will become. If picked without stems, the fruit should be used straight away. Eat fresh, in pies, or preserves.

Pears (*Pyrus communis*)

Pears are delicious when they are eaten straight from the tree, but some types need more time than others to ripen fully before the juice runs freely. Plant different cultivars so that the fruit will be ready from midsummer through to mid-autumn. The size of a pear tree will depend on the rootstock that the cultivar has been grafted on, and when you are buying, remember that a pear tree will require another pear tree to be flowering at the same time to pollinate the flowers.

Site and soil Pears like a sheltered spot; they need warmer conditions than apple trees do.

Cultivation Pears have similar planting requirements to apple trees. Topdress with plenty of well-rotted manure, but make sure that it does not touch the stem.

Care Water well and keep weeds at bay. Once established, winter prune as apples to keep plants in shape and encourage fruiting spurs. Trained forms may need extra pruning in summer. Blossom is early and may be susceptible to frost damage, so cover with cloth if necessary. Thin fruits if there is a bumper crop.

Problems Aphids and leaf blister mite.

Harvesting Judge picking time by cupping the fruit in the palm of your hand and gently twisting. Not all picked pears are ready for eating, and they may need to be left for about 3 weeks in a cool place to ripen fully. Pears will not keep as long as apples, but later cultivars can be stored in a cool, frost-free place where they should keep well into spring.

Grapes (*Vitis vinifera*)

In cooler regions grapes are best grown in greenhouses or polytunnels. They are hardy plants, but need sunshine and warmth for the fruit to ripen. Dessert grapes will ripen more quickly than wine cultivars.

Site and soil Grapes prefer a slightly alkaline soil and good drainage. Outside they need a south-facing position.

Cultivation Improve the soil with well-rotted manure and a little bonemeal before planting. Plant to the original soil mark. Train against a wall or wires. Erect posts and wire support with 2 wires, one 12 inches from the ground and the other 30 inches up. Cut back stems to 6 inches in the first year. In summer tie in the vertical leading shoot and cut back sideshoots to 5–6 leaves. Cut back to a bud about 16 inches from soil level in winter. Allow 3 buds to grow in the second year and tie these to the vertical stake. Pinch back sideshoots as previously. In winter tie shoots along the bottom wires and cut them back to 2 feet. Prune the central shoot to 3 buds. In the following season the new growth from the horizontal growths should be tied in vertically. Pinch back shoots when the necessary height is reached and also the sideshoots. Keep 3 new shoots from the central shoot to tie vertically, then tie these to the horizontal wires the following winter. In the greenhouse give support and tie in in a similar manner. Remove foliage around grapes in late summer for grapes to have more access to sunshine.

Problems Gray mold and powdery mildew.

Harvesting Cut through the stalk to remove each bunch when grapes are fully colored. Eat dessert types soon after or prepare wine.

A pear tree requires another for pollination.

Strawberries (*Fragaria spp.*)

The strawberry is a favorite summer fruit. Include different cultivars to extend cropping from early summer through to autumn.

Site and soil Strawberries will grow on all kinds of soil. On light sandy soils extra attention to watering will be needed in hot, dry weather. On heavy clay soils poor drainage could lead to disease and rotting of the roots. Preparing the soil appropriately first or planting strawberries in a raised bed will help to overcome this problem. Strawberries may lack iron and manganese on limestone soils, so adding sequestrone (chelated iron) to the water would be beneficial. Strawberries should be planted in a sheltered site away from the prevailing winds, neither facing north nor under tree shade.

Cultivation Strawberries can be grown outside, under glass, in polytunnels, raised beds, growbags, hanging baskets, or strawberry pots. If grown outside or in raised beds, prepare the soil for the crop to last 4 years. Dig it over to a depth of 10 inches, fork over the bottom of the trench, and remove any perennial weeds. After replacing the soil, incorporate well-rotted manure into the top 6 inches. Poultry manure is a strong fertilizer and should be added only in small quantities. Plant the strawberry plant in a hole large enough to take the roots comfortably and so that the crown is level with, or just above, soil level. In traditional rows, plant 12–18 inches apart in rows 30 inches apart. In a raised bed or under protection, plant rows 12 inches apart. Standard growbags will take 10 strawberry plants. Planting in other containers will depend on their diameter and depth.

Care Water well after planting and when fruits are developing, especially during hot, dry weather. Remove runners so that the plant can concentrate on fruiting. Place straw or matting under the plants to protect the fruits from mold and soil damage. After fruiting, cut back the foliage and remove all debris to encourage new growths. In early autumn propagate some runners for replacement plants and dispose of the remainder.

Problems Strawberry mosaic virus, powdery mildew, gray mold, slugs, aphids, and birds. Buy stock that is certified virus free.

Harvesting Pick the fruits when fully colored. They are best eaten straight from the plant, used in desserts or tarts. Strawberries make good jelly, but do not store successfully in other ways.

Black currants (Ribes nigrum)

A nutritious fruit, which is full of vitamin C and worth growing for its reliable cropping and versatility. Buy virus-free stock.

Site and soil Black currants will grow in most soils but appreciate plenty of well-rotted manure mixed in. Clear the site of perennial weeds.

Cultivation Bare-rooted bushes should be planted during late autumn through to late winter. Container-grown plants can be planted throughout the year. Black currants should be planted so that 3–4 inches of the stems are below soil level. The plants should be 5 feet apart with 5 feet between rows.

Care After planting cut back each branch to within 2 buds or 1 inch above soil level. Keep plants well watered. After the first growing season cut out only weak shoots and one strong shoot back to 1 inch above soil level. In following winters cut out branches of more than 45 degrees from the vertical. Mature bushes should have 3–4 of the oldest branches either cut back to strong shoots or to the base to encourage new shoots. Black currants fruit on wood that is 2 years old, so retain these branches while encouraging new growth. In early spring mulch with well-rotted manure or general fertilizer.

Problems Black currant gall mite, black currant leaf curling mite, aphids, gooseberry sawfly, red spider mite, tortix moth larvae, American gooseberry mildew, gray mold, leafspot, black currant reversion, rust, and birds.

Blackcurrants are usually a reliable crop.

Harvesting Pick when strings of fruit are fully colored. Eat fresh, in pies, crumbles, ice creams, sorbets, jams and jellies, cordials. Can be bottled or frozen.

Red currants (Ribes rubrum)

Redcurrants are tangy fruits that can be made into various preserves for use over winter.

Site and soil As gooseberries.

Cultivation As gooseberries.

Care Prune sideshoots to 5 leaves in late summer and again to 3 buds in winter because red currants produce fruit on spurs. In winter also prune the leading shoots back by a half. Keep plants weed free and mulch if necessary. Water well until established and in dry periods.

Problems As gooseberries.

Harvesting Red currants are produced in strings, and they are ready to pick as a bunch, when all the fruits are colored. They can be mixed with other fruits for dishes such as summer pudding, but they also make excellent jelly, which is a traditional accompaniment for roast lamb, as well as other preserves.

White currants (Ribes rubrum)

White currants and pink currants are treated in the same way as red currants (see page 121).

Gooseberries (Ribes uva-crispa)

One of the first fruits of the summer season and one of the most versatile, gooseberries need to be thinned in late spring—use these surplus fruits in pies or crumbles. Those left on the bushes will grow larger after thinning, and if left to fully ripen will be sufficiently sweet and juicy to eat straight away. Gooseberries have the same requirements as red and white currants, so these plants should be grown together.

Site and soil Gooseberries will grow in most soils, but appreciate plenty of well-rotted manure mixed in. Plant in an open site where the air can easily circulate around the plants.

Cultivation Gooseberries can be bought as bare-rooted bushes or container-grown plants. Bare-rooted bushes are planted from autumn through to spring at the same depth as the soil mark on the stem; container-grown bushes can be planted at any time with the rootball just below soil level. Plant gooseberries 4–5 feet apart in rows 5–6 feet apart. Cordons should be 12–15 inches apart, and fans should be placed at 5-foot intervals. If you are growing cordon and fan gooseberries, erect post and wire supports similar to those for raspberries.

Care Water well until established and in dry periods. Gooseberry branches can droop, so insert some stakes and tie the branches to these for support. Prune sideshoots back to around 6 buds in late summer and again in winter to 4 buds. In winter prune out branches in the center of the bush to allow air in. Gooseberries will continuously produce suckers. Do not cut these off but pull them off the stem or roots in early summer.

Problems Gooseberry sawfly, American gooseberry mildew, leafspot, green capsid bugs, tortix moths, aphids, caterpillars, and birds.

Harvesting Best eaten after picking as fresh, stewed, in pies and compotes, jams or jellies. Gooseberries can be bottled or frozen.

Blackberries (*Rubus fruticosus*) and hybrid berries

The commercially produced varieties of blackberry are heavy cropping and taste very similar to the wild blackberry. They are easy to grow if supported on wires like raspberries, and a selection of cultivars will provide fruit from midsummer to mid-autumn. Blackberries have also been crossed with raspberries, resulting in a wide range of hybrid berries, including

loganberries, tayberries, tummelberries, boysenberries, silvanberries, and veitchberries. The hybrid berries have similar growing requirements, but generally fruit after raspberries and before blackberries. Always buy certified virus-free stock.

Site and soil Blackberries will tolerate some shade, but hybrid berries need full sun. All will grow in most soils, but add plenty of well-rotted manure to the soil before planting.

Cultivation At either end of a row erect posts 4 x 4 inches and about 8 feet long into the ground to a depth of about 30 inches. Between these, posts 2 x 2 inches wide should be erected at 13 feet intervals. The horizontal wires secured between the posts should be 10-gauge and positioned at heights of 3, 4, 5, and 6 feet. Allow up to 16 feet between the plants. Bare-rooted cultivars can be planted from late autumn through the winter, and container-grown plants at any time. Blackberries and hybrid berries should have each stool planted so that the roots are just below soil level.

Care During the first year of growth spread out the new canes evenly across the wires, to one side of the plant in a serpentine manner. Tie in the canes. In the second year new growth can be trained in a similar way. Up to 24 canes are required per bush for a good crop. Remove excess canes in late spring.

Problems Blackberry mite, raspberry beetle larvae, raspberry leaf and bud mite, aphids, blackberry purple blotch, gray mold, cane spot, rust, spur blight, stamen blight, and birds.

Harvesting Blackberries and hybrid berries should be harvested when they have fully colored. Eat fresh or in pies, crumbles, or summer pudding. They can be made into jams or jellies and will freeze well.

Loganberries (*Rubus hybrid*)

Treat as raspberries (see right).

Raspberries (*Rubus idaeus*)

Another favorite soft fruit, raspberries thrive in colder regions. There are summer-fruiting raspberries, which produce fruit on canes grown the previous year, and the increasingly popular autumn-fruiting cultivars that produce fruit on canes grown in the current year.

Site and soil Raspberries will grow in most soils as long as it is well drained. They thrive on organic matter, so add plenty of well-rotted manure when preparing the soil for planting. Remove all perennial weeds. Insert posts 2 x 3 inches and 6½ feet long into the ground to a depth of about 20 inches. Between the posts secure 3 horizontal strands of 12-gauge wire for tying in the canes. As long as they stay clear of virus, raspberries should crop satisfactorily for 10–12 years before needing to be replaced.

Cultivation After the area has been fully prepared, plant the stools (individual raspberry canes) so that the roots are just below soil level from late autumn to late winter, but not during frost. Place 16 inches apart in rows 6 feet apart.

Care Keep the rows free of weeds. Tie in the canes as they grow and remove any flowers during the first year. In following years cut down old canes and tie in new. Cut off new shoots that grow outside the row area and limit the number of canes grown to 10 to a yard or 7 to each stool. Water well in dry weather.

Problems Raspberry mosaic virus, gray mold, powdery mildew, cane spot, raspberry die-back, root rot, rust, spur blight, stamen blight, aphids, leatherjackets, raspberry beetle, raspberry cane midge, raspberry leaf and bud mite, wireworms, and birds.

Harvesting Raspberries can be picked when fully colored. They will come away from the plant easily, leaving the center core of the fruit on the plant. Raspberries are best eaten fresh, straight from the plant, but also freeze well, so there is no need for any to go to waste if you have a glut.

Blueberries (*Vaccinium corymbosum*)

A popular fruit in many countries, especially in North America. Blueberries bear 2 crops a year, and pollination is better if 2 cultivars are grown.

Site and soil These plants require a sheltered site in full sun and an acidic soil with a pH of 4.5–5.5, which is well drained but moisture retentive. Can also be grown in 15-inch diameter pots.

Cultivation Incorporate composted bark and sawdust into the soil 12 months before planting together with some sulphate of potash and sulphate of ammonia. Plant in late autumn 4–5 feet apart with a 5–6 feet distance from other fruits.

Care Trim off tips of branches and any flower buds after planting. In future years cut out new branches where fruit could touch the soil and take back any thin, bushy wood to strong side branches or ground level. Water little and often with rainwater, but do not allow to dry out. Mulch with plenty of bark mulch, rotted sawdust, or leaf mold.

Problems Drought; use tapwater if no rainwater is available during dry spells. Birds.

Harvesting Pick when fruits are dark mauve with a gray bloom and detach easily from their stalks. Eat raw or cooked.

Cranberries (*Vaccinum macrocarpon*)

A dark red, very tart fruit that is related to the blueberry.

Site and soil A raised or sunken bed with acidic, moisture-retentive but free-draining soil.

Cultivation Soil as for blueberries. For a raised bed place 6 inches of acidic soil on top of the prepared area. A sunken bed should be excavated to 6–8 inches, and if drainage is not good it should be slightly deeper. Sink a plastic drainpipe into the base to protrude from the bed and release surplus water. Cover

Raspberries can be picked when fully colored.

the base with 1-inch stones to a depth of 3 inches and then polythene or plastic bags with lots of holes to prevent soil clogging the drainage process. Fill with acidic compost. Plant cranberries in the spring, then cover the bed with 1 inch of coarse sand.

Care Water with rainwater through a very fine hose on a watering can until the bed is saturated. A sprinkler is best, but the water must not be alkaline. Feed with a lime- or calcium-free fertilizer in mid- and late spring. The vines creep horizontally over the surface, and upright shoots produce the flowers. Prune overcrowded shoots and vines and trim the edges of the bed in early spring, then water to saturate the bed.

Problems The bed must be well watered.

Harvesting Hand-pick the fruit from early autumn when it is fully colored. Cranberries are eaten with turkey and game as jelly. They can be dried and freeze well.

Herb directory

No kitchen garden should be without at least one or two herbs, and even if you have just a small patio or a windowbox, you can accommodate some. They will enhance a wide range of dishes, and you can also use them for medicinal and cosmetic purposes.

Pests and diseases

Herbs don't usually suffer from pests or diseases as much as vegetables and fruit, but slugs and greenfly may cause problems during spells of wet or dry weather, and frost and wind can also damage the plants. Mints are susceptible to mint rust, a disease that lives on the soil over winter, and if a plant is affected, its shoots will appear distorted with orange pustules when they emerge in the spring. Powdery mildew will also attack mint and tarragon, especially during damp weather. Buy healthy plants or fresh seed, and once the herbs are growing well, give them a liquid feed every two weeks throughout the summer.

Chives (Allium schoenoprasum)

The narrow, hollow leaves of onion-flavored chives are used in summer salads. It is a perennial with small bulbs and attractive tiny, pink flowers. Plants grow to a height of 12–16 inches.

Site and soil Any moist but well-drained soil in a sunny position.

Cultivation Sow seeds in early spring. Once established, divide clumps every 4 years in spring or autumn.

Care Water well during hot periods; do not allow to dry out.

Harvesting Cut chives with scissors when needed. They can be chopped and used fresh in salads, sprinkled on soups, added to omelets or pickled in white wine vinegar.

Dill (Anethum graveolens)

An attractive herb with feathery foliage and yellow flowers that grows up to 2 feet high. An annual, it often seeds itself.

Site and soil A sunny position in well-drained soil.

Cultivation Sow seed in a fine tilth in drills 12 inches apart in mid-spring and thin to 12 inches apart. Sow every month until early summer for continuous cropping.

Care Water when required and hoe weeds.

Harvesting Pick and use the leaves fresh. When the flowerheads are brown, cut the plant down and complete the seed-drying process indoors. Dill leaves make a good sauce for fish. Add seeds to stews, soups, or pickles. Dill seed tea helps to promote sleep.

Onion-flavored chives have pink flowers.

Chervil (*Anthriscus cerefolium*)

A biennial herb with parsley-like leaves, umbels of tiny white flowers, and a spicy, aniseed flavor. Plants grow to 1–2 feet high.

Site and soil A cool, slightly shaded part of the garden in moist but well-drained soil.

Cultivation Sow seeds in succession from early spring to autumn in drills 8 inches apart and thin plants to 6 inches apart. Chervil can be grown in windowboxes if trimmed.

Care Plants grown later in the year will need protection under a cloche in winter.

Harvesting Cut chervil leaves when 4 inches high and use chopped in soup, egg and cheese dishes and as a garnish.

Horseradish (*Armoracia rusticana*)

Horseradish is a hardy perennial with leaves similar to those of docks (*Rumex* spp.) and growing 2–3 feet in height.

Site and soil An open sunny site with rich soil and plenty of room for the long taproots.

Cultivation Plant root cuttings in early spring 12 inches apart. Horseradish is invasive, so contain it in a raised bed or large pot sunk into the ground.

Care Keep the plant from spreading.

Harvesting Lift roots as they are needed. It is used raw grated into cream as a condiment with beef or smoked mackerel. Horseradish is a good embrocation for chilblains and stiff muscles.

Tarragon (*Artemisia* spp.)

There are two types of tarragon, French tarragon (*Artemisia dracunculus*) and Russian tarragon (*A. dracunculus* subsp. *dracunculoides*). French tarragon is a fragrant, half-hardy plant that can grow to 3 feet high. Russian tarragon is more vigorous than French tarragon, but has an inferior flavor.

Site and soil A sunny site in any good, well-drained soil.

Cultivation Tarragon does not set seed in temperate climates, so buy young plants or take cuttings from existing plants in spring. Grow plants 12 inches apart. Divide established plants every 3–4 years in spring.

Care Weed and water throughout the growing season. Cut down in autumn and cover with leaf mold or straw to protect plants from frost in the winter. Tarragon will grow in containers and can be brought indoors to extend the season.

Harvesting Pick fresh leaves for salads. Leaves can also be added to French dressing, meat, poultry, and fish dishes, and added to white wine vinegar to make tarragon vinegar. They lose their flavor when dried.

Borage (*Borago officinalis*)

Borage is a hairy-leaved annual, 1–3 feet tall, with blue flowers, which are borne for many months of the year.

Site and soil Plant in an open, sunny site because borage does not like shade; it will grow in moist soils as long as they are well drained.

Cultivation Best grown from seed sown 2 inches deep where they are to flower. Thin seedlings to 2 feet apart. The plant will die down in winter, but any seeds in the soil will grow in the spring. Borage is not suitable for container growing.

Care Trim plants regularly so that they do not get leggy.

Harvesting Pick leaves and flowers, both of which taste of cucumber, as required. Chop the leaves and add to pickles and bean soups. Add leaves and flowers to green salads or put into fruit cups and leave for an hour before straining. The flowers can be crystallized or frozen in ice cubes.

Caraway (*Carum carvi*)

Caraway is a feathery-leaved biennial mainly grown for its seeds and roots. It grows up to 2 feet high and has small white flowers that produce fruit in the second year.

Site and soil A sunny site with well-drained soil.

Cultivation Sow seeds in spring, early summer, or autumn in rows and thin plants to 8 inches apart. The plants will not reach their full height until the second year. Caraway can be grown in a container in a sunny position.

Care Protect younger plants in winter by covering with a mulch.

Harvesting Remove seedheads after they have turned brown and continue to dry indoors. Use seeds to flavor pork, liver, vegetable stews, baking, and confectionery. The roots can be dug up after harvesting the seeds and boiled as a root vegetable. The leaves can be added to soups and salads.

Camomile (*Chamaemelum nobile*)

A low-growing, sweetly scented evergreen perennial, which, in the form *Chamaemelum nobile* 'Treneague,' is sometimes used as an ornamental lawn instead of grass. It is also a healing and cosmetic plant.

Site and soil Camomile prefers a sunny position in well-drained soil.

Cultivation Sow seeds in early spring directly where they are to flower. The seeds are tiny, so mix with sand before sowing. Thin the plants to 6 inches apart. If the flowers are left on the plant it will self-seed around the garden. Camomile grows well in containers.

Care Water seedlings well until leaves appear. Divide established plants in spring.

Harvesting Pick the flowers when the petals have turned back and dry them whole in a cool place. Camomile tea helps relieve indigestion; add honey for a tasty tonic. An infusion of camomile can be used as a herbal rinse for fair hair, a face wash, eyebath, and mouthwash. The dried flowers and leaves can be used in pot-pourri.

Coriander (Coriandrum sativum)

This annual herb has fine foliage (known as cilantro) and small white or mauve flowers. The plants have a pungent smell and are not suitable for growing indoors.

Site and soil In a sunny position in rich, well-drained soil.

Cultivation Sow seeds in early spring and thin to 4–6 inches apart. Coriander needs a long growing season for the seeds to ripen.

Care Keep weed free.

Harvesting Pick young leaves to use fresh as required or to freeze. Cut down plants when the seedheads have turned a pale brown and leave in an airy place to dry further. Shake out the seeds and store in an airtight container. The spicy, aromatic seeds are used in curries and other spice mixtures and, when ground, to flavor cakes, cookies and chutneys.

Fennel (Foeniculum vulgare)

A perennial herb with an aniseed flavor, which should not be confused with the vegetable Sweet fennel (see page 103). It grows to 5 feet tall and has graceful, feathery foliage and mustard yellow flowers.

Site and soil A sunny position in any moist, well-drained soil.

Cultivation Sow seeds in rows in early spring or autumn and thin the plants to 12 inches apart. Fennel will self-seed.

Care Divide established plants every 3–4 years. Trim to provide young leaves, but leave some stems to produce flowers.

Harvesting Pick and chop leaves for use in fish sauces or to sprinkle as a garnish. Harvest some stems and hang them in a cool, airy place for the seeds to dry. The seeds can be used, whole or ground, in bread, crackers, soups, and pickles. An infusion of fennel seeds soothes tired eyes, is a diuretic and laxative, and helps alleviate cramp.

Hyssop (Hyssopus officinalis)

A hardy evergreen or semi-evergreen perennial with spikes of purple-blue flowers. It grows to 2 feet and can be grown in a pot. The strongly aromatic leaves are an ingredient in the liqueur Chartreuse.

Site and soil A sunny position in light, well-drained alkaline soil.

Cultivation Sow seed in moist soil in spring and thin plants to 2 feet apart. Alternatively, take stem cuttings in spring or divide roots in autumn. Can be successfully grown in a container.

Care Hyssop can be used to make a good hedge around the herb garden if it is kept well trimmed.

Harvesting Pick young leaves as required and add to meat pies, lamb stew, fruit tarts and pies. An infusion of hyssop helps to clear catarrh and a chesty cough.

Bay (Laurus nobilis)

Also called sweet bay or bay laurel, this is an evergreen perennial in tree form, which is often seen in containers, when it is usually clipped to maintain a particular shape. In the garden trees can get to 30 feet or more tall. Note: the leaves of the sweet bay may be eaten, but ordinary laurel leaves are poisonous.

Site and soil Bay trees will grow in any soil in a sunny or semishaded position.

Cultivation Buy a tree or take cuttings from half-ripened shoots in summer.

Care Keep well-watered. Containerized plants should be overwintered indoors.

Harvesting Pick leaves as required. Bay is used in bouquet garni, a collection of herbs used to flavor savory cooking, and also used to flavor a court-bouillon in which to poach fish.

Lovage (Levisticum officinale)

A vigorous perennial, lovage grows to 6 feet tall. It has large, deeply divided leaves and yellow flowers, whch are followed by brown, oblong seeds. The plant has a celery-like taste.

Site and soil A sunny position in moist soil. Prepare the soil with plenty of well-rotted manure to retain moisture.

Cultivation Sow seeds in summer for the following year. Alternatively, divide roots in spring as leaves emerge and plant 2 feet apart, making sure sure that each root has a shoot.

Care Mulch with well-rotted manure over winter when the topgrowth has died down. Water as necessary.

Harvesting Pick leaves in summer and autumn as required for use in stocks, soups, and stews. Young stems can be candied and used for decoration.

Do not confuse the herb with Sweet fennel

Mint (*Mentha* spp.)

A perennial herb, the foliage dies down each winter. There are several species and many cultivars, the most common being apple mint (*M. suaveolens*), spearmint (*M. spicata*), and peppermint (*M. x piperita*). Mints grow to between 18 inches and 2 feet tall.

Site and soil In partial shade and any soil.

Cultivation Plant young plants in spring 8–12 inches apart. Mint will grow easily from root cuttings. The roots can be invasive, so grow in large, sunken pots in the ground or place concrete slabs around a hole. The container should be 2 inches above soil level when planted.

Care Pick leaves and trim stems regularly. Dig up some roots in the autumn and pot up indoors for winter use.

Harvesting Pick when required and use fresh in mint sauce or preserved as jelly. Mint sauce is a traditional accompaniment for lamb. Leaves can also be used in fruit salads and wine cups and to decorate cakes and desserts.

Basil (*Ocimum basilicum*)

The main cultivars are sweet, bush, and opal, and they are generally grown as annuals, even though basil is a perennial plant. Sweet basil has shiny leaves, white flowers, and grows 1–2 feet high. Bush basil is compact and only 6 inches tall. Opal basil is a hybrid with purple-bronze leaves and pink flowers. Because basil grows so easily from seed, it is not worth buying the small container-grown plants often seen in supermarkets.

Site and soil A sunny position in fertile, well-drained soil.

Cultivation Sow seed outside when fear of frost has gone or indoors in pots; harden off before planting out 8 inches apart. Bush basil is ideal for growing in containers. In cooler areas grow under cover or outside under cloches.

Care Keep plants moist, but do not overwater. Pinch out the growing tips to encourage bushy growth.

Harvesting Pick the leaves as required or hang to dry. Leaves can be frozen in ice cubes. Use in tomato, egg, and pasta dishes. Fresh leaves are also used in salads and vinegar dressings.

Marjoram (*Origanum* spp.)

Several types of marjoram are cultivated: wild marjoram (*Origanum vulgare*), pot marjoram (*O. onites*), and sweet marjoram (*O. majorana*). Sweet marjoram has the best flavor and is grown as a half-hardy annual in all but hot climates. It is a compact plant, growing to 8 inches high, with small leaves and flowers that look like little knots. Wild marjoram is sometimes called oregano and is a perennial that grows to 75 cm (30 inches) high and has the strongest, spiciest taste of the three. All marjorams are widely used in cooking.

Site and soil All marjorams like a sunny position in well-drained but moist soil. Add plenty of well-rotted manure when preparing the planting area.

Cultivation Sow seed of sweet marjoram mixed with sand in heat indoors in spring and plant out after fear of frost, spacing plants 8 inches apart. Sow seed of pot marjoram in early spring or take cuttings from established plants in spring or autumn; it will do best in a sheltered position. Wild marjoram is easily grown from seed sown in spring or by root cuttings taken in spring or autumn. Sweet and pot marjorams are ideal container plants.

Care Pinch out the growing tips to keep the plants compact and water when necessary. Lift and pot up some plants to put indoors for winter use. Divide perennials every 3 years.

Harvesting Pick fresh leaves as required. Sweet marjoram dries well, and all types will freeze. All are used in meat and vegetable dishes; use wild marjoram sparingly because it is so strong.

Basil is easy to grow from seed.

Parsley (*Petroselinum crispum*)

A versatile hardy biennial, parsley is usually treated as an annual. It has either plain or crinkled leaves and can vary in height from about 8 inches to 2 feet high.

Site and soil A sunny position in rich, well-prepared soil.

Cultivation Sow seeds indoors from early winter and outside in drills from spring through to autumn. Soak seeds overnight before sowing to improve germination. Thin the seedlings to 8 inches apart. Grow in pots indoors over winter for all-year use.

Care Remove weeds and water well. Parsley will quickly run to seed if the roots get dry.

Harvesting Cut a few leaves from different plants as required. Chop and use in salads, soups, and sauces. A popular garnish. Hot parsley tea is believed to be diuretic. Store chopped-up leaves frozen in ice cubes.

Rosemary (*Rosmarinus officinalis*)

An evergreen shrub, it can grow to 6 feet. The leaves are short and narrow, and the tiny flowers are pale blue, although pink- and white-flowered variants are available.

Site and soil Choose a sheltered, warm, sunny position in well-drained, yet moisture-retentive soil.

Cultivation Buy container-grown plants because rosemary is slow growing from seed. Set out 2 feet apart. Cuttings taken in summer root easily.

Harvesting Pick leaves all year. Use with lamb, but also fish, eggs, cookies, jams, jellies and fruit cups.

Sage (*Salvia officinalis*)

An evergreen shrub with blue–purple flowers and leaves from gray to purple. Sage grows to 2–4 feet tall.

Site and soil A sunny position in any well-drained soil. Add grit to clay soil to improve the drainage.

Cultivation Sow seeds indoors in spring and transplant in late spring or buy young plants and space them 2 feet apart. Easily grown from summer cuttings 3 inches long. Good in containers.

Care Pinch out the growing tips or cut back in mid- to late summer to keep the plant well shaped and compact.

Harvesting Pick fresh leaves as required. Hang shoots in a cool place to dry. Sage is often combined with onions in a stuffing for roast pork, duck, and chicken. Add chopped leaves to salads, tomato dishes, fruit drinks, and cider cups. An infusion of sage makes a good hair conditioner.

Savory (*Satureja hortensis*)

A herb with long, narrow leaves and dainty blue and white flowers, which are attractive to bees. Plants grow to a height of 9–12 inches. There is also a perennial form, *S. montana*.

Site and soil A sunny position in a rich, well-drained soil.

Cultivation Sow seeds in drills in late spring and thin to 6 inches apart. It is an excellent herb for containers or windowboxes.

Care Keep weed free and water the plants when necessary.

Harvesting Pick leaves when required. Use chopped in meat, fish, and egg dishes and sprinkled on meat and vegetable soups. Put fresh sprigs in wine vinegar to infuse.

Rosemary leaves can be picked all year round.

Thyme (*Thymus vulgaris*)

A sweetly scented, shrubby plant, growing to 8–12 inches high. The clusters of tiny flowers attract pollinating insects, and lemon thyme (*T. citriodorus*) and its cultivars are especially good for bees.

Site and soil A sunny position in any good, well-drained soil.

Cultivation Although you can grow thyme from seed, it is easier to buy young plants or take cuttings from established plants in summer (from lemon thyme in spring). Space pot-grown plants 12–18 inches apart. Can be grown in containers.

Care Pinch out the tips to keep plants compact and cut back hard after flowering.

Harvesting Pick leaves as required, but the most intense flavor is from dried leaves. Cut shoots before flowering and hang up in a cool place to dry. Use in soups, sauces, stocks, and meat dishes. Add lemon thyme in cheesecloth bags to bathwater. Used in pot-pourris.

Sage is a good container-grown herb.

Growing cereals

Growing our own vegetables and fruit is something that most of us can aspire to, but you could also take self-sufficiency a stage further and grow your own cereals, provided that you have a large enough plot of land to do so.

Growing cereals for your own household consumption will not involve mass production —it is more likely to resemble how farm workers would have gathered in the harvest in years gone by. It is, however, undeniably hard work. The smaller the area planted, the less overall work there will be, but even a modest few square yards should provide sufficient wheat for a few loaves of bread.

Preparing the ground

If you have the growing space, a working horse or a small tractor, disk harrows, seed drill, and binder, most of the hard work can be done by machinery. However, even without those items you can prepare an area of land in early fall, work it until the topsoil is a tilth and then sow some winter wheat.

If pigs have been reared on the land beforehand they will have done a lot of the hard work for you. About 55 pounds of seed will be required to plant up an area roughly 165 x 65 feet. If you have double this area, it could provide you with around half a ton of wheat after harvesting. The yield you get will depend on the type of soil: wheat will do well on heavy loam or

BELOW Wheat can be sown in either autumn or winter depending on the crop and climate. Spring wheat is the main crop in countries with severe winters.

clay, but on light, sandy soil you will get good-quality grain but less of it.

Sowing

Weather permitting, winter wheat gets off to a good start in the still-warm soil of early fall and then lies dormant over the winter, growing quickly once spring has come and producing an early crop. In some areas spring wheat is sown in spring and harvested later than winter wheat, and in countries with severe winters spring wheat is the main crop.

The variety of wheat you need will also depend on when it is grown and the yield you are after. The modern strains have full ears, but require chemical treatments to enable them to produce heavy yields. To grow wheat for your own use it is worth going back to an old variety, such as 'Maris Widgeon', which produces an ideal bread-making flour.

The easiest way to sow a small area of land is to broadcast the seed, which is the traditional way. The seed is in a bag hanging from a strap going over the shoulder, and a handful of seed is scattered on the ground. The sowing continues in this way until the area is complete. A seed drill actually drops the seed down pipes in the soil, but broadcasting leaves it on the surface, so it is vulnerable to theft by birds.

With winter wheat, green shoots will appear quite quickly, but will remain in that state throughout the winter. By the time it continues to grow again in the spring, weeds and grass will be growing among it as well. It will be an impossible job to clear all the weeds, but if wild oats appear, which look like very tall grasses, you can pull them out by hand, but do wear some thick gloves.

Harvesting

When the crop has matured, a scythe is probably the best way to cut the golden-colored wheat, but it will be slow work. When all the wheat is cut, it needs to be gathered in bundles and tied with thick twine. These bundles, called sheaves, are then placed upright in stooks of five or six, with their heads resting against each other. Harvesting in this ancient way is best done with some help. Gather all the stooks and cart them to an outbuilding where the ears of wheat can dry out further and fully ripen.

LEFT Domestic electric grinders can turn 22 pounds of wheat into whole wheat flour in a matter of minutes, but manual grinders can be very efficient for smaller amounts of grain.

Threshing and winnowing

As soon as the wheat starts to drop from the ears, it is ready for threshing. Place a large tarpaulin at the bottom of a wall or other suitable place and bash a sheaf against the wall so that the grain falls onto the tarpaulin, then you can gather it up into burlap sacks.

The next stage is winnowing the grain—that is, separating the wheat from the chaff. Choose a windy but dry day. Take a scoop of grain from a bag and hold it above a bucket, gradually letting it fall down into the bucket. The wheat will collect in the bucket, but the chaff will have blown away. This takes time to do and is another task where additional help will be appreciated.

Grinding

The final stage is grinding the wheat. Rather than the original way of grinding between two large stones, today you can buy a small electric grinder, which you can use year after year. An electric grinder can turn 22 pounds of wheat into 22 pounds of whole wheat flour in a matter of minutes.

The smell of bread being baked made from flour you have grown and milled will be immensely satisfying (see pages 226–31), even though it may not be very cost effective as far as labor goes.

You can grow and harvest oats in a similar manner and you can then add oatmeal and oat cakes to your self-sufficient menu.

Raising your own

Livestock to the land

For many people the opportunity to keep poultry and sheep or dairying with goats or cattle is the most important element of being self-supporting. But what type of livestock, which breeds, and how much time and knowledge will it take?

Keeping livestock of any kind is a great responsibility, financial, practical, and, to some extent, emotional. The amount of knowledge that you have, multiplied by the amount of time that you can spend, together with the facilities, including land and buildings, that are available will help you come up with the factor of what is likely to work for you and your animals.

Knowledge

Knowledge is the most important aspect of livestock keeping, and it can, to an extent, outweigh the financial factors. An experienced stockperson will be able to prevent things like the occurrence of expensive problems, such as an outbreak of disease, an infestation of worms, or birthing problems, by using their husbandry skills to ensure high standards of welfare for the stock. Time spent at this stage researching the management of your proposed livestock will save you money and heartache, and keep your future stock content and healthy.

This chapter is designed to get you to question what you want to keep, the facilities that you will need, and to be a primer for the steep learning curve that will follow. You will also need to get some practical experience through courses, from established small-scale farmers, or at open farms, and you should take every opportunity you can to visit livestock shows and sales where you will be able to talk to people who are expert in keeping a particular type of stock.

Knowledge translates into good stock-keeping skills, and no matter how suitable your animals are, the quality of your grass, and the excellence of your housing, welfare is also dependent on good stockmanship This can only be achieved with knowledge and continuous learning.

Money

Although the ultimate aim will be for your livestock to repay you with their produce—eggs, milk, meat, honey, and fiber, for example—there will be start-up costs. The earliest part of your stock keeping, when you choose breeds, adapt buildings, erect fencing, and get the land in good order, is such an important time. If you make the right choices now, the future will be so much easier and more rewarding. If you do not, you will probably spend time in future playing catch-up, and any inadequacies in your system soon show up in the form of injuries, disease, or lack of produce. This is where you need to know how to choose the best stock for your purposes and provide fully for their needs, to allow them to do the job they have to do in producing food for you and your family.

Be accurate in planning start-up costs and make allowances for extra veterinary visits when you begin—you will learn from these visits, and as time passes there will be more situations that you can handle without calling the vet.

Time

How much time you can give to your livestock will determine what type and how many you keep. Top of the list for time-consuming stock must be dairy animals—goats, cows, or sheep—which must be milked every single day, usually twice a day, while their offspring (removed from the mother to allow you to access her milk) will have to be raised separately, often from a young age, when they will require several feeds a day.

Then there are the animals that need training, such as a working pony or horse. A young and inexperienced animal will require regular and, ideally, daily sessions to educate them, as well as exposure to the outside world, such as trips to shows or walking out, to learn to cope with traffic. There are no short cuts. It all takes time.

All livestock requires daily care. You have to check them in the field or provide twice-daily care, such as letting them into the field, cleaning out the pen, and putting them back in the house at night. Some livestock care is seasonal, too. Breeding time—lambing or kidding, for example—needs 24-hour observation to be really successful, and it's important to plan the mating so that the birthing occurs in a period when you can be fully available. Shearing for fiber animals is an intense day or so and needs to be planned, and routine tasks, such as vaccinating, hoof trimming, or worming, can be scheduled around time off if you have a job.

The production side of keeping livestock also needs careful planning—plucking and dressing turkeys for Thanksgiving or Christmas will take time and people to do it, and harvesting honey and spinning it off the combs has to be done at the appropriate time.

Land

Your choice of livestock will also be affected by the amount of land you have and where it is situated. Steeply sloping land simply will not accommodate some types of stock. Grazing animals require acreage of grass, and if your land is in an area with harsh winters, you will have to house your livestock during the worst of the weather. Some areas lend themselves to particular breeds—after all, many native breeds became established through being the breed that adapted best to regional circumstances. It may be difficult to keep poultry in some areas because there are too many predators, and you simply cannot give the birds the security they need.

Your needs

Finally, think hard about what you want to achieve. Full self-sufficiency will require dairy and meat animals plus eggs, but you might not want to raise meat although you will want to take the vegetables, bees, and egg route. For many of the people making the first moves to self-sufficiency, the choices will depend on all the factors above, although they are likely to include poultry and supplement their home-produced food through wild foraging.

There is no specific "right" combination, but the overriding fact must be that you need to manage the stock for their best welfare and produce food that you are able to process and eat. Don't forget, though, that you should also enjoy the work involved.

ABOVE With some knowledge it's possible to fit bee care into evenings and weekends.

Keeping chickens

Poultry are probably the most adaptable and easiest of livestock to keep, and they make a huge contribution to our diet in the form of eggs and meat. Poultry are not only productive if kept correctly but also pleasurable to own.

What type of chickens?

There are numerous breeds, most developed for specific reasons—to produce more eggs or a certain type of egg, for hardiness, or for the table. In the mid-20th century there was an interest in utility poultry—birds that would produce both a respectable number of eggs, while the cockerels would provide a decent-size table bird. Many breeders concentrated on developing strains to meet these requirements, and the Rhode Island Red and White Wyandottes, both breeds originating from the USA, met this demand.

These days the requirements have changed, and an egg-laying hen is expected to produce many more eggs, while the modern table bird is bred to weigh in at far more than the traditional Rhodie. Pure-bred birds have been superseded by high-performing hybrids, which are bred to reach table weight in a few weeks, and by egg layers bred to lay large quantities of eggs for an economic input of feed. The male chicks in the laying birds are killed at a day old (for the exotic pet market), and the table bird hens don't reach egg-laying age before they are killed.

With this came a change in management. Small poultry farms with their arks, semi-intensive laying houses, and ability to produce a reasonable income for a family from a few acres were replaced by intensive units on small acreages but with huge numbers of hybrid birds.

Why do we need to know this? Because the old pure breeds with the magic names associated with war-time survival are not always the ideal choice for self-supporters. The utility strains have been largely replaced by exhibition strains, which are beautiful but without a proven egg or table record. Some 60 years ago laying trials would tell you all you needed to know about a breeder's birds' performance and you would be able to see if one breeder had a strain that would out-lay another. Now it's almost impossible to tell with pure breeds unless the breeder is keeping records—and most don't.

Hybrids have moved out of intensive farming and into the self-sufficiency market, and there are many guaranteed "egg a day" varieties to choose from, bred to lay, to be kind and docile (as befits a semi-industrial management system), and to

RIGHT An attractive group of Barnvelder hens—a brown egg-laying pure breed that originated in Holland.

make good use of their feed ration, converting quality food to eggs. It's the same for table birds. Most hybrids do not go broody.

As increasing numbers of people want to keep poultry in their backyard, hybrids have been developed specifically for the purpose, from blue egg layers to free-range table birds.

If egg production is your goal and you are relying on a given number per week, you will need to look closely at hybrids. If you want pure breeds, find a breeder who can provide an accurate guide to their egg-laying performance, and then you will need to learn to become an egg recorder yourself and develop the strain just as breeders used to do.

Identifying a suitable breed

There are hundreds of poultry breeds, and all have merits. Get the list of poultry standards for your national poultry club and visit the big shows, where most will be on display. Owners of these exhibition birds are usually more than happy to talk with interested people, and seeing the birds in the feather is a really good way of deciding what to keep. They come in different sizes, different styles and colors of feathers, and have distinctive temperaments, with some breeds being known as flighty—that is, they are lively and don't settle easily—while others are placid.

A **large fowl** is the original size of a hen and ranges from around 4 pounds for a Hamburgh to 13 pounds for a Jersey Giant.

A **miniature** is a scaled-down replica of its large fowl counterpart—the Hamburgh has a bantam that weighs in at around 1½ pounds for a hen, while the Rhode Island has a miniature. In reality they are usually referred to as bantams.

A **bantam** is a breed of poultry that has no large fowl equivalent, such as the Dutch Bantam, which are known as true bantams.

Chickens are also divided into hard and soft feather. **Hard feather** are game-type birds, once used for fighting, with tight feathering and sometimes areas of skin showing through. All others are **soft feathered**.

They are also often referred to as light and heavy breeds. The **light breeds** tend to be the good layers originating from around the Mediterranean, including the Leghorn. The **heavy breeds** are generally table birds, such as the slow-maturing Brahma, although these are

generalizations, and cross-breeding was used to produce the utility breeds of their day.

The characteristics of pure breeds were selected and used to produce hybrids. These continue to be developed. The increased demands for organic and free-range poultry has promoted the development of different characteristics, and hybrids are selected for newly desirable characteristics, such as hardiness, which is another reason why we need to maintain good numbers of the pure breeds. Who knows what will be needed in the next century?

Choosing a breed

Some of the top poultry breeds for self-supporters are described below, but many other breeds are both beautiful and useful.

Araucana

Originating in Chile, these are large fowl, a light breed and soft feathered. They have a distinctive appearance with their head crests and face and ear muffs. But their prized characteristic is that they lay blue or green eggs, where the color permeates through the strong shell. The number of eggs laid varies from strain to strain, but is usually between 80 and 150 a year, although old records show much higher numbers. A light breed classification, they are not ideal table birds.

Bantams

Bantams are useful for smaller areas, and as can be seen in the large fowl breeds, many dual-purpose breeds have a bantam counterpart. There tend to more ornamental breeds among the bantams, including the range of colors and types that make up the **Belgian Bantams**, the charm and prettiness of the **Japanese Bantams**, the color markings of the **Sebright,** and the distinctive combs of the **Rosecomb**. The **Cochin Bantam**, as well as producing a respectable number of eggs, is a docile bird, which is ideal for families, but even more importantly it is such a good mother that it can be used to incubate eggs from the less-reliable breeds.

The hard-feathered **Old English Game Bantam** comes in such a wide range of colors that there is a saying that there is "no such thing as an OEG of a bad color." It is really a miniature of the bigger bird, but most people tend to think of it as a bantam in its own right. It is a useful bird for small gardens, although extremely active, is "chatty," sociable, and endearing, and lays a good number of eggs—up to 120 or so in a season. It also rears chicks effectively. Although it is called a game bird, it has an excellent temperament.

Barnvelder

Developed in Holland in the 1920s, this bird lays large, brown eggs. A good example will lay around 170 eggs a year, but the darker the egg, the lower the number laid. A large fowl with bantam counterpart, they are heavy birds and soft feathered, and also dual purpose. It is a good-natured bird, bred from domestic backyard flocks, but it can be bullied by other breeds.

Leghorn

Like many Mediterranean breeds, this bird was known as a prolific layer when it evolved into the Utility Leghorn. It fell out of favor because it produces pure white eggs, but now there is more of a demand for these eggs. It is a flighty bird and not for beginners. They are not good broodies. Today's exhibition strains have huge, floppy combs, which are not ideal in the backyard where they can get injured or frost bitten. This breed has had a huge influence on high-laying hybrid strains, and the lightness of the breed makes them economical in feeding.

BELOW A famous breed developed in America to be a utility (meat and egg) bird. Check the egg-laying record of the modern birds with the breeder.

Marans

A French table bird originating in the 1920s, this lays a varying number of dark brown eggs, some with speckles. It is hardy and likes to be free range, but sometimes the males can be aggressive. It's not keen on being handled, but the color of the eggs makes this breed worth keeping, even though some strains are poor layers.

The Welsummer from Holland, developed from breeds including the Cochin, Wyandotte, and Leghorn, also lays deep brown eggs.

New Hampshire

This useful, dual-purpose bird was developed from the Rhode Island Red, and laying trials in the USA showed that it could produce 332 eggs a year. This has now dropped to around 150 eggs a year, but it is still a good backyard bird, docile and friendly, the archetypal "little, red hen," with the bantams being especially popular for backyarders. They are good broodies and good mothers, and more and more people are breeding these to try to improve the egg-laying score.

Orpington

This breed, especially the Buff Orpington, is beloved of people beginning in poultry, but although the birds are docile, they are large and need plenty of space, including plenty of headroom and good-size entrances to their houses. The profusion of soft feathers needs attention so that the birds do not attract external parasites and maggots. Some strains are particularly poor layers, with small eggs in proportion to their size, but a good strain can lay 150 eggs in a season.

Rhode Island Red

Developed in the USA in the mid-19th century, this bird became the watchword for a meat and egg-laying bird. They are docile, but the large fowl need to be able to range. A good laying strain can produce up to 200 eggs a year, and the cockerels will make a medium-size table bird.

Silkie

This unique breed of chicken was first described by Marco Polo during his travels in the Far East as a "furry" chicken. It looks like a ball of fluff, has dark skin underneath and blue earlobes. It is an ideal broody which makes it invaluable as a

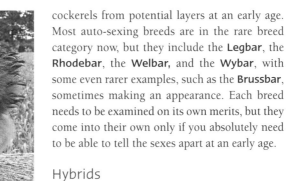

natural incubator for other breeds. It is gentle and does not fly. Because of its compulsion to go broody, it only lays up to about 100 eggs a year. Its unique feathering is also susceptible to wet conditions and easily attracts parasites, and the birds seem to be susceptible to scaly leg and need regular inspection and treatment.

Sussex

As the name suggests, the breed was developed in Britain and was present at the first poultry show in 1845. It reached its prime with the Light Sussex around the mid-1900s, when it was an ideal utility breed, producing meat and eggs. A docile, hardy breed and also a good broody, but the eggs vary according to the strain. A good layer will manage around 180 eggs a year.

Wyandotte

A bird with a huge range of color combinations, this was developed in the USA and named after a tribe of Native North Americans. As a dual-purpose breed, the body should be deep, and a good layer could produce 200 eggs in the first year. The silver-laced variety is usually the best layer. They are robust, hardy, and good broodies, but they need space.

Other breeds

Breeders in the 21st century have continued to develop breeds of bird that are commercially useful.

Auto-sexing breeds

This is where the sex of the chicks at hatching can be identified by their down coloring, and it was useful when people needed to separate cockerels from potential layers at an early age. Most auto-sexing breeds are in the rare breed category now, but they include the **Legbar**, the **Rhodebar**, the **Welbar,** and the **Wybar**, with some even rarer examples, such as the **Brussbar**, sometimes making an appearance. Each breed needs to be examined on its own merits, but they come into their own only if you absolutely need to be able to tell the sexes apart at an early age.

Hybrids

There are numerous hybrids to choose from, and it would be sensible to choose hybrids for guaranteed egg laying, while at the same time keeping a small flock of pure breeds (and recording their performance). If you can only have a few chickens and rely on the eggs, choose hybrids. If you are producing solely for the table, such as for Christmas, choose hybrids.

They are still delightful birds, and they will fulfill their purpose to the letter. The **Black Rock** originates from the Harco/Arbor Acres breeders of America. They are a true first-cross hybrid from specially selected strains of Rhode Island Red (male line) and a Barred Plymouth Rock (female line). It is arguably the most successful hybrid for modern, free-range conditions with its dense feathering, highly developed immune system, and good body weight. Many other types of hybrid followed this successful bird, including variations on Marans, which lay brown eggs, and colored-egg layers, including some attractively colored hybrids, such as the blue-gray **Bluebell**.

Becoming a poultry keeper

The best way to buy pure breeds is direct from the breeder, who is usually an expert in the breed and can tell you their laying performance. Hybrids tend to come direct from specialty chick rearers. Poultry sales vary, ranging from sales of "carded" (prejudged for breed type) birds from breeders to auctions, where anything and everything is sold at various ages and states of health. If you buy from an open sale, remember to keep the new birds away from any existing birds to allow for a period of quarantine.

Point of lay

Hybrids begin to lay at 12–16 weeks if they are given the correct feed. Pure breeds have a laying cycle that goes with the seasons, and they come

ABOVE If you want to rear chicks the natural way, check that the brood you buy has a good mothering record—hybrids do not go broody.

can reach a table weight from six weeks onward, it makes economic sense to rear them yourself. However, most self-sufficient households try to rear them more slowly and on a semi-free-range system with the aim of reaching table weight at 10–14 weeks. Pure breeds will take longer and not reach such high meat to bone weights.

Eggs

Buying eggs, which are then incubated either by hen or by machine, is not the best beginner method of acquiring stock, as it also involves rearing management as well as incubator skills, but it will become a useful replacement method as your poultry-keeping skills grow, especially if the eggs are from your own flock and you know exactly their age and how they have been stored.

Ex-battery hens

Battery hens are high egg-laying hybrids, and although the first season will have passed, they will have many more eggs still to lay. They will have been closely confined, so when you collect them you should ensure they are in a warm place with a heat lamp if necessary. Allow them to feather up, letting them out in a controlled space on warm days. Continue with their feed if it can be obtained from the farmer, and gradually change to the pellets from your supplier. Add some vitamins to their water and let them slowly adapt to their new environment. It will take them as long as it will take—you can't hurry the process —but keep them warm, dry, and protected. Eventually they will be ranging like normal hens.

Housing for hens

Hens can be kept in comparatively small gardens, or they can be allowed to range freely in orchards and fields, but they all require the same basic, everyday management.

They need enough space to be able to exhibit their natural behavior and to be able to escape from those higher up the pecking order. A run needs to be large enough to allow scratching, stretching, and natural movement.

They will need protection from predators, from wild animals such as foxes to domestic pets. Unless the run is totally predator proof (which includes those that can climb and dig), your chickens must be shut into the house at dusk and let out at first light. You can buy automatic pop-

into lay as the days lengthen. A pure breed that reaches point of lay (POL) in age in the fall may not, therefore, produce an egg until early spring.

POL is the best way for beginners to start. It is also the time to "mix" poultry, as they will be the same age and new together, and a pecking order will not have been established. Never mix new young birds with old, established flocks.

Day olds

The big disadvantage of buying day-old chicks is that unless they have been pre-sexed they will include males, which will have to be removed when identified or grown on to the table. Keeping extra cockerels or selling them is not an option because there is scarcely any demand for them.

Day olds require careful management under heat in the early weeks, correct feeding, and attention to their growing needs. It is usual to buy in poultry destined only for the table as day olds, although some stockists also supply one- and two-week-old stock. As hybrid table birds

Gardens and hens

Gardens and hens don't always mix! In winter, when nothing much is growing and as long as you don't have any special plants in the border, you can let the hens into the garden, and they will do a wonderful job of clearing it of slugs, snails, and any

other insects they can find. Keep them out in spring, when your seedlings are growing, however, because they will eat these and find a dustbath they like—usually somewhere your plants are struggling to grow.

hole closers if you cannot always do this, but if you don't do it they will be killed. Even if you let them out to range during the day, you must still shut them up at night and let them out in the morning. Roosting in trees won't protect them.

Arks are a traditional method of moving poultry around land so that they can clean grass. Some of these are wedge shaped, with the base the largest point, reducing the chickens' head-room, which can be a problem for larger fowl.

Within the house there should be a perching area and a nestbox area. Hens prefer to lay in a secluded, darkish place. Laying in an open area encourages egg eating. You will have to clean out and replace the bedding regularly, so make sure it is easy for you to get into. Most housing is wooden, which is attractive but harbors mites. You must remove the birds to another house twice a year so that you can clean the house thoroughly and apply an anti-mite solution.

Dustbaths are important to poultry, so make a sand bath in the run if the poultry are not free range and can choose their own bath.

A range of purpose-built poultry houses is available, but a good-size garden shed, with the window removed and replaced with strong wire netting, perches, and a nest area in the darkest corner, perhaps partly hidden by sacking, makes an excellent house. You can build a run at either side so that one can be rested at a time. Existing buildings around the farm can also be adapted for poultry, as long as you remember that they will also need cleaning for mites at regular intervals. Secure, light stables make a particularly good environment for rearing table birds, which can be let out to range as they get older.

Food for fowl

A hen is born with the ability to lay a given number of eggs and it will mainly be the level of nutrition (combined with good management) that will allow her to do this. If a bird is able to lay 300 or more eggs a year yet poor feeding stops her from doing this, it is a real waste of potential and, potentially, a welfare issue.

Fully balanced poultry feeds were developed at the same time as the hybrid breeds, and the two go hand in hand. These high-performing birds need a well-balanced diet for them to fulfill their genetic expectations, and they must receive the right amount of vitamins, minerals, and grit

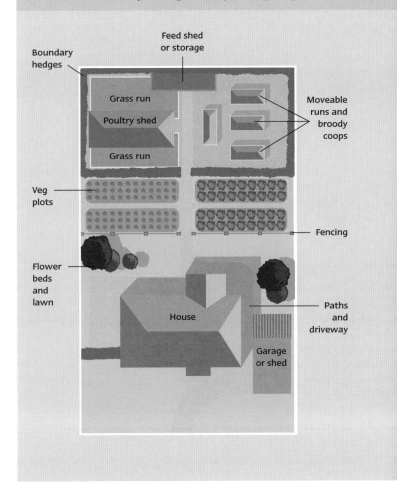

Plan for backyard poultry keeping

Boundary hedges

Feed shed or storage

Grass run

Poultry shed

Grass run

Moveable runs and broody coops

Veg plots

Fencing

Flower beds and lawn

House

Paths and driveway

Garage or shed

as well as nutrients. You will find all this in ready-bagged feeds, which will help you get the best from your poultry. Pure breeds also require a balanced diet, although they can manage with less high nutrition. However, if you want them to perform well, you should offer them a quality, balanced ration.

All poultry go through a molt at some point during the year and will go off lay. You must carry on feeding a high level of nutrition so that they can re-grow their feathers and maintain health.

What food you offer your poultry will depend on their age:

- Day olds to five weeks old—chick crumbs
- Five weeks to 14–16 weeks (POL)—growers' pellets (gradually change them over)
- POL (throughout laying life)—layers' pellets

Table birds should be fed as on page 139 until a couple of weeks before killing, when they should be on a finishing ration.

You can obtain poultry food in organic, free-range, or garden mixes and as mash or pellets. If mash is mixed with water, you must clear away any that is not eaten in a day or it will go sour. Dry mash will keep hens busy for longer, thus helping to avoid feather pecking.

Mixed corn

Poultry love mixed corn (wheat and maize grits), which is usually fed in the afternoon, often as a "scratch feed"—that is, it is thrown for the birds to scratch up. It must not be fed until after the birds have had their morning balanced ration of pellets or mash.

Scraps

Although scraps have their place in poultry feeding, different countries have different regulations about what can and cannot be fed. Whatever the rules, you should never feed meat to poultry. Scraps should be regarded as a treat rather than as a nutritional feed.

Grit

All poultry need grit. A bird's gizzard is its "teeth" and needs grit to work. If they are free range, most poultry will pick up an adequate amount, but if you keep them in a run, provide a bowl of grit. Calcium, for hard shells, will be included in the pellets.

Feeders

You must provide enough feeders for all your birds or shy feeders won't get their full ration and cannot be expected to lay productively. Err on the side of too many rather than not enough and they can be hung within the house or placed on bricks to stop them getting contaminated with soil.

Water

An egg is 65 percent water, and a mature bird is up to 55 percent water, so it is very important your birds have access to clean water during daylight hours. You must provide sufficient drinkers, suspended or supported on legs or bricks to stop contamination, so that hens lower down the pecking order will be able to drink as much as they need. During stressful times, such as molting, moving, mid-lay, or in hot or cold weather, supplementary soluble vitamins can be given in the water, which must be changed daily.

Both water and feed should be placed within the house or the run to discourage wild birds and possible infections.

Parasites

Poultry suffer from a number of parasites, but they can be easily controlled. Internal parasites, such as worms, are controlled with worming products, given on veterinary advice and often administered in the water.

You must be on the lookout for external parasites, which are controlled in several ways. Houses must be cleaned regularly and thoroughly to keep them clear of mites, and dustbaths and nestboxes be treated with a suitable powder, either from your vet or feed merchant. A broody hen must be kept clear of mites because she will have to desert her eggs if she becomes infested. Mites are life threatening: they can drain the blood overnight and make birds at best anemic and at worst ill to the point of death.

If you come into contact with poultry mites, put all your clothes in the washing machine and shower thoroughly. If they get into your home, they can be difficult to eradicate.

Scaly legs, tiny burrowing mites to which feathered-leg breeds, such as Silkies, are particularly susceptible, can be treated with a

BELOW Free-ranging birds on good pasture will have access to grit and invertebrates, which will help to keep them healthy.

specially formulated product and petroleum jelly, which suffocates the mites. Be gentle with this treatment and don't attempt to remove the scales, because the bird's legs will already be sore.

Vaccinations

You will probably buy birds that have already been vaccinated, but if not, get veterinary advice. It is not possible in all countries to vaccinate against avian flu. Most birds will survive well without any vaccinations if they are kept in clean conditions, are not overcrowded, and have access to balanced food and plenty of clean water.

Produce from your chickens

Your aim in keeping chickens is to get produce in the form of eggs and meat, especially to have a surplus that you can sell.

Eggs

Eggs have to be collected every day—preferably twice a day—and stored, pointed end down, in a cool place. Check local regulations on selling eggs, although if you are selling direct at the gate without prior grading, there are normally no regulations. Your customers might want to know how old the eggs are, so keep the eggs in date order so that you can easily check.

You can sell fertile eggs for eating, but they must be collected the same day as laying and not be semibrooded. You don't need to keep a cockerel for a hen to lay, and it might be best to keep hens only, especially if close neighbors are likely to object to the early-morning noise.

Table birds

There are many rules and regulations governing the slaughter and sale of birds for the table, and if you intend to sell or give your birds to people outside your household, you should do some research. Slaughter must be done humanely, ideally by stunning first. However, it is hard to source home stunners, so quick neck dislocation is the preferred method, and you should learn how to do this from an expert before you attempt it yourself. Do not use any other method. It's important that handling prior to slaughter is calm and gentle. Everyone who keeps poultry should be able to undertake emergency slaughter for sick or suffering birds, or have access to a neighbor who is able to do this.

Health check

Check your birds every single day. A bird that is not eating or reluctant to leave the house may indicate poor health. Look out for bullying and damage to the body. At least once a week do a thorough check:

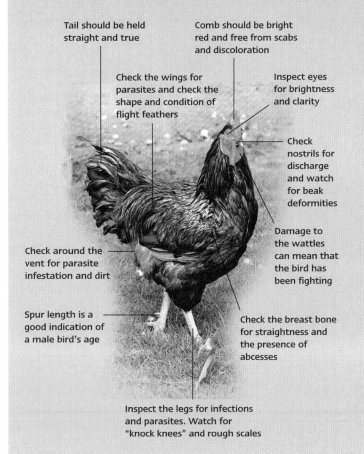

Tail should be held straight and true

Comb should be bright red and free from scabs and discoloration

Check the wings for parasites and check the shape and condition of flight feathers

Inspect eyes for brightness and clarity

Check nostrils for discharge and watch for beak deformities

Check around the vent for parasite infestation and dirt

Damage to the wattles can mean that the bird has been fighting

Spur length is a good indication of a male bird's age

Check the breast bone for straightness and the presence of abcesses

Inspect the legs for infections and parasites. Watch for "knock knees" and rough scales

Allow plenty of time for plucking and dressing, especially at first. Chickens should be hung neck down for the blood to drain downward, and they can be plucked wet (dunked in hot water after death) or dry.

When is a table bird not a table bird? Old layers, young cockerels of laying breeds, and partially grown birds will not produce a carcass fit for roasting, no matter how creative the cook may be. They can all have some use, however, from making stock to making a curry. If you have one of the light breeds, consider "breasting"' only—that is, removing the breasts without plucking. Some birds will taste quite gamey, and adapting recipes for game birds often works well.

Keeping ducks

Domestic ducks not only produce a large number of good-size, rich eggs but they also make good table birds. They are increasingly popular with self-supporters, and they can also help you rid your land of slugs and snails as they forage.

Choosing a breed

All domestic breeds, except the Muscovy, originate from the wild Mallard, but they have been developed for specific purposes. Most ducks still have a strong utility element—they provide meat and eggs—although there are exceptions. Like chickens, ducks are divided into bantam, heavy, and light breeds, with the heavy breeds being better suited to the table and the light breeds providing the high egg layers.

Bantam breeds

The best known of the bantam breeds is the **Call** duck, so named for its loud and persistent quack. It makes a great pet, but is not a good layer. The **Crested Miniature**, which is an exhibition type, lays a useful 100 eggs a year, but the **Silver Appleyard Miniature** not only lays well but is also meaty for its size. The **Australian Spotted** also lays well and matures fast. Bantam breeds are good flyers and need to have their wings clipped.

Light breeds

This group includes the really good layers, such as the **Indian Runner**, an upright duck that cannot fly but is a superb forager on pasture and should not be confined to a small area. The **Campbell** was bred for egg laying—it can produce 300 a year—and also makes a good table bird. The **Welsh Harlequin** is another dual-purpose, hardy bird with a placid nature.

Heavy breeds

These are the table birds, and top of the list is the **Aylesbury**. The true Aylesbury is rare, and most such-named ducks are really white, heavy, Pekin-type hybrids. The **Pekin** is a semi-upright, quick-maturing, high meat-yielding bird, but a

low layer in Britain, although US keepers can expect up to 200 eggs a season.

The **Rouen** and **Rouen Clair** are kept for their looks, but still produce a good carcass and 100 or so eggs a season. The **Silver Appleyard** was developed to be a good foraging, dual-purpose bird, but it is also colorful in appearance.

Heavy breeds are not good flyers, with the exception of the **Muscovy**. It originates from a tree duck, and with its crest, its hissing, and the red, fleshy protuberances on its face and bill (carbuncles), it looks quite different from other ducks. It makes a good table bird (though it is dark meat) and is a moderate layer, but it can be aggressive and also eats small mammals.

Among the established commercial breeds are hybrids, such as the high-laying Rhode Island Red/Sussex hybrid **Daisy Belle**, but there are many other types.

Buying

You can buy ducks direct from breeders, from quality shows and sales, and from hatcheries.

Buy POL at 21–24 weeks, and they can live for 8–10 years. Day-old ducklings require heat and starter crumbs as well as drinking water. Restrict access to swimming water until the birds' preen glands come into play, which is not until they have passed the downy (fluffy) stage, because ducklings reared away from their mothers are not waterproof and will drown or get chilled.

Feeding

Offer a balanced ration according to age or type—starter crumbs for ducklings, growers' pellets for four to six weeks old, finishing pellets up to slaughter, breeders' pellets for breeding ducks, and layers' pellets for egg producers. If they are foraging on ground that is not overgrazed, they will pick up lots of invertebrates and other grubs to supplement their diet. Provide plenty of water.

Water

Ducks need water in order to splash, activating their preen gland, keeping their feathers well oiled and healthy, and clean their eyes and nose. The heavy breeds appreciate swimming water for mating, but the lighter ducks can manage with a small pond. The water must be deep enough for them to be able to get their heads under the water and ideally to be able to float.

The water will become foul and must be changed regularly unless it flows naturally. All ponds need to have sloping sides or ramps so that they can get in or out.

Housing

Ducks must be shut in a house at dusk to protect them from predators and let out in the morning. They are ground-roosting birds and need a secure, well-ventilated shed with a large entrance so that they do not get damaged. High windows will allow air to circulate above the birds, and the house should be at least 3 feet high. For night-time confinement only, ducks need around 4 square feet of space each, but if they have to be confined for longer periods they will need more space, together with a pond that can't be knocked over.

Ducks are messy creatures, so you need to be able to clean out their pen and hose it down. They also suffer from "bumble foot," which is caused by infections resulting from injuries on their webs by sharp stones or rubbish. It can be fatal, so smooth surfaces or grass are preferable.

Predators

Ducks are at risk from foxes and other predators, and ducklings from winged predators. Young birds should be protected in a covered run, while adults need protecting at night and, sometimes, during the day. The protection may take the form of electric fencing or wire sunk into the ground and sloped at the top. If you are using natural water, look out for water predators, such as mink.

Diseases

If they are kept well, with access to water and room to forage, ducks are hardy. Worming and mite treatment are essential, and respiratory problems are often caused by a stuffy, over-hot house with moldy bedding. Crop binding is caused by long grass or grass clippings getting stuck in the gizzard or by gizzard worm, so make sure you provide grit.

The sudden death of more than one bird from your flock should always be investigated by a veterinary surgeon in case they have a notifiable disease, such as avian flu or Newcastle disease.

Produce from your ducks

Collect the eggs every day and keep them clean. It's hard to get ducks to lay in a nestbox, but they do often lay in the house, so keep the bedding clean. Table ducks need to be slaughtered at seven weeks for hybrids or ten weeks for pure breeds, before they go into their juvenile molt. After this they will be harder to pluck, although the meat is unaffected. As with chickens, slaughter is usually by neck dislocation, but it requires more skill and determination than for chickens, and you must learn from an expert or get a professional to do it for you to ensure a humane death.

Plucking is time consuming. They can be wet or dry plucked, and small-scale plucking machines are available.

Keeping drakes

Do not keep more than one drake to a flock because they have high libidos and will damage the ducks with their constant attention. You don't need a drake at all for the ducks to lay eggs.

BELOW Strong, well-ventilated housing should also have a large door, as ducks all try to come out at once!

Keeping geese

Geese have been domesticated and bred, mainly for meat, for generations, but have resolutely resisted efforts to be kept really intensively. A goose's natural inclination to utilize good grass and to forage makes it a very useful bird.

These hardy birds have been useful to humans for many years, from guard birds to the modern hybrids for the table. For a small-scale farmer or self-supporter, geese do best when they can forage on good grass. They are ideal birds for an orchard, clearing up windfalls and getting much of their nutrition from good-quality grass in summer and early fall.

Choosing a breed

Although they are kept primarily for the table, some people like to use the birds as guard geese—Chinese geese in particular are suitable for this. In the past their feathers were used for quills for writing and down for quilts, and the birds were also a source of grease and fat.

Goose breeds are divided into light, medium, and heavy.

The light **Chinese** goose originated from the Asiatic Swan goose. It is incredibly noisy, making it a superb guard goose. It's the best layer, producing up to 80 eggs a year.

Originating in Germany, the heavy **Embden** is a large, hardy white goose, with a gander weighing in at up to 34 pounds. Their size makes them good table birds, and they produce 20–25 eggs a year. They can be protective, so should not be kept if you have small children or pets.

The **Roman** and **Roman Tufted**, both light breeds, are compact, pure white geese. They are great for beginners, being kind, good all-rounders, and easy breeders. They lay 30–60 eggs a season, and one gander can breed up to five geese.

The **Pilgrim** and **West of England**, both auto-sexing breeds (the sexes are different colors), are good examples of breeds that were developed by small farmers to graze rough

ground while producing good carcasses. The **American Buff** is a large breed, developed to be a heavy table bird, and it will put on weight with good grazing.

Commercial breeds tend to be white and there are some well-known breeds. They grow quickly and produce up to 50 eggs a season. They are excellent to keep, as long as you don't mistake them for the pure breeds.

Buying geese

Geese can be purchased at all ages, but goslings are bought in late spring and grown on grass for the Christmas market. Young goslings need heat if they don't have parents and they are not waterproof until their preen glands are activated, so must not get wet and chilled when "fluffy" (in down). It's often hard to be sure of the sex of some breeds of adult geese.

Feeding

Goslings begin on starter crumbs, but by two months old good grass should be providing much of their ration. By four months, depending on the quantity and quality, they can survive on grass alone with perhaps some grain. In late summer to early fall, when the quality of grass diminishes, they will also require a balanced supplementary feed such as a finisher pellet if they are heading for the table. Breeding birds will need a breeder feed—a sitting goose cannot get her nutrition and still sit on the eggs. Don't ever underfeed your birds—give them as much as they will clear up. Laying birds and young birds especially need extra food.

Grit for the gizzard to work properly will be available naturally to grazing geese, but it's still best to put some out in a dry feeder.

Goose and gander

If you have a goose and gander and the goose dies, do not expect the gander to immediately accept any another goose—they are selective.

LEFT Chinese geese are excellent guard geese, as they are very vocal, but they also lay the most eggs of any goose.

Water

The heavy geese appreciate water that will hold their weight, but the lighter breeds can manage with a pool in which they can immerse themselves. Like ducks, they need to be able constantly to clean their heads by dipping them under water and to be able to splash.

Housing

The house must have sufficient headroom with ventilation above and be solid, so that predators cannot get in. A strong wooden shed with wire windows sited where it is not exposed to strong sun would provide good, safe shelter, but you can adapt small barns and existing buildings. The doorway must be wide enough to let more than one bird through at the same time. Use shavings or straw for bedding. Moldy bedding and poor ventilation will cause respiratory problems.

Predators

Geese are at risk from predators, including comparatively small ones like mink or foxes, and they need protection, particularly at night when they must be shut up safely from dusk until the morning every day. During the day predator-proof fencing may be needed around an orchard in some areas—use small-mesh wire netting sunk into the ground and high enough with the top bent over to discourage climbers. You can also use electric fencing to deter predators. If they have access to natural water, watch out for water-based predators, including mink.

Diseases

All the diseases that apply to ducks (see page 143) apply also to geese. They suffer from bumble foot if they step on something sharp and the wound becomes infected, and this can be incurable. Prevention is better than cure, and geese do best if they are kept as naturally as possible but protected from predators. Correct feeding, water provided, and sufficient exercise will ensure that this naturally hardy bird thrives.

Produce from your geese

Geese are large birds and are not at all easy to kill. You must make sure that you are able to slaughter your birds quickly and humanely. You must seek expert advice and guidance before you attempt to kill a goose.

If you want to save the down, the bird must be at least 16 weeks old and be dry plucked. They are hardest to pluck at 12–16 weeks, when they are molting their first set of juvenile feathers. However, many small-scale producers prefer wet plucking, when the bird is dunked into hot water for a couple of minutes. There are also plucking machines that you can use. Don't underestimate the time it will take you to pluck your geese, at least when you are doing it for the first time.

The eggs are in demand for cooking, hatching, and for decorating, and they will command good prices if marketed correctly. Although a good laying goose will produce only a quarter the number of eggs of a high-laying chicken, the eggs can be worth up to ten times more.

Keeping turkeys

As long as they have adequate housing, good pasture, and proper feed, turkeys will provide you with excellent eggs and meat, and they are not as difficult to keep as is sometimes said.

Before you even think about keeping turkeys, you must check any rules and regulations. In Britain, for example, you can't keep turkeys on some allotments, and if you have near neighbors they might be annoyed by the noise—male turkeys gobble loudly. In the USA there are local rules and covenants on land use, so check with the local authorities before proceeding. However, if you have plenty of space for them, turkeys are hardy, rewarding birds.

Choosing a breed

There are several breeds of turkey. The standard heritage varieties include the **Bourbon Red** and **Norfolk Black** (also known as the Black Spanish), and there are commercial hybrids, such as the **Broad Breasted Bronze** and **Broad Breasted White**. The standard breeds grow more slowly than the commercial hybrids, but their meat has an excellent flavor.

Buying

You can purchase turkeys from private breeders, through markets, or from commercial hatcheries. Buying day-old poults is the cheapest way, but they will need a heat lamp for the first six weeks and should be offered turkey starter crumbs and a drinker with a rim.

Feeding

Young turkeys need rations with a higher protein content than chicks, so chick crumbs are not suitable. From six weeks of age feed them turkey grower pellets.

Turkeys love to graze and will snack on grass, insects, leaves, and berries. So that they produce eggs and meat, you will also have to give them conventional feed. For adult birds this will be a turkey breeder ration for egg laying or a turkey finisher ration for table birds, given from 12–16 weeks upward. This is fed in the morning, while a grain feed, usually wheat, should be offered in the afternoon. Fresh, clean water must be available at all times.

Housing

These hardy birds can be penned outside if the weather is warm during the day, but they need a house at night when it is cooler. You can keep up to six turkeys in an adapted, good-quality garden shed that is sized about 9 x 6 feet. This is not large enough for them to be kept inside all the time, but it is ideal for overnight housing. You will have to make sure that there is plenty of ventilation near the roof, and you should replace any windows with small-mesh wire. Place a round pole, 3 inches across, about 30 inches from the ground across the inside to make a perch for your birds.

Depending on your property, you might have to erect a fence, about 6 feet high, around an area for the birds, although it's possible for hen turkeys to fly over and out if they want to. Generally, however, they will be well behaved as long as there is sufficient space and vegetation to keep their interest.

Turkeys need to be kept clean, and dust-free shavings make a good litter in their house. The cleaner they are kept, the healthier they are likely to stay. Stale feces allow bacteria to build up, and turkeys will then succumb to respiratory and fungal diseases. Ventilation in the house is always vital because lack of fresh air will bring on respiratory problems. Drinkers and feeders should be washed in a suitable disinfectant at least once a week.

Predators

Despite their size, turkeys are vulnerable to foxes and raccoons, so they must be safely housed at night. You need to be one step ahead of them when it comes to shutting them up at night—if you leave it too late they may fly up and be perched on the roof or up on another building. Don't leave them there, because of severe weather in winter and light mornings in the summer, when predators will be around. However, they soon get used to routine and are easy to manage when accustomed to human contact.

Breeding

If you are planning to breed from your turkeys for future stock, you will have to protect the females (hens) with "saddles" in midwinter so that the males (toms) do not harm them during mating. Keep the saddles on until the end of the mating season in early fall. Eggs appear about 28 days after mating has started, and a hen turkey will lay 50–80 eggs a year, which should be placed in an incubator or under a broody turkey for hatching.

Pests and diseases

The main worry for turkey keepers is the disease known as blackhead, which is caused by a protozoan worm that chickens can carry but turkeys suffer from. If you have had poultry on the land before or if the turkeys are going to be kept near or with other types of poultry, you will have to worm everything about every six weeks. Regular worming interferes with the life cycle of the parasitic worm *Heterakis gallinarum*, which if allowed to get through the gut damages the liver and is usually fatal. Ask your veterinarian to prescribe a suitable proprietary wormer.

Produce from your turkeys

Turkey eggs are wonderful to eat by themselves or in baking.

Turkeys mature at around 5–6 months, depending on the breed, and this is when they are killed for meat. These large birds are not easy to kill humanely. Make sure that you get professional help and that you obey all local regulations about slaughtering and processing in preparation for the table.

BELOW Norfolk Black turkeys surrounded by a 6-foot high fence. They won't fly out if there is sufficient space and vegetation.

Keeping quail and other fowl

There are several other fowl that you could consider. Most of these are quite small, but if you have space, you might want to consider some of the larger, more exotic birds.

Quail

Quail (*Coturnix coturnix*) are small birds that can produce a large number of eggs and also tasty carcasses for the table, and for their size they are productive and low cost.

They are members of the pheasant family. Many bird breeders keep them in aviaries where they pick up dropped seed. The Japanese and Italian strains are normally kept for meat and eggs, although there are many other types. They will lay up to 200 eggs, coming into lay at about 45 days old. The larger bobwhite is often kept for meat but is not a good egg layer. A quail can live for up to two years.

Quail are good flyers and must be confined. They will sit in the wet, so it's best to keep them in a wire-fronted aviary or a movable ark with a wire run. Shavings can be used for bedding. They are ground dwellers and roost on the floor, which must be dry. Like chickens, they need dustbaths.

They are shy birds and like having places to hide, such as boxes lined with hay or shavings. In winter, if their house is not waterproof, move it into a building to keep them dry. If there is no access to grass, grow some in pots or dig turf for them. They are particularly vulnerable to predators—even a small rat can take a quail.

They don't eat much—about 5 ounces a week—and specialty food is available. Vary the diet with mealworms and millet, and spread it around so that they have to look for it. They need grit like all poultry, but it might need crushing to make the pieces small enough for them. They must have access to clean, fresh water at all times, and they hate old or stagnant water.

Collecting eggs can be difficult because they are not tidy layers, and although you can provide secluded areas for laying, they do spread their eggs all over the pen. Collect regularly and make sure the pen is constructed so that you can open it to collect eggs without losing the birds. Domestic quail are not great breeders, and you may need to incubate their eggs, producing chicks the size of bumble bees, which need heat and a pen that will keep them safe from predators of all sizes and from which they cannot escape.

Guinea fowl

Guinea fowl (sometimes known as guinea hens) are inquisitive, noisy birds, alerting their owners to visitors, welcome and unwelcome. Recently, people have discovered that they also make good table birds, and they are excellent gardeners, eating insect pests without doing much damage to the plants. In the USA they are noted for the control of ticks. Because they are so noisy, they may not be suitable if you have close neighbors.

There are several species, all hardy and prefer free-range conditions, although if you get them young you might persuade them to roost in the rafters of a building rather than in trees. They are safe in trees in the dark, but they are vulnerable to predators in the early morning when they come down to feed, and if possible they should be kept in a large run with some height for them to fly. They do not suffer from the same diseases as chickens and can be safely kept with them.

You can buy guinea fowl as day olds (keets) or as young birds, and it is difficult to get adults to settle, although initially confining them in a large barn may work. As with all poultry, they will need heat, protection from predators, and suitable feed for youngsters. Adults nest on grass and are easily frightened off their nests. They will lay 25–35 eggs before sitting, but you can collect the eggs if you want to use or sell them.

Pigeons

Pigeons (*Columba* spp.) have been domesticated for centuries as a source of protein, and until fairly recently all farms and estates had a dovecote. Meat pigeons are sometimes known as utility pigeons, and the meat is referred to as squab, probably because in commercial rearing squabs are killed at four weeks before they fly. Look out for breeds such as Kings, Modaines, and Carneau, all big, meaty birds.

The birds can be kept fully confined—this will be necessary if killing young—but it may be both practical and pleasant if they are able to fly, not only for their welfare but also because they will find a large proportion of their own food. They will need a safe place to breed and roost, such as a dovecote or pigeon loft, and like all poultry will need protection from predators, a balanced feed, clean water, and grit.

Slaughter can be carried out when the population is sufficient for you to remove some birds without affecting the breeding and can be done by removing the bird or birds at roost.

Pheasants

If you have some woodland, you might consider rearing a few pheasants (*Phasianus colchicus*) or partridges (*Perdix perdix*) to release for shooting in season.

The best source will be a local gamekeeper who is breeding replacement birds and may be able to provide eggs for hatching or young poults. These will probably be vaccinated and wormed. You can then grow them on to maturity, using a "release" pen. If you wish, you can continue to put food in a specific place in winter to keep them on or near your land. Don't try to confine pheasants in the long term unless you have a large aviary. They can be surprisingly aggressive to each other as well as toward people.

Ostriches and other exotics

At the other end of the scale are the really large birds, such as rheas and ostriches. These are creatures for experts and will require a license in most areas. They need careful handling in terms of both their welfare and your safety, and their slaughter also requires particular expertise because most abattoirs are unable to handle them, and home slaughter must be carried out humanely and under local regulations.

They also need specialized outlets for the selling of the produce, and even though ostrich meat is a healthy, low-fat choice, there may not be a demand for it in some areas where people are not used to eating it. Ostrich eggs are more usually used for decorative or breeding purposes than for eating. The feathers do have a value, as does the hide of ostriches.

If rearing these birds interests you, look into the management carefully and make sure that the costs of keeping them will be met by the market for the produce.

BELOW Ostriches are for experts, as they need careful handling. Check the demand for their produce before investing in them.

Hatching and rearing poultry

It's easy to raise poultry from an egg as long as you provide all the things that the egg and hatchling need to thrive. It's also satisfying and can save you money on breeding replacements.

What is incubation?

If a male bird is present in the flock, the eggs will be fertile. The natural process would be for the female to lay a certain number of eggs according to her species and when she feels there is the right number she will sit on them. Until she covers them and provides warmth, they cannot begin to hatch and are quite safe to eat.

If she has partially sat an egg, it will begin to hatch. If the egg cools, it cannot hatch because the embryo inside will die. The bird will sit on her eggs for a given number of days (see below), during which time she will turn the eggs and her body will provide the right amount of moisture. As they hatch, she will continue to sit.

The hatchling will live off the yolk that it has absorbed for the first 24 hours of life outside the egg, and you can safely leave the mother for this time to complete the hatch, even though some chicks have hatched.

Natural incubation

This is the bird hatching her own eggs or a "broody" hatching another bird's eggs. This is the simplest and most effective method, but it will only hatch a limited number of eggs at a time—the number a bird can cover and keep warm. The bird also has to be in a broody state so that she sits for the allotted time. Not all breeds of poultry are good at this, and some, such as hybrids, have been bred to discourage it altogether.

You can identify a broody because she sits on eggs and she will fluff out her feathers and become agitated and noisy if you approach. If you take her off the eggs, she will swiftly return. Check the number of eggs—often other birds lay into the nest, leaving an impossibly high number for the hen to cover, and these will then hatch at different times. Leave her only the number she can cover. She will need to be protected from predators and have access to high-quality food and clean water. If you have to move her to a safe place, be aware that she might stop sitting, but sometimes it's the only thing that can be done to keep her and the eggs safe. Transfer her and the eggs to a small area in the dark, and then extend this in the daylight. An infestation of mites will cause a broody to get off her eggs.

Geese and turkeys may have to be protected from predators and bad weather because they cannot easily be moved. The gander takes an active part in guarding the goose and bringing up the family, so take care with him at this time.

On hatching, continue to protect the mother and chicks. Keep her away from other poultry, because she will defend her family, often crushing them in the process. Provide chick crumbs for the chicks and make sure that they do not drown by using suitable water containers—a shallow dish with stones will do for the first days. If a bird appears with a brood, which she has managed to keep safe so far, you should still take steps to protect her and to give appropriate food. She will

Incubation periods

Hens (bantams and large fowl)—21 days

Ducks (except Muscovy) - 28 days

Muscovy ducks—35 days

Pheasant—23-24 days

Geese (small breeds)—30 days

Geese (large breeds)—33-35 days

Japanese quail—16-17 days

Bobwhite quail—23-24 days

abandon the chicks when she considers they are old enough.

Pigeons are different from other poultry in that the parents feed the young birds directly, and they should be reared by their own parents.

Artificial incubation

It's possible to provide everything the female bird would do, but artificially. An incubator normally comes with a hatcher, and you put the eggs in the preheated cabinet, following the manufacturer's instructions for the incubation period. As with natural incubation, the chicks have 24 hours in which they don't need to eat and drink and can be left in the hatcher until they have dried off and become lively.

Carefully select eggs for artificial incubation. Ideally they should be naturally clean, of a normal shape, and no more than a week old but not fresh. Store them in a cool, not cold, room.

In a manual incubator you will have to turn the eggs by hand up to seven times a day, but at least three times a day. In an automatic incubator the eggs are turned by the machine, and you should stop the turning three days before the hatch. Machines can be still air or forced air, where a fan circulates the warmth. The correct temperature for an egg is 100°F; still-air machines are set at 103–104°F, and forced air at 100°F, but you must check the instructions for each machine. They are affected by outside conditions and changes in temperature; you may need to add water to increase the humidity. It is important to keep a record of everything you do and the result of the hatch so that you can improve the hatching rate.

Candle the eggs to check that the embryo is developing and to see the air space. At the end of the hatching period this air space will be about one-third of the egg. A small air space indicates that there is not enough moisture, while too large a space suggests that there is too much; both indicate an unsuccessful hatch. Destroy clear eggs, which will not develop. Although you need to candle at regular intervals, do not do it too often because it's important to maintain the temperature.

You should then transfer the day-old chicks to a brooder, a machine providing even heat. Alternatively, put them in a homemade brooder, normally a dull infrared light (bright light doesn't allow the chicks any rest) over a draft-proof box (put blocks in the corners so that chicks cannot get trapped) or a circle of hardboard with shavings as litter. Chicks spread away from the light if it's too hot and huddle together if it's too cold, so adjust the lamp up and down, being careful not to "cook or chill" the chicks and watch their behavior. Make sure that starter crumbs and water are available in safe containers.

LEFT Incubators come in various sizes and are manual or automatic—select the best model for your situation and budget.

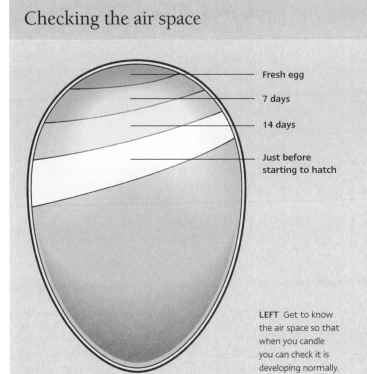

Checking the air space

- Fresh egg
- 7 days
- 14 days
- Just before starting to hatch

LEFT Get to know the air space so that when you candle you can check it is developing normally.

Keeping bees

For most people bees mean honey, but these insects play a major part in food production through pollination, and a hive on your small farm will increase yields. A colony can also provide beeswax, which can be crafted into candles and polish.

The honeybee is a truly amazing social insect. Individuals cannot survive on their own but must live in a colony. This has a single queen which, in normal circumstances, lays all the eggs in the hive. Fertilized eggs develop into female worker bees, making up the bulk of the colony, and unfertilized eggs develop into male drones. Drones are produced only during the active season so that they are available to mate with virgin queens, usually produced as part of colony reproduction or swarming. At the end of the season they are killed or ejected from the hive by workers, as they serve no further useful purpose.

The nest

The species of honeybees kept by beekeepers nest in cavities, originally hollow trees or rock cavities. Humans took advantage of this and provided beehives in which their colonies could live. Within the cavity, the bees build parallel hanging combs using beeswax secreted from glands on the underside of the abdomen. The wax scales are molded into hexagonal cells using the mandibles or jaws. These combs form the basis of the nest.

The brood nest

The next generation of bees is reared in some of these cells—the brood found in the brood nest. Worker brood forms the majority of this. The egg hatches, is fed, and grows rapidly. The cell is then sealed with a beeswax capping and the larva pupates to emerge as an adult.

Drones are larger than workers, so their cells are bigger, with a domed capping. Queens are raised in large cells, usually hanging on the face of the comb, and when beekeepers find occupied queen cells, they know the colony intends to swarm. The queen usually lays eggs in a spiral pattern, working out from the center of the comb, a habit that helps beekeepers ascertain that the situation in the colony is "normal."

The cells are also used to store pollen in an arc above the brood nest. Honey, the carbohydrate, is stored in cells above the pollen.

The life cycle of worker bees

When a worker bee emerges, she begins life as a house bee and her first job is to clean cells, ready for the queen's eggs. As her glands develop, she starts feeding the brood and then helps to tend the queen.

RIGHT This nest shows the parallel comb structure of the nest, but it is unusual for a wild colony to build such a large nest and survive in the open.

Her next job is to receive nectar and pollen from incoming foragers and pack these into cells. As her wax glands become active, she helps to build comb. Then she helps ventilate the hive by fanning her wings at the entrance, and she guards it against intruders, such as robber bees or wasps (yellow-jackets). Finally, at about three weeks old, she becomes a forager.

In the active season her life ends some three weeks later, but in winter a worker bee can live up to six months and help to develop the colony the following spring.

Bees forage for nectar and pollen as well as water and propolis:

Nectar

Nectar is sucked from a flower through the tongue. It is transported to the hive in the honey crop inside the abdomen, regurgitated and passed to house bees. Nectar is converted to honey by reducing the water content through evaporation and inducing chemical changes by adding enzymes secreted by a gland in the worker's head. When the water content is sufficiently lowered, the honey is placed in a cell, which is sealed with a wax capping to store it until required.

Pollen

Bees actively collect pollen for food, particularly in spring. Pollen is also deposited on their hairy bodies as they collect nectar. Stiff hairs on each pair of legs are used to comb this off and it is collected in specially adapted baskets on the back legs. Back at the hive, pollen is packed into cells by house bees. Enzymes and other substances are added to preserve it and prevent mold.

Pollination is the most important honeybee activity, for both food crops and wild flowers.

Water

Water is essential for the life of the individual, but the colony uses it in several other ways. Honey stores are diluted for use with water. Water is a major constituent of brood food, fed to larvae, and it is evaporated to cool the hive in hot weather. It is not stored within the nest.

Propolis

Propolis is a resin exuded by tree buds and conifers, and bees use it to fill cracks in the hive to exclude drafts. It is used to varnish the inside of the cavity and to strengthen beeswax combs. A colony may build a propolis "curtain" across the entrance to reduce its size, making it easier to defend. Propolis has antiseptic properties and cells are varnished with it before the queen lays in them. It is also used to cover any large intruders, such as slugs, that die within the hive so that they do not decay and pollute the nest.

The bee dance

Bees communicate by dancing. A bee that has found a nectar source runs along the vertical face of the comb, waggling her abdomen. She turns to the right and returns to the start of her run. The next time she turns to the left. At intervals she regurgitates nectar and feeds it to her followers. The angle of the waggle run to the vertical corresponds to the flight direction relative to the sun at the hive entrance. The number of waggles indicates the distance to be flown. Recruits learn the position of the source and start foraging there.

Preparing for your bees

Before you get your bees, your best preparation is to join your local beekeeping association and attend a beginners' course. Many associations link beginners with more experienced mentors, and this is an excellent way of getting help and support, particularly in the early days. It is also worth reading one good basic beekeeping book, which your mentor can recommend.

Beekeeping equipment

There are threee essential items of equipment for all beekeepers—a veil, a smoker, and a hive tool —and most beekeepers wear protective clothing.

Veil

This is designed to protect you from possible bee stings. Veils come in different designs and you should find the style that suits you. It must be bee proof and comfortable, and you must be able to see what you are doing, especially when you need to check eggs and larvae in the brood nest.

Smoker

You will use a smoker to control the bees while you inspect the hive. Smokers come in different shapes and sizes. Choose one with a good air flow from the nozzle and one where you can pump the bellows easily.

ABOVE A good smoker is an essential part of the beekeeper's kit.

Hive tool

Get into the habit of never putting your hive tool down during a colony inspection. Select one that is comfortable to hold. Try out both the standard and J-type patterns before choosing one.

Protective clothing

Overalls will help protect you from stings and keep your clothes clean. Rubber boots will protect your ankles and gloves will protect your hands. You can buy leather gloves with gauntlets or you can use dishwashing gloves. Make sure that your gloves do not make your movements clumsy because bees react to sharp movements, and their defense is their sting.

The sting

Worker bees defend their colony in several ways. They may fly upward off the frames when you open the hive or fly round your head, emitting a high-pitched buzz. These are warnings. If you do not heed them, the bee's last defense is her sting. The worker's barbed sting catches in the flesh and the sting mechanism is left behind when she flies off. As a result, she dies, but her death in defense of the colony is insignificant in the overall picture. Drones cannot sting.

Getting stung hurts. Your body will react by swelling and itching. Most beekeepers become immune to the venom, but sometimes stings produce a severe reaction, which can lead to anaphylactic shock and, on rare occasions, death. If you are allergic or are afraid of being stung, consider carefully whether beekeeping is for you.

The hive

In 1845–50 Rev. Dr. Jan Dzierzon discovered that bees build combs a fixed distance apart, allowing them to just pass between them. In 1851 Rev. L.L. Langstroth discovered that bees leave a space between their combs and the cavity wall. This "bee space" is the basis of all hive designs. These discoveries allowed beekeepers to use frames that can be lifted out of the hive.

The Langstroth hive is the most popular design around the world, but other designs are available. You would be wise to look at different hives, especially those that are widely used in your area, before making your choice. Generally, frames are not interchangeable between hive types, so you must choose one design and stick to it.

Working from the bottom, the hive stands on a floor or bottom board. This is often fitted with a small-hole mesh as part of disease monitoring and control. Next is the brood box, within which the queen is confined with a queen excluder, a grid with gaps that allow workers through but not the larger drones and queen. Honey supers are placed on top of the queen excluder during a honey flow, and they are covered with a crown board or inner cover. The hive is completed with a roof. The brood box and supers contain frames of appropriate sizes.

All parts of the hive must fit closely to prevent access by robber bees or wasps. The thickness of the wood used is immaterial, although it should be reasonably robust. What is vital is that the internal measurements are correct. If they are not, the bees will fill gaps with propolis and wild or brace comb, making manipulations difficult.

For your safety and comfort, your hives should be placed on sturdy stands and the top of the brood box should be level with your hands. Lift boxes correctly so that you do not damage your back. The boxes are heavy when they are full of brood or honey and may be awkward to handle.

Obtaining bees

You can buy a small nucleus colony from a dealer, or a local beekeeper may have colonies for sale. Check that the bees are disease free and easy for you to handle.

You could also collect your bees as a swarm (see right). This is great fun, but you will know nothing about the colony's health or temper.

It's best to start with two colonies, to compare their performances and be warned if something is going wrong. A problem, such as the loss of a queen, can usually be solved by using young brood, for example, from the second colony.

Inspecting the colony

During the active season you should inspect your colonies every seven to nine days, particularly to check for signs of swarming. Other checks are:

• Is there enough room?
• Is the queen present and laying?
• Is the colony building up like the others?
• Does it have enough food?
• Are there signs of disease?

Keep a record of your observations from the start. At the end of the season you need to treat against varroa (see page 156) and make sure that the colony has sufficient winter stores.

Swarming

Swarming is colony reproduction. Some bees are genetically more inclined to swarm than others, but there is general agreement that a major swarming trigger is congestion, particularly in the brood nest. One way to prevent it is to add supers to the hive, giving the colony more space.

When a colony decides to swarm, the queen lays fertilized eggs in queen cups. Soon after the cells are sealed, the original queen leaves the hive with about half the bees. They occupy another cavity and establish a new colony.

In the original colony the first virgin to emerge leads out an after-swarm, or cast, with around half

BELOW A traditional-looking hive—make sure you choose your style carefully.

Harvesting honey

- Use a comb or a knife to uncap the cells in the honey frames. The uncapping comb is more efficient.

- Load the extractor so that all the spaces are filled. Make sure the drum is evenly balanced.

- When the extractor is full, start the motor (or turn the handle) slowly so that it does not shake. Gradually increase the speed to maximum. The extraction process can take 2–3 minutes. Check both sides of the frame to ensure you have extracted all the honey.

- Once extracted, replace the frames into the super box and, in the evening, put this back on the hive

for the bees to reclaim the last droplets of honey for their own stores.

- Once the honey has settled and the air bubbles have risen to the top, you can run it off into a food-grade bucket or honey jars. This can be quite a sticky process.

- The cappings will be full of honey. Store them in a colander or a warm gravity extractor to get the last drops of honey from them and finally use the remaining wax by washing it thoroughly in plenty of soft water to remove any remaining sweetness.

the remaining bees. This is repeated until the colony "decides" that to lose more bees threatens its survival. The next virgin to emerge kills the occupants of any remaining queen cells. She then flies out to mate on the wing with 10–20 drones, or more, at a drone congregation area. She stores the sperm and uses it for the rest of her life. She then returns to the hive and heads the colony.

When you see occupied queen cells, take swarm control measures. There are variations, but if you regard the colony as consisting of the queen, brood, and foragers, the principle is to separate any one of these from the other two.

Pests and diseases

Sadly, honeybees are subject to pests and diseases. Brood diseases, such as American foul brood, European foul brood, chalkbrood, and sacbrood, affect the larval and pupal stages. Adult bee diseases include a range of viruses and the microsporidian *Nosema*, which affects the bee's gut. The acarine mite fouls the bee's tracheae or breathing tubes, and the varroa mite enters a brood cell just before it is sealed and feeds on the larva/pupa while going through its reproductive cycle. Varroa mites have become resistant to authorized pyrethroid chemical treatments and beekeepers are now using integrated pest

management (IPM) to keep mite levels low. Without treatment, a varroa-infested colony will die in around five years.

A new pest causing problems in the USA and Australia is the small hive beetle (SHB). When feeding, the larvae secrete a substance that makes the combs slimy, and the heat generated by large numbers of larvae can cause combs to collapse. To date, SHB has not been identified in Britain.

A potential pest, not currently identified outside Asia, is the *Tropilaelaps* mite, which has a similar life cycle to varroa and is causing just as much damage.

Other pests include mice, wasps, birds, livestock, and vandals. Wax moths cause problems, particularly in stored comb, and empty comb is best kept in a cool, well-ventilated place, where mice cannot gain access.

A recent problem experienced in the USA is colony collapse disorder (CCD), when the colony population crashes over a few days or even hours. The queen and a few nurse bees remain, but cannot maintain the colony. No dead bees are found near the hive. Robber bees and wax moths do not invade the hive immediately. It appears that CCD is caused by a number of factors yet to be positively identified.

If you suspect that your colony is suffering from a disease or pest, seek advice on what action to take from an experienced beekeeper.

Extracting honey

If the weather has been kind and your colony is healthy and has not swarmed, it should end the season with surplus honey in the supers. You can remove and extract the honey, but you must make sure that sufficient food stores remain to feed the colony during winter or a dearth period. You can leave a super of honey on the hive or replace the honey with sugar syrup, which the bees store in their combs, ready for later use.

Only remove honey super combs that are capped. Uncap it with a knife and place the frames in a centrifugal extractor. In the radial extractor cage, frames radiate like spokes in a wheel. The cage rotates and honey is extracted from both sides at once. It runs down the barrel to a sump and is drawn off through a tap. In a tangential extractor, the combs face the central spindle. The cage is rotated to remove most of the honey from the outside cells. The frames are then turned through 180 degrees, and the second side extracted. This process can be repeated until the cells are empty.

Extracted honey contains wax and other particles, so it is strained. The clean honey can be bottled immediately or stored in bulk in a bucket until later.

Most honeys granulate naturally, often forming large crystals. Naturally granulated honey can be hard. You can produce a soft-set or creamed honey by distributing a naturally fine-grained honey throughout liquid honey, providing centers of crystallization. Such a honey has a smooth texture and can be removed from the jar easily.

Honeys from different plants have different aromas, colors, and flavors. You can extract them separately if you wish to produce speciality monofloral honeys.

Recovering wax

After draining the honey from the wax cappings, you can wash them with clean, soft water. The washings can be fermented to make mead. The wax can be melted and filtered clean before being used to make candles, polish, or foundation.

ABOVE Fresh honeycomb from your hives can be sold alongside your honey.

Flowers for bees

If you decide that beekeeping is not for you, you can plant "bee-friendly" flowers, particularly those providing pollen and nectar in early spring when the colony is building up, ready for the main honey flow. It is a great pleasure to watch your bees visiting your flowers, pollinating your crops, and collecting honey for you.

The beekeeper's year

This is a guide to beekeeping activities during the year. The actual timings of events will be dependent upon geographical location and on the prevailing weather conditions, and appropriate adjustments will need to be made.

Early spring
- Check that pollen is being taken into the hive
- Check colony stores; feed if necessary
- Prepare equipment for swarm control
- Replace old frames and comb

Spring/early summer
- Inspect the brood nest regularly
- Check for swarming preparations
- Carry out swarm control
- Extract early honey crops

- Attend apiary meetings
- Increase stocks if required

Late summer
- Extract surplus honey
- Unite colonies if necessary
- Treat against varroa

Autumn
- Check colony stores; feed if necessary
- Reduce entrances against robbers

Winter
- Protect hives against livestock, woodpeckers, and rodents
- Clean and repair equipment
- Buy new equipment
- Check colony stores by hefting or lifting the back of the hive just off the stand to estimate its weight
- Review the year and plan for the subsequent one

Keeping rabbits

Raising rabbits is a great way of producing healthy meat on a small scale. Some breeds are kept for fiber producing, but although there used to be a strong market for pelts, curing rabbit skins is often more for home use and crafting.

Popular breeds

Rabbits are pleasant and straightforward to keep, but, as with all livestock, the more you know about their needs, the better their health and your return will be from them.

The fiber rabbit is the Angora rabbit, which has a long, silky coat ideal for luxury yarn and hand spinners. It comes in various colors and it's important to buy stock from someone who is breeding for fiber quality. Obviously, surplus stock can be used for the table.

If you are planning to keep rabbit for meat you will want large rabbits with a high proportion of lean meat.

Californian

As the name suggests, the breed was developed in the USA. It is white with black ears, nose, feet and tail. It weighs 9–13 pounds at maturity, and the body tends to be plump. It is often crossed with the New Zealand breed (see below), another primary meat breed, by breeders trying to achieve hybrid vigor.

Flemish Giants

These were popular meat breeds, but the meat is not as lean as other meat rabbits and they reach weights of 12–20 pounds, making them too big for some requirements.

Florida White

Also from the USA, this rabbit weighs only 4–6 pounds at maturity, making it suitable for a small family. The body is compact and meaty.

Lops

These large rabbits, which come in a variety of colors, have ears that hang downward. Some exhibition strains have large ears, which can easily get injured or frost bitten. A mature animal will weigh 11–13 pounds.

New Zealand

These come in a variety of colors, but the most popular for meat is the White. A fully grown animal weighs 10–13 pounds, but you can produce rabbits weighing 5 pounds at eight weeks. Despite its name, the breed was developed in the USA, and the body is well muscled, an essential characteristic in a meat rabbit.

Housing

The costs of setting up a commercial rabbit business with cages is quite high, but for the self-sufficient and self-supporters, the best method is to use a hutch and a run, as you would for a pet rabbit. There is no more reason for rabbits to be kept intensively than any other livestock on the home producer's land, and they can be allowed to enjoy a good life before they are slaughtered.

Choose a strong, predator-proof hutch that is raised above the ground, ideally with a ramp to a run where they can exercise, which can be moved around fresh grass. The alternative is to have a separate run with a shelter included (still predator proof) for dry and warm days. Large rabbits need large hutches, and they must be able to take several hops, stand up, and stretch out. Do not overcrowd them.

Think about where you will site the hutches. They must be well ventilated but draft proof, and they must never be in direct, hot sunlight. Provide your rabbits with a bedding of straw (which they don't eat) or shavings.

Cleanliness is hugely important, and you will have to clean out your rabbits at least a couple of times a week, more if the bedding is soiled. Look out for maggots in the bedding when you take it out. Rabbits are much healthier if they inhabit a clean environment.

Feeding
Rabbits need access to fresh hay, which must not be moldy or dusty, fresh fruit and vegetables, and a well-balanced, dry rabbit mix fed in an earthenware bowl. Clean water, from a clip-on bottle, must always be available. An adult will eat 4–6 ounces of pellets or mix a day.

Rabbits have delicate stomachs, so watch out for loose droppings, which can prove fatal and stain wool-producing rabbits. Introduce new vegetables gradually—stop feeding any that cause diarrhea. Rutabaga (sliced), carrots, cabbage, and kale are particularly acceptable, and wild food, including grass, dandelions, deadnettles, comfrey, sow thistle, and trefoil, are all good. Make sure that you collect from a clean place.

Health
In some countries wild rabbits infect domestic rabbits with myxomatosis, which is thought to be due to insect carriers. Owners should look out for rabbits with swollen eyes, swollen genitals, and breathing problems. If you notice any of these signs you should seek veterinary attention as soon as possible. Keep domestic rabbits away from wild rabbits and be careful in selecting wild food. There is a vaccination, but it may not be appropriate for meat rabbits, although you might consider vaccinating breeding does and bucks. Consult your veterinarian.

Breeding
It might be cheaper and easier to buy young rabbits and raise them to meat weight, but if you want to breed your own, you will need a doe and a buck—take the doe to the buck's cage. The large meat breeds should not breed before they are eight months old. Watch them for aggression. Mating should take place immediately. If it does not, remove the doe and try a couple of days later. The gestation period of a rabbit is 31 days, so keep a careful record of mating.

You need to supply a nestbox for her three days before kindling (giving birth) with nesting materials of clean straw or shavings, but you can use shredded newspaper, too.

Keep other animals away from her before she gives birth. She will busy "making" the nest, including pulling fur from her belly. After kindling, gently look to see how many offspring are present, remove any dead, and kill deformed ones (see below). When you handle them (and if all is well leave for a few days), rub your hands over the mother first to get her scent. By the tenth day they will have enough fur to keep themselves warm and will open their eyes. The doe will need extra feed during and after pregnancy. You can wean at four weeks and the doe can be mated when her litter is seven to ten weeks of age. She can produce three to four litters a year. Taking a couple of young rabbits out daily until they are all gone will gradually reduce her milk supply.

Produce from your rabbits
As with any stock, you must learn how to kill humanely before you keep rabbits. It's normally done by a strong blow to the base of the head behind the ears, but you must make sure that you know how to do this correctly.

You will need to be able to skin a rabbit. Take off the feet at the first joint and remove the head below the skull at the first joint. From a point between the forelegs and the hind legs, slit the skin of the stomach and remove the innards, and then slit the skin from the opening in the stomach to the other side. Hold the back of the rabbit and pull the skin from the hind and then forelegs.

You can cure the skin for hats, gloves, sewn together as vests, or many other home uses.

BELOW Meat rabbits should be kept in a humane way with space to move around.

Keeping pigs

The obvious reason for keeping pigs is to provide pork and bacon for the family, but pigs can also help you clear rough ground if you harness their natural desire to root and dig, and they will also leave valuable fertilizer in the form of dung.

There has recently been a return to home pig keeping, facilitated perhaps by easier to obtain, ready-built pig housing and a more relaxed approach generally to "growing your own."

Most new pig keepers begin by buying and raising two weaners (newly weaned piglets) for home-produced pork. It is easy to make sausages from this meat and also to try your hand at curing bacon. It used to be said that "the only thing from a pig that cannot be used is its squeak," and today dishes that were once regarded as for poor people, such as pigs-feet, have come back into fashion.

Choosing a breed

If you are planning to raise weaners just for eating, you don't need to buy the best breeding-quality stock, although you still want something that is healthy and will grow on. A suitable cross-bred animal will do the job. However, if you keep a pure breed, even for eating, you will be helping to preserve these beautiful breeds for the future. If you later decide to go into breeding, it is important to buy the best pure-bred stock you can so that you establish a herd from which the finest-quality weaners will find a ready market for further breeding at a premium price.

All pigs like to root, but some do this more than others. Those with snub noses, such as the Middle White, tend to graze, and therefore do less damage than those with long snouts, such as the Tamworth. Lop-eared pigs (whose ears cover their eyes) are usually more docile than prick-eared breeds, and it's no coincidence that the well-known cottager breeds, such as the Oxford Sandy and Black and Gloucester Old Spot, are lop eared. If you have only limited space, select a relatively small breed, such as the Berkshire.

Visit agricultural shows to look at the range of breeds and talk to their owners and breeders.

RIGHT Choose a breed such as a Gloucester Old Spot that is suitable for outdoors foraging and make sure you have enough space to accommodate their behavior.

Berkshire

This black and white pig has attractive white feet and a white tip to its tail. Prick eared, it is reasonably small and placid. It is dark skinned, hardy, and well suited to living outdoors, but is more often used for pork than for bacon. Berkshires are good mothers with up to 12 piglets when fully mature. A mature pig will weigh 660–770 pounds.

Duroc

A modern breed, the Duroc is a mixture of the Red Duroc and the Jersey Red. It came into its own with the emergence of outdoor pigs at the end of the 20th century because it is hardy and resistant to sunburn. Heavily muscled, it is versatile enough to produce light pork and heavy hog production. The sows are good mothers with litters of 8–12 piglets.

Gloucester Old Spot

These hardy and thrifty pigs naturally grow a fatty carcass and do well in cold conditions. The breed was sometimes known as the "orchard pig" because they were often kept in apple orchards in Gloucestershire, England. Gentle and comparatively docile, this is a good breed for beginners. They make excellent mothers, producing an average of 9–10 piglets. A fully mature pig weighs about 770 pounds.

Kune Kune

The breed comes from New Zealand, but is not indigenous to that country. The name means "round and fat," which is a great description, to which could have been added "and hairy." It is usually kept as a delightful pet, but it is also good to eat, although it may have to be kept longer than other breeds to get a decent-size cut. Kune Kune pigs range from 24–30 inches high and weigh 140–220 pounds. Because of their small size they do not cut the land up as much as larger pigs. Females, which should not be mated until they are 12 months old, are good mothers, but the litters vary in size.

Large Black

Popular in the early 20th century, the breed fell out of favor with the rise in demand for white pigs. Hardy and sunburn resistant, these docile pigs love being outdoors. They are suitable for beginners. The sows produce 10 piglets from basic rations and are excellent mothers.

Large White

The breed originated from the Yorkshire pig, as does the American Yorkshire. Both are popular in indoor commercial farms, but they are suitable for small-scale keeping, although they do suffer from sunburn. They also get large. Sows normally have big litters of 12–14 piglets and are good mothers.

Oxford Sandy and Black

Also known as the Oxford Forest Pig. It is a natural browser and forager, but doesn't put on as much excess fat as some other breeds, making it easier for a beginner to "finish" correctly. It is docile and friendly and is a good mother, producing six to nine piglets.

Tamworth

The breed is thought to resemble the pig from the forests of ancient Britain. It produces a white-fleshed carcass with long sides and big hams, ideally suited for bacon. It is a lively pig and not for the beginner. Because of its enthusiasm for rooting and its hardy disposition—including being resistant to sunburn—it is often used for clearing ground. They make good mothers, but have small litters, between five and nine piglets. A mature pig weighs 550–770 pounds.

Where to buy

Buying from local breeders is best, although you may have to travel further if you are looking for specific breeding stock. Advertisements in small farming magazines are a useful starting point.

You must follow all the relevant rules and regulations covering identification, movement, and transportation before you take the pigs home.

Housing

Pigs are strong animals that dig, root, and generally push and shove, and they require robust housing. A purpose-built ark is ideal. It should be sturdy and made of strong, pressure-treated lumber. For ease of movement it should come with skids (ski-like structures) on the bottom or a loading bar on the top for lifting. They come with fixed floors, but it is best to have a removable floor that makes thorough cleaning easy and allows access in the case of an emergency.

Following are sample ark sizes for housing different numbers of pigs:

6 x 4 feet—2 Kune Kune pigs

8 x 6 feet—1 sow and litter; up to 2 dry sows; 6–8 porkers

8 x 8 feet—up to 4 dry sows; 10–15 porkers

8 x 10 feet—up to 6 dry sows; 15–20 porkers

8 x 14 feet—up to 8 dry sows; 20–25 porkers

Existing buildings, well-built stone barns or stables, may be adapted, but you must make sure there is a strong gate out onto a yard or fenced-off paddock so that the pig is not shut in and unable to see out. Whichever type of house you use, make sure it is well ventilated. Pigs like a wallow and will need shelter from hot sun.

Bedding is usually straw, and the more the better, except for newborn piglets, which can get buried. Plenty of clean, dry straw will allow the pigs to keep themselves clean. Wood shavings or shredded paper are also used but are not edible, so deny the pigs the pleasure of snuffling for tidbits, and they get very soggy quickly.

Fencing

The fencing must be strong enough to withstand a strong, digging pig. Loose pigs are difficult to catch and could be a real danger to those around them. Don't skimp on area and never keep more than six pigs to an acre. Even this will become "ploughed," especially in wet weather.

Make sure the gates are wide enough to fit a trailer and that they open in and outwards. Have a small gate for everyday access. Post-and-rail fencing with high-tensile pig netting or stock netting as a filler is the first choice, and you should use posts that are at least 8 inches in circumference. Electric fencing is excellent within the outer fence to strip graze and rotate the pigs. It also has a place inside the outer fence to stop them rooting or pushing on the fence.

If you are using pigs to clear ground, electric fencing will enable you to move the pigs around. Make sure the energizer is always working because your pigs will soon discover if it is not.

Spending time and money on getting the fencing right at the start will save much heartache and expense later on.

Feeding

Pigs have a reputation for living on waste products, but these days feeding kitchen waste is banned in many countries, and meat waste must never be fed. If you are offering vegetables, don't expect them to make up for proper pig food. Beginners should stick to compound food—a balanced ration that comes in a bag and varies according to the stage of life. Creep feed (tiny pellets with a high protein content) is for piglets from three weeks onward, but for raising weaners to the plate you should use select growers' food, which can be fed up to finishing.

Quantities vary according to breed and the amount of foraging, but as a guide you will be looking to feed 1–2 pounds for eight-week-old weaners up to 12 weeks, increasing by 8 ounces each month until the pigs are ready to go for slaughter. Most feeds also come in meal form, which must not be fed dry—pigs like wet feed—and you can add surplus goat's milk to a feed in a trough.

In the wild pigs eat little and often, so feed at least twice a day or have feeders that will dispense as the pigs need it while keeping feed fresh. The smaller Kune Kunes can do well on good grass alone and should not be overfed. Put smaller nuts in galvanized or rubber troughs, or scatter large nuts around so that the pigs can hunt

BELOW Electric fencing must be working at all times—check daily, as your pigs will soon discover if it is not!

for them. If a pig does not want its food, consult your veterinarian immediately.

Water must be available at all times. Because pigs will knock over buckets and play with them, use a rubber bucket on a clip or a bucket wedged into a car tire. Ultimately, however, you should provide nipple drinkers or automatic drinkers. Make sure the water is always clean.

Handling

Get to know your pigs and always handle them quietly. They enjoy being scratched, and you can teach them to follow a feed bucket.

The secret of moving pigs lies in preparation, and you will need a pig board, a stick, and a bucket of food. Ideally, plan a fenced walkway (even if it is just a temporary structure) to your destination, such as up into a trailer. Pigs are big, strong animals and they can be dangerous; they can have a savage bite when they feel threatened. Don't allow children or domestic pets to go in with them. Be especially careful if you are breeding pigs or have to get close to a sow with piglets. Make sure you experience handling live pigs before you take up keeping them.

Health

When they are kept correctly, pigs are hardy and healthy, but they do suffer from heatstroke, which can be prevented if you provide a wallow in hot weather and somewhere for them to shelter. Don't spray affected animals with cold water; instead, cool them down by sponging and dabbing vinegar behind their ears. Sunburn is a problem for young pigs and pale-skinned breeds.

All pigs need worming at eight weeks and about every six months afterward; follow the instructions on the package and note the withdrawal time for meat animals. Scouring has several causes, from bad hygiene to overeating or worms. Consult your vet, because the pig may dehydrate and die if it goes on for too long.

External parasites such as lice need to be controlled with an antiparasitic wash. Mites can be a problem, and your vet may recommend an injection to kill the pests. Pigs can also get colds and pneumonia, which will need antibiotics.

They are also susceptible to poisons because they will eat anything, even plants that will do them harm, including rhododendron, laburnum, ragwort (*Senecio jacobaea*), and deadly nightshade (*Solanum dulcamara*). Prevention is better than cure, and it is time to call the vet when your pigs are not behaving in their usual manner—lack of appetite or appearing dull, for example.

Produce from your pigs

Getting your pig to the right weight is a skill, and a weigh tape might help you to keep track. When you decide at which stage you are going to kill the pig—porker, cutter, or baconer—make sure you have identified a local abattoir. Make arrangements well ahead of time and check what paperwork is required and any other regulations. Remember that the pig does not know it is going for slaughter, so behave as you would on any other day, handling the pig quietly and kindly throughout the journey and offloading.

Most abattoirs have a butcher who will cut the meat to your requirements, so make sure you know what you want. If planning to butcher the pig yourself, you will need a large, clean area, and if you are selling any of the pig, you may need to register with your local authority. Attend one of the butchery courses that are organized now, and it's a good idea to get some practical experience before you attempt to deal with your own pig's carcass.

Meat categories

These stages of production are not set in stone, although most owners send off their pigs at the porker stage and often ask the butcher for bacon and sausages, as well as the more usual joints.

- **Suckling pig** Usually a young pig still on the sow, weighing around 33 pounds; popular with the restaurant trade.

- **Weaner** A newly weaned pig, usually 8–10 weeks old and weighing around 45 pounds; often sold to small-scale farmers who wish to fatten the pig themselves or sent on to finishing units to fatten for the commercial trade.

- **Porker** A pig 5–6 months old and weighing approximately 120 pounds.

- **Cutter** Kept for longer than a pork pig, usually up to about 9 months, and weighing around 145 pounds.

- **Baconer** A pig grown on specifically for bacon; it tends to be 9–12 months old and weighs around 175 pounds.

- **Sausage pig** Pigs used specifically for sausages tend to be older sows or pigs that are no longer required; finding an abattoir to take such a large animal can be difficult.

Keeping goats

You can keep goats for their milk and dairy products, for their meat, and for their fiber. They are, therefore, good-value animals for self-supporters and small-scale farmers, and they are also sociable creatures that are fun to keep.

Buying

You should buy goats direct from a breeder, who will be able to show you records of milk or fiber production and will have a full veterinary history, including worming and vaccination. Joining your local goat club will be helpful, not only in buying stock but in sharing knowledge. Most countries have identification and movement regulations, and these must be up to date before you move goats from one place to another.

There is no need to keep an entire male for a small number of goats, as they are extremely smelly and have some other dubious habits. It's better to take your goat to a male for mating or rely on artificial insemination.

Choosing a goat

There are specialized breeds for dairy, meat,` and fiber, but a dairy goat can be crossed with a meat-producing goat to produce kids for meat or with a fiber goat for kids with a useful fleece.

Dairy breeds

These goats, which can produce large quantities of milk for their size, were an important feature of British life before and during the Second World War. Essential to the war effort, they were easier and cheaper to keep than dairy cows and their milk was unrationed. However, a really high-yielding dairy goat may produce too much milk for your family, and it will eat more food than a more modestly producing breed.

If you decide on a dairy goat, get an older animal that is used to being milked—one of you needs to know what you are doing. They are herd animals, so you should keep at least two, and it's best to buy animals that are used to being together. Unless you want a lot of milk, you could

have one pregnant animal or a younger goat that is not yet in milk and then dry off the older goat when the younger one is in milk.

See page 174 for how to milk a goat, in the same way as you would milk a cow.

One of the most popular breeds is the **Saanen**, which gives around 4 quarts of milk a day, a large amount in proportion to the animal's size. These white goats are placid and have a long lactation, even in winter. They require good nutrition to produce this quantity of milk, and you will need to watch out for mastitis and other udder problems.

The smaller **Toggenburg** has a long lactation and produces similar quantities of milk to the Saanen. These goats may or may not have tassels —fleshy, hair-covered protuberances—from their necks, and they are cheekier than the Saanens.

The **British Alpine** (not always available in the US) is also a heavy milker, but these goats are more active than other breeds.

Anglo Nubian goats have distinctive floppy ears and are the breed of choice in arid areas. They cope well with the dry desert, also milking well and provide a decent-size carcass for meat. The milk contains a high proportion of butterfat.

The **Golden Guernsey** has a more compact frame and does not yield so highly, which makes the breed suitable for a small family that doesn't want to make huge quantities of dairy produce. They are an ideal goat for a cottage garden and are a delightful golden color.

Meat breeds

As their name suggests, **Boer** goats originated in South Africa. They are solid-looking animals, and they produce a comparatively large quantity of lean meat.

Fiber breed

The **Angora** goat has a lustrous coat of curls and was developed in New Zealand, Tasmania, and Canada. The tighter the curls, the better quality the fiber. There is a market for the fleece, but the best outlet is probably for home spinning and knitting, with the money being in the finished garment. They need to be clipped twice a year. The Angora also produces a reasonable carcass for eating, but because they are not kept for milk, the males can be castrated and still produce fiber.

Pet goats

The small, compact **Pygmy** goat, originally from Africa, is usually kept as a pet. They are lively, intelligent, and amusing animals—and are great escapers. Their size makes milking difficult, although some keepers do succeed. They need the same care as any other goat, and all the same regulations will apply.

Housing

Goats need protection from rain and sun, so you must provide at the least a rudimentary shelter. Ideally, they need a dry, draft-free but well-ventilated house. You could adapt a stable or other outside building or use a well-built shed.

Horns or not

Angora goats have quite impressive horns, which are not normally removed. Dairy goats, however, are routinely disbudded as kids, usually by a vet. This is because of the damage a horned goat can do to another goat's udder.

Some people disagree with this procedure, but whatever your decision you should never keep horned and unhorned goats together. Horned goats do get tangled up more readily in fencing, especially electric netting.

Pens need to be at least 5 x 6 feet for a single milker or two kids. You can partition an area from a store—take great care that the goats cannot get at the feed—and you also need an area for the milking stand, which must have room for a bucket and be well lit. Goats prefer to be able to look out of the building. Make sure the house is erected on concrete and that there is concrete round the entrance.

Provide fresh straw for bedding and clean the house regularly. The waste can be composted for use in the garden.

Any fencing must be strong enough for a goat to stand on it, close enough together so that the goat cannot get through it and high enough to

BELOW Good fencing is the key to successful goat keeping, as they are born escapers. These dairy goats are well protected in their paddock.

Tethering

Regard tethering as a last resort. If you do tether a goat, provide a swivel collar and chain, and check from time to time to make sure the goat is not hanging itself. Move your goats regularly and make sure they have access to water at all times.

You must also provide shelter for goats in bad weather.

stop the goat jumping over it. It also needs to be safe—the last thing you want is for your high milker to rip one of her udders—so never use barbed wire. Goats are determined escapers, but a couple of strands of electric fencing in front of the fence will usually keep even the most determined goat from the fence. Be careful with sheep netting, either plain or electrified, because a goat might get its horns or even its head stuck. A thick hedge is ideal, although goats will get through really quite small gaps, and they can also browse it, keeping it well trimmed.

How much space?

Zero-grazing is a system of keeping goats, popular in the late 20th century, when all food, including branches, is brought to confined animals. But goats are natural browsers rather than grazers, and they are intelligent, lively creatures, that should have access to a paddock space, ideally offering a combination of grazing and browsing (feeding on woody fibers, such as leaves and branches). If you keep them in a paddock, they really like a platform to jump on.

Feeding

It's not true that goats can eat anything and everything, and to keep them healthy you must supply the correct diet. They need a good supply of fibrous food, such as hay, but they also like lucerne (alfalfa), haylage (see page 35), and, if you can find it, clean pea straw. Depending on their enclosure, they may get some nutrition from browsing or grazing, or from branches cut for them. Beware of poisonous plants, in particular laburnum, yew (*Taxus*), and rhododendron.

A high-yielding dairy goat needs a well-balanced ration. You can grow lucerne, comfrey, and kale and it is worth establishing a hedgerow simply to supply branches for the goats. Choose species that are of particular liking or value to them, such as willow (*Salix*), hawthorn (*Crataegus*), and birch (*Betula*). You can also cut nettles and dry them to feed to goats. To supply other nutrients, choose a bagged dairy goat mix, and if you cannot get good-quality forage or are not using haylage or lucerne, you will have to offer more of this. Provide a mineral block, making sure that it is suitable for goats.

Fiber goats need a balanced diet but can get more of this from quality grazing.

The best hayracks are those with a lid and that are too high for goats to get in or on them. Goats climb when they can, so don't use haynets, because their feet and horns will get caught.

Water

It is highly important to have clean water available all day to a dairy animal. They have to take in water in order to produce milk. Fix buckets that cannot be knocked over.

Healthy goats

Hoof trimming is essential. You will need to check the hooves every two months, and after a practical session with an experienced goat keeper you will be able to do this yourself.

Goats are susceptible to a number of fatal diseases, including enterotoxemia, tetanus, and clostridial diseases, but all are preventable by vaccination. Seek advice from your veterinarian. Routine worm control is also necessary, especially if your goats are kept on a small acreage or with sheep. Using clean pasture can help keep down infestations, the method in organic systems, although it is not usually practicable on small plots. Lice are more attracted to goats than to other livestock, so keep a lookout for these and treat immediately if found. Take care in areas where ticks are a problem, and always look out for blowfly strike (maggots form in soiled fleece, which is more likely in longer-fleeced fiber goats). These will be fatal unless caught early.

Although it's not strictly necessary, it is a good idea to groom your goat from time to time and thoroughly check her all over.

Goats do not bear pain well and immediate veterinary attention should be sought for any sick, off-color, or off-food animal. Good nursing, tempting food, warmth, and painkillers will all be necessary for a full recovery. Beginners

particularly should not hesitate to seek veterinary advice at an early stage; experience comes with years of goat keeping.

Breeding

There is perhaps no young animal quite as pretty as a lively kid, and you will get hours of pleasure watching them play. Unlike other dairy animals, a goat can "run through"—that is, she can milk for at least two seasons without kidding—so you need to mate her only every other year.

Females come into heat every three weeks from late summer until early spring. She should be at least 18 months old. If you want a younger goat to mate, you must offer plenty of nutritious food so that she can grow and produce young, but it's best not to risk stunting her growth and milking career. Signs of heat are that the vulva will redden and appear swollen, and she will wag her tail and bleat more frequently. A "billy rag" (a rag rubbed around a male goat and hung in her pen) will encourage her to show more strongly.

Mating will take less time than it takes you to write the check to the male goat's owner. Write the dates down and look carefully in three weeks time for signs of heat—this is when a billy rag is helpful. If she is in milk, dry her off six weeks before kidding—that is, stop milking gradually by maybe only milking once a day and then infrequently before stopping. Take care not to cause mastitis.

Gestation is 150 days, but a week either side is not unusual. If all is well at kidding it will go quickly and the presentation should be front legs and head. If kidding is delayed or you notice any other presentation, call your veterinarian immediately to avoid losing her and the kids. If you can, go on a lambing course before your goat kids so that you know what to expect.

Looking after kids

Make sure the kids take the colostrum (the first thick, yellow milk, which is full of nutrition and antibodies). An older goat may have large, swollen teats from being milked, and the kids will have trouble feeding, so milk a little out and bottle feed it to them. Check a couple of times a day that they are feeding—never assume that if the goat has milk the kids are getting it.

You will have to decide whether to remove the kids after a few days so that you can have all the milk from the goat, rearing them with a milk replacer or some of her milk, or whether to leave them and milk her but not have so much milk or leave them and not start proper milking until they are weaned, which will be at about three months. Choose what is the easiest course of action for you in terms of time and need.

Male kids should be castrated. They are destined for the freezer, so don't sell them as pets or they may end up neglected. Ask your vet to disbud female kids at around five days; if you leave it any longer it becomes a bigger procedure.

Your goat will be hungry in the weeks after giving birth, so be sure to provide plenty of nutritious fiber and a balanced mix.

Keeping sheep

In recent years the practice of keeping a small flock of sheep has grown in popularity, and self-supporters often keep a few sheep to provide meat for the freezer and fleeces for spinning. Sheep milking has also enjoyed an increasing following.

There is no doubt that sheep do need good, clean (ungrazed) grass in plentiful supply and do not do well if confined in a small space and fed forage.

Don't exceed the number of sheep that your acreage can support, which will only be from as low as two to six to an acre if they are going to stay on the land all year round.

Choosing a breed

In general, sheep can be divided into four categories: the long-wooled breeds, which were once prized for their fleeces but now largely feature in the rare breed category; the short-wooled breeds, commercially successful because they are more "meaty"; the mountain breeds, adapted to living on rough grazing; and the primitive breeds, which are small and active. There are also breeds that have been developed for dairying.

Long-wooled breeds

This group includes the **Wensleydale**, which is a large sheep that produces a fleece of outstanding quality and quantity. Because of its size, it is not considered ideal for beginners. The **Border Leicester** is another large sheep, white in color, that produces a heavy, good-grade fleece, as does the **Teeswater**. The **Dartmoor** is a grassland ewe that produces a long, curly, lustrous wool of good quality. The **Lincoln Longwool** is the largest of all, with the heaviest, longest-stapled, and most lustrous fleece, ideal for hand spinners. The **Merino** is an economically influential breed that is prized around the world for its wool. Merinos are regarded as having the finest and softest wool of any sheep.

All long-wools produce a slow-maturing, large, lean carcass, but the emphasis has been on

their wool, leaving more meaty breeds to take over as the demand for wool has decreased.

Short-wooled breeds

This category includes most of the lowland or downland breeds. They tend to be smaller and stockier, with good-size limbs for producing family-size joints. They include the black-faced **Oxford Down**, the **Hampshire Down**, the **Dorset Down** (also useful as a dairying breed), and the **South Down** (of which there is a miniature variety), which look like teddy bears with a leg at each corner. The South Down and Oxford Down are renowned for their placid natures. The placid **Suffolk** grows to a large, commercially meaty carcass, known for early maturity, but it may require more supervision when lambing.

All lowland breeds need good-quality grass in order to produce meaty carcasses.

Upland and mountain breeds

The **Welsh Mountain** is able to live in testing conditions, as is the **Shetland**. Both breeds are small and, although lively, are lighter to handle. The fleeces are good for hand spinners and the Shetland comes in a number of colors. The **Badger Welsh Mountain** comes in white and black. The **Exmoor Horn** is a hardy, white-wooled breed, a good producer on lower ground. The fleece of the **Herdwick** produces a good carcass of dark, fine-grained meat from low-value grazing. The latter three are more common to Europe than the US.

Primitive breeds

Keepers of these sheep claim a well-flavored meat, but the carcass will be small and take time to mature. They are remarkably hardy, difficult to domesticate and tame, and the fleeces can be rather sparse, although they are valued by home spinners. They are nearly always horned, and the some breeds can grow up to six horns. Difficult to categorize but also able to be multihorned, the distinctive black and white **Jacob** is kept for its lovely colored wool, which produces fine colored garments, its longevity, its lean but slightly gamey meat, and its striking looks.

Other specialized breeds

The **Wiltshire Horn** is a large, placid, white-faced breed that produces good carcasses. It loses its wool without shearing, saving on costs if the wool isn't required. The **British Milksheep** and the **Friesland** have been developed for milk production and can produce more than twice that of other breeds. The Friesland produces milk with a high butterfat content for up to 10 months of the year. The **Dorset Down** can produce three lamb crops in two years if well managed and fed and is sometimes used as a dairy animal.

Commercial sheep

If a hardy hill ewe is crossed with a long-wooled ram she will produce a half-breed ewe. These are then crossed with what is called a terminal sire, a breed that stamps fast growth of a meaty carcass on the stock to produce meat lambs for the market. If you are selecting purely for the freezer, consider a commercial breed. Perhaps the best known of these are the Mule cross-breeds, which are formed from various crosses. The **Scottish Mule**, for example, is the progeny of the Blackfaced ewe and the Bluefaced Leicester ram.

Rearing a couple of orphan lambs from a commercial farmer is not only a good way of producing meat for the freezer if you have sufficient time to spare but is also an excellent way to prepare for breeding your own sheep.

How much space?

Sheep need to be able to graze and will quickly use up a small area. How many you are able to keep on your land will depend entirely on the quality of your grass and the amount of management you are prepared to do, including using fertilizer. You can increase the amount of grass by moving your sheep to other grazing by using electric fencing or by moving on to root tops, if available.

At first, at least, it's best to have no more sheep than your own land can support. If horses or other animals are sharing the grazing, this will reduce the number of sheep still further. It is possible to overwinter sheep indoors if you have a large, airy building or covered yard. Although lambing outside is fine in good weather, it is much more practical to bring them indoors for lambing, especially in bad weather or early spring days when the day is short, so you can observe them. The key to successful lambing is good observation 24 hours a day. .

Fencing

You must use sheep netting—wire that is divided into small squares so that nothing can get through it—inside a post-and-rail fence or electric fencing. A sheep in full fleece simply doesn't feel electric fencing and can walk through it. If the charge gets low or stops, the sheep will soon be out. They don't have any respect for the fence as horses do. Be careful if electric fencing is the only fence onto a road, although it's ideal to use in conjunction with an outer fence.

Both wire and electric fencing come in the form of sheep netting, and horned sheep can get their heads and horns stuck in it. The three-reel system was developed in Australia to get around this because running three strands of electrified wire close together is safer.

If you are using railings or wire, they must be low enough to prevent the sheep from squeezing under, high enough to stop them climbing over (electric can be lower), and close enough together to prevent them from pushing through. A good,

BELOW Sheep require clean grass in plentiful supply, which is why so many breeds have developed to live well on grasslands and extensive pastures.

Tip

A good shepherd is one who constantly observes the health, condition, and behavior of the flock and increases feed as and when necessary.

Lambs are weaned at about three months and then finished to slaughter weight, ideally on good grass, but extra feed will be needed in most cases in the form of a finishing pellet or grain with a mineral lick. A ewe needs little feed immediately after weaning, so her milk dries more quickly, but then she will need feeding up and "flushing" (extra feed) just before she is put to the ram.

The better quality your grass, the less feed you will need, but it's false economy and bad animal welfare to deny sheep extra feed.

Water

Water is essential and must be available at all times. They also require a mineral lick (some sheep licks are dangerous to other stock).

Sheep systems

There are other methods of sheep keeping, other than rearing weaned lambs, that are more economical but require more knowledge.

Orphan lambs

If you have limited space or don't want to overwinter them, orphan lambs are a good introduction. It's handy to have them close to the house if you are bottle feeding, but there are mechanical feeders that will save time. Simple sheep hurdles could contain a couple of lambs as you move them around the farm, or you could use electric fencing to keep them under control.

Get the lambs from a local farmer. Make sure they have had the colostrum and are old enough to suckle and have been taking bottles. Make sure, too, that they are tagged.

At first you will have them penned, but the aim is to get them out on good grass as soon as possible, at least during the day. Check with your vet for vaccination and worming advice.

The lambs will be tame, which might make it hard for you to slaughter them, so be prepared for this. Keep their housing clean, and add their bedding to your compost heap.

Breeding ewes

Buy older ewes that have already had at least one set of lambs. Sheep can live for 20 years, but commercial sheep are often slaughtered at six to seven years. You don't need a ram for a few sheep. Instead, take them to a local owner or borrow a ram. Don't let the ram into the ewes until you

thick hedge is ideal and provides shelter, but because it is edible gaps will soon appear.

Shelter

Sheep do need shelter from hot weather in the form of trees or a shelter—straw bales tightly bound together will be sufficient. In theory they should survive cold weather, but they get miserable when wet through—in the wild they would shelter in hollows and hedges—so provide something for winter, too if they are not housed.

Feeding

In early pregnancy the number of lambs a ewe will have is not only determined genetically but by the amount of food available. If there are three embryos and food is scarce, two (or even all three) will die. In late pregnancy the ewe needs a balanced compound to supplement her plus a high-energy lick. The more commercial breeds of sheep and the more lambs that are expected, the higher the feeding requirement will be.

have thought about when you want to lamb. It's best to lamb in mid- to late spring when the grass is coming through, so early winter would be the time to ram. Make sure you have a vet to advise you. Pen ewe and lamb(s) together—the rough guide is one day for one lamb, two days for two and so on.

Health

The great demands placed on them in multi-lambing make them susceptible to a number of metabolic diseases caused by unbalanced or poor feeding. They also suffer from parasites, such as tick or blowfly (maggots), which can easily be controlled by preventative treatment. If you don't do this you must "crotching" (remove the hair round the bottom) and watch them for signs of problems. Maggots are usually fatal once they get a hold.

Vaccinations are necessary for the clostridial diseases and fatal illnesses. Worming can be a problem if the animals are staying on the same pasture. Foot care is essential, and if one of your sheep is lame, seek advice from your veterinarian.

Shearing

For their own health sheep must be sheared in early summer. It's not a good idea to shear in late pregnancy, though they will need "crutching out" (see left). Speak to your local small farm society or sheep farmer for information about shearers, but if you are planning to do it yourself, go on a course. It's extremely hard work. Treat any cuts with an antiseptic spray.

The shepherd's year

Throughout the year the flock will need to be vaccinated, so check with your vet for optimum times—for example, the protection given to a ewe will be passed to her newborn lambs, but lambs will need their own protection after two or three months. Check in your local area what is needed. Combine with another management procedure, such as shearing or foot trimming.

Autumn

- Feed ewes extra pre-ramming
- Check their feet are in good condition
- Make sure they have been wormed

Late autumn

- Put ram in with ewes, bearing in mind that they will lamb about five months later
- Fit harness to ram with marker on brisket so that it will mark the ewe when she is covered; change the color every month

Winter

- Remove ram when all ewes have stopped returning to the ram; if they have only one mark, they should be in-lamb

- Supplement pregnant ewes and make sure all sheep have sufficient forage if grass is not available
- Bring ewes inside if necessary, but make sure the quarters are well ventilated and that each ewe has trough space

Spring

- Before lambing, build lambing pens or have materials available (sheep hurdles)
- "Crotching" sheep
- Ideally, put ewes in pens to lamb or immediately afterwards to allow her to bond with her lambs; mark the ewe and lamb so that you know which lambs belong to which ewe
- Turn ewes and lambs out as soon as possible into a sheltered, grassy paddock where you can keep an eye on them

- Before turning out, check and trim her feet
- Rear orphan lambs on the bottle

Early summer

- Shear sheep and treat with a pour-on to prevent blowfly or parasites
- Continue to monitor condition of ewes and lambs, and provide forage or supplementary feeding if necessary or if a dry summer reduces grass

Mid- to late summer

- At 12–16 weeks remove lambs to wean them
- Temporarily remove ewes to poorer pasture until the milk has dried off, then put them onto grazing to improve their condition
- Finish autumn lambs to reach slaughter weight

Keeping cows

Small-scale farmers and self-supporters will want to keep cows for both meat and their dairy produce, and it is possible to keep a single cow and calf for dairying or a few young cows that you feed up for their meat.

Cattle have a comparatively low requirement for labor and are not too technically demanding, but they can bring their keepers a great deal of pleasure and enjoyment.

Cattle are good for utilizing grassland, but they need a large area and high capital investment for the financial return. They are herd animals and are really suited only for small farms with 8–10 acres or more of grassland, where maximizing income is not an issue.

There are several ways of keeping cattle, and each has different requirements for the amount of grazing and housing. However, all cattle need plenty of good grazing, a strong building, and an integrated handling system.

Breeders have developed cattle that are specifically designed to produce either milk or beef but that are unsuited to produce both. Self-supporters who want milk should, therefore, seek out one of the traditional, dual-purpose breeds, the calves of which will fatten to produce excellent beef, while the mother can be milked.

Most people should find it possible to milk a cow once a day, while the calf sucks for the rest of the 24 hours, but some cows object to this and resent being milked when they have a calf to feed. A bucket-fed calf will not grow as quickly as one that sucks his mother whenever he needs, even when that bucket contains his mother's milk. It's a good compromise if both the household and the calf can share the milk, especially as there is usually too much for one family to use.

Selecting a breed

A dual-purpose breed that was indigenous to your area a century ago would be ideal for a self-supporter, providing both dairy produce and meat. Look for breeds that are used to being kept in your local climatic conditions—for example, the Ayrshire and Aberdeen Angus, which originated in Scotland, are hardier than the Jersey and Guernsey, which came from a much warmer climate. Remember, too, that the more traditional breeds tend to be both smaller and more docile.

Dairy breeds

Popular breeds include traditional breeds that are unsuited to beef production. That's not to say you can't eat the offspring, but the meat to bone ratio will be low, and they will cost money to fatten for what is achieved in terms of meat. The hardy **Ayrshire**, a horned breed from southwest Scotland, calves easily and is suitable for difficult terrain. The **Jersey** is an attractive, high-producing dairy breed with a high butterfat content in its creamy milk. The short-horned breed is usually de-horned, although there is a **Polled Jersey** in the USA. Also from the Channel Islands, the **Guernsey** is another dairy cow, but it is, sadly, fast declining in numbers.

Dual-purpose breeds

The **Shorthorn** is a milky, hardy breed that was historically hugely important to the dairy industry. A real success story, the **Dexter** is an Irish breed. It is compact, often only waist high, and a favorite family cow. In years gone by it was also used as a draft animal.

The **Red Poll** does not have horns and is a motherly breed. The red coat is particularly resistant to the sun.

Beef breeds

Among the traditional beef animals that are less suited to milk production is the **Hereford**. The distinctive white face is stamped by bulls on all breeds of cows, but the true Hereford originated from the borders of England and Wales and is famous for its outstanding beef. The cows' motherliness makes them ideal suckler cows.

The renowned **Aberdeen Angus** from Scotland produces early-maturing, prime marbled beef, and it passes on the polling (non-horned) gene to its cross-bred offspring.

Housing

Although cows spend most of their time on grassland, you will have to provide a shelter for the worst of the weather, and it's important to be able to move them to a dry, well-ventilated barn in winter. You will also need an area for milking.

You will have to erect strong fences, up to 6 feet high depending on the breed, with up to six strands of electrified wire.

Keeping cattle for milk

Before you become involved with dairying, whether it be with cows, goats, or sheep, think seriously about the commitment. The milking must be done every day, usually twice a day, preferably at 12-hour intervals. If you are the only person available, you can never be more than a few hours' journey from the cattle, and unless you can make alternative arrangements, you will have no vacations, no weekends off, and no long trips anywhere. You won't even be able to be ill. If your partner is the relief milker, you will have a little more freedom—but never together. The number of helpers who might be prepared to do the milking will be limited.

If you have only one cow you will probably milk by hand although small milking machines, suitable for a single cow, are available. The machines must be kept scrupulously clean.

Having a "house cow" sounds such a lovely concept, but most of the above comments apply to one cow as much as to ten, except that cows do have a "dry" period, when they have no milk, when you could have a vacation.

A cow's milk production cycle is designed around the demands of her calf. It is quite low when a calf is born but increases for 8–10 weeks to keep pace with the demands of a growing calf, after which time it decreases as the calf begins to live off grass. Milk will reduce to a trickle at 9–10 months, when she can stop producing and have a rest until the next calf arrives.

A house cow will require an acre of grass to graze in summer and 1 ton of hay to eat in winter, plus forage (see page 175).

Remember that you have to get her in calf again, because without a calf there will be no milk. Gestation take nine months, so it is best to get her in calf again when the first calf is three months old. She will come into season at three-weekly intervals and will need to run with a bull for a period covering at least one, preferably two cycles. Artificial insemination (AI) is difficult to get right with suckler cows.

It is strongly recommended that you buy an experienced milker so that one of you knows what to do. Do not buy an unhandled maiden cow and expect to be able to milk straight away.

Keeping cattle for beef

There are four possible ways of raising cattle to produce beef.

Calves from the house cow

The calf would be milk fed for the first 10–12 weeks, but after this you should gradually introduce a grass/hay and concentrate diet, at considerable cost, until the animal is ready for the butcher at about 30 months.

If you assume a six-month winter and one cow having a calf each year, with the calves leaving for the butcher at 30 months of age, you will require 1.8 acres of grassland for grazing, about 2 tons of purchased hay, and 1 ton of concentrates

BELOW Choose a breed suitable for your situation— an Ayrshire thrives well, is hardy and a comparatively easy calver.

How to milk by hand

The process is the same whether you are milking a cow, a goat, or a sheep. Sit on the right side of the animal and milk the nearest two udders (one in each hand).

1 Clean the udder with a medicated wet wipe.

2 Swirl the first few drops of milk in a dark-colored container to check for signs of mastitis.

3 Squeeze high up the teat with the thumb and forefinger to stop the milk from going back up into the udder.

4 Then bring in your third and little fingers, squeezing progressively downward to expel the milk. Repeat the process using a rhythmic motion.

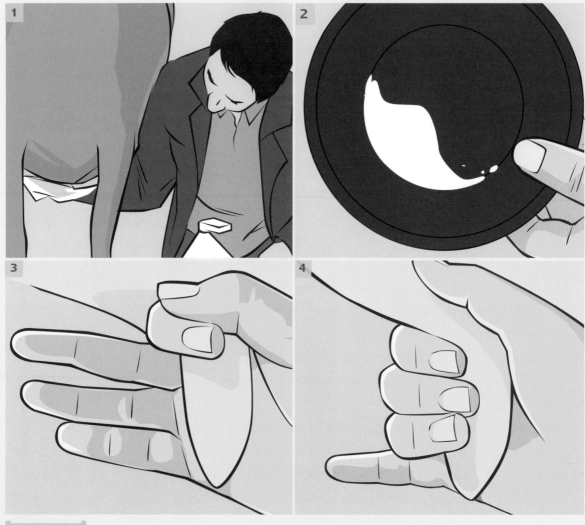

to provide winter feed for the cow and her calf. You might want to house the growing cattle over the winter, in which case you will also need a large, airy building where they can move around easily.

Suckler herd

A suckler herd is just several house cows as above but with no milking. The calves will grow much more quickly, having had all their mother's milk to themselves, and you can achieve quite good profits when the meat is sold. A rare breed, which will fatten with little cereal, can produce beef with a "name," which will sell to discerning customers at a healthy profit. The downside is the long wait and the capital you will have invested in the animal before it finally goes off to the butcher. You will also have to think about a building, as mentioned above, for overwintering.

Buy calves and fatten them

Buying good calves can be difficult for newcomers to keeping cattle because you have to be able to recognize quickly, at the time of the

sale, which of the available calves will thrive and which will never get fit for slaughter.

Starting with the right calf is critical to having an animal that will produce lots of meat, but a poor calf will cost a fortune in vets' fees and never ever make beef you can be proud of. If you want to do this, find a knowledgeable friend who will

ABOVE Cleanliness is extremely important when milking: udders must be wiped, sterilized utensils used, and hands well washed.

How much land will you need?

Use the chart below, which gives the weight of forage for each category of cattle plus the amount of land needed to produce it. If you have less land than this, you will need to buy in the forage. Bagged feed and bedding is also shown—bought in from outside.

Category of cattle	Silage fed	Hay fed
Suckler cow **(producing milk for a calf)**		
Summer grazing (6 months)	0.85 acre	0.85 acre
Winter forage (6 months)	3.0 tons silage	0.75 tons hay
Concentrate feed (winter)	220 pounds	330 pounds
Bedding (winter)	1.0 ton straw	0.8 tonn straw
Calf, 0–12 months **(spring born, hand reared)**		
Milk substitute	30 pounds	30 pounds
Weaner ration	240 pounds	240 pounds
Rearer ration	630 pounds	630 pounds
Summer grazing (3 months)	0.1 acre	0.1 acre
Concentrate feed (winter)	440 pounds	660 pounds

Category of cattle	Silage fed	Hay fed
Winter forage (first winter)	2.0 tons silage	0.5 tons hay
Bedding (suckling and winter)	0.7 tons straw	0.5 tons straw
Yearling, 12–24 months		
Summer grazing (6 months)	0.85 acre	0.85 acre
Winter forage (6 months)	3.0 tons silage	0.75 tons hay
Concentrate feed (winter)	660 pounds	880 pounds
Bedding (winter)	0.75 tons straw	0.6 tons straw
Finishing a spring-born beef animal, 25–30 months		
Summer grazing (6 months)	1.2 acres	1.2 acres
Concentrate feed (summer)	110 pounds	110 pounds

go with you when you purchase the calves to help you select the good ones.

Feeding young calves can be difficult. The milk or milk substitute has to be just the right temperature and fed in the right quantities and at the right time. If it is not, the animal will scour (have diarrhea).

The calves will need a warm, well-ventilated, draft-free building. Provide clean straw for bedding and keep the floor dry and clean.

Buy two-year-old stores in spring

This method of beef production is the least demanding of stockmanship skills. All you have to do is buy the right animals and at the right price and then market them profitably. It's a good way to gain some experience of cattle without committing yourself too deeply to begin with.

Each animal will require about 0.6 acres of good grazing. They will consume 0.5 tons of silage and 110 pounds of concentrate each month in winter.

When you try to buy these animals you will find that almost every farmer in the land will be competing with you for good animals to graze their grass in spring, and they will all be more experienced than you, so get some help, or you will end up with the unwanted leftovers, which will never make money.

As a small-scale farmer, however, you will have an advantage when it comes to marketing because you will be able to retail the meat direct to your customers, making a good profit. Farmers have so many animals that they have to sell them into the wholesale market, for which they receive a much- reduced income.

Feeding

Cattle require grass as a major part of their diet. When no fresh grass is available, they enjoy silage, haylage, or hay and will eat small amounts of straw to help their digestion. Although they can survive on grass and hay or silage alone, they are unlikely to thrive and "finish" to meat weight unless they are given additional feed in the form of concentrates. It is possible, but requires skill and experience, to produce exceptional forage in the form of clover-rich grazing and silage.

The feed must be clean and dust free. Clear away old feed, and never allow your cows to eat anything that is moldy or musty.

Fresh, clean water must be available at all times, and a full-grown cow will need about 35 gallons every day.

RIGHT Cattles are ruminants and require forage as a major part of their diet in the form of grass, hay, silage or haylage.

Managing calving

Managing calving requires care. It's important for the cow and calf's health, but difficult calvings can also be expensive in terms of your vet's bills but also because cows might not breed afterward and the calves might be slow to "get going."

The most important factor is to make sure that the cows are given the correct feed in the two to three months before calving. You must monitor their condition and, if necessary, ration the feed to prevent them from getting fat in the later stages of pregnancy. If their diet is too rich, they will lay down fat in the pelvic aperture, restricting the birth canal. The same good diet will also lead to a big calf, which, given adequate nutrition, will dramatically increase in body weight during the last few weeks of pregnancy.

Over-generous rations in the latter stage of pregnancy can, therefore, be disastrous for both the cow and her offspring, when a large calf has to pass through a passage restricted by fat.

The breed of bull will also, of course, affect the size of the calf, and beef breeds with double-muscled hindquarters, such as Charolais and Simmental, tend to produce big calves.

Immediately before calving, keep the cow calm and in a place where she has plenty of space, feels at ease, and is on a nonslip surface.

A grass field is as good as anywhere because the surface is naturally nonslip and has been disinfected by the weather.

Never transport an animal that is due to calve within two weeks.

Pests and diseases

Good grassland is the key to healthy animals, and you must learn to keep the grass growing well and to be able to move your cattle to fresh grazing when it is necessary.

Seek your vet's advice about vaccinations and deworming schedules, which will vary according to breed. One of the unfortunate side effects of keeping cows is that they attract flies. You can get ear tags that contain an insecticide, and there are also pour-ons and sprays that you can use. Again, your vet will advise you on suitable treatments.

Get into the habit of checking your cows' hooves regularly. They will need trimming every two or three months, and you can learn to do this yourself or have a professional visit your small farm to do it for you. Foot rot, a bacterial infection, is a serious problem, which can lead to lameness. Don't let your cows stand in mud, and check regularly to make sure they haven't got any cuts or scratches on their hooves through which infection can enter.

ABOVE If you have a sheltered field close to your house, calving outside can be cleaner and easier but watch the weather.

Keeping horses, ponies, and donkeys

Today horses, ponies, and donkeys are used as companion animals and in sport and leisure. But in some circumstances these working animals still have a place on the small farm.

Using horses and ponies on your small farm does require a level of knowledge if you are to train the animal to be useful, and the larger the animal, the more precise your training methods must be for safety's sake. The training of a youngster can't be skimped or taken lightly. Shire horses are not foaled knowing how to plow a field and their quiet dignity is a result of years of patient training.

Choosing horses or ponies

To be truly self-sufficient you don't need more than a couple of strong ponies for farm work, probably a mother and her offspring to bring on. However, if you decide to have your own horses, remember that they will substantially reduce the amount of grazing available to all other livestock. Although sheep and cattle eat some grass that horses don't touch, that doesn't mean that when a horse has finished grazing sheep or cattle can live only on the rough stuff left to them.

Horses and stock don't often mix—cattle eat the tails of horses, horned animals can cause damage to horses, and horses can injure smaller livestock such as lambs. Some licks are toxic between species, so always check the label, especially for copper.

Working horses and ponies need thorough, knowledgeable training, and a young, untrained animal can be dangerous. Decide what you want your working animal to do. Does it need to pull a cart of produce? Does it need to help harrow a paddock? Will it need to cultivate land? Will you want to ride to inaccessible places to check on stock? You need to match your needs to a breed.

For many purposes a strong 14.2-hand pony will be more than sufficient to do most jobs, but if you are planning to haul heavy timber or plow clay ground, you will need the strength of a draft horse.

If you are a beginner, never buy a young horse or pony. Instead, choose an older animal, 12–20 years old. Experience pays, and you should try to gain this with someone who is knowledgeable. Buy from a private seller who cares about the future of their animals and will let you try them in harness before you buy, and ideally go to a buyer who will be available to answer your initial queries. Best of all, join a driving club and buy your animals through the contacts you make. It's unkind to keep a horse, pony, or donkey on its own, so you will need to have a companion, perhaps a smaller pony or a younger animal, to bring on as your knowledge increases.

Popular breeds

Draft power

These breeds or breed crosses are short-legged, stock-bodied animals with plenty of power. They are normally 15–17 hands, with the big Shires making 18 hands, although for most purposes 16 hands would be the preferred height. The Belgian Draught horse or **Brabant** is one of the most popular American breeds, while in Britain there is the clean-legged **Suffolk**, the world-famous **Shire**, the **Percheron**, and the **Clydesdale**, which are all used for pulling. The **Ardennes** is another powerful breedm, more common in Europe.

Pony power

When it comes to ponies, it's not so much the breed as the type. They should be short legged, full bodied, and as wide as they are high (but don't mistake fatness for this). The legs should be large in circumference, and the hooves strong. Most native breeds have played their part on small farms. Look out for breeds like the **Haflinger**, the **Highland**, or the **Fell** or **Dales**. Be careful with the Welsh Cob: although it is a strong, powerful pony, it can be quite lively in temperament and needs expert handling. Traditional colored ponies make excellent working ponies and have a naturally placid temperament.

Small pony and donkey power

Some families are left with a pony after the child has grown up, and they have found that the pony can do lightweight jobs around the garden, such as some light harrowing on small paddocks, carrying produce to the house, or helping to clear up fields by pulling a cart to take the weeds or collect droppings. Donkeys are also good at this sort of work, and it's possible to plow small plots with smaller animals as long as the ground is not too hard or has already been broken up—say, a big vegetable plot. Do be careful not to overload any size of horse, pony, or donkey—if they are struggling, stop and remove the load.

Equipment

It is getting easier to obtain equipment for all sizes of working horses, ponies, and donkeys as the demand grows. Visit any agricultural show that features plowing or heavy horses and you will find stands that offer a selection, although some may have to be ordered in specially. The USA is leading the way at the moment with contributions from the Amish, among others, and is making it possible for more small-scale farmers to work a wider range of horses and ponies.

Driving harness is obtainable, either second hand (check the stitching carefully) and through tack shops. It's important to get the correct fit for both the animal's comfort and your safety, so seek expert advice the first time you harness up.

Housing

The ideal situation for a horse, pony, or donkey is in a sheltered paddock (with a hedge or mature trees) with a field shelter, although if the weather is particularly bad, the ground can become waterlogged and the animal may need restricting. Some people bring their horses in at night, but they need to be outside for some time every day, except in extremely bad weather.

The stable is a loose box; stalls where the animal is tied are no longer acceptable. The stable must be large enough for the animal to walk round easily, and the door must be high enough to keep them in but low enough that they are able to see over. Plenty of ventilation is essential, and the top door should never be shut except in special circumstances.

LEFT Horses and ponies do better living outside— a hardy, native type with a wide body and short legs makes an excellent working animal.

RIGHT If the horse
or pony is working
hard, they will need
a bucket feed in the
form of a properly
balanced ration
according to their
type and work.

You will need at least an acre of grass for each horse or pony. Any less, and you will need to feed hay all year round. You might have to restrict the grass available to smaller ponies and donkeys at peak growth time to prevent them from becoming dangerously fat.

Fencing

A post-and-rail fence is ideal, but horses are adaptable, and as long as it is strong, they cannot get their feet stuck in it, and it forms a definite boundary, they are usually good at staying put. A strip of electric tape inside the fence will stop them leaning on it, and you can use this for strip grazing a field. Most horses will continue to respect an electric fence even if it is not actually working. Never use barbed wire.

Feeding

How much food you have to offer will depend on the amount of work that your horse, pony, or donkey is doing and its size, but good grass will support a native pony nearly all year round, and it can be supplemented by good-quality hay in the winter when the frost is on the ground or the grass is not growing.

Good grass and quality hay are the most important factors in the diet and they must be present. Haylage can be fed in place of hay, but you must make sure that it comes from a reputable source. Avoid silage. If the animal is working, a bucket feed will be needed and there is a wealth of bagged feeds available, from mixes for low work to high-energy competition nuts. Choose a balanced bag ration, preferably based on forage such as lucerne (alfalfa).

Horses are designed to eat leafy or fibrous food, not cereal feeds, though cereals play a part in providing energy for hard-working horses. Use a tape measure to measure your horse just behind

the withers, keeping a record of any weight gains or losses and adjusting the feed accordingly. Feed more in cold weather if the horse is living out.

A horse's stomach is small, so although you can feed as much hay as it will eat, bucket feeds should be split into at least two feeds a day if you have to feed any more than a small bucketful.

Health

Prevention is better than cure, and keeping a careful eye on its weight will stop your horse being either debilitated from not enough food or getting laminitis through having too much. Horses, ponies, and donkeys must be vaccinated for tetanus, and your vet will be able to advise you about other vaccinations you may need.

Feet

Regular foot care and trimming are essential, but shoes may not be needed if the animal has good feet. Not all do, so you should be guided by your farrier or vet. If the animal is regularly working on stony ground or tarmac, you will have to have shoes fitted every six to eight weeks, and this must be done—in most countries it is a legal requirement—by a qualified farrier.

Donkey difference

Donkeys have fluffy coats, and water gets straight to their skin, unlike ponies, which have naturally oily, tight coats. Some native ponies even have whorls to help water run off. Donkeys must have access to shelter at all times. You can keep two donkeys in the same stable.

As much as 90 percent of lameness is always in the foot, so watch out for abscesses. Never work a lame horse and seek advice from your vet.

Worming

Regular worming is necessary because a small worm migrating internally can kill a large horse. Check for external parasites, especially with donkeys, which suffer from biting flies and lice.

Laminitis

This disease exhibits itself in the feet, but it is caused by a number of triggers, including a toxic reaction and being overweight. It shows with severe lameness, the front feet often being pushed forward, and should always be treated as life threatening. Seek veterinary advice immediately.

Colic

You must always contact your vet if you suspect colic. The horse will look uncomfortable, get up and down, roll and look at its sides, and will be in obvious pain.

Coughing

This is usually caused by an infection or by dusty or moldy hay. You must deal with it promptly and remove the source of the problem.

Handling

Remember to wear protective footwear when you are handling horses, especially when working them. If you are riding, wear a hard hat. Many people recommend that you should wear a riding hat when you are training on the ground as well.

Handle your horse, pony, or donkey regularly, and if you are planning to undertake work or an event, get them fit gradually. You cannot just pull an animal out of the field, work it hard, and put it back. Even if you have bought experienced animals, you need to fit the harness and work them on a regular basis, so set aside time once or twice a week to do something with them, even when you are not actually working them.

If you are training you will need to plan regular sessions that progress from leading to driving to pulling, making sure the horse, pony, or donkey understands each step as you move on to the next one. Bullying, shouting, and using the whip have no place in basic training. Seek help from an expert if you cannot make progress.

Alternative draft horse harnesses

There are many different types of harness for pulling instruments, but its purpose is to enable the power of the horse to be harnessed to the best advantage. Do not use anything that does not fit properly. The pulling power is in the collar or breast collar, the hames and traces, the belly band or saddle that prevents the traces lifting, the breeching that stops the vehicle running into the animal, and the steering parts, which are the lines or reins, the bridle, and the bit. The bridle normally has blinkers, and you should adjust these so that the horse has vision forward. Some people prefer to use an "open" bridle with no blinkers, so that the horse can see the load behind it, but you will have to train your horse for this. When unharnessing, leave the bridle on until last because if a horse is used to blinkers it might be scared to see a cart behind it.

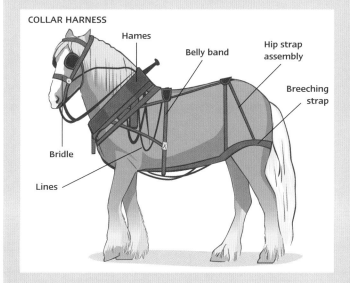

COLLAR HARNESS
Hames · Belly band · Hip strap assembly · Breeching strap · Bridle · Lines

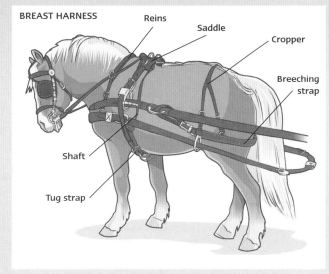

BREAST HARNESS
Reins · Saddle · Cropper · Breeching strap · Shaft · Tug strap

Keeping camelids

Camelids are unusual and attractive animals. They are kept by self-supporters for their wonderfully light, soft, and warm fiber, and llamas can be used for trekking. You will also have great enjoyment just watching them in the paddock.

These animals are native to the high South American altiplano and they therefore have to be hardy. They are herd animals, and you must not keep a single alpaca or llama. They can be used as guard animals, protecting their group, which can include sheep or poultry. The fleeces come in a range of natural colors.

Before you buy

Before you buy these creatures you must have a clear idea of why you want to keep them. If you decide to keep llamas for trekking you need to get easily led creatures. A couple of geldings could keep the grass down, a breeding herd could produce champions, or you could produce high-quality fiber. Whatever you choose, remember that you will get a fleece from each alpaca every year and will have to deal with it.

Camelid breeders often offer introductory days. Look out for courses on assessing camelids, which will tell you what you should be looking for when you purchase them.

Llamas

The Ccara llama has a short- to medium-length coat with short fiber on the legs and head. It tends to be larger than the Tampuli llama, which is more heavily wooled and has a coat extending down the legs. The Tampuli often has a woolly "topknot."

Llamas weigh up to 400 pounds and stand about 4 feet at the shoulder. They usually live for 12–18 years, but can exceed 20 years. They are strong, intelligent, inquisitive, and gentle animals. They can be kept as field pets, with other stock, and they are often used as pack animals, particularly for treks. Brushing will remove the fine, soft undercoat that is sought

after by hand spinners. The outer guard hair can be used for products such as bags and rugs.

Alpacas

There are two types of alpaca. The Huacaya has a fine, dense, crimped fleece, and the Suri has a fleece that parts along the back line and falls in long, silky ringlets. Adults weigh 130–175 pounds and stand approximately 3 feet at the withers. They can live for 15–25 years. Outside of South America they are kept for their luxurious fiber, which can be on a par with cashmere. Huacayas must be shorn annually, yielding a fleece of 7–11 pounds, but Suris may be shorn annually or every other year.

Where to buy

Where possible, buy stock registered with the national breed society because this ensures that minimum standards have been met. Learn as much as possible about the animals from the society and talk to as many breeders as possible. Visit farms to look at as many animals so that you can compare characteristics and quality. Check each animal's vaccination, worming, and other health records. If one exists, join the regional group of your national breed society.

Pasture management

You must have sufficient land. The recommended stocking rate is between five and six alpacas and four or five llamas to an acre. You will need adequate grazing, ideally allowing stock rotation. Check that your pasture does not contain any plants that would harm your animals.

Paddocks should be cleaned regularly, but the animals' tendency to use specific soiling areas makes this task relatively easy. Foot rot is not common, but make sure animals have access to drier ground in lengthy periods of wet weather.

Alpacas and llamas can be contained with sheep netting, post-and-rail or electric tape fencing 4 feet high. Fencing should be dog proof and all barbed wire removed.

Camelids can live outdoors all year, but they must have some form of shelter such as hedges, trees, or a custom-built field shelter. A catch pen is useful for routine examinations.

Feeding

They will require hay or haylage, particularly in winter. Specially formulated camelid feeds are available. They must also have a constant supply of fresh, clean drinking water. A supplementary concentrate feed is advised for pregnant and lactating females and for other animals in winter.

Handling

You should handle your animals authoritatively but gently and calmly. You can halter train them, and this is essential if you are going to use your llamas for trekking or are going to show your animals. Halter training usually starts at around six months.

Transportation

Llamas and alpacas can be transported in a livestock trailer or horsebox. They must have sufficient room and not be tethered, as they will cush during transit. Entire males and females should be transported separately or a solid partition placed between them. You need to stop regularly to give them clean water and food and to allow cria to suckle.

Before you move the animals, check whether you need a health certificate from your vet to allow them to travel to your destination.

Health

Before you decide to keep camelids, find out if there is a specialized vet in your area. Camelids give little indication that they are sick, and so that you spot problems early, you should get into the habit of checking your herd every day.

Camelids do not have hooves but have soft pads on their feet. Llamas generally do not need their toenails trimmed, but this should be done for alpacas three or four times a year. Teeth should be checked twice a year and advice sought to correct any anomalies. From about 18 months, males develop fighting teeth in their lower jaw and these should be removed by a professional.

Animals should be vaccinated against clostridial diseases and the entire herd wormed every six months. In "at risk" areas, camelids should be vaccinated against Bluetongue. They are also susceptible to tuberculosis (TB). There is no TB vaccine at present, but avoid moving animals from "hot spots" to disease-free areas. In all cases, you should check the legal requirements relating to animal movements and vaccinations.

In winter, animals will benefit from a boost of A, D, and E vitamins. This is especially beneficial for cria, as it helps bone growth and development.

Breeding

Alpacas and llamas can be bred at any time, as the act of mating induces ovulation. You can keep your own stud male, or stud services can be purchased from other breeders. Gestation is around 11½ months, with the single cria usually being born in the morning. Cria are weaned at six months and generally wormed at the same time.

Produce from your camelids

One of the main reasons for keeping alpacas is for their fiber. Many breeders are now developing the fiber side of their businesses.

LEFT You can halter train camelids from six months—essential if you are going to use them for trekking or if you are going to show your animals.

Keeping rare breeds

Rare breeds can provide the ideal animals for small farms. Chosen carefully, the breed will be adapted to the climatic conditions in a particular area, and value arises from being able to attach a breed name to the source of the produce.

What are rare breeds?

Rare breed farm animals and poultry are categorized in most countries and are brought together by organizations that work to keep them and, therefore, their gene pool alive. These organizations cooperate, exchanging knowledge and expertise, and the endangered stock they are concerned with represents stock indigenous to their country as well as stock bred for purpose.

No rare breed began life as a rare breed. It was once bred for a purpose or roamed as semiferal. Some of today's rare breeds achieved huge numbers, and whole sections of the community depended on them for their livelihoods. Others reflected the life and times of their area. We are beginning to realize that their future is important to our future, and many self-supporters and farmers are looking at ways to change the intensive agricultural system that has developed in the West. We have come to recognize that some of the breeds that we "outgrew" with our modern farming methods are now perfect for less intensive, small-scale husbandry.

What makes a rare breed?

A breed becomes "rare" simply through a lack of demand for its produce or for its method of production. But what causes this to happen?

Public tastes change according to perceived health issues or fashion, or a "superior" product comes onto the market and creates a demand for something new.

Old pictures of livestock show round, fat animals, but modern fashion requires lean meat. Out go Gloucester Old Spot pigs as a commercial proposition. Intensive farming removed the need for a hardy, maternal, rooting pig. Exit the Tamworth, the Large Black, and a host of others.

Cattle were bred for utility purposes, and dual-purpose meat and dairy cows were the norm. The increasing specialization of the late 20th century meant that dual-purpose cows could not compete with either the specialized meat or dairy breeds. Farms were getting bigger, and there was just no space for the traditional dual-purpose cow. The Gloucester, Shetland, and Red Poll fell into this category, while the traditional Hereford was superseded by fast-growing, high meat-producing European breeds.

Poultry keepers found that white eggs had fallen from favor as the public demanded brown eggs. Intensive systems were introduced, and, as with cattle, the dual-purpose bird was not needed in a world where male chicks of hybrid laying breeds are killed as day olds because they are unsuitable for rearing for the pot.

The story is the same for waterfowl. The Aylesbury duck is rarely seen in its pure form, and is often mistaken for the commercial white duck (see page 142), yet in the past a whole village and an industry depended on this duck for their survival.

Sheep suffered from the drop in value of their fleece. Breeds prized for their fleeces, such as the Leicester and Lincoln Longwools, the Cotswold, and the Wensleydale (see page 168), were once so valuable that huge churches were built from the wealth they created. Today they have only a small place in our largely meat-producing needs, but even meat-producing breeds have been pushed to the brink of extinction by the enormous popularity of breeds like the Suffolk.

In addition to native pony breeds in all countries, the big draft horses, such as the Suffolk, suddenly found themselves without a place as mechanized farming gathered pace, leaving them as dog meat and no replacements being bred. Even the donkey does not escape unscathed. The Poitou donkey from France became redundant when the need for a large donkey to breed big mules disappeared.

If we learn anything from this, we must learn how changes in farm production affect the gene pool in every country. Luckily, a few enthusiasts in every country kept a handful of many of these rare breeds going until we came to our senses and realized what we were losing or—sadly in many cases—have already lost.

Why keep rare breeds?

Rare breeds have special characteristics that make each and every one unique, and they have a particular place in small farming, from which most of them originated, where their hardiness, docility, and ability to thrive on lower-value forage are positive advantages.

A dual-purpose cow is just the thing for the self-sufficient, while a hardy, foraging pig, such as the Gloucester Old Spot, which produces succulent meat, is an attractive proposition. The Leghorn's white eggs can be sold with blue ones from the Araucana and dark brown ones from Marans or Welsummers to achieve a premium price, and home spinners relish the quality and beauty of the natural long wool fleeces.

If your property is in an area of difficult terrain or is subject to extremes of weather, there is more than likely a rare breed that is suitable for you. Slower maturing, hardy, and able to utilize food local to your area—grassland, upland grazing, or,

in the case of one unusual sheep, seaweed—this livestock is finding its place once more on the small farms and in the cottage production that is increasing again around the world.

Why preserve rare breeds?

In addition to their individual characteristics and their attractive appearance, rare breeds have one advantage over hybrids: they hold the future gene pool. Who in the 1970s could have predicted that there would be a need for outdoor pigs? Yet it took the remaining stocks of rare breed pigs to produce the commercial outdoor pig. Who could have foreseen the distaste for battery cages and wanting their chickens to range outside? Breeders had to revisit the poultry gene pool to find hardy hens with a docile temperament that they could develop into the new hybrid free-range hen.

The new interest in slow food favors the fatter pig and the slower-growing cattle, while the smaller families can now find smaller joints from hill breeds that were once considered too small for a mass market. Meanwhile, small, hardy, weight-carrying ponies, nearly wiped out when the working horse came to an end, have found a new life carrying small adults at weekends in leisure activities.

Once a breed is gone, it has gone. It can't be brought back. So keeping a few rare breeds and breeding them intelligently and to high standards, while at the same taking the trouble to find or create a market for the produce, will help to keep these breeds where they should be—in the farming practices of their respective countries.

LEFT Many breeds of sheep became almost redundant as the value of their fleece dropped with modern meat-producing types taking over.

Breeding date chart

This chart gives you the dates of the average periods of gestation for a nanny and ewe (see pages 164–7 and 168–71), a sow (see pages 160–3), a cow (see pages 172–7), and a mare (see pages 178–81). Please note that for a leap year you will need to adjust the due date by one day.

January

Served on	Goat/ewe due	Sow due	Cow due	Mare due
1	28 May	26 Apr	11 Oct	7 Dec
2	29	27	12	8
3	30	28	13	9
4	31	29	14	10
5	1 Jun	30	15	11
6	2	1 May	16	12
7	3	2	17	13
8	4	3	18	14
9	5	4	19	15
10	6	5	20	16
11	7	6	21	17
12	8	7	22	18
13	9	8	23	19
14	10	9	24	20
15	11	10	25	21
16	12	11	26	22
17	13	12	27	23
18	14	13	28	24
19	15	14	29	25
20	16	15	30	26
21	17	16	31	27
22	18	17	1 Nov	28
23	19	18	2	29
24	20	19	3	30
25	21	20	4	31
26	22	21	5	1 Jan
27	23	22	6	2
28	24	23	7	3
29	25	24	8	4
30	26	25	9	5
31	27	26	10	6

February

Served on	Goat/ewe due	Sow due	Cow due	Mare due
1	28 Jun	27 May	11 Nov	7 Jan
2	29	28	12	8
3	30	29	13	9
4	1 Jul	30	14	10
5	2	31	15	11
6	3	1 Jun	16	12
7	4	2	17	13
8	5	3	18	14
9	6	4	19	15
10	7	5	20	16
11	8	6	21	17
12	9	7	22	18
13	10	8	23	19
14	11	9	24	20
15	12	10	25	21
16	13	11	26	22
17	14	12	27	23
18	15	13	28	24
19	16	14	29	25
20 Feb	17 Jul	15 Jun	30 Nov	26 Jan
21	18	16	1 Dec	27
22	19	17	2	28
23	20	18	3	29
24	21	19	4	30
25	22	20	5	31
26	23	21	6	1 Feb
27	24	22	7	2
28	25	23	8	3

March

Served on	Goat/ewe due	Sow due	Cow due	Mare due
1	26 Jul	24 Jun	9 Dec	4 Feb
2	27	25	10	5
3	28	26	11	6
4	29	27	12	7
5	30	28	13	8
6	31	29	14	9
7	1 Aug	30	15	10
8	2	1 Jul	16	11
9	3	2	17	12
10	4	3	18	13
11	5	4	19	14
12	6	5	20	15
13	7	6	21	16
14	8	7	22	17
15	9	8	23	18
16	10	9	24	19
17	11	10	25	20
18	12	11	26	21
19	13	12	27	22
20	14	13	28	23
21	15	14	29	24
22	16	15	30	25
23	17	16	31	26
24	18	17	1 Jan	27
25	19	18	2	28
26	20	19	3	1 Mar
27	21	20	4	2
28	22	21	5	3
29	23	22	6	4
30	24	23	7	5
31	25	24	8	6

April

Served on	Goat/ewe due	Sow due	Cow due	Mare due
1	26 Aug	25 Jul	9 Jan	7 Mar
2	27	26	10	8
3	28	27	11	9
4	29	28	12	10
5	30	29	13	11
6	31	30	14	12
7	1 Sep	31	15	13
8	2	1 Aug	16	14
9	3	2	17	15
10 Apr	4 Sep	3 Aug	18 Jan	16 Mar
11	5	4	19	17
12	6	5	20	18
13	7	6	21	19
14	8	7	22	20
15	9	8	23	21
16	10	9	24	22
17	11	10	25	23
18	12	11	26	24
19	13	12	27	25
20	14	13	28	26
21	15	14	29	27
22	16	15	30	28
23	17	16	31	29
24	18	17	1 Feb	30
25	19	18	2	31
26	20	19	3	1 Apr
27	21	20	4	2
28	22	21	5	3
29	23	22	6	4
30	24	23	7	5

May

Served on	Goat/ewe due	Sow due	Cow due	Mare due
1	25 Sep	24 Aug	8 Feb	6 Apr
2	26	25	9	7
3	27	26	10	8
4	28	27	11	9
5	29	28	12	10
6	30	29	13	11
7	1 Oct	30	14	12
8	2	31	15	13
9	3	1 Sep	16	14
10	4	2	17	15
11	5	3	18	16
12	6	4	19	17
13	7	5	20	18
14	8	6	21	19
15	9	7	22	20
16	10	8	23	21
17	11	9	24	22
18	12	10	25	23
19	13	11	26	24
20	14	12	27	25
21	15	13	28	26
22	16	14	1 Mar	27
23	17	15	2	28
24	18	16	3	29
25	19	17	4	30
26	20	18	5	1 May
27	21	19	6	2
28	22	20	7	3
29	23	21	8	4
30	24	22	9	5
31	25	23	10	6

June

Served on	Goat/ewe due	Sow due	Cow due	Mare due
1	26 Oct	24 Sep	11 Mar	7 May
2	27	25	12	8
3	28	26	13	9
4	29	27	14	10
5	30	28	15	11
6	31	29	16	12
7	1 Nov	30	17	13
8	2	1 Oct	18	14
9	3	2	19	15
10	4	3	20	16
11	5	4	21	17
12	6	5	22	18
13	7	6	23	19
14	8	7	24	20
15	9	8	25	21
16	10	9	26	22
17	11	10	27	23
18	12	11	28	24
19	13	12	29	25
20	14	13	30	26
21	15	14	31	27
22	16	15	1 Apr	28
23	17	16	2	29
24	18	17	3	30
25	19	18	4	31
26	20	19	5	1 Jun
27	21	20	6	2
28	22	21	7	3
29	23	22	8	4
30	24	23	9	5

July

Served on	Goat/ewe due	Sow due	Cow due	Mare due
1	25 Nov	24 Oct	10 Apr	6 Jun
2	26	25	11	7
3	27	26	12	8
4	28	27	13	9
5	29	28	14	10
6	30	29	15	11
7	1 Dec	30	16	12
8	2	31	17	13
9	3	1 Nov	18	14
10	4	2	19	15
11	5	3	20	16
12	6	4	21	17
13	7	5	22	18
14	8	6	23	19
15	9	7	24	20
16	10	8	25	21
17	11	9	26	22
18	12	10	27	23
19	13	11	28	24
20	14	12	29	25
21	15	13	30	26
22	16	14	1 May	27
23	17	15	2	28
24	18	16	3	29
25	19	17	4	30
26	20	18	5	1 Jul
27	21	19	6	2
28	22	20	7	3
29	23	21	8	4
30	24	22	9	5
31	25	23	10	6

August

Served on	Goat/ewe due	Sow due	Cow due	Mare due
1	26 Dec	24 Nov	11 May	7 Jul
2	27	25	12	8
3	28	26	13	9
4	29	27	14	10
5	30	28	15	11
6	31	29	16	12
7	1 Jan	30	17	13
8	2	1 Dec	18	14
9	3	2	19	15
10	4	3	20	16
11	5	4	21	17
12	6	5	22	18
13	7	6	23	19
14	8	7	24	20
15	9	8	25	21
16	10	9	26	22
17	11	10	27	23
18	12	11	28	24
19	13	12	29	25
20	14	13	30	26
21	15	14	31	27
22	16	15	1 Jun	28
23	17	16	2	29
24	18	17	3	30
25	19	18	4	31
26	20	19	5	1 Aug
27	21	20	6	2
28	22	21	7	3
29	23	22	8	4
30	24	23	9	5
31	25	24	10	6

September

Served on	Goat/ewe due	Sow due	Cow due	Mare due
1	26 Jan	25 Dec	11 Jun	7 Aug
2	27	26	12	8
3	28	27	13	9
4	29	28	14	10
5	30	29	15	11
6	31	30	16	12
7	1 Feb	31	17	13
8	2	1 Jan	18	14
9	3	2	19	15
10	4	3	20	16
11	5	4	21	17
12	6	5	22	18
13	7	6	23	19
14	8	7	24	20
15	9	8	25	21
16	10	9	26	22
17	11	10	27	23
18	12	11	28	24
19	13	12	29	25
20	14	13	30	26
21	15	14	1 Jul	27
22	16	15	2	28
23	17	16	3	29
24	18	17	4	30
25	19	18	5	31
26	20	19	6	1 Sep
27	21	20	7	2
28	22	21	8	3
29	23	22	9	4
30	24	23	10	5

October

Served on	Goat/ewe due	Sow due	Cow due	Mare due
1	25 Feb	24 Jan	11 Jul	6 Sep
2	26	25	12	7
3	27	26	13	8
4	28	27	14	9
5	1 Mar	28	15	10
6	2	29	16	11
7	3	30	17	12
8	4	31	18	13
9	5	1 Feb	19	14
10	6	2	20	15
11	7	3	21	16
12	8	4	22	17
13	9	5	23	18
14	10	6	24	19
15	11	7	25	20
16	12	8	26	21
17	13	9	27	22
18	14	10	28	23
19	15	11	29	24
20	16 Mar	12 Feb	30 Jul	25 Sep
21	17	13	31	26
22	18	14	1 Aug	27
23	19	15	2	28
24	20	16	3	29
25	21	17	4	30
26	22	18	5	1 Oct
27	23	19	6	2
28	24	20	7	3
29	25	21	8	4
30	26	22	9	5
31	27	23	10	6

November

Served on	Goat/ewe due	Sow due	Cow due	Mare due
1	28 Mar	24 Feb	11 Aug	7 Oct
2	29	25	12	8
3	30	26	13	9
4	31	27	14	10
5	1 Apr	28	15	11
6	2	1 Mar	16	12
7	3	2	17	13
8	4	3	18	14
9	5	4	19	15
10	6	5	20	16
11	7	6	21	17
12	8	7	22	18
13	9	8	23	19
14	10	9	24	20
15	11	10	25	21
16	12	11	26	22
17	13	12	27	23
18	14	13	28	24
19	15	14	29	25
20	16	15	30	26
21	17	16	31	27
22	18	17	1 Sep	28
23	19	18	2	29
24	20	19	3	30
25	21	20	4	31
26	22	21	5	1 Nov
27	23	22	6	2
28	24	23	7	3
29	25	24	8	4
30	26	25	9	5

December

Served on	Goat/ewe due	Sow due	Cow due	Mare due
1	27 Apr	26 Mar	10 Sep	6 Nov
2	28	27	11	7
3	29	28	12	8
4	30	29	13	9
5	1 May	30	14	10
6	2	31	15	11
7	3	1 Apr	16	12
8	4	2	17	13
9	5	3	18	14
10	6	4	19	15
11	7	5	20	16
12	8	6	21	17
13	9	7	22	18
14	10	8	23	19
15	11	9	24	20
16	12	10	25	21
17	13	11	26	22
18	14	12	27	23
19	15	13	28	24
20	16	14	29	25
21	17	15	30	26
22	18	16	1 Oct	27
23	19	17	2	28
24	20	18	3	29
25	21	19	4	30
26	22	20	5	1 Dec
27	23	21	6	2
28	24	22	7	3
29	25	23	8	4
30	26	24	9	5
31	27	25	10	6

Food from
the wild

Natural abundance

The countryside is crammed with edible plants, fungi, and animals, free to anyone with the skills to recognize, find, and harvest them. The rediscovery of seasonal eating is also an important lesson for the forager.

It may be possible to buy cultivated asparagus, lamb, and eggs around the year, but wild garlic, crayfish, blewits, and venison can be harvested only when they are naturally available, serving to heighten our enjoyment and appreciation of these seasonal delicacies. In many cases wild foods are infinitely better than their domesticated versions. None of the most delicious species of wild mushroom, for example, can be cultivated—truffles, ceps, and chanterelles are all wild. Similarly, farmed pork or salmon that have been reared on commercial pellets are poor reflections of their free-range, organic cousins.

Conservation

There is nothing intrinsically wrong with gathering food from the wild, but using common sense is vital. Some once-abundant foods have been devastated by over-harvesting—in Europe, for example, wild oysters and salmon were once staples of the poor, but both are now rare luxuries. In other cases pollution and habitat loss have forced plants and creatures into isolated pockets. Elsewhere some native plants or animals may be threatened, while an introduced near-relative is deemed a pest—as has happened, for example, in Britain with signal crayfish.

It is a good idea to ask farmers, fishermen, and environmental groups for advice. Always respect local customs: there is little competition for wild mushrooms in most English-speaking nations, for instance, but the Poles, Italians, and French jealously guard their fungi.

Remember that when it comes to wild foods sustainability is key—you should always make sure that you leave enough for the plant or animal to restock naturally. Even where a food is abundant, other creatures—and often people

—depend on it, too, so collect in moderation, gathering only what you intend to use.

Many wild foods are also strongly flavored, so quality is often more important than quantity.

The law

Most countries have legislation in place to protect wild plants and animals. In many cases the plants and animals automatically belong to the landowner, but there are often public areas, such as communal woods and commons, where foraging is permitted—for example, anyone can forage between the tidelines in some countries. In addition, there is often specific protection for endangered species, and you must always observe hunting seasons and licensing systems. In some countries these can vary from locality to locality, so always check because even an honest mistake can be an offense.

It is up to you to take all reasonable steps to avoid harming the wrong species. Where this is a danger there are usually means of avoiding accidents—for instance, by setting a trap in a location where only the target species can gain access or by using a particular mesh size when you are fishing.

It is extremely important to establish local rules and laws before you gather from the wild. The police will usually be able to help, but hunting and conservation organizations are often fountains of useful advice.

In the case of wild animals and fish you must make sure they are humanely slaughtered, whether you are shooting, fishing, or trapping.

Safety

Unfortunately, in many areas pollution presents an invisible risk. Farm discharges can leak into watercourses, and plants may concentrate heavy metals on waste ground. In addition, some coastal towns discharge sewage into the sea, contaminating filter-feeding shellfish. It is always worth seeking local advice.

The powerful weapons needed to kill large mammals humanely can be lethal to humans, too, so always observe scrupulous safety measures. Similarly, strongly sprung traps can injure the hunter, and water always carries a risk of drowning, particularly where nets and weighted ropes are in use. Even simple fish hooks and penknives are capable of causing painful injuries.

Weather conditions can also rapidly pose risks, especially when you are concentrating on studying the ground or water immediately in front of you. When you are working in mountain regions or along the seashore, it is particularly important to familiarize yourself with weather forecasts, snow reports, tide charts, and local currents. It is often safest (and most fun) to work in pairs.

Efficiency

Harvesting from the wild can be time consuming, and this usually comes at a premium for the self-supporting smallholder. There are ways of countering this, however. Traps, nets, and long lines take only a few minutes to set, but once they are in place they work 24 hours a day (although they will still need to be checked regularly).

It takes time to find rich sources of plants, fungi, or shellfish, but you can reduce the time you spend on research by asking for advice and studying field guides and maps to identify likely hot spots. Provided you are not too greedy, most wild produce returns year after year.

Cooking

Many people dismiss wild food as tough, inferior, or indigestible. In some cases there are good reasons to turn to cultivated alternatives, but in many instances the real problems stem from fear or ignorance. Fungi are an obvious instance of this. A few are certainly very poisonous, but far more are edible—and the vast majority are neither one nor the other. Even those known to be edible should be treated with respect, but more because most of them are very rich than because of possible misidentification. Use them as a flavoring rather then a staple ingredient— 2 ounces per portion is a good rule of thumb.

BELOW Freshwater fish—such as this trout—are delicious and as free-range as one could desire. Catching them can be fun, too.

Fields contain vegetables and game. Woods produce berries, nuts, salads, roots, fungi, birds, and mammals. Fish, crustaceans, roots, and vegetation lurk in rivers and lakes. Richest of all, perhaps, is the seashore, where vegetation, roots, and shellfish are available around the year, while offshore fish and crustaceans can be caught.

Fields

Intensive agriculture means that farmland is no longer as rich in wild food as it once was. Weeds have been heavily controlled in most arable fields for decades, while ancient pasture has often been plowed and reseeded with more productive grasses. This management not only reduces the edible plants available but it also drastically reduces biodiversity at the microscopic level. Fewer bugs mean fewer insects, and fewer insects mean fewer birds. Similarly, heavy grazing by livestock cuts the amount of food available for game. Many "weeds" and "pests" are remarkably resilient and can still be found in the margins or thriving in patches of overlooked open ground, while rabbits and deer are even more partial to cultivated crops than to their wild alternatives.

Woods

These are often a rich source of delicious wild foods, not least because even well-maintained woodland is neglected compared with farmland. Foresters use few chemicals, and harvesting for timber allows in light and churns up the ground to produce an explosion of berries, leaves, and fungi. Deciduous woodland generally provides the richest foraging grounds. Scrubby coppices of hazel (*Corylus*) or birch (*Betula*) are often full of fungi and salad plants, while older stands of oak (*Quercus*) and beech (*Fagus*) provide subtly different conditions where a range of different foods thrives among the leaf mold and rotting wood. Many guidebooks dismiss conifer woods as dark deserts, but they can often provide rich hunting grounds. This is particularly true of mature plantations—particularly those of "red softwoods," such as Scots pine (*Pinus sylvestris*) and larch (*Larix*)—where the ground is covered with a thick, mossy blanket.

Waste ground

It is easy to overlook the underused scraps of land that surround us, but nature hates a vacuum, and

ABOVE You can find a range of habitats for wild food in every landscape, from fields and waste ground to rivers and the sea.

Many plants are too strong to make a salad on their own. Beef up a cultivated lettuce with wild garlic (*Allium ursinum*) and dandelion (*Taraxacum officinale*) leaves, scattered with a few tips of fireweed (*Epilobium angustifolium*).

Most wild meats are very low in natural fat. While this means they are healthy, they can also quickly dry out and become tough if cooked conventionally. So broiled venison steaks and pheasant and pigeon breasts are all best served rare, but if you like your meat well done, a stew is usually more successful than roasting.

Where to look

Every landscape contains a range of habitats, each producing a distinct range of wild foods.

plants and animals will rapidly colonize any neglected areas. Disused factory sites can provide rich pickings in the form of berries, fungi, and even game. Invasive plants, such as brambles (*Rubus*) and nettles (*Urtica*), are usually among the first to arrive, but railroad tracks and canal towpaths act as "wildlife highways," allowing rabbits, squirrels, and even deer to move relatively freely between city and field. The rough areas on golf courses are another potential mine of free food—porcini and parasol mushrooms love conditions around the quick-growing birch trees (*Betula*) that are beloved of course designers.

Road edges
The broad bands of vegetation that border our highways and country lanes are natural oases. They are rarely sprayed, there is no competition from livestock, and the occasional grass cutting allows light in to the understory, encouraging wild flowers and fungi. They are also often rich in "wildings"—feral apples that have sprouted from discarded cores. All this draws in wildlife, which rapidly learns to ignore passing vehicles (and the occasional fatal errors provide roadkill protein). Because of the easy visibility, the forager can easily and quickly check a huge area from a moving vehicle. Would-be gatherers are, however, often warned to avoid road- and railside vegetation, but the banning of lead additives in petrol means this is no longer an issue.

Rivers and lakes
Most freshwater contains plants and animals that are good to eat, although you should remember to be wary of possible contaminants from farming and industry. Sheep, for example, can infect watercress with liver fluke, while eels build up organic pollutants in their fatty tissues.

Although freshwater fish are often dismissed as too "muddy" for modern tastes, this can be solved by keeping the catch for a couple of days in clean water or by soaking the flesh in a light brine solution. Some delicious fish, including pike, contain myriad small pin bones, but this can be tackled by steaming the flesh and passing it through a sieve.

Shore
The seashore is probably the richest source of wild food. Furthest inland are the marsh and

mudflats, which are sometimes described as the rainforest of the temperate world. These are rich in invertebrates, drawing fish in along the creeks with every high tide. Edible plants, like marsh samphire (*Salicornia europaea*) and sea kale (*Crambe maritima*), grow there, while a little lower seaweeds, limpets, and mussels cling to rocks around the tideline. Rockpools can contain crabs and lobsters, while shrimps patrol the shallows. And at low tide cockles and clams can be dug from the drying sand near the water's edge.

Sea
Most inshore waters are rich in fish. These are attracted by the tiny animals and plants that thrive in the shallow water on the plentiful nutrients and abundant light. Some white fish, such as bass and flounder, can often be caught with pole and line from the shore, but a small boat can be invaluable, particularly for catching shoaling fish, such as mackerel. In addition, bigger species such as halibut, turbot, cod, and haddock are usually found further away from the shore.

Similarly, crabs and lobsters can sometimes be found in rockpools, but the biggest specimens are usually around submerged rocky outcrops further out to sea. Their smaller cousins, scampi, live in even deeper water. Catching any of these is best done with baited traps or "pots" and requires the services of a boat.

ABOVE Crabs and lobsters are abundant and easy to catch in rockpool crevices, although the finest lurk further out to sea and are best trapped in baited "pots."

The wild food calendar

Most wild produce is seasonal. Productivity in the vegetable patch and in the wild peaks in late summer, but there is always something available if you know where to look.

Spring

As temperatures rise and day lengths increase, everything speeds up quickly. Tender green shoots and young leaves are the dominant theme. Hop (*Humulus*) sprouts start to curl up from hedge bottoms, forcing their way through the light green of young nettles (*Urtica*). Alongside these, alexanders (*Smyrnium olusatrum*) and hogweed (*Heracleum sphondylium*) are producing altogether more substantial shoots. Protected from all but the hardest frosts by its damp habitat, watercress (*Nasturtium officinale*) puts on vigorous early growth that is crammed with precious vitamins and minerals. Out in the fields rough rings of St. George's mushrooms (*Calocybe gambosa*) appear on ancient pasture. Along the coast the fleshy shoots of marsh samphire (*Salicornia europaea*) spread like a green carpet across the saltmarsh. This is mirrored in damp woods by wild garlic (*Allium ursinum*). The first young of the year emerge, too. Baby rabbits, which were born underground in late winter, now hop into the light, pigeon squabs are leaving their nests, and in rivers and lakes torpid fish begin to stir.

Early summer

This season is marked by volumes. Nettles (*Urtica*) are in full growth and are beginning to toughen, while florets of elderflowers (*Sambucus*) dangle above. As the water warms, it is time to set traps for crayfish and search for crabs in rockpools. On warm days, patrol the warm shallows at low tide with a shrimping net. Meanwhile, the fungal crop is also getting into full swing: scotch bonnet or fairy ring champignons (*Marasmius oreades*), chicken of the woods (*Laetiporus sulphureus*), and chanterelles (*Cantharellus cibarius*). Wild strawberries are now at their most abundant, shortly to be followed by feral raspberries growing wild in hedgerows.

Late summer

The foliage is now coarse and most is past its best, but regularly cutting nettles will stimulate fresh new growth. Meanwhile, roots are starting to fatten and come into their own. Gardeners may hate the stubborn persistence of biennial weeds like horseradish (*Armoracia rusticana*) and burdock (*Arctium minus*), but below ground their 2 foot long taproots are at their prime. Wild fruit is also beginning to peak as the bilberry season reaches its height. Giant puffballs (*Calvatia gigantea*) lurk deep in nettle patches, and on the moors the grouse season has started. Trout are running in the rivers, while off the coast huge shoals of mackerel and pollock are swimming into the shallows to spawn.

Autumn

This is the season of plenty for the forager. Many plants and fungi have been building up reserves all spring and summer to fruit before the frosts arrive. Blackberries need no introduction, while feral apples are also easy to recognize and make the perfect accompaniment to the black fruit growing below. This is the peak of the mushroom season: saffron milk caps (*Lactarius deliciosus*), porcini or ceps (*Boletus edulis*), field parasols (*Macrolepiota procera*), ink caps (*Coprinus*), beefsteak (*Fistulina hepatica*), and the last chanterelles flush in the autumn rain.

This is the height of most game seasons, and even if you don't want to shoot your own, wandering around the edge of sporting estates will often yield casualties from the previous day's action. Pheasants, rabbits and even deer casualties

can be found on the road edges in the morning but it is not recommended that you gather them for your own consumption. If you don't want to hunt them for yourself, seek out a hunter or purchase from an accredited meat-packer.

Salmon are now breeding, running upstream to lay their eggs in shallow gravel beds where herons, otters, bears, and humans have feasted on both fish and their caviar for centuries.

Early winter

The fall in temperatures and shorter days herald the end of the annual bonanza. Finding easy pickings is becoming increasingly difficult as the "hungry gap" begins. This is when food is most elusive, yet calories are more important than ever. There is also plenty of competition from wildlife for what little there is. Food is still out there, however, if you know where to look. Wood and field blewits (*Lepista nuda* and *L. saeva*) are prompted to fruit by frost, while another mushroom, the velvet shank (*Flammulina velutipes*), will happily grow through snow.

The cold does have a silver lining, however, because it forces hungry animals into the open as they search for food. Huge flocks of pigeons gather to ravage winter crops, and deer browse along field margins at dawn and dusk. Ensure that any deer you hunt are wild and you are not poaching from someone else's land.

Midwinter

By now the land is lying apparently dormant, but food is to be found. The easiest pickings are to be had along the coast where the salt water keeps the land frost-free in all but the harshest of weather. Limpets, clams, and mussels are present, as is fresh seaweed dredged up by winter storms. Many fish nose up creeks at high tide looking for morsels washed downstream by winter rains, while sea bass can be caught from the rocks and lobsters hauled from the depths in pots.

Late winter

Although everything is apparently largely lifeless, sap is stirring, and birch (*Betula*) and maple (*Acer*) trees can be tapped to produce a sweet liquid to make beer and syrup. The green shoots of bittercress (*Cardamine hirsuta*) and chickweed (*Stellaria media*) are among the first plants to emerge, but they are soon followed by edible blossoms. Morels (*Morchella*), which mark the beginning of the fungal year, appear on alkaline waste ground and around bonfires.

Identification guide

Our fields and woods are full of edible plants. Many make indifferent eating, but some are superior to any cultivated versions and make a delicious addition to a home-grown meal from the smallholding.

The dimensions of plants are given in the form height x spread. The maximum height and spread are those that might be achieved by the plant when it is growing in ideal conditions. Plants that do well in full sun will not do as well if they are found in a shady position, and plants that have a restricted root run will rarely achieve their full potential. At first you should use a guidebook to help you identify some species. Make sure you don't take vast amounts of any plant and leave enough for it to restock naturally.

Trees and shrubs

American chestnut

A tall deciduous tree, the American chestnut (*Castanea dentata*), 100 x 10 ft, is native to the eastern United States. The species is very similar to the European sweet chestnut. The American chesnut is a prolific bearer of nuts and they are a rich source of nutrients. Chestnuts are edible raw or roasted, though preferably roasted, and are perfect for roasting on the embers of a fire. Alternatively, you can boil them for half an hour, after which the tough skins and hairy inner layer peel off easily. Their rich, creamy flavor works brilliantly when mixed with steamed Brussels sprouts to make an unusual stuffing for turkey or stir-fried with pork belly and soy sauce.

Juniper

A rather variable evergreen shrub, juniper (*Juniperus communis*), 6–12 x 30 ft, is often found on poor alkaline soils, although it will grow in more acidic conditions. The fruit takes two years to mature and is ripe when it blackens, usually in winter, when it is rich in oils. It is valued more as a drink flavoring than as a food. It is used to produce beers and schnapps in Scandinavia and Alpine regions, but is best known as the base for gin. The dried berries also accentuate the gaminess of venison, or they can be stewed with pork to produce "wild boar."

Common crab apple, wild crab apple, wildings

A rather thorny tree, the common crab apple (*Malus sylvestris*), 28 x 22 ft, bears pink-white flowers in spring. In summer and early autumn the red-flushed yellow-green fruits festoon many hedges and highway edges and are often mistakenly called crab apples. In fact, these are usually the descendants of discarded apple cores and thus more properly known as wildings. The small, hard fruits vary wildly in taste. Most are too bitter to eat, but they make good cider and have a high pectin content, which is perfect to set jams and jellies. The taste can be a little bland, however, so make it more interesting by slipping a sprig of rosemary or chili into each jar to create the perfect accompaniment for lamb or pork.

Wild rose, dog rose

The dog rose (*Rosa canina*), 10 x 10 ft, is a common climbing shrub of woods and hedges. It flowers briefly in early summer and fruits in autumn. The bright red berries are extremely high in vitamin C—they contain four times as much as black currants—and this can be harnessed by boiling with sugar and water to make syrup, which can be bottled for use as a winter tonic.

Blackberry, bramble

The blackberry (*Rubus fruticosus*), 12 x 12 ft, is one of the few edible plants that is universally and instantly recognized. The fruit is borne from midsummer to mid-autumn, but because of the wide genetic range of the parent briers, the quality of the crop varies hugely from area to area. When you are harvesting you should concentrate on the best bushes rather than becoming obsessed with quantity. The fruit makes a superb jelly, and it also goes well in desserts when it is combined with apples.

Common elder

The widely found common elder (*Sambucus nigra*), 30 x 15 ft, is a variable deciduous tree that needs no introduction to anyone who has walked along country lanes in spring, and elders are a common sight along canals, railroads, and on waste ground. The frothy cream-colored flowers, borne in dense panicles, impart a wonderful aroma to drinks—elderflower pressé, wine, and "champagne" are wonderfully refreshing on a summer's evening—but the blooms are much more versatile than just as a base for drinks. The flowerheads can be eaten raw in salads or dipped in frothy batter, deep-fried for a few seconds in light oil and served dusted with confectioners' sugar as an unusual dessert.

When they are eaten straight from the tree, elderberries are a little bland and sour, but they make an interesting, port-like, hedgerow wine. They are rich in vitamin C and viburnic acid (which stimulates mild sweating). Our ancestors made a natural cure for aches and colds by boiling berries with a few cloves in just enough water to cover for 30 minutes, straining the juice and then mixing it with an equal amount of sugar before bottling. The resulting cordial can be taken by the teaspoon as a tonic, used like cassis to flavor wine, or mixed with honey and whiskey as the basis of a hot drink.

Herbaceous perennials and annuals

Wild garlic, ramsons, wood garlic

The perennial wild garlic (*Allium ursinum*), 16 x 12 in, grows profusely in damp woods. The large, glossy, dark green leaves and star-shaped white flowers make it easily recognizable, but any doubts you have will disappear when you rub the leaves between finger and thumb and smell the strong garlic scent. The taste is mild, however, and it is best treated as a substitute for chives or scallions.

Hairy bittercress

One of the first plants to start growing in late winter and early spring, hairy bittercress (*Cardamine hirsuta*), 8 x 8 in, loves bare and freshly turned soil, so it is one of the commonest annual weeds. It has a fine peppery flavor that is reminiscent of watercress. The leaves are probably a little strong to use on their own, but they make a great addition to a green salad.

Wild strawberries

The long runners of wild strawberries (*Fragaria vesca*), 10 x 8 in, root easily, making propagation simple. The small, sweet berries taste nothing like the larger fruit of familiar cultivars, which mostly derive from North American varieties. They share the same characteristic trefoil leaves, however, and are locally common, particularly on limestone soils and in woodland after felling has disturbed the soil. They also often grow along old railroads, where the runners straggle across the track, benefiting from the warmer microclimate. The berries have an intense flavor, but picking them can be tedious, so treat them more as an herb than as an ingredient. Try simmering a handful with a little wine, then pureeing the mixture before drizzling it over smoked duck breasts.

Hogweed, cow parsley

A biennial, hogweed (*Heracleum sphondylium*), 6 x 4 ft, grows in huge, large-leafed clumps and produces the characteristic umbels of white flowers in midsummer. The young shoots are one of the great hedgerow delicacies. Try steaming them and serving with melted butter, black pepper, and sea salt or with a Béarnaise sauce of lemon-tinted melted butter thickened with egg yolks.

Hop

The shoots of hop (*Humulus lupulus*), to 20 ft high, are among the earliest to emerge each year. Today we associate hops with beer, but they were first cultivated by the Romans for their delicate tendrils. These have a wonderful aromatic flavor and are a worthy alternative to asparagus, as long as you gather them early in spring before they become coarse and hairy.

Marsh samphire, common glasswort

Not to be confused with rock samphire (*Crithmum maritimum*), marsh samphire (*Salicornia europaea*), 8–12 in high, is a strange-looking primitive perennial, which thrives in the brackish water and mud of saltmarshes. It grows all year round, but the

The bitter-sweet taste of the wild strawberry makes a wonderful savory dressing.

tender young stalks are best picked in spring and summer. Make the most of its flavor by steaming the shoots quickly to accompany fish or white meat. Alternatively, samphire can be eaten on its own dressed simply with butter or a light vinaigrette.

Stinging nettle

These perennials (*Urtica dioica*), to 5 ft high, are one of the most reviled of garden weeds, but they have their uses. Their deep roots drag up nutrients from far underground, so the foliage is full of vitamins, minerals, and trace elements. When the young leaves are cooked, the acid sting is instantly neutralized and the leaves taste like nutty spinach. They are particularly good as a thick soup, or try nettle mousse with cream and goat cheese. Unfortunately, older nettles have a decidedly laxative effect, so cut them back repeatedly to produce a steady supply of young tips.

Fungi

Wild fungi are particularly valuable because, despite having some of the most fantastic flavors known to man, the majority cannot be cultivated. They are available throughout the year, most are found globally, and they are a good source of protein. They have long been valued by chefs in Europe and Asia, but English-speaking nations seem curiously wary of their culinary qualities. A few are certainly extremely poisonous, so you should never eat a mushroom without being absolutely certain of its identity; a good guidebook and, preferably, expert advice are essential. That said, even beginners can easily recognize some of the best.

Cep, porcino, penny bun

Undoubtedly the world's most commercially significant wild mushrooms, ceps or porcini (*Boletus edulis*) grow around the world, but always near trees, appearing from late summer to autumn. They are easy to recognize thanks to the spongy gills and thick white to beige stalk. Although they are superb when fresh, drying intensifies the flavor and allows the autumn glut to be used at any time. The dried slices are reconstituted in boiling water to produce a nutty stock, which deepens the flavor of stews, soups, and risottos.

Chanterelle

Egg-yellow chanterelles (*Cantharellus cibarius*) can grow through summer and autumn in almost any deciduous woodland, but they are commonest in birch, beech, and oak scrub. They begin as a little button pushing out of the soil on stalks, before the caps spread out into an irregular funnel perched on a deeply veined stalk. Another tell-tale indicator is the distinct whiff of apricots.

Shaggy ink cap

Groups of the distinctively torpedo-shaped, white shaggy ink cap (*Coprinus comatus*) burst into view on roadside edges in early autumn. The flaky white cap quickly dissolves into black ink—in the Middle Ages monks used the soggy remains to illustrate manuscripts—so hurry home with your haul and cook them immediately, discarding the fibrous stalks. The texture can be a little slimy, so these are generally best in soups, where the rich flavor comes into its own. Try pureeing them with spinach, shallots, and garlic and a generous helping of cream.

Hedgehog fungus, wood hedgehog, pied de mouton

The common name of the cream-colored hedgehog fungus (*Hydnum repandum*) derives from their curious spine-like gills. They grow beneath trees in summer and autumn and are well worth searching out, because they can emerge in large numbers and the firm flesh is delicious, going particularly well with cheese or cream on fresh pasta.

Saffron milk cap

Fairly large, buff-colored mushrooms, the saffron milk cap (*Lactarius deliciosus*) appears in summer and autumn in conifer woods (especially pine and spruce) and on sandy heaths. The name comes from the light orange, milky sap that exudes from the damaged gills. Many experts rank this highly, not least because it has a great texture, is fairly common, and grows in large numbers.

Chicken of the woods

One of the most easily recognized edible species, chicken of the woods (*Laetiporus sulphureus*) emerges as bright yellow lumps from the trunks of deciduous trees, usually oak, beech, or willow, in early summer, swelling until it resembles a stack of yellow plates. Pick them while they are still bright yellow, because the flesh toughens as it ages. Young specimens have a fantastic flavor and meaty texture, and they are perfect additions to a range of vegetarian dishes.

Field parasol

The pale brown field parasols (*Macrolepiota procera*) emerge like drumsticks in grassland in late summer and autumn. As they grow, the "heads" unfurl to resemble frilly umbrellas. The stalks are fibrous and woody, so are best discarded, but the fresh caps are superb when fried in butter and served on toast. More commonly picked in Europe than the US.

Cep or porcini mushrooms grow around the world.

Fairy ring mushroom

A familiar and not altogether welcome sight to gardeners who tend their lawns carefully, fairy ring mushrooms (*Marasmius oreades*) grow in circles in short-cropped grass. They appear in flushes through summer and autumn, particularly after rain. Care needs to be taken not to confuse this mushroom with the deadly poisonous false fairy ring mushrooms (*Clitocybe dealbata* and *C. rivulosa*), but the two can be distinguished with a glance at the gills. Those of the edible species curl up into the cap; those of its dangerous lookalikes curve down the stalk toward the ground.

Morel

Large mushrooms, which can get to 10 in tall, morels (*Morchella esculenta*) appear in spring on alkaline soils. They are particularly partial to fire-ravaged waste ground and used to grow in profusion on London's bomb sites during the Second World War. More recently huge crops have been reported after forest fires in the USA, while Turkey and India are major exporters. This strange, honeycomb-like mushroom grows on a thick, hollow stalk (the only poisonous lookalike has a multichambered stem). Its musty, delicate flavor goes particularly well with white meats. It also dries well, allowing you to harness a spring glut throughout the year.

Cauliflower fungus

One of the easiest of all fungi to identify, the cauliflower fungus (*Sparassis crispa*) more closely resembles a marine sponge than a cauliflower. It is a parasite of mature conifers, fruiting in late summer and autumn from the roots and the base of the trunk. It comes up year after year, and large specimens can reach 12 in across and weigh over 4 lb. It has a wonderful crunchy texture and is particularly good deep-fried in batter and served with a squeeze of lemon and a grind of black pepper.

Chicken of the woods is an easily recognizable fungi.

Truffle

The well-known truffle (*Tuber aestivum*) grows underground on the roots of deciduous trees and has a fantastically pungent aroma. Truffles are often cooked with egg and cream dishes. European hunters use trained pigs and dogs to locate the tubers, but you can find them by looking for bumps in the leaf mold below trees or by looking for tiny plumes of forest fruit flies hovering above the buried treasure.

Game shooting and fishing

Humans have always hunted wild animals for food. Hunting for pleasure and pest control is still common and self-supporters can use it as a valuable source of delicious protein.

Hunting considerations

There are important things to consider before you embark on hunting. If you intend to shoot any game, you must be well-practiced so that you don't just wound the animal. Go out with an experienced guide who will show you how and when you can shoot. Check the rules on the licensing and storage of shotguns.

If you are using traps and snares, then you must check them at least twice a day so that you don't cause any unnecessary suffering. Make sure your traps are legal and that you are able to quickly dispatch the animal. Use clean shooting or killing methods in preference to trapping.

In all cases you should check what the most up-to-date humane method of slaughter is. There are strict seasons in many countries as to when you can hunt or shoot different groups of animals and birds. Check your local regulations to make sure you are abiding by the law.

You must also remember that you cannot take animals or fish from other people's land without permission; this is known as poaching.

BELOW Sportsmen spend a fortune every year releasing game birds to shoot. The result is a bonanza of delicious, free protein for neighbors.

Top birds

The best game birds for hunting and taste are:

Pigeon, wood pigeon

Pigeons (*Columba palumbus*) can be a serious pest on arable land; they are capable of devastating delicate young shoots and can do almost as much damage to ripe cereals. Their rich dark breast meat is delicious, however, and a winter pigeon casserole is a good way of compensating for their raids on the vegetable patch earlier in the season.

Pheasant

Every year millions of this chicken-size game bird (*Phasanius colchicus*) are released by shooters to provide autumn sport. Unless they wander onto your land, they belong to someone else and you will need shooting rights.

Partridge or quail

Smaller versions of the pheasant, partridges (*Perdix perdix*) (also known as quail in some parts of the US) live in family groups on open ground. Make sure you can tell the difference between the farmed and wild birds or think about joining an organised hunting group who will ensure a safe and productive shoot, and make sure you are abiding by any local regulations.

Top mammals

There are several mammals that can be hunted for food, but the most popular are:

Deer

For centuries the right to hunt deer was jealously guarded and restricted to the aristocracy. Today, however, they are more likely to be viewed as a menace to agriculture, not least because in many areas alien species, such as the dog-size muntjac (*Muntiacus reevesi*), have been introduced. Their flesh is rich and dark—and, better still, it is extremely healthy, almost completely lacking saturated fat and cholesterol. They are very strong and capable of running long distances when wounded, so they are generally shot from a vantage point or hide with a high-powered rifle.

Rabbit

Rabbits (*Oryctolagus cuniculus*) were spread around the world by the Romans and Normans as a source of meat and skins. They have long been fully naturalized in areas around the globe. They can be shot, snared, trapped, netted, or bolted with ferrets.

Freshwater fish

Rivers and lakes are home to some beautiful and very edible freshwater fish:

Carp

During the Middle Ages the vegetarian carp (*Cyprinus carpio*) was a staple food during Lent, and monks farmed it in lakes and stewponds. Although some people find its white flesh "muddy," to this day it is highly prized in parts of Central Europe, where it forms the centerpiece of festival feasts.

Trout

There are many species (*Salmo*) of this fast-swimming creature, and anglers have long valued the challenge of luring it onto a hook decorated with an artificial fly created from wool, feather, and tinsel.

Crayfish

These freshwater crustaceans look and taste like miniature lobsters. They are readily caught in "pots" (traps with funnel entrances and baited with meat), and it is possible to catch hundreds in just a handful of traps each night. In Britain the native crayfish (*Austropotamobius pallipes*) is protected by law and is under threat from the American signal crayfish (*Pacifastacus leniusculus*), which is farmed and has escaped into the wild.

Sea fish

If you live near a coastline, try fishing for:

Bass

A marauding carnivore, which lurks in shoals around reefs and wrecks, bass (*Dicentrarchus labrax*) also hunts around the incoming surf. It can be caught from the shore with a pole baited with a spinning treble-hook or on a multihooked line garnished with colored plastic or feathers.

Halibut

A large flatfish, halibut (*Hippoglossus hippoglossus*) can grow to 8 foot and weigh 450 pounds, although 27 pounds and 32 inches is usual. It is a greedy feeder, snapping up meaty baits both on and off the bottom.

Mackerel

Huge shoals of beautifully dappled blue-green-gray mackerel (*Scomber scombrus*) gather offshore to spawn each summer, although numbers seem to be steadily dwindling, probably thanks to over-fishing for animal feed by deep-sea trawlers. They are easily caught using "feathers" (as with bass).

Shellfish

Delicious shellfish that can be gathered include:

Lobster, crab, and scampi

These creatures are generally caught in deeper water using baited pots (as crayfish), but edible crabs and even lobsters often lurk in crevices in rockpools. These are scavengers and sometimes betray their presence with piles of discarded mussel and shore crab shells. Make sure you can quickly slaughter them— traditional methods are being superseded by more humane methods.

Mussels

Rocks around the coast are often festooned with mussels, but those between the tidelines are usually both small and festooned with barnacles. Bigger, cleaner relatives tend to be found around and beyond the low-water mark. They are easy to gather and quick to prepare.

Cockles

Cockles lurk just below the surface of the sand around low tide. The beds can be difficult to find, but look for discarded shells and flocks of shellfish-loving seabirds. Use a blunt-tined rake to scour the sand and leave them in a bucket of seawater overnight to discard residual sand.

From crop
to kitchen

Preserving

Learning how to make the most of surplus produce so that it is available in leaner times and how to add value to your cereals and dairy is one of the most important aspects of your new, self-supporting life.

Using up surpluses

Modern methods of food production and storage have made preserving our own food something of a neglected skill, but even some 50 years ago, the mass ownership of refrigerators was still in its infancy and the practice of flying out-of-season foods from far-off places was yet to be truly exploited. If you wanted to eat plums in winter, you bottled them. If you had too much of a vegetable, you pickled it. Other methods, such as salting beans, drying herbs, or candying fruit, were also practiced. In order to survive, our ancestors had to be experts in keeping food all year round.

But it's not just about practicality. As you preserve what you have grown, it is not only the actual foodstuff that you are capturing in the bottle or jar but also the satisfaction of having produced it from a seed and having nurtured the plant and harvested the crop. That jar of green tomato chutney represents hours of watering, weeding, and picking, while that jar of plums at the winter dinner table brings back the sights, smells, and sounds of summer, if only fleetingly.

Preserving your produce

There are several ways to preserve foods—freezing, drying, pickling, and so on—but all are straightforward and on the whole work well. Different methods suit different produce, but once you have grasped the basic principles, you will be able to experiment with different produce.

Choosing the appropriate storage method will allow you to keep fresh food fresh for varying lengths of time. For example, if you wrap apples in paper and store them in a cool place, they will keep for months. You may have a root cellar, where vegetables can be stored fresh for weeks or months. If you leave the stalks in place and allow them to sit in the sun for a couple of weeks, squash can go into the cellar at around 50°F for four to six months. Onions and garlic can be lifted, dried in the sun, then plaited together for storing in a cool outhouse.

Before you consider other, more complicated methods of preserving produce, think about providing cool, well-ventilated storage space with some humidity (but not damp) for those vegetables and fruits that can be stored in their original form. Pick produce at its freshest and make sure that everything is dry and completely undamaged. A single damaged vegetable will give off ethylene, which will ruin the others. Make sure that the fruit and vegetables are in good condition and are not overripe, and continue to check regularly, even if it is only by carefully smelling the storage area, while produce is in store. Damaged vegetables can be chopped and pickled or you can simply remove and discard the damaged parts and freeze the remainder.

BELOW Learning the correct techniques for food preservation will extend your harvested produce into the winter.

From crop to kitchen

Some older houses have a cool pantry with a window that can be covered with a fine-mesh wire to keep out the flies. These are invaluable, even today, especially if you have a glut of produce and cannot process it all in the same week, let alone the same day. Look around your house and any outbuildings to see if you can create a suitable space for storage. It must be dry, well ventilated, cool but frost-proof and dark. It must also be as vermin-proof as possible because you will be using it to store produce for several weeks, so you don't want to share it with a family of mice or nest of insects. If you can provide this type of area, it will take the pressure off while you deal with more vulnerable produce.

Long-term storage

You can dry, freeze, pickle, preserve (as in jam making), salt, and bottle to prolong the life of produce, and all methods are surprisingly easy to do successfully. The enemies to long-term storage or what makes foods "spoil" are enzymes, molds, yeasts, and bacteria, and not only can these ruin food but also, if eaten, can make you ill.

Enzymes

Each plant or animal contains enzymes that help to control its life cycle, and one of their functions is decomposition. They begin to work soon after harvesting, but their action is slowed down by cold (hence the success of freezing) or by extreme heat (as in boiling for canning).

Molds

These fungi show themselves as the soft fuzz on food. They cannot grow below freezing point and cannot survive boiling, although there are temperatures between these that actively encourage their spread. Although they are not believed to be too dangerous to eat, mold is still a strong indication that the food is no longer in good condition and that it is time for it to become compost. There is a risk of what are known as mycotoxins, some of which can be very bad for you. Of course, molds are deliberately introduced into some blue cheeses to make the blue veins, but these are controlled and safe.

Yeasts

Yeast is essential for making bread and, of course, in alcoholic drinks, but not what we want in fresh foods, because it renders them inedible and unsafe. As with molds, freezing and extreme heat destroy yeasts, but they can be a problem in opened preserves, so always store open jars in a cool place, preferably the refrigerator, and don't leave them uneaten for too long.

Bacteria

The idea of bacteria rightly strikes fear into many would-be food preservers, and because the micro-organisms can come from anywhere—soil, water, air, on hands or on equipment—it is important that all bottles and equipment are kept scrupulously clean, that you wash hands regularly to avoid cross-contamination, and that you boil briskly or freeze quickly as appropriate. Salmonella and botulism are serious illnesses, and you should be on guard against them at all times. Do not leave food at room temperature for a second longer than necessary.

BELOW Bottled fruit seems to bring back the sights and sounds of summer.

Drying

Drying is a basic but effective method of food preservation and it is still of practical value in today's kitchens, especially for herbs. What could be better than a winter compote of dried fruit or having dried vegetables available all year round?

You will need

Drying must be done as quickly as possible, but without "cooking" the produce. In dry, sunny weather you can leave foodstuff outside, although you might have to cover them to keep off birds and insects. Alternatively, use a pantry, a warm oven, or even a cool part of the kitchen range. Don't be tempted to try to dry herbs and flowers by hanging them up in your kitchen; the atmosphere is far too steamy.

You will need some string and flat trays. Traditionally, basketwork or willow trays are used, but wooden ones are fine. Wire cooling trays and sieves can also be pressed into service, although they are not as efficient as wicker or wood. You will also need clean, airtight storage jars and labels. Covering the bottom of the trays with a piece of cheesecloth or flimsy cotton will help protect the produce from becoming marked.

If you are going to do a lot of drying, you can buy a special cabinet, and it's now possible to buy solar-powered versions that carry on drying even in cloudy weather. Alternatively, you could make your own. A drying cabinet is an enclosed box with a heat source, ideally a fan (although you can turn the produce manually), and racks for the fruit and vegetables. Most home-built food dryers use a 100 watt light bulb as the heat source. They should have a temperature range of 120–140°F. If you are making your own make sure that the bulb is not so close to the sides that it catches fire, and never leave the cabinet unattended while it is switched on. Most cabinets take between four and seven hours to dry food. It's tempting to start off with a high temperature, but that will only harden the foodstuff or even trap moisture inside.

How to dry

Whether you are working inside or outside, you need heat to draw out the moisture, dry air to absorb the moisture, and circulating air to take the moisture away.

Choose fresh produce that is in good condition and completely ripe: unripe produce does not dry well. You will need to prepare each type of food in a different way, and the best approach in deciding this is to think about how the fruit or vegetable looks when you buy the dried equivalent.

For example, you should core, peel, and cut **apples and pears** into rings, removing any discolored flesh. Immerse them in a solution of 1 tablespoon salt to 4 cups water for a few minutes to prevent discoloration and pat them dry. Cut large **figs** in half. Apart from removing any compost, **mushrooms** need little preparation. Smaller **beans** can be dried in their pods, although larger ones, such as fava beans, must be shelled. One of the simplest of all to dry

Why dry food?

- You can preserve a wide range of foodstuffs.
- Radically reducing the moisture in a foodstuff inhibits the growth of the enzymes that cause food to spoil.
- In hot, dry, sunny weather it is a natural and low-cost method of preservation.

- It creates lightweight foodstuffs that can easily be stored and transported.
- Dried food is highly concentrated and the flavor is often enhanced.
- Dried foods, especially herbs, can smell gorgeous and make a kitchen look homely and productive.

is **garlic**. Dig up the bulbs when the stems turn yellow and shake off the soil, trim the tops, and hang them in bunches in a warm, airy place.

Once you have been successful with the more usual produce, you can experiment with other types of foodstuff.

Add a label giving the date and type of foodstuff; dried herbs in particular can be hard to identify. Don't store dried herbs in full light, because they will fade and lose their flavor. Keep them in airtight jars in a cool, shady place.

Drying outdoors

Choose a shady spot in the garden. Drying can take several days, but you must remember to move the produce indoors at night because the dew will disrupt the process. Spread the produce loosely on flat trays raised above the ground or hang them on strings. It's a good idea to experiment with smaller quantities first. Apple rings and onion rings can be strung up like paper chains, and you can use a large needle to help you string mushrooms. You can dry peppers whole or sliced, and they are best hung up to dry, although you can arrange them on trays.

Herbs of all kinds are among the easiest plants to dry. Pick them before they flower on a dry day. Tie sprigs of small-leaved herbs, such as rosemary, thyme, or marjoram, in bunches, then tie a piece of cheesecloth over the bottom to catch the falling leaves. When they are dry, rub off the leaves and, if you wish, grind them. Dry mint and sage in a similar way, though it is usually better to remove the leaves and put them in cheesecloth bags to dry. Blanch bay leaves in boiling water for one minute, pat them dry, and dry in cheesecloth.

A word of warning: if there is pollution nearby, such as a major road or crop spraying, don't dry outside because the food will be tainted.

Drying indoors

Ideally, you need to start fruit and vegetables off at 120°F and increase the temperature to 140°F. It's quite possible to dry in an pantry or in an oven as long as you can achieve these temperatures. Be particularly careful if you are using wooden trays in an oven: keep a careful eye on the trays at all times and don't let the temperatures get too high. The process can take a couple of days. After drying, it's a good idea to

ABOVE Apples lend themselves to drying and can be eaten as a snack or used in a dried fruit salad, cakes, and even pork dishes.

LEFT Herbs have traditionally been dried for winter use and retain their smell and flavor for use in a range of dishes and also for medicinal purposes.

expose the produce to fresh air before packing it into airtight jars.

As with all forms of preserving, mold, a bad smell, or signs of fermentation mean that the produce is not fit to eat. Discard it and review your methods. Keep a record of what you did: when you harvested the crop, the temperature on the day of harvest, how long you dried the produce, the temperature in the oven or drying cabinet, and when and how you stored it. This will be a guide to what works and what does not.

Freezing

The ability to freeze fresh produce at its peak is great for keeping it in perfect condition to last through the shortages of winter. Most frozen foodstuffs not only taste as good as when they were harvested but also retain many nutrients.

Processed food can be frozen just as well as fresh produce, so pies made from seasonal fruit (such as blackberry and apple) can be frozen. Carcasses and bones from a roast joint can be simmered into stock that is then frozen and used in winter as the basis of nourishing soups and stews. Large cuts of meat can be cooked in casseroles or curries and frozen in various portion sizes. It's usually just as cheap to cook several meals as it is to cook one, so making extra to freeze for later consumption saves on energy, too. It's so convenient when you are busy with harvest, for example, to be able to take one of your own pies or casseroles from the freezer for a quick supper.

Why freeze food?

A freezer that is working at the correct temperature will slow down the bacterial growth that makes food rot. This means that the food will be as safe to eat when you defrost it as it was when you put it in the freezer. But what a freezer does not do is kill bacteria, so when food is thawed, the bacteria will resume their growth until killed by a high temperature in the oven. If the temperature in your freezer rises, it will allow bacteria to become active again, the food will spoil, and it becomes dangerous to consume.

A freezer should operate at 0°F; this compares with a normal refrigerator, which runs at 35–39°F.

RIGHT Frozen food, including stock, will retain a high level of vitamins if treated correctly and mean that locally grown summer produce can feature on the winter table.

A refrigerator is for safe, short-term storage, while items in a deep freeze can be stored for longer than the recommended matter of months. As the temperature of a freezer rises, the food spoils more quickly, and the length of time it can be stored will fall dramatically, even if the freezer is out by only a few degrees. The rise in temperature will also affect the quality of the nutrients and taste of the food, but what is more serious is that bacteria may begin to develop and be harmful when consumed. Check the temperature of your freezer to make sure that everything in it is kept in good condition.

Choosing a freezer

Most home producers will need one or two chest freezers, kept in a cool outhouse, to store their produce. If you have two freezers, you can use one for meat and one for fruit and vegetables. Bear in mind that freezers are at their most efficient when they are full, so don't get a huge one if you are not going to use all of it. Alternatively, fill up the empty space with plastic bottles filled with tapwater until you have sufficient produce to fill it.

It's a good idea to have a freezer as part of your refrigerator in the kitchen as well as a separate chest freezer. You can transfer small quantities for cooking when you need them so that you don't have to go out to the outhouse in the dark or cold. Don't site a freezer in a warm place, and if you have one in the kitchen, place it as far as possible from the stove. Having a large refrigerator in the kitchen will allow you to store produce that you cannot immediately process.

New freezers are more efficient than old ones in terms of energy consumption, and they tend to be produced in a more ecologically friendly way. However, many people's first chest freezer will be a second-hand one from a family that is downsizing or from a commercial source. If you are going to use a second-hand freezer, you must be certain that the wiring is good and that produce is frozen consistently in all parts. You should use a thermometer to check that the correct temperature is maintained in all sections, and you should freeze smaller batches of food until you are sure that it works properly. Clean it thoroughly inside and out.

Many freezers have built-in thermometers, but it is worth purchasing one and checking your freezer regularly. Most insurances will pay if frozen goods spoil because of a power cut (and so will some electricity companies), but it is best to try and plan ahead and spot any temperature changes resulting from mechanical failure.

You will need

In addition to the freezer, you will need a selection of freezer bags that can be written on and, if the bags are not the self-seal type, you will need freezer ties. A waterproof pen is useful.

If you are freezing a large amount of your produce, you need to keep records. A simple book or list on the computer that can be updated with the produce, date, and any comments (such as "overripe—cook with this") will help prevent you from scrabbling in the depths of your chest freezer for old produce that you've overlooked.

What to freeze

Although most foods freeze well, there are some you should avoid, including cooked eggs, salad leaves, bananas, celery, and tomatoes (unless pureed). Do not freeze mayonnaise made with raw eggs. Frozen cooked whole boiled potatoes are disappointing, but mashed potato freezes well. Homemade yogurt doesn't freeze well, but stirring in a teaspoon of honey makes it freeze better.

Freeze fruits and vegetables that are young and freshly picked. You want your frozen food to be a taste of summer at its best, and any items that are

Help! My freezer has failed

If you have a lot of produce stored in your freezer and live in an area with an erratic power supply, you should consider having a standby generator in case of emergency. For everyone else, frozen food will keep for 24 hours or more if you don't open the freezer door. If you know in advance that there is going to be a power cut, stuff newspaper into any gaps and make sure that the freezer is at its highest temperature—that is, at its coldest. If a power cut persists and produce starts to defrost, you can probably claim at least some of the cost on your insurance.

It's safer to refreeze some foods than others. Fruit is a reasonably safe bet, as are cooked vegetables and bread, but you should cook fish and meat before refreezing. Any defrosted food that is refrozen should be fully cooked to destroy any potentially harmful bacteria. Never refreeze ice cream.

How to blanch

Select fresh, recently harvested produce and make sure it is clean and free of all insects and caterpillars.

- Prepare appropriately—for example, slice beans or cut root vegetables into chunks of the same size. Different vegetables can take different times to blanch.
- Plunge the vegetables into a large saucepan of boiling water. A blanching basket—a wire basket a bit like a fish fryer—will make it quicker and easier to get the vegetables in and out of the water.
- Cool in a bowl of ice-cold water

or in running water (though this wastes water and may be unsuitable if your water is metered).

- Label the bags while it is easy to write on them and remember to add the new produce to your freezer stock list.
- Allow to cool completely and either open-freeze and then pack into bags or pack into bags, seal, and then freeze.

old, discolored, starting to spoil, or tough will be in the same state when you take them out of the freezer. If some of your produce is less than perfect, you could freeze it, but think about whether you will be wasting freezer space. You can semiprocess less than perfect fruit and vegetables before freezing by pureeing or stewing.

How to freeze

You normally have the option of freezing produce as separate items or making them into a meal, such as a pie or casserole, or an ingredient, such as stock. Never put food into the freezer while it is still hot, and do not place unfrozen food next to frozen food. Some freezers have special sections for freezing, but if there isn't one, its worth creating a special area for the purpose.

There are two basic methods of freezing: freezing raw is better suited to fruit, while blanching suits most vegetables.

Freezing raw fruit

Spread out the fruit on a baking sheet, making sure that it is not touching, so that each piece freezes separately. When the fruit is frozen, seal it in a plastic bag and label it. Open-freezing works especially well with raspberries and currants, although strawberries tend to turn mushy.

You can also pack fruits with sugar, allowing about ½ cup sugar to every pound of fruit. Add the sugar in layers.

Blanching

Blanching is the process of scalding vegetables briefly in boiling water, then cooling them before freezing. You can open-freeze some vegetables at this point if they won't stick together—blanched cauliflower or broccoli florets are ideal for open-freezing. Blanching is the preferred method for most vegetables because the heat inhibits the enzymes that cause decomposition, making them keep better in the freezer.

LEFT Blanching is the process of scalding vegetables in boiling water, then cooling them before freezing.

You can try freezing raw vegetables, though you should be aware that this is something of an experiment and you might have to use them for further processing, such as pickling or in a casserole, if they don't freeze well. Note that small onions don't need blanching.

You will need a saucepan (or more) of boiling water, at least one colander, and a clean bowl of cold water to which you keep adding ice cubes. Alternatively, you can transfer the hot vegetables to a colander and cool them under running water.

Blanching times vary, but in general small vegetables, such as peas, cut flat beans, or dwarf beans, take 1 minute, larger ones, such as fava beans, take 2 minutes, and chopped rutabagas, celeriac, and other root vegetables take 3–4 minutes depending on size. Corn ears take up to 8 minutes. Mushrooms can be fried lightly (sautéed in butter) and then frozen; you can freeze small mushrooms raw and whole, but they won't keep for long.

Freezing herbs

This is a great method of preserving herbs, though they won't keep as well as dried herbs. As with drying, pick the herbs before flowering, when the dew has gone but before the sun is really strong. Wash the herbs and remove any bugs or discolored leaves.

Pack them loosely in small, clearly labeled plastic bags. It's a good idea to put the correct quantity for a single dish in each bag because they will soon spoil after defrosting and cannot be kept. They also become brittle when frozen. You could freeze small bundles of herbs—a frozen bouquet garni—to use in stews and casseroles. Basil freezes well and keeps its flavor for at least three months.

Some people recommend freezing herbs in ice cubes so that they can be used for garnishing, but it is fiddly and other people prefer to blanch them, which can be done quickly and easily.

RIGHT Herbs freeze very well, as they will keep their flavor, but they do become brittle and lose their shape—use them for cooking and not for decoration.

Freezer checklist

- Start every season with an empty freezer. In theory, you shouldn't need to keep food for longer than 12 months (in fact, it's recommended that many foods shouldn't be kept in a freezer for more than three to six months, even though they will usually keep much longer). If you grew green beans last year, you should have eaten them all by the time the new harvest comes, and it would be ridiculous to be eating last year's frozen beans when this year's crop is ready to eat.

- Be strict about using produce and remember to rotate your menus so that some items don't fall to the bottom and become older and older.

- Defrost and thoroughly clean your empty freezer each year before adding the new season's produce.

- Label everything clearly, or you will struggle to remember if that brown liquid is chicken stock or vegetable broth and you will perhaps upset a vegetarian friend in the process.

- Remember that liquids expand as they freeze, so allow some room in the packaging. Plastic milk containers are useful as long as they are thoroughly clean.

- If you have only one freezer, use a color code, such as simple stick-on spots, to help you easily identify fruit, vegetables, and meat.

- Collect used plastic cartons, such as those for ice cream and butter, for freezing produce throughout the year, but make sure they don't have any trace of smell from their previous contents.

- Buy a freezer thermometer and use it regularly.

- Remember that, once defrosted, frozen food deteriorates more quickly than fresh food, so use it as soon as possible. There is no need to defrost vegetables, which can be plunged into boiling water while still frozen.

Preserves and chutneys

Turning fresh produce into an attractive product that will keep is very satisfying, and learning how to use your produce to create a salable product can be a useful source of income.

Jellies, jams, and chutneys are used to enhance and add flavor to everyday foodstuffs from toast to cheese or cold meats, and they can be used in cooking and creating imaginative menus. They can be made following traditional recipes or with new and interesting combinations of ingredients to give lavender-flavored preserves, for example, fruit chutneys, and marmalades made from combinations of citrus fruits.

Once you have mastered the basic principles, you can personalize any recipe to suit your own taste and to use your own produce.

Know your preserves

There are many different types of preserves, both sweet and savory:

- **Conserves** are preserves with a slightly softer set and are generally made with a mix of whole and crushed fruits. Serve them spread on bread or toast, or add them to fruit desserts.

- **Chutneys** are a cross between a pickle and a jam with a sweet and sour taste. Like jam, they require boiling, but all the ingredients are added to the pan at once and then simmered until thick, rather than until a set is reached. Serve with savories such as cheese, cold meats, or broiled sausages.

- **Crystallized fruits** are fruits soaked in sugar syrup over 10–14 days, then dried and rolled in sugar. They are most often served as petits fours.

- **Candied fruit** are similar to crystallized fruit, but are finished by dipping the fruit into a thick sugar syrup to achieve a glossy finish.

- **Jams** are made from crushed fruit and should have a slightly runnier set than a jelly.

- **Jellies** are clear preserves made from cooking diced fruit, with its seeds, skins, and cores, in just enough water to cover. It is then strained to make a clear juice and boiled with sugar until set firm. Spread on bread or toast. Rowan, quince, or cranberry jellies are traditional.

- **Fruit butters** are made from fruit purees cooked with sugar until the consistency of thick cream. Serve with thickly sliced bread or toasted muffins or crumpets.

- **Fruit cheeses** are made in the same way as fruit butters, but are cooked until very thick. Serve with cheeses as part of a cheese course.

- **Fruit curds** usually contain butter and eggs and are cooked in a double boiler or in a bowl set over a pan of simmering water. As they contain eggs, they must be stored in the refrigerator and used within one month.

- **Marmalades** are a jam made exclusively from citrus fruits. The rinds may be pared from the fruit and then mixed with the squeezed juice, or the fruits may be cooked whole and then cut into fine shreds. Serve at breakfast, spread on thick toast.

- **Mincemeat** is not minced meat at all, but made with minced dried fruits and grated or cooked apples and flavored with sugar, alcohol, and spices. It is traditionally served at Christmas as a filling for small or large tarts.

- **Pickles** are made from vegetables or fruits and preserved in sweetened vinegar. Most often, vegetables are pickled raw after soaking in salt. Serve with cold cuts, salads, and cheese.

- **Relishes** are of Indian origin and may be cooked or uncooked; they are more highly spiced than a chutney. Serve to accompany curries, cold meats, or barbecued food.

Jams

Making jam is a great way to preserve summer fruit for later use, and a day spent in the kitchen can result in a shelf full of jars filled with colorful jams and jellies that capture the flavor of summer. These make excellent gifts, and, as long as you always observe local hygiene laws and regulations, they can be sold for extra income.

Although ideally you should use perfect ingredients, you can often use slightly damaged fruits and cut out any blemishes. Choose firm, ripe fruits or those that are just underripe for maximum pectin content. You can also use vegetables: gourds, carrots, beets, pumpkins, and tomatoes all make good jams.

You will need

The first essential is a clean kitchen with clean working space, free of flying insects (it's amazing how many you can attract), and no children or animals. Second, make sure you have plenty of time because you can't go off and do something else, leaving your jam to its own devices.

If you do not have a **boiling-water canner** that is at least 10 inches across and 4½ inches deep, use a large saucepan with a thick base. You need to use a wide pan because the mixture has to evaporate and the jam must be able to boil without boiling over. Never fill your pan more than half full, and you must be careful that the mixture does not burn on the bottom or it will contaminate the whole batch and you will have to throw it away.

You can make jam without a **sugar thermometer**, but it's much easier and safer to use one. Check its accuracy from time to time by putting it into cold water and bringing it to a boil for 2 minutes, when it should read 212°F.

You will also need several **spoons**, including a long-handled wooden spoon for stirring, a flat, stainless steel slotted spoon for skimming, and a teaspoon for testing setting on a saucer.

A **funnel** will reduce spills and mess, and it is safer to use a funnel to pour the jam into a jar. Funnels are usually made from metal rather than plastic because they have to be able to withstand high temperatures. Check that other materials can withstand hot fluids.

When you are making jams and chutneys, you can recycle you own **jars**. Inspect them carefully before using them and discard any that are not perfect, especially those with chips or dirty lids. Sterilize them in a warm oven for 10 minutes or on a standard wash cycle in a dishwasher. Make sure they are completely dry.

Each jar of jam needs a **covering**. Place a disk of waxed paper, waxed side down, on the surface of the preserve while still hot, then add a cellophane cover, secured with a rubber band, or a sterilized screw-top lid. Allow to cool. As the preserve cools, the heat kills any bacteria or mildew spores from the air that may be trapped between the lid and waxed disk.

Remember to add a **label** to each jar showing the type, the date made, and any other comments you feel necessary. If you are making for sale, the label might need to carry other information, so check with your local food health department.

What is jam?

The scientific principles of preserving produce in the form of jam are that the boiling kills any micro-organisms and deactivates the enzymes, while at the same time the large amount of sugar used inhibits the growth of the bacteria that would cause the jam to deteriorate. It's difficult

ABOVE Although you can use a large saucepan, do try to buy a boiling-water canner if you are intending to regularly make jam or chutneys.

LEFT A jelly bag (or some fine cheesecloth) is necessary to make jellies where cooked fruit needs to strain slowly through a fine mesh.

to make low-sugar jam, and you should bear in mind that it may have a shorter storage life than traditional jam.

Pectin is what gets the jam to set. This natural, gum-like substance is found in varying amounts in seeds, cores, and skins of fruit, and when fruits are crushed and heated, the pectin is released and mixes with the natural acids to produce a jello-like set. The amount of pectin in fruits varies, so if you are making your first batch of jam, choose fruit that is high in pectin for almost certain success. In general, fruits with firm skin—black, red, and white currants, damsons, gooseberries, citrus fruit, and apples, for example—are all high. Apricots, early blackberries, most plums, raspberries, and morello cherries are medium, and strawberries, elderberries, peaches, and so on are low. If you are using low-pectin fruit, you can add pectin in the form of 2 tablespoons freshly squeezed lemon juice or 1 teaspoon citric acid to each 2 pounds of fruit.

The type of sugar you use is also important. You can buy jam or preserving sugar, which contains pectin and dissolves quickly, but it is more expensive than other sugars. Otherwise, use ordinary granulated white sugar, unless you are darkening the jam for a special finish.

Testing for setting

While you are testing the jam for setting, either remove the saucepan from the heat altogether or keep a careful eye on it so that it does not boil over or burn.

Flake test Dip your wooden spoon into the jam and let it cool a little by turning or holding it in a cool draft. Hold the spoon over the mixture and watch how the jam falls off the edge. If the jam is ready to set, it will partly set on the spoon and the drops will form a flake together, which will fall cleanly off the spoon. Runny jam is not ready.

Saucer test Drop a small spoonful onto a chilled saucer. Return the saucer to the refrigerator for 2–3 minutes, then gently push the mixture with a spoon or your finger. It should wrinkle and feel stiff. If it is liquid, the jam is not ready and you need to continue boiling.

RIGHT Pectin is the key to getting jam to set. Some fruits naturally contain high levels, while others need it adding—all preserves need to be tested for setting point before bottling.

Safety first

- Never turn your back on the jam and make sure it does not burn, or you will have to discard it.

- Take care when you handle the hot, sticky liquid and keep children and animals out of the kitchen.

- Be prepared. Have everything you need ready before you start and allow plenty of time.

Pectin stock

Once made, pectin stock will keep for up to a week in the refrigerator or for about three months in the freezer.

Roughly chop 2 pounds cooking apples, including the cores, peel, and seeds. Bring to a boil and then reduce the heat and simmer for about 45 minutes or until extremely soft. Strain through a jelly bag set over a bowl (it can take two to three hours to go through the bag). Boil the strained juice again for about 20 minutes to reduce the volume by one-third. Allow to cool and then freeze or store in the refrigerator as above. Use 1 teaspoon to improve the set of jam.

How to make preserves and jellies

Method

1 Choose and prepare the fruit, which should be just ripe or nearly ripe. Overripe fruit contains less pectin. Wash and dry the fruit carefully, then remove the stalks or top and tail. It's usual to remove the pits from stone fruit, although you can crack a few pits open and add the kernels for extra flavor.

2 It's a good idea to weigh the pan before you start so that if you have to re-weigh any cooked fruit, you can do it in the pan. Cook the fruit until soft with a little water. A rough guide is half the volume for soft fruit, an equal volume for harder fruit, such as black currants, and two to three times the fruit volume for citrus fruit. Strawberries and raspberries will require little water, but stir them to make sure they don't stick or burn; they will cook in 10–15 minutes. Harder fruits may take up to an hour and will need more water. If you add too much water, you will have to boil to evaporate it, and although this isn't a total disaster, it does mean that the jam will lose color and flavor. If there is too little water, the fruit will burn, which is a total disaster and you will have to discard the jam.

3 Test the fruit and add extra pectin (see opposite). If you are using fruits known to be low in pectin, such as strawberries, you can add extra pectin at the beginning.

4 If you are making a jelly, you should strain the fruit though a jelly bag or a piece of cheesecloth held over a collecting bowl. Make sure that the bag is sterile, which you can do by boiling it.

5 Prewarm the sugar in a large roasting pan in the oven at 325–350°F. Take care that the sugar doesn't burn. You will usually use the same weight of sugar as the raw fruit you have prepared. As the fruit simmers, add the sugar carefully, stirring well, then boil rapidly for 10–15 minutes. (A rapid boil is where the jam continues to bubble even when it's stirred.) If you boil it for too long, the jam will pass the "setting point" and be dark and overcooked. Stir it to stop the sugar sticking, but don't overstir.

Thermometer test If you have used a sugar thermometer as you boiled the jam, you can check the temperature: setting point is 221°F.

Bottling your jam

Remove the jam from the heat, then skim off any scum. A teaspoonful of butter or oil in the pan will disperse some of the scum, but will make jellies become cloudy.

Fill the jars, which you should prewarm in the oven, taking great care that the hot mixture does not cause them to shatter. Also take care that you do not get any of the hot mixture on yourself. Using a wide funnel and a pitcher is the safest way to handle the really hot liquid, which will stick to you. Fill the jars almost to the rim, the mixture will shrink after cooling by up to ¼ inch.

Seal each jar as you fill it with a waxed paper disk, wax side down, and screw on the lid. Allow to cool.

Other methods

You can make jam by using a pressure cooker to cook the fruit. You then remove the cover and cook in an open cooker after adding the sugar. Advocates of this method say that not only does it reduce the cooking time but it helps to retain the flavor and color of the fruit.

You can also use your microwave oven, but not recommended by the USDA. It is essential to use the right amount of sugar and lemon juice. The principle is to microwave, uncovered and on high power, the fruit, sugar, and pectin until it is boiling (this takes about 4 minutes in most microwaves). Reduce to medium power and cook for an additional 5–15 minutes, checking for set during this period. Skim and bottle when hot as above. Some supporters of this method increase the cooking time a little, but stir the mixture every couple of minutes. It's important not to try and microwave large quantities—about

How to make chutney

Prepare the fruit and vegetables. Chutneys frequently, but not always, also include onions, dried fruit, such as raisins, and spices. Garlic is also often featured, but can be left out if you prefer.

Method

1 Put everything in a large saucepan, ideally a boiling-water canner, with the appropriate amounts of vinegar, sugar, and salt. Because the vinegar will act as a preservative, you won't need as much sugar as you do for jam: in general, work with 1 cup sugar and 1–2 cups vinegar for every 4 pounds fruit or vegetables.

2 Bring to a boil and simmer until tender (the timing will depend on the basic ingredients). Take care that it does not burn; stir often and don't go away and leave it. The mixture will thicken as the vinegar evaporates, but don't let it dry out altogether. It's ready when the fruit or vegetables are soft and there is no excess liquid.

3 As with jam, transfer immediately into warmed and sterile jars. Cover the surface with a waxed paper disk, waxed side down, add an airtight lid and seal. Label and store in a cool, dark place and don't be tempted to eat it for at least a month.

13 ounces is the maximum, and less is probably ideal—and you must use a large bowl so that the mixture cannot boil over. As with any jam, handle it with extreme care when it's hot.

The microwave method is perfect for making smaller quantities, and you can easily experiment to find your favorite recipe.

Chutney

Making chutney is an effective method of preserving fruits and vegetables, and they can be used to add flavor to all kinds of food. Once you have made a basic recipe, you can experiment with different ingredients and combinations of ingredients. A great advantage of making chutney is that you can use less than perfect produce. After processing they will taste delicious. Chutney is also easier to make than jam because you don't have to worry about pectin levels and setting points.

What is chutney?

The word chutney derives from the name of an Indian relish, *chatni*, a spiced side dish served with the main course. It's obviously evolved over the years, and there is now an almost limitless number of variations.

The underlying principle is that fruit or vegetables are combined with vinegar to inhibit the actions of the micro-organisms that cause rotting. Chutney will store for a long time in a cool pantry, and the flavor often improves with age. Once opened, chutney should be kept in the refrigerator.

You will need

You will need much of the equipment that you need for making jam (see page 213), but you mustn't use copper, brass, or iron pans, which react with the acid in vinegar. It is best to use stainless steel pans.

RASPBERRY AND REDCURRANT JAM

If you do not like too many seeds in your jam, then cook half the fruit separately and press it through a sieve before adding it to the remaining fruit.

4 cups raspberries
4 cups red currants
1¼ cups water
juice of 2 lemons
4 cups sugar

1 Put the fruit into a large pan and mix together. Add the water. Bring to a boil, then reduce the heat and cover the pan. Simmer for 20–30 minutes until the red currants are really tender.

2 Add the lemon juice and sugar and stir over a low heat until the sugar has completely dissolved.

3 Increase the heat and bring to a boil, then boil hard to setting point. Remove the pan from the heat and, using a slotted spoon, carefully skim off any scum.

4 Transfer the jam to warm, dry jars. Cover the surface of each with a disk of waxed paper, waxed side down, then top with an airtight lid or cellophane cover. Label and allow to cool, then store in a cool, dark place. It will keep for 3–4 months.

GREEN TOMATO CHUTNEY

If you grow tomatoes, you will probably be left with some unripened fruit at the end of the season. But don't throw your green tomatoes away; chop them up and make a tempting chutney.

2 lb green tomatoes, finely chopped
1 lb onions, finely chopped
1 lb cooking apples, peeled, cored, and chopped
2 fresh green chilies, halved, seeded, and finely chopped
2 garlic cloves, crushed
1 teaspoon ground ginger
generous pinch of ground cloves
generous pinch of ground turmeric
¼ cup raisins
1 cup soft dark brown sugar
1¼ cups white wine vinegar

1 Put the tomatoes, onions, apples, and chilies into a large pan and mix together. Add the garlic, ginger, cloves, and turmeric, then stir in the raisins, sugar, and vinegar.

2 Bring to a boil, then reduce the heat and cover the pan. Simmer, stirring frequently, for 1¼–1½ hours or until the chutney has thickened.

3 Transfer the chutney to warm, dry jars and cover the surface of each with a disk of waxed paper, waxed side down, then top with an airtight lid. Label and leave to mature in a cool, dark place for at least 3 weeks before using, or store, unopened, for 6–12 months.

Pickling, salting, and preserving in oil

Some of the traditional methods of preserving have become popular again and even with the modern methods of canning and freezing, they still have an important place in the kitchen.

Pickles

Pickles are a tasty accompaniment to other foods and are a glimpse of the summer in winter. Some people confuse pickles and chutneys, but pickling is a good way of preserving perfect produce in a whole or recognizable form—cauliflower florets, for example—while chutneys are made from chopped produce and cooked.

You can turn a wide variety of produce into impressive pickles. As well as old favorites, such as pickled onions, red cabbage, beet, and cucumbers, you can try more unusual fare. Pickling young walnuts makes them into more than a simple dried nut, and freshly gathered samphire still tasting of the sea can be captured in a pickle bottle to enjoy in cold weather.

It is the vinegar that preserves the food by inhibiting the micro-organisms that make fresh food deteriorate. In some circumstances, brine (salt and water) can also be used, but it is less effective for long-term storage.

You will need

You should always use good- to top-quality fresh produce, ideally recently picked or gathered. Because fresh food loses moisture and you are pickling these vegetables in their (usually) raw and original form, you don't want them to be hollow centered or shriveled.

As with making jams and chutneys, work in a clean kitchen, free from insects, pets, and children, and with lots of space. Allow plenty of time.

You will need a good selection of sterile jars with self-sealing metal lids, funnels, a ladle and slotted spoon, colanders for draining, scales and measuring cups. You will also need thick pot holders and some clean dish towels and dish cloths. Use a knife to prepare the produce so that

it isn't crushed or torn. You will need a large, heavy pan or preserving pan, and because vinegar reacts with certain metals, do not use copper, brass, or iron utensils. You might also need some pieces of cheesecloth to hold herbs and spices.

How to pickle

You can pickle most produce, but they must be of good quality and young; don't use vegetables that are past their best. Prepare the produce according to how you want it to be when you eat it—that is, sliced cucumbers, cauliflower florets, seeded and quartered bell peppers, whole baby beet, sliced beet, green tomatoes, and so on. Some vegetables, such as beet, need cooking first, but most are fine raw.

Most pickling recipes require the vegetables to be soaked in brine for 24 hours to draw out excess water. Brine is normally a 10 percent solution of water and salt, and you should use pickling or canning salt rather than iodized table salt, which will contain additives. Remember that some produce won't need brining. For example, you can remove the moisture from mushrooms by placing them in a small amount of water and then simmering with some salt; drain and dry before proceeding as for other pickles.

The basic method is to pack the prepared vegetables into jars and cover them with vinegar. The better the vinegar, the better the flavor. Wine vinegar gives the best results, but is more expensive. Cider vinegar is also good and remember that white vinegar produces a less strong taste than dark vinegar. Make sure that the acetic acid content is at least 5 percent so that it preserves the produce effectively. If the result is too tart, you can add sugar. Fill the jars almost to the top (leave ½–1 inch). Add pickling spices, dill weed or whatever herbs and spices you like. Seal with waxed paper to keep the vinegar away from the metal lids. Remember to store in a cool place for at least a month, preferably longer, to allow the flavors to mature and develop.

Prepare a spiced vinegar before you begin pickling, experimenting with the spices to make your own tailor-made taste.

Cold method You need to make this pickling liquid in plenty of time. Take 2 tablespoons of the spices of your choice and steep them—that is, pour cold vinegar over them and leave them for a couple of months. You can tie the spices in cheesecloth to keep them together if you wish. A basic recipe includes 1 tablespoon peppercorns, 1 tablespoon cloves, and a small piece of fresh ginger root or a cinnamon stick, and some allspice, but you can vary these according to taste and depending on the produce you are pickling.

Hot method If you haven't left time to make the spiced vinegar by the cold method, you can heat the ingredients. Put them in a stainless steel saucepan and bring to a boil, then simmer for a few minutes and remove from the heat. Cover the pan and allow to cool. Take out the cheesecloth bag or, if the spices are loose, strain the vinegar.

ABOVE Making a cold pickling vinegar is easy, but do remember that it needs time to stand. Use a basic recipe to start with and then try out your own variations.

LEFT If you need a pickling vinegar more quickly, blend the flavors by heating. If you want a clear vinegar, then put the spices in a cheesecloth bag that can be removed.

Sweet pickles

You can also make sweet pickles in which sweetened vinegar is used. This is suitable for fruit such as apples, pears, and plums, which are delicious with cold meat, especially in the middle of winter. They make great presents, too.

To make the sweet vinegar, add 3–4 cups sugar to each 2½ cups vinegar. Do not use malt vinegar. Prick the whole fruits, but there is no need to soak them in brine. The fruits tend to shrivel when they are cooked in vinegar, and if you want to preserve them more perfectly, consider bottling them (see pages 222–3). Add

(see pages 222–3)

suitable spices—cinnamon, cloves, and nutmeg, for example—as well as orange or lemon rind, rosemary, bay, or a vanilla bean. Remember that the herbs and spices must be whole; if they are ground or powdered they will make the vinegar murky, although it won't affect the fruit, which will be fine to eat.

Salting

Historically, salting has been the most important method of preserving food for the hungry seasons, and for this reason salt was a valuable commodity—indeed, the word "salary" derives from the Latin word *salarius*, meaning salt. Salted meats and fish still form a small part of some people's diet, but other methods of preserving, such as canning, freeze-drying, and freezing, have become far more widely used. However, some people still like to salt surplus green beans, especially if freezer space is at a premium, and sauerkraut, the well-known dish from Eastern Europe, is, in essence, salted cabbage.

If you intend to salt some produce, remember to use pickling or canning salt; ordinary table salt contains additives to make it pour smoothly and is not suitable. Choose rock salt (not the sort you put on snow) or sea salt.

Vegetables preserved in salt have to be soaked before cooking in several changes of water to remove as much salt as possible.

Basic recipe for salting

You will need about 1 pound salt for every 4 pounds vegetables. Take a clean glass container

BELOW Salting was one of the few ways that food could be preserved before the advent of freezers—useful if you run out of freezer space or have problems with power supplies.

Preserving in alcohol

The great thing about using alcohol is that you don't have to use a really expensive liqueur. A bottle of cheap gin or vodka combines perfectly with peaches, plums, and damsons or even strawberries, and brandy with plums or apricots makes an impressive combination and a delicious gift.

Leave small fruits whole and slice larger fruits. As a basic guide, add two-thirds alcohol to one-third sugar, top up with your chosen fruit and leave for at least a month

(although they will last for up to a year). You can drink the alcohol, which will have taken on the flavor of the fruit (this is the principle behind sloe gin) and eat the fruit with cream or in a trifle (but don't eat the sloes). Remember, though, that the fruit will be high in alcohol and is not suitable for everyone.

and add a layer of salt in the bottom. Layer the vegetables and salt alternately until you reach the top. Put a plate on top and hold it down with a can or the weights from old-fashioned scales. This will keep the vegetables enveloped in the salt, which will eventually turn to brine as it draws out the moisture. Add a tight-fitting lid and it should keep for up to a year.

Preserving in oil

Jars containing produce such as lemons, small cheeses, and olives in oil always look appetizing, and this is an excellent way to preserve them.

Simply pack the produce into a sterilized jar or bottle and choose some suitable flavorings to complement it—fresh herbs, baby onions, or garlic go with a lot of savory produce. Top up with good-quality olive oil, tap or shake gently to get rid of any air bubbles, and seal with screw-top lids. Keep cheeses in your refrigerator and other produce in a cool place.

Herbs are ideal for preserving in this way, and although it's more expensive than drying or freezing, the infused oil will add a wonderful flavor to Mediterranean dishes. Choose whole, medium-sized leaves—basil, for example—and then pack into a small, sterilized jar. Sprinkle each layer with salt, add oil, and seal. Store in a cool, dark place or the refrigerator, where they will have a long life although the leaves may darken.

PICKLED ONIONS

You will need small onions that are all the same size for this recipe. If you prefer, you can use ordinary malt vinegar instead of spiced vinegar, and if you like sweeter pickles, add up to 1 cup sugar and use white vinegar instead.

3 tablespoons salt
2½ cups water
2 lb small onions
2½–3¾ cups spiced vinegar (see page 219)

1 Make the brine by mixing together the salt and water. Peel the onions and transfer them to a bowl. Cover with the brine and make sure you keep them fully immersed by putting a plate on top. Allow to stand overnight.

2 Drain the onions, wash off any excess salt in cold water, and then drain again.

3 Pack the onions into warm, sterilized jars (see page 213) and pour the vinegar over them. Keep them in a cool, dark place for between four and six weeks before opening.

PICKLED PLUMS

You can use damsons in this recipe, but check the taste because you might want to adjust the amount of sugar you use.

2 lb plums
2 cups sugar
1¾ cups vinegar
1 tablespoon mixed spice, such as whole cloves, allspice, and ginger root
stick of cinnamon
rind of 1 small lemon

1 Wash and prick the plums and place them in a clean, dry bowl.

2 In a large saucepan, dissolve the sugar in the vinegar over a gentle heat. Wrap the spices in cheesecloth and add to the vinegar with the cinnamon stick and lemon rind.

3 Bring to a boil until the mixture becomes syrupy. Allow to cool, then pour over fruit. Cover and leave for a day.

4 Strain the plums, reserving the syrup, and transfer to clean jars. Return the syrup to a saucepan and reboil. Pour over the plums.

5 When they are quite cold, cover and seal. Store for up to two months before using.

SAUERKRAUT

Remove the outer leaves and stalk (which will make the sauerkraut bitter) to give the desired weight of cabbage. If you are making a larger quantity, you will need about 3 tablespoons salt to every 5 pounds cabbage.

1 lb cabbage hearts
½ tablespoon salt

1 Finely shred the cabbage, mix it with the salt, and pack into a clean crock or jars. Push down and add a weighted saucer.

2 Leave for between two and four weeks to ferment. During this time skim off any scum that rises to the surface. Top up the salt if necessary with a brine solution made from mixing 1 tablespoon salt with 4 cups water.

3 Use the sauerkraut as it is, but it won't keep for more than a few days. To keep it longer, sterilize by draining the brine off into a saucepan. Bring to a boil and simmer. Transfer the cabbage to large, clean jars and cover with the boiled brine. Cover the jars and process in boiling water for 25 minutes (see page 223).

Bottling

Bottling is a traditional method of preserving mainly fruits by using syrup and heat to destroy or inhibit the microorganisms that cause food to deteriorate. It must be done carefully to keep the fruit in good condition and safe to eat.

Bottling is the forerunner of canning, and in some countries the process is often known as "canning." Of course, bottling uses glass bottles and does not require the equipment needed for metal canning.

The principle behind bottling is that the produce and jars are heated to a high temperature and then sealed to kill the bacteria and to stop any enzymes from spoiling the food.

Bottling is more suitable for fruit than vegetables, which have to be heated to a higher temperature to destroy dangerous organisms, but if you do want to bottle vegetables, pressure cooking is the recommended method. Vegetables are bottled in brine and are blanched first.

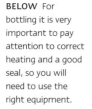

BELOW For bottling it is very important to pay attention to correct heating and a good seal, so you will need to use the right equipment.

Why bottle?

It's so easy to freeze fruit these days that you may wonder why it's worth bothering to bottle any. One reason is that some fruit still tastes better when it's bottled, and it often looks better, too. In addition, rows of glass bottles full of wonderfully colored fruits bring warmth to the dark days of winter. It is an ideal method of preserving a special crop when there are only a small number of fruits. Bottling is a way of recognizing that these are precious. Of course, it's just as suitable for dealing with large quantities of fruit from a bumper crop of plums or greengages.

You will need

As well as the equipment you need to make jam (see page 213), you will need special, sterilized jars with rubber seals (which will be used only once). Because of the nature of the process, you will also need some thick, heatproof gloves. Check that there are no children or pets in the kitchen, and that you have a heatproof surface to work on and, ideally, a wooden surface for the hot bottles to stand on while they cool.

How to bottle

The timing and control of the heat are essential factors in the process because there is a slight risk of botulism, which is, of course, a serious illness. If you intend to use some bottled fruit and you notice that it is bubbling, smells odd, the lid is loose, or there is any evidence of mold, then discard it immediately.

There are four methods of bottling: in the oven, in the pressure cooker, and the cold water and hot water bath methods. The most popular are the cold water and oven methods. The strength of the syrup that you use will depend on both personal taste and the fruit that you are bottling. Peaches, for example, are best in a heavy syrup, but plums are better in a light to medium syrup. The lighter the syrup, the better the appearance of the fruit.

- **Light syrup**—½ cup sugar to 2½ cups water
- **Medium syrup**—1–1¼ cups sugar to 2½ cups water
- **Heavy syrup**—1½–2 cups sugar to 2½ cups water

Make the syrup by boiling the sugar and water together, stirring continuously, until the sugar has dissolved. If the syrup is slightly cloudy, strain through strong cheesecloth.

Before you begin, dip the rubber rings in boiling water to soften them and make them easier to put on the jars.

Cold water bath method

Put the prepared fruit in sterilized jars and pour over the cold syrup. Tighten the lids, but not so much that air cannot escape or the jar could explode during processing. Stand the jars on a wire rack in the bottom of a large, deep pan. Add cold water to come up to the necks of the jars.

Put a sugar thermometer into the pan. Slowly heat the water over the course of an hour until the water temperature reaches 131°F, then continue heating for 30 minutes until the temperature is 165–190°F, the lower temperature being suitable for fragile berry fruits and the higher for larger, denser fruits such as pears. Maintain this temperature for an additional 10–30 minutes according to fruit type. If you allow it to heat too rapidly, the fruit will be overcooked and will lose color.

Ladle some of the water out of the pan, then use jar lifters to lift out the jars. Tighten the lids and allow to cool. Always check the seals before putting the fruit in store (see right for instructions).

Hot water bath method

Put the fruit in sterilized jars and pour over the hot syrup. Tighten the lids, but not so tightly that air cannot escape. Stand the jars in a pan and cover with warm water at 100°F. Slowly heat the water, increasing the temperature to simmering, 190°F, over 30 minutes, and maintain at simmering temperature according to the type of produce—2 minutes for berry fruits, 10 minutes for damsons, and 40 minutes for pears. Remove the bottles from the pan as for the cold water bath method.

In the oven

This method is not suitable for fruits such as pears and quinces that require longer cooking times. Put the fruit in jars, cover with boiling syrup, and loosely fasten the lids. Jars filled with cold syrup might crack in the oven, so you must use hot syrup for this method. In addition, don't use large jars because it takes longer for the heat to penetrate the jar, and the top layer of fruit might discolor before it is cooked.

Stand the jars on a baking sheet, spacing them well apart—at least 2 inches—and cook in the center of a preheated oven at 300°F for 15–40 minutes depending on the size and firmness of the fruit. You can check the timing by noticing when the fruit just begins to rise in the syrup.

Pressure cooker method

Put the prepared fruit into clean jars and add the boiling syrup to within ½ inch of the rim. Fit the rubber rings, lids, and clips. It's vital that some air is able to escape during cooking to reduce the pressure, so check the instructions in your pressure cooker manual. Usually, however, you should move the clips slightly to the side of the lid. Cover with boiling water, making sure the cooker is not more than two-thirds full, and follow the instructions for bottling in the manual for your model. Remove after the appropriate time, tighten the seals, and allow to cool.

Testing for a good seal

Whichever method you have used, leave the jars until they are cool, which will be at least 24 hours. Remove the screw bands or clips from the jar and then carefully hold the rim of the lid and lift the container. If it is sealed, it should hold its own weight, with the lid remaining firm. If it does not, the vacuum has not formed and the contents should be eaten immediately or reprocessed with fresh syrup.

There are several reasons for a vacuum failing to form:

- The bottle, jar, lid, or ring is faulty.
- The jar wasn't sealed promptly enough after being removed from the heat.
- A seed has lodged in the rubber ring.
- The lids have been disturbed before the contents have cooled.

Grains and bread

Growing grain for bread today may not be one of the most obvious routes to self-sufficiency, but increasing numbers of self-supporters are finding it worthwhile to grow grain, to provide cereal and wheat from which to make bread.

BELOW Yeast cookery does not have to be in the traditional bread shape—once you have mastered the recipe, then experiment with form and flavorings.

Using grains

In the past in the West, bread was used to supplement the diet and provide bulk for people who couldn't afford to buy meat. Today most people's meals are balanced, and the idea that protein is accompanied by a larger amount of a carbohydrate is widely accepted. As countries become richer, they tend to turn to processed grains, such as white flour. However, people are increasingly looking for a diet that contains a larger proportion of whole grains, especially as research seems to reveal the health benefits of a diet that includes more fiber from the grain.

Daily bread

The easy availability of processed bread in the developed world has rather devalued the idea of grains and bread in many people's minds, and most of us take its cheapness and availability for granted. Yet the rise of artisan-type breads, a willingness to experiment by even commercial bread makers, and an understanding of the value of whole grains in the diet are paving the way to something of a comeback for bread and grain in the diet.

Growing your own grain

Growing grain on a small scale on your own plot is quite possible (see pages 128–9), but if you are going to make bread, you must plant a "hard" variety, such as the heritage 'Maris Widgeon' (which grows a huge length of straw), 'Avalon' or 'Mercia.'

When the grain is ready for harvest, you will need to winnow it—that is, separate it from the wheat plant to leave just the grain (hence the expression "separating the wheat from the chaff"). You can do this by rubbing it through your fingers on a breezy day and letting the wind take the chaff. You will be left with the whole grain, from which you want to extract the soft kernel inside from the hard outer coat, so it needs grinding. In white flours the outer husk is separated, but home grinders tend to grind the whole grain to produce a nutritious, high-fiber whole wheat flour. You can either grind it with stones by hand, which is extremely time consuming, or purchase a home mill.

Barley has to go through a pearling machine, which removes the outer husk. Pearl barley can be added to soups and stews to create filling and nutritious dishes.

It's quite difficult to remove the husk from oats, and they are best purchased already husked or as oatmeal.

Millet grows in dry areas and in poor soil, but it might not ripen in wetter countries, although you can cut it and dry it. It's quite easy to strip out the small grains, and they have a number of uses, such as giving some substance to soup or thickening a casserole.

Rye also thrives in poor soils, but it is a cool-climate cereal and is much hardier than wheat. Process it in the same way as other grains and use rye flour in place of wheat. It doesn't absorb moisture as well as wheat flour, so you must remember to adjust your recipes accordingly to ensure you get a good result.

Making bread

The act of breaking bread with someone is an old symbol of friendship and of reconciliation between enemies. This reflects bread's long significance in human life—it was found in ancient Egyptian tombs to provide food for the "traveller." Today bread is still an extremely important part of most people's staple diet, and

Frumenty

Some people believe that frumenty is the medieval forerunner of muesli. It is actually a traditional British farming dish, but it makes an appearance in many forms around the world. There are numerous recipes, but they are all variations on the following. Simmer whole or chopped wheat for 12 hours (if you have a pressure cooker, check the manual; it will save a lot of time). Add butter, mixed spice, dried fruit (such as currants and raisins), sugar, cream, and rum (if desired). It is like drinking a rich fruit cake and is traditionally enjoyed at Christmas time.

Fluffin, a close relative of frumenty, is made by simmering pearl barley and milk until soft and liquid and then adding grated nutmeg, sugar, and some brandy.

WHOLE WHEAT CASSEROLE

This is an ideal casserole for using whatever vegetables are in season. You can add root vegetables—carrots, parsnips, rutabagas—if they available, but you should make sure that you chop them into even-sized chunks so that they cook evenly. You can cook the entire casserole on the top of the stove and brown the cheese topping under a preheated hot broiler once the vegetables are tender.

½ cup whole wheat grains

about 2½ cups stock or tomato juice

selection of chopped vegetables, such as 2 onions, 3 celery sticks, 2 leeks, and 2 zucchini

1 garlic clove, chopped (optional)

1 bay leaf

grated cheese

1 Wash, rinse, and drain the whole wheat grains and add to the stock or tomato juice in a large saucepan. Bring to a boil and then simmer until the wheat is tender, which might take up to 2 hours. Take care that it doesn't burn and add more liquid if needed.

2 Add the chopped vegetables, garlic, if using, and bay leaf and simmer on the top of the stove until the vegetables are cooked. Transfer to a casserole dish, sprinkle over the cheese, and cook, uncovered, in a preheated oven, 400°F, until the cheese is bubbling. Serve the casserole with whole wheat bread.

MILLET DUMPLINGS

Serve these dumplings with a thick sauce, such as homemade tomato sauce, as a meal in themselves or add them to a thick soup. Instead of onion you can add any chopped vegetable of your choice, such as leek, parsnip, or a firm zucchini.

¾ cup millet

2 tablespoons butter or 1 tablespoon corn or olive oil, plus extra oil for frying

1 onion, finely chopped

2 cups stock

1 egg, lightly beaten

2 heaping tablespoons bread crumbs

chopped fresh herbs, such as chives, parsley, and basil, to taste

sea salt

1 Wash and drain the millet.

2 Heat a little oil in a skillet and cook the onion. Add the millet. Pour the stock into the pan and simmer until the millet is soft and has absorbed the stock. Allow to cool.

3 Transfer the millet to a bowl and add the egg, bread crumbs, and the herbs. Mix together and season with salt to taste. Form into balls or, if preferred, flatten them between floured hands.

4 Heat the butter or oil in a large skillet and cook the dumplings on all sides until brown. Serve hot.

making your own bread is one way in which you can take control of that part of your nutrition.

There are now some excellent flours on the market, sold in even the big food stores and supermarkets, and organic flour is relatively easy to obtain. Alternatively, you can visit a local flour mill—many have now been restored—where traditionally ground flour is sold. You can also, of course, grow your own wheat and grind it yourself for a truly homemade bread. The actual act of making bread is therapeutic: the kneading and the baking as well as the rich smell of the baking loaf soothe the soul; a good enough reason to make your own bread.

What is bread?

Bread means different things to different peoples in different countries. It can range from the flat bread of Asia to the soda breads of Ireland and from the black rye bread of Eastern Europe to the yeasty bread that is so familiar in our supermarkets.

The expression "to leaven" bread means to lighten it. Unleavened breads include tortillas and chapattis, and they are flat and thin—they have to be so in order to cook through properly. Bread is "leavened" with either soda (baking powder) or yeast. For some reason people often feel that cooking with yeast is going to be too difficult or too time consuming to achieve anything worthwhile. Making bread is not an exact science, and you'll probably find that your results will sometimes be outstanding and sometimes less so, but that's part of the charm of homemade bread. It's true, too, that the more bread you make, the more successful you will be. As for being time consuming, it's true that you have to allow the bread to rise, but you can do something else while this happens.

Baking bread is an everyday pleasure that you can easily make part of your day-to-day life.

You will need

When you start to make your own bread, you will probably find that you already have most of the equipment you will need in the kitchen, especially if you enjoy baking. Some people like to bake loaves on stones, and you can buy special baskets for "proofing" (getting the bread to rise), but many people manage perfectly well without these. You will definitely need:

- Large, heavy baking sheets
- Loaf pans if you want a change from cottage-style loaves
- Wooden boards
- Cloths to cover the dough
- Large mixing bowl—use the largest bowl you have because the dough needs space to rise; earthenware, metal, and plastic are all fine, and you can even use a large, clean dishpan if you can't find anything else
- Bottle to spray on water—you can find these in garden centers and hardware stores, where they tend to be less expensive than sprays sold specifically for bread making
- Cooling racks
- Somewhere warm and draft free to put the dough to rise
- A timer with a buzzer if you get easily distracted

What is bread made from?

Basic yeast-based bread is made from flour, salt, yeast, sugar, and water or milk or a combination of water and milk. It's also common to add a piece of butter or lard or a dash of oil.

Yeast Yeast is a living substance that needs particular conditions in order for it to ferment

BELOW Bread making only requires very basic equipment and you can get loaf pans in all shapes and sizes.

and produce the gas that causes the bread to rise. In order to do this it needs warmth, food, and liquid and time.

Yeast comes in both fresh and dried forms, and it's often much easier to obtain dried yeast these days, although you may be able to buy fresh yeast from your local health food store or local baker. Fresh yeast does not keep for long, although some people claim they have kept it in the freezer successfully. It looks like a block of putty and is moist with a distinctive but not unpleasant smell. To be used it has to be mixed with liquid and sugar until the mixture is frothy.

Dried yeast is sold in ¼-ounce envelopes or jars and comes in various forms. It's important to read the package carefully in order to reconstitute it by dissolving the granules in warm liquid, when it starts to release the carbon dioxide that makes bread rise. Yeasts sold as "instant" or "rapid rise" are ideal for use with bread-making machines. They are also available in ¼-ounce envelopes, and this type of yeast is mixed with the dry ingredients without being dissolved first. Check the package, because some work faster than others and you won't need to leave the bread to rise so many times.

Flour There is now a wide range of flours on the market, and most indicate on the package how they should be used. Some are helpfully labeled "bread flour," but you will also come across:

- **Whole wheat**—flour that has been milled from the whole wheat grain with nothing added or taken away
- **Stoneground**—flour milled with traditional stones, which give it a distinctive texture
- **Strong white**—flour usually made from very hard Canadian wheat, which has a high protein level, extra strength, and tolerance for baking
- **White**—flour from only the creamy middle of the wheat, which is milled with the outer husk and wheatgerm removed (this goes on to be bran, which may feature in animal feed or as a breakfast cereal ingredient depending on the wheat variety)
- **Brown**—flour that has some of the wheat bran but that is lighter than whole wheat flour, which makes it easier to get a light-textured loaf from it
- **Malted brown**—flour that includes kibbled

malted grains and malt flour to give it a good flavor and texture
- **Organic**—flour that could be any of the above forms but that has been grown under organic conditions, without artificial fertilizers or pesticides, and that is independently certified as such by a certification body

All the flours have distinctive characteristics and their own advantages and disadvantages. For your first experiments with baking, begin with a white flour, which is easier to work with, and then progress to other types.

Liquid This can be water or milk or a combination of both, but whatever you use it should be warm when it is mixed with the yeast or the yeast cannot ferment. The liquid should feel warm but not hot, which would kill the yeast.

Salt Salt is added to give flavor to the bread, and you shouldn't be tempted to leave it out. Don't let it come in direct contact with yeast—salt will kill yeast—but if you add it to the flour, it will be diluted enough for it to be safe. It is supposed to have a scientific effect as well in that it will tighten the mixture and enable the gas bubbles to be trapped and so more effective. Table salt is fine, but you can also use sea salt.

Sugar Ordinary white superfine sugar will do.

ABOVE There are several different sorts of flour to choose from. Start by using a white bread flour and move on to other types as you gain experience.

Basic loaf

As you get more confident about making bread, you can add a wealth of ingredients to the basic recipe, including herbs, onions, honey, nuts, and seeds.

Ingredients

1 cake fresh yeast or ¼ oz dried yeast

2 teaspoons superfine sugar

1¼–1¾ cups warm water or water and milk
 mixed

3 cups white bread flour

2 teaspoons salt

1 tablespoon olive oil or butter or lard

Method

1 If you are using fresh yeast, blend the yeast with 1 teaspoon of the sugar, add the warm liquid, and stir well. If you are using dried yeast, make it up according to the instructions on the package. Mix together the flour, salt, remaining sugar, oil (or blend in the butter or lard), and, if using, the dried yeast according, to the package instructions.

2 Make a well in the center of the flour mixture and pour in the liquid, either with the fresh yeast or the liquid alone. Mix to a soft dough with a wooden spoon. It should start to leave the side of the bowl and stick together.

3 Turn the dough out of the bowl onto a lightly floured surface and knead well for about 10 minutes until it feels elastic, smooth, and firm, and no longer sticky. Shape it into a round, dust with flour, transfer to the container and cover it with plastic wrap or a clean dish cloth. Allow it to ferment in a warm (but not hot) place, such as the kitchen, for between 30 minutes and 2 hours. The dough will double in size, so make sure your container is large enough.

4 Knock back the risen dough to remove uneven air pockets and re-establish the texture. Some people like to bang the dough with a fist, but others say that squashing and squeezing it is more successful. Knead the dough again for a couple of minutes to get it back into shape. It will reduce in size.

5 If you wish, you can allow it to rise again and repeat the previous step. For simple loaves divide the dough into bread pans or shape it into loaves and allow it to proof (rise) again. Keep an eye on this, as the time taken will vary from 20 minutes to over an hour. The dough should look plump, but not overblown. Bake in a preheated oven, 450°F, for 20–30 minutes. If you have a fan-assisted oven, check with your handbook; you might need to reduce the time or temperature to prevent the loaf from burning.

6 Remove loaves from the pans and tap the base of each with your knuckles or with a wooden spoon; if they sound hollow, they are done. Take care that you do not burn your hands, as they will be hot. Allow to cool on a wire rack.

How to knead

When you have turned the dough out on to a lightly floured surface, hold it with one hand and stretch it by pushing the dough away from you with the other hand—you are stretching the gluten. Then fold it back toward you and turn the bread slightly and repeat. You will need to keep your hands well floured. As you knead dough, it changes in texture from sticky to smooth and elastic.

Dairying

Many self-supporters find that the dairy becomes one of the most important parts of their self-sufficient life, providing milk but also cream, yogurt, ice cream, butter, and cheese, all foods in themselves and also the ingredients for other dishes.

Dairying is often regarded as a rather complicated activity, and indeed it can be so for commercial producers of hard cheeses. However, dairying on a small scale will quickly become part of your everyday life. Making soft cheeses is not difficult, nor is collecting cream, and then you will soon be thinking about making some butter. As with so many of the skills you will have acquired as you become more self-sufficient, if you begin with simple but effective recipes, you will quickly gain the confidence to expand your repertoire.

You will need

Before you can begin you must have a **dairy area**. That sounds rather grand, but if you are processing milk every day, you will either have to arrange your kitchen so that there is a specific area where you can keep all your equipment or have a completely separate area for working and storage, which can be kept perfectly clean and that is cool. Because it is so important to keep your dairy area spotlessly clean, be careful not to keep anything in it that can gather dust or attract any sort of flying insect. Keep the contents to a bare, cleanable minimum. It's a good idea to start in a small way, and you will soon learn how much space you need and the most appropriate layout.

You must be able to keep insects out, and it's common to fit **fly screens** over dairy windows. You will need milk **bottles** and **labels**. A specialized **dairy thermometer** will be essential for all but the smallest-scale production, and no matter how much milk you process, you will need some **dairy sterilizer**, which is available in liquid or tablet form. Make sure that all cloths in the dairy are perfectly clean.

You will need to be able to cool the milk and have somewhere to put a **cream separator**. A

separate **refrigerator and freezer** will be useful, and you will also need somewhere to set out your **cheese-making equipment** and store the cheese at the various stages of its manufacture. Make sure that there is a large **sink** with hot and cold water and a number of electrical points, including one for a kettle so that you can boil water.

Your **milking pail** should be stainless steel so that it can be sterilized. After each milking you must rinse the bucket, then wash it in very hot water and detergent, then rinse it again with a dairy sterilizer. Finally, rinse it thoroughly with clean water and leave it upside down to drain where it cannot be contaminated by insects or dust. If the bucket is not scrupulously clean, it will cause the milk to sour from bacteria.

The milk will arrive in your dairy having been strained into a **collecting vessel**, which should have a lid—hence the design of the traditional **milk churn**—or if you are milking on a small scale, you could carry the bucket into your dairy area for processing and strain the milk at that point into a lidded vessel. You can buy **dairy strainers** or use nylon sieves with a milk filter between them.

The milk must then be cooled immediately after milking. You can buy special **cooling equipment**, but as long as what you use can be easily sterilized and allows the milk to cool rapidly, it will do the job. Half-fill the sink with cold water, put the container into it and then trickle cold water over the lidded container. Cool the milk to 41°F.

If you haven't got a specialized cooler, you can use a little ingenuity. Make a series of holes in a hose and arrange the hose round the lid of the churn so that cold water cascades evenly down the outside. Alternatively, you can buy whole tubes, known as in-churn coolers, that are fitted within the churn in order to cool the milk, but you must take great care to clean them very thoroughly after use.

Keep milk in a refrigerator until it is consumed. Goats' milk freezes well, but be sure to label each day's supply with the date.

Treated milk

After cooling, the milk is unpasteurized. Pasteurized milk is milk that has been heated to kill all bacteria, and this can be done by heating it to 192°F for a second and then quickly cooling it to 70°F. To do this you can use ice cubes in water if necessary. If you are going to pasteurize on a daily basis, it will be far easier and much more effective to purchase a home pasteurizing machine. Milk that is subjected to prolonged boiling is known as ultra heat treated (UHT) milk.

Pregnant women and anyone classified as vulnerable, such as invalids or young children, should always drink pasteurized milk, but the debate for and against pasteurization continues, with strong supporters on both sides of the argument. Whatever the rights and wrongs of the process, unpasteurized milk must come from healthy animals that are kept and milked hygienically, and the milk must be consumed within a few days of production.

Working with milk

Now you are ready to progress to processing the milk. There are differences in the make-up of goats' milk and cows' milk, so you will need to alter recipes slightly to suit your type of milk. In addition, the butterfat content of cows' milk varies according to breed and the time of lactation, so be aware of this. As you gain experience, you will be able to make adjustments to take account of these variations.

Milk is a perfect medium for growing bacteria, and it's essential that you practice excellent hygiene and that your dairy area always reflects this. In reality, your dairy starts with the milking process (see page 174). This area must be spotless, and when the milk reaches the dairy it must be free of any foreign bodies, such as straw or shavings. Contaminated milk must be sterilized or discarded.

Although you will not need any specific qualifications to produce milk and dairy products for your family, depending on where you live, you might need a food hygiene certificate or its equivalent if you are producing on a larger scale. Relevant courses are widely available, and you will probably find them useful anyway, but check local regulations in case they are mandatory for you.

LEFT You will need a clean area to process your milk. Milk must be produced and processed away from contamination in the form of dust or dirt.

Making cream

The word "cream" has come to mean the best of something, and it is often associated with luxury and special occasions. Yet if you have dairy animals, especially cows, you will be able to produce your own cream remarkably easily, and from that it is but a short step to making butter. At some points during the cows' lactation cycle and depending on the breed, cream will be quite plentiful, and this deliciously fresh, thick cream will have a distinctive flavor.

You can use cream for further cooking—to enhance homemade produce such as vegetables in a cream sauce, for example—and, of course, it is the perfect accompaniment for soft fruits, such as strawberries and raspberries. Some creams will freeze quite well—cream based on Jersey milk is one of them because it has a higher fat content than other milks—but creams with less than 35 percent butterfat will freeze if you whip them with confectioners' sugar.

Remember that you will have skim milk left over from making cream, and you need to have a use for this—feeding pigs was the traditional use. If you are feeding goats' or cows' milk to youngsters, keep a full-fat quantity for them before processing.

There are several types of cream. **Light cream** has an extraction rate of about 2½ cups from 1 gallon of milk. **Heavy cream** has an extraction rate of 1¾ cups from 1 gallon of milk. You can also obtain **Devonshire or extra thick cream**, which is made by standing the separated cream in a shallow pan. After 12–24 hours it is slowly heated (but not boiled) until the top crinkles. It is then cooled again. Devonshire cream has to be eaten quickly. If it is to be kept for longer, it should be heated in a water bath (double boiler) to 181°F for 30 seconds and then cooled. It used to be said that the more slowly it was heated, the more effective were the results.

BELOW
Homemade cream is the perfect accompaniment for your luscious home-grown fruits.

You will need

It is important to remember that cream rises to the top of milk, so you must be able to collect it from the surface, either by hand skimming or by a mechanical method. As with most dairying processes, the equipment you buy will depend on the quantity you want to produce, on the regularity with which you wish to do it, and on the time you have to devote to the procedure.

Ideally, you will need a **cream separator** (see opposite), although it is possible to manage with a wide-topped pan or bowl.

Separating milk by hand

If you are using a pan rather than a special cream separator, do not move the milk around too much before pouring it into the receptacle because this seems to delay the cream rising. It's important that the milk is fresh and clean (see page 231), and as it stands in the pan, you must keep it cool and free from flying insects, as well as from the family cat.

There are several methods of collecting the cream manually:

- You can use a skimmer (a ladle with small holes that allow the milk to run out) and scrape the cream off the top, transferring it to a clean pot or pitcher.
- You can place some kind of straining material in the bowl before you add the milk, then pull it up so that the cream remains on the material. This method is quite quick if you can get it right, but it can be very messy and you need to be able to sterilize the material or keep replacing it.
- You can use a bowl that has a hole or holes in the base, which can be plugged. When you remove the plugs, the milk will drain into another bowl set below, leaving the cream to be scraped from the upper bowl. Make sure that you can clean the holes properly.

Using a mechanical separator

If you are making cream regularly, a mechanical separator will be a good investment. Choose a model carefully, however. Some separators consist of a series of scoops that work by centrifugal force, and these can be extremely fiddly and time consuming to clean after use. Look for a model that is relatively easy to clean properly, even though it might be more expensive initially. Take care if you are buying a second-hand one, and never buy one that shows the slightest sign of rust because it will be impossible to clean and will taint the cream.

The next decision is between buying a manually operated separator or a powered model. If you are making cream occasionally, you might find the charm of hand cranking quite attractive, but if you are making it every other day, the energy and time you will need to spend on a hand-operated machine will soon make you yearn for a powered model. Try working with a hand-operated separator to find out exactly how long it will take to use. Be honest about your requirements from the start, because it might be better to spend a little more now rather than have to rethink your needs in a few months' time.

Goats' milk cream

Some people say that you cannot make cream from goats' milk because its composition is different from cows' milk. They will tell you that goats' milk has no cream separation because the fat molecules are smaller, although it is richer than cows' milk, with an average of less than ½ ounce fat per cup, compared to ⅓ ounce for the same amount of cows' milk. However, you can make cream from goats' milk, and if it is your main requirement, choose a breed or strain of goat that is known to have a high butterfat content in the milk, even though the milk from most goats can be used to produce cream. Cream and butter from goats' milk is white in color.

RIGHT Cream naturally rises to the top of milk and all methods of collecting cream are based on that fact.

Making butter

Fresh butter has an incomparable flavor, and if you are already making cream in your dairy, you will easily be able to make your own delicious butter. The principle underlying the process is that cream is moved around until the butterfat particles show themselves as little granules, which separate from the buttermilk.

It will take you as much effort and time to make a small amount of butter as to make a larger quantity. Bear in mind, too, that commercially produced butter has added ingredients that are designed to improve its shelf life, so you will have to eat your own butter relatively quickly. Salting will help to prolong its life, or you can store the surplus in your deep freeze.

RIGHT Churning butter by hand is hard work, but satisfying. The churn must be kept scrupulously clean.

BELOW The butter can have a distinctive pattern put on it by using a special mold.

You will need

To make butter you will need a **churn**, which can be the simple, age-old design of a large glass jar with paddles inside and a handle to turn or a modern electric churner. Churning by hand is hard work, but deeply satisfying, although it is probably not practical if you are regularly producing a large quantity, when you will need to source more mechanical equipment. As with cream making, the model you choose will depend on how much butter you intend to make and the time you have available.

Some people claim to have made butter with a hand whisk or an electric mixer set at low speed. Very small amounts can even be made in a jam jar or bottle, which is shaken by hand or rolled backward and forward. Egg mixers can also be used, but they are slow and messy. Whatever you use, you must be able to clean and sterilize the equipment.

You will also need a **bowl** and **sieve or strainer** to remove the buttermilk—these, too, must be sterilized—as well as **butter pats** to shape the butter. You can also obtain molds with various designs on them. Dairies used to stamp their butter with a mark—such as a flower—to show who had made it, and this indication of the maker has been picked up by people who sell through farmers' markets.

In addition to the equipment, you will also need patience. Butter does not happen quickly, and if you are churning by hand, it can take up to what will feel like a very long 30 minutes.

How to make butter

Different makers interpret the steps to making butter in different ways, but the basic process is unvarying:

• Collect the cream and ripen it
• Churn the cream
• Wash the butter granules
• Dry the granules
• Work the butter, then wrap and store it

Some makers like to add salt—either at the end of the churning stage or at the working stage—and the usual quantity is 4 teaspoons to 2 cups, but you can add more or less depending on your taste. The saltier the butter, the longer it will keep, but not everyone likes salted butter.

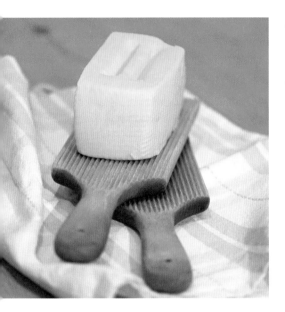

LEFT Working the butter into pats is one of the most enjoyable steps in butter making.

Ripening the cream For the natural chemical process to take place in the cream, it should be about 24 hours old and at a temperature of 54–61°F, depending on the outside temperature —cream will churn at a lower temperature in hot weather. Don't use cream straight from the refrigerator, and if you have an Aga or similar range in your kitchen, you could stand it near the stove overnight in very cold weather.

Churning the cream Using whichever type of churn suits you best (see opposite), agitate the cream, which will thicken until the butter granules appear and the liquid goes thin again and becomes buttermilk. Some people, but by no means all, like to add "breaking water" at this point—about 1 cup of water to 2 cups of cream. The water should be cold if the weather is warm, and 61°F if the weather is cold. Keep churning slowly, but don't allow the lumps to become too big. Any lumps that are bigger than peas will be hard to wash properly.

Washing

You must wash every trace of buttermilk from the grains—if you do not do this, the butter will taste rancid and not store properly. You can strain off the buttermilk and keep it separate because it does have other uses: if you are not feeding it to pigs, you can drink it (it contains beneficial proteins), or you can include it in recipes, including farmhouse buttermilk cake (see right).

At this stage you can put the butter lumps back into the churn and cover them with water—don't use water that is too cold or the grains will shrink, and make sure that it is not too warm or the butter will melt. Churn again and drain, repeat until the water is clear and contains no buttermilk. Or, wash the grains in cold running water, although this method does waste water.

Drying One of the easiest ways of drying the grains is to drain them over cheesecloth and to squeeze the cloth gently to remove the water. Put the butter on a clean board placed on a surface from which water can drain away. Press and work the butter to remove more water. If the water is still coming up as milky, add more clean water and keep rinsing the pat until the water runs clear. It cannot be overstressed how important it is to get all the buttermilk out. Butter pats are ideal for working the butter at this stage, but if you don't have any, use big spatulas or flat wooden spoons.

Working the butter

This is one of the most enjoyable steps in making butter. Keep working it until it is smooth, then form it into pats, put it in jars, add your own stamp, and then cover and keep in a cool, dark place. Wrapping it in waxed paper covered with foil will keep it fairly airtight, or you can place it in glass or earthenware containers. Don't use plastic containers, which can taint the butter.

FARMHOUSE BUTTERMILK CAKE

Instead of currants and raisins you could use some of your own dried fruits, such as black currants.

1 cup butter
4 cups self-rising flour
2½ cups raisins or currants
pinch of ground cinnamon
pinch of mixed spice
pinch of ground ginger (optional)
1 cup buttermilk
1 tablespoon molasses
1 cup brown sugar

1 In a bowl, blend the butter into flour. Add the dried fruit and spices.

2 Meanwhile, warm the buttermilk, then add it to the molasses and sugar, stirring until the mixture is frothy.

3 Stir the buttermilk mixture into the flour mixture. Transfer to a greased and lined 9-inch cake pan and bake in a preheated oven, 400°F, for about 25 minutes. Allow to cool in the pan before turning out onto a wire rack.

Making yogurt, kefir, junket, and ice cream

Fashions come and go in dairying. Today yogurt is more likely to be chosen in preference to cream for a light dessert or as a snack rather than junket. The popularity of ice cream is enduring, however, and having a source of cream from your own cows will enable you to create some delicious flavors.

There is a revival in interest in making ice cream on a small scale, often by artisan producers who use milk from named cattle breeds—Jersey ice cream, for example—as well as from goats' milk. It's also possible to make ice cream from sheep and buffalo milk, but all these ice creams have one thing in common: a diverse and innovative range of flavorings, from traditional vanilla to chili and everything in between.

The great thing about making your own dairy products is that your imagination is the only limit on the flavors and textures you can create. Take the basic recipes and play around with them. At first you might prefer to make small quantities, using the fresh fruit and produce you have on hand, before moving on to large batches and more elaborate concoctions. But do remember to write down the successful combinations so that you know what quantities you used.

Yogurt

Whole milk makes the best yogurt, but you can make it from all milks—sheep and goats' milk are ideal—including skim milk and even soya milk. You can strain it through cheesecloth first if you want an even thicker product.

Yogurt is straightforward to make, and there are several useful machines on the market that make the process even easier. The basic recipe is that a "starter" culture is added to warm milk. You can either buy the starter or simply use part of a carton of plain yogurt. Put the milk and culture in a warm box, which is where a special machine makes everything simple. You can also use a wide-mouthed thermos flask (the sort you use for soup rather than tea) or stand the container in a box lined with hay or even on a warm but not hot kitchen range overnight. The milk will thicken, and the longer you leave it, the thicker it will become. You can add the flavoring at the same time as the culture or later, when the plain yogurt is ready.

Some makers think that the milk should be boiled before it's used to make yogurt, and it does seem sensible to sterilize it because the process involves introducing a culture and allowing the milk to sit in a warm place, the ideal conditions for less welcome bacteria to develop. The milk and culture plus any flavorings should be kept at a temperature of 100–120°F for between 12 and 48 hours, depending on how thick you want the yogurt to be. Take care that the temperature does not exceed the recommended range; the ideal is probably about 113°F.

Take out some of each day's culture to make the next batch, but you will have to get a new starter, either a fresh plain yogurt or a culture, after a few weeks because the yogurt bacteria are taken over by other bacteria.

BELOW Yogurt has become popular as an alternative to cream and as a snack or dessert. Making your own is very satisfying.

Safety first

If you are using eggs in any recipe, remember that vulnerable groups, including young children and pregnant women, should avoid eating raw eggs. Make sure that the eggs you use are fresh and that they have clean shells when you collect them. If you are making ice cream for commercial purposes you may want to pasteurize the mixture. Remember that ice cream is one of the few foods that is really dangerous to refreeze once it has been allowed to defrost.

Kefir

Like yogurt, kefir is a fermented milk product, which originated in the Caucasus region. The bacteria used are present only in kefir grains and in cultures prepared from these grains. Kefir can be left plain or flavored.

The culture and mix are put in a glass jar with a rubber seal that will allow pressure to escape. They are then strained, and the culture is removed and used again. It is perhaps more of an acquired taste than yogurt, but its supporters claim it has health benefits.

Junket

Junket is milk to which rennet (an enzyme from a calf's stomach, which clots the milk to make it digestible) has been added. It was popular in the late 19th and early 20th centuries and was often given to invalids. You can buy vegetarian rennet from health stores, but you can make your own from the lining of the paunch of newly dead calves. Junket separates into curds and whey (looking like unstrained yogurt), and you can add nutmeg, jelly, cinnamon, and sugar or even alcohol to flavor it.

Ice cream

There are variations on the basic recipe for ice cream, some sticking purely to cream, sugar and a flavoring such as fruit, some including egg yolks and some gelatin. Other recipes add whole milk. A basic recipe is given here, but you should experiment to see what suits your milk best, bearing in mind that heavy cream makes the best ice cream. You can create ripple effects or combine flavors and colors for a marbled effect.

Whichever recipe you decide to follow, there are two basic ways to make ice cream: with and without churning the freezing mixture. The first method involves using your freezer, while the second requires the aid of an ice cream machine.

Basic ice cream

If you have an ice cream maker, transfer the cooled mixture (at the end of step 4) to the machine for churning and follow the instruction manual for your particular model.

Ingredients

2 eggs, separated
1 cup confectioners' sugar
1¼ cups heavy cream
vanilla extract, to taste (optional)
fresh fruit, to taste (optional)

Method

1 In a bowl, beat the egg whites to soft peaks and beat in the sugar. In a separate bowl, whip the cream. In another bowl, beat together the egg yolks and vanilla extract, if using.

2 Combine the egg yolk mixture with the cream, then add the egg white and beat again. Add fresh fruit, if using.

3 Pour the mixture into a freezer-proof container, cover with a lid, and leave in the refrigerator for a couple of hours to chill.

4 Transfer the ice cream to the freezer and leave it until it has begun to freeze from the outside but not in the middle. Put the container on a flat surface and beat the mixture thoroughly until it is smooth.

5 Repeat step 4 twice more at about 40-minute intervals, depending on your freezer, to give a smooth ice cream without churning.

Making cheese

Cheese making can be as simple or as complicated as your time and skills allow. Soft cheese is easy to make, and once you have mastered the technique, the next step is to try a basic hard cheese. After perfecting that skill, there is a whole world of flavored, textured, and veined cheeses to explore.

Cheese has played an important part in food from the earliest times, being a convenient way to store excess milk and a terrific source of concentrated nutrition. It is probably the most locally defined food in the world, and people who have never visited another country will know something of its regions from the cheeses produced there. In recent times, artisan cheese makers have begun to revive the old recipes from their areas and to create new ones, and today the range of cheeses is wider than ever. You can use milk from cows, goats, and sheep, and some makers use buffalo milk. The composition of the milk from some breeds is better suited to making cheese than others—milk that has small fat globules is more suitable than milk that contains a high percentage of fat.

It is encouraging to think that only 60 years or so ago, during the Second World War, many households regularly produced small amounts of cheese as a matter of course to supplement their household. There is no reason why we shouldn't take the same approach today and allow cheese making to be part of our dairy routine.

What is cheese?

Basically, cheese is made from curdled milk—that is, milk that has become acidic, usually through an additive or acid (lemon juice), although any milk left in a warm place will break down. It's best to use a starter, which will give you greater control over the flavor and final result. The science underlying cheese making is that it is produced by the coagulation of the milk protein casein. The curd (solids) separates from the whey (liquid), and the solids are pressed into the final form. The variations are caused by the origin of the milk (including what the animal has eaten), the type of milk, the butterfat, whether or not the milk has been pasteurized, the aging process, and various flavorings, from smoking to additions such as herbs, spices, and even fruit cake.

You will need

The most important qualities for a cheese maker are persistence, perseverance, patience, and the ability to keep good records. You must also be scrupulously clean and well organized. As far as equipment is concerned, as long as you have a special area for dairying (see page 230), you won't need much to start with because your first attempt will be to make soft cheese.

You will need **stainless steel buckets**, which are much easier to clean than plastic ones. If you do use plastic buckets, make sure they are good quality and don't put anything but milk in them or they will carry a taint. For the same reason, use plastic **boards** to work on rather than wooden ones. You will need plenty of clean **dish cloths** (or cloths made from old pillowcases, duvet covers, or sheets) and **cheese cloths** to strain soft cheese.

A **thermometer** is essential if you don't already have one from your other dairy work.

BELOW Artisan cheeses are increasingly sought after but you can actually make your own from your dairy animals.

Make sure that everyday **kitchen utensils** such as colanders, sieves, and measuring cups are perfectly clean and on hand, but do not use wooden spoons for stirring because they might carry a taint. If you progress to making hard cheese, you will need specialized equipment, such as **curd brushes** and **cheese curd knives**, as well as some form of **cheese press**. An **pH meter** to measure the acidity of a cheese will prove useful if you are going to make cheese regularly.

Thinking of milk

To make a good, clean-tasting cheese, you need to start with high-quality, efficiently cooled, clean milk that is no more than two days old. The slightest taint will show up in the cheese, at best affecting the flavor and at worst leading to a cheese that is not safe to eat.

Bear in mind that the milk will be affected by the point in the animals' lactation cycle—for example, in early lactations the protein and fat levels are high, and this is better for cheese. If you are just making cheese for the household, you should plan to make most of it around this time. Similarly, if the animals are on good, fresh grass, the milk will be more suitable for cheese than winter milk, especially if the animals are being fed on roots or beet. You might get away with winter milk if they are having haylage or well-conserved, good-quality spring grass.

The animals' health also has an effect on the milk, and it is absolutely essential that you keep any milk from an animal with mastitis out of the food chain, particularly away from cheese making. The milk from any animal on medication must also be discarded. Not only is it extremely bad practice to use milk from an animal receiving antibiotics but their presence in the milk will hinder the starter cultures.

If you are using unpasteurized milk, you must be even more careful about hygiene. Remember that it is recommended that some vulnerable groups, including pregnant women, the elderly, and very young, should not eat cheese made from unpasteurized milk.

Making hard cheese

You should be able to make around 1–1½ pounds of hard cheese from about 2 gallons of milk. You will also need a starter, some rennet, and some salt. Pour the milk into a wide-mouthed

container, such as a stainless steel boiling-water canner or a large bowl.

The purpose of the starter is to activate the lactic acid bacteria, which raise the acidity of the milk and make it a suitable environment to introduce the rennet. It is possible to make your own starter, but when you are beginning to experiment with cheese making, it is probably better to buy the small amount you need. Add the starter to the milk, following the instructions on the packaging, and slowly heat the milk to 90°F. Remove the milk from the heat and leave it to stand. Add rennet, as you did for the soft cheese, again following the instructions on the packaging. You need only a small amount of rennet; take care that you do not add too much.

The curd should have formed after 30–45 minutes. Gently place the back of your clean hand on the curd and press lightly. Properly formed curd should not feel sticky and should show some firmness. Carefully cut through the depth of the curd, first across your container and then at right angles. Be firm but gentle; it's important that you don't mash the curds.

Gently heat again, this time to about 104°F, a process rather misleadingly known as scalding. If you have a large enough pan, you could stand the container in it and add boiling water around the sides as you would in a water bath. It should take up to an hour to reach the optimum temperature. During this time some people like to scoop out some whey, heat it, and gently stir it back into the mixture; others prefer to remove some of the whey and replace it with boiling water, slowly pouring it into the side of the bowl. This is where the mechanical cheese vat plays such an important part in commercial cheese making. Use your kitchen thermometer to check the temperature.

The cheese is then pitched—that is, the curd sits in the pan to absorb some whey and build up some acidity. People who make hard cheese on a large scale will use an pH meter (see page 239) at every stage to check the levels, but this is useful only when you know what the acidity should be in the first place, and this will vary according to the type of milk that has been used. It is normally in the range of 0.17–0.19.

At this stage you can do one of two things. You can pour off or ladle out the whey. Transfer the curds to a bowl, add 2 teaspoons of salt for every pound of curd and stir it to break the curd

into small pieces. You can use a cheese mill if you have one to break up the curd.

Alternatively, you can transfer the curds to a cheesecloth-lined colander, then pull together the ends of the cloth in what is known as a Stilton knot (see panel below left). Suspend the cloth over a bowl and allow to drain. After draining, cut the curd into pieces and rebundle, repeating this process, known as cheddaring, several times. Don't let the curd become chilled during this process. Then break the curd into small pieces with clean hands and add salt. If you have one, use a cheese mill at this stage.

Transfer the cheese to a cheesecloth-lined mold, leave it to rest for an hour and then put on the follower (the lid of the mold). Add weights, such as canned food, large stones wrapped in a clean cloth, or even a jack or vice. If you are using a proper cheese press, adjust the pressure, starting low at first and increasing it gradually. The aim is to drain out whey, not to crush the cheese. Turn the cheese over and keep adding more weight or pressure. Do this for two or three days, and then wrap the cheese in clean wrapping (strips of cotton sheets, for example, or purpose-bought calico or cheesecloth). Continue to turn the cheese daily. Keep checking the wrapping, and when white patches appear, remove it and leave the cheese to dry where there is a draft. You can coat the cheese in a light covering of fat or olive oil to help exclude air. Leave it to mature for a month or so. Homemade cheese should keep for at least three months.

Always be guided by the smell and taste of a cheese, and if you have the slightest doubt, do not eat it. Cheese should never be covered in mold or show any signs of rot, and it should not smell unpleasant.

A "blown" cheese is one in which gas has formed as a result of contaminating bacteria or yeasts. There are small gas holes and a definite smell of taint. The top will be "blown up" with gas, and if you do taste the cheese, it will be sweet and sickly. Do not eat it.

If, as is more likely, you have managed to produce a successful homemade cheese, you can tackle more complicated recipes, such as blue-veined cheese or very hard cheeses, and you can experiment with textures and rinding. Alternatively, you can simply continue to perfect your very own smallholder's cheese.

Cheesecloth knot

A bundle made from cheesecloth with a knot can easily be made to drain the curds into a bowl.

1 Hold three corners.

2 Wrap the fourth around the other three corners.

3 Pull the fourth corner tight.

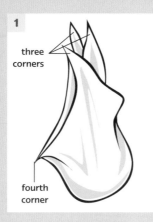

1

three corners

fourth corner

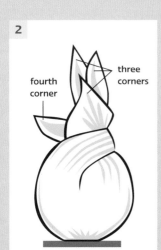

2

fourth corner

three corners

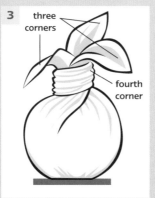

3

three corners

fourth corner

Making soft cheese

This is the simplest cheese to make, and you can flavor the basic cheese with black pepper or herbs for a more interesting flavor. You will be able to make ¾–1 pound of cheese from about 1 gallon of milk. You will also need some rennet (see page 237) and some sea salt. Although you can omit salt, using the unsalted soft cheese in sweet recipes or as an alternative to cream, if you want a savory cheese it is better to add a little.

that are too heavy, you will only succeed in flattening the cheese rather than allowing it to continue to drain slowly, which is what should be happening. Leave for an additional 24–48 hours and you will have a semihard cheese, though a smaller quantity than the soft cheese from which it was made.

Method

1 You can use a large, open casserole dish if you don't have a special pan, but make sure that the dish does not carry a taint. You can warm the milk in a saucepan and then transfer it to a shallow bowl or casserole dish. Most recipes will suggest that you slowly heat the milk to body temperature, allow it to cool for a few hours, and then add the rennet, but other people simply add the rennet to the milk. The amount of rennet you add will depend on the type you are using, and the appropriate quantity will be specified on the packaging. In general, however, you need add only a small amount, usually a few spoonfuls. If you stir the milk gently one way and pour in the rennet mixture the other way, you won't need to disturb the milk too much.

2 Allow the mixture to stand for a couple of hours and the milk will begin to "set"—that is, the curds form. You can either ladle the curd out of the pan, straining it through clean cheesecloth, or make some criss-cross cuts across the surface to break up the curd, thereby releasing more whey. Sprinkle salt on top to encourage this. Then you should slide or gently pour the mixture into a cheesecloth-lined colander. Be careful that you do not break it up too much.

3 Check the flavor and add a little more salt if necessary. Gather in the sides of the cheesecloth into a bag shape and suspend it over a basin. Allow it to drain for 12 hours or more. You can then mix in the herbs or flavoring of your choice, and the cheese is ready to eat.

4 To transform this soft cheese into a "smallholder" cheese, you can transfer it to a special mold and press it according to the instructions that come with the mold. Remember that if you use weights

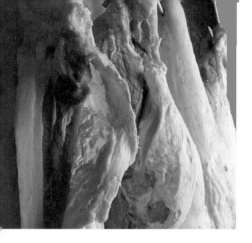

Meat

Raising animals for the table is not easy. There are many health and safety and welfare regulations to observe, and you will also need an understanding of the basic elements of butchery, even if you are not slaughtering your own stock.

A knowledge of basic butchery is essential for anyone who is rearing animals for the table for two main reasons. First, you will be in a position to recognize a good carcass on the living animal in order to "finish" it to slaughter weight and to know when it is ready for killing. Second, your knowledge will enable you to joint a carcass yourself or instruct the slaughterhouse in the cuts that you want to have. From this comes an ability to be able to process the meat further—into bacon or ham and sausages or burgers.

In the 19th century, it was said that the only part of a pig that was not eaten or used was its squeak, which is a long way from the joint- and chop-centered cooking of today. Even people who buy meat rather than raising animals will find that a working knowledge of the various cuts and their qualities will enable them to eat well for less money because they will be able to choose less expensive cuts and make them go further. Using a range of cuts also creates more variety and choice when it comes to cooking.

Livestock for the table

There are numerous regulations surrounding the slaughter of livestock, from the welfare of the animal to health and hygiene considerations. In some areas, health and safety issues have to be taken into account. In some countries, home slaughter for sale or for your own consumption is not allowed. Whether or not home slaughter is allowed, it's essential that you observe welfare and hygiene laws, that your animals are not caused unnecessary pain or suffering, and that the meat is safe for human consumption.

It is your responsibility to make yourself fully aware of the legislation concerning slaughter in your area, and that includes keeping the relevant paperwork, which may involve transportation documentation before you start.

Home slaughter

There is a big difference between attempting the slaughter of a chicken and killing a bullock. The slaughter process includes the restraint, stunning, and bleeding of the animal, and if you decide on home slaughter, you must be fully trained in the method you intend to use and to have witnessed and assisted in an approved method of slaughter for the livestock you intend to kill.

Slaughtering an animal is not something to be undertaken lightly. You cannot learn how to do this from a book; it is a practical skill that must be learned practically. Go on an accredited training course and prepare yourself fully with the necessary equipment and a safe slaughter area. It is a big undertaking, because not only will you have to be able to butcher the carcass into cuts of meat but you must also bleed the carcass, and skin and gut the animal.

In some areas, licensed slaughterers are prepared to undertake home kills. Make sure that anyone you employ is suitably qualified, and before you come to any agreement, make sure you have discussed fully the facilities they need and who is going to bleed and gut the animal. Talk to people who have used the slaughterer and attend a home kill before you commit yourself. Don't forget that you will have to have facilities to dispose of the by-products—you can't just put them in the trash.

Small animals, such as rabbits and table birds, are often slaughtered at home, but the same considerations apply. The usual method for home killing is neck dislocation, but prestunning the animal is ideal. There are various gadgets that you can use, but there is no substitute for learning the correct manual method. In fact, some of these gadgets can actually cause more suffering by crushing the vertebrae rather than dislocating.

Do not attempt to kill anything until you have done so under the supervision of a competent person and until you feel confident that you can bring about death quickly. Remember that you will also have to be able to prepare the carcass and pluck and draw it, and, if it needs hanging, know when to hang and for how long.

Using a slaughterhouse

Most livestock owners will send their bigger animals to a local slaughterhouse. Unfortunately, in some places, there are far fewer of these than there were, which means that some small farmers have to travel a considerable distance to their nearest facility.

As with killing at home, the welfare of the animal is of paramount importance. This is the last but perhaps the most important aspect of care that you can do for your animal. If you've never been to the slaughterhouse before, it might be a good idea to visit by appointment and find out exactly where your animal is going and how you can make the whole experience as stress free as possible. Just by knowing the route, arriving in good time, and providing a comfortable journey will help reduce the stress of your animal.

You will have to be calm and handle the animal as you usually do. If you really don't like the lairage (the place where the animal is to be kept overnight), make arrangements to bring the animal straight into the slaughterhouse with as little time between delivery and killing as possible. It is better if you can take more than one animal at the same time, as they will be more settled in familiar company.

Remember that the animal will normally be inspected by a veterinarian and that the slaughterhouse will expect it to be clean—that is, not covered in dirt and not wet. Slaughterhouses can refuse to kill for reasons of ill health or dirt, and they can even take more punitive measures.

Before the animal is slaughtered, you must establish how you want your carcass returned. Most slaughterhouses offer good cutting services, and at the very least it is a good idea to have it returned divided in two because it will be easier to handle. In the case of beef, you will probably

want it cut into smaller sections, because even a fore quarter may prove too heavy for normal handling. Discuss your requirements with the slaughterhouse. You might prefer to have the animal back in recognizable cuts, and most cutters will also label the meat so that you can easily identify it.

Slaughter of farm livestock must include prestunning, which is carried out by a captive bolt, followed by bleeding the animal by cutting its throat. (The point of prestunning is that it will not feel pain when its throat is cut.)

Whichever method of slaughter you choose, you must make sure that the end is swift and that the way the animal is handled before death is humane and calm. This often gets forgotten with poultry, for which the stress of catching and rough handling can arguably be as terrifying as the death itself.

If you have found it hard to part with an animal you have raised, having it returned in pieces rather than as a carcass can make the process a little easier.

ABOVE When sending an animal to a slaughterhouse, make sure you decide in advance how you want the animal to be jointed.

From carcass to cuts

Before cutting up a carcass, you will need to have some idea of the basic anatomy of the animal because you will be cutting through bone and will need to know where and how to create clean cuts. Remember that meat is jointed, not hacked.

A sheep or goat is probably the most straightforward carcass with which to start, and it is quite forgiving in that you are not cutting for specific uses. Unless a pig is for pork only, you have to remember that you are also cutting for hams and bacon. Don't attempt a beef carcass without practical experience of working with an expert. Not only is it an awful lot of money to get wrong but it is physically demanding work. When you are dealing with beef, you also need to decide whether to hang it and for how long, and your decision will depend on whether you have a large, cold area where this would be possible.

When you are butchering your meat you will find there are numerous cuts and pieces, from feet to innards, that don't normally feature on supermarket shelves. Nearly everything is edible if you know how to cook it. The main ingredients of pig's haslet, for example, are liver, heart, and sweetbread, and many people enjoy tripe with onions. Stuffed heart is considered a delicacy by some, and blood sausages are a traditional part of breakfast in some areas. If you do not like variety meats, you can always feed the cuts you can't face to your dogs or cats. They, at least, will be pleased with your efforts.

BELOW Learning how to correctly truss a chicken for the oven is a skill that needs to be mastered.

You will need

Your requirements will largely depend on the size of the carcass, but you will need to work in a cool, clean area that is well away from your livestock, pets, children, and crawling insects. The area must be one that can be washed down easily, and you will need plenty of space.

Butchers have thick wooden tables for a good reason, and although you might not be able to replicate this, you will need a **robust, cleanable surface** that will withstand blows.

Make sure you have plenty of **containers**, such as washable plastic crates, to hold the cuts of meat and a good supply of **freezer bags** and **labels** for them.

You will need several sharp **knives**, including a boning knife, a large butcher's knife, a cleaver, and a butcher's saw. Cleavers are great for breaking through bones along the grain, while saws also cut through bones but should be used against the grain. Your knives should be of the best possible quality, and a good set will be a worthwhile investment. Don't forget that they will need sharpening from time to time, so you will need to have **sharpeners** on hand as well.

Wear thin plastic (medical) **gloves** when you are dealing with the carcass. If you cut yourself, cover the wound and put on some new gloves. You should also wear clean, washable **clothes**, such as a full apron or a butcher's type "coat" overall. Make sure that your hair is confined by a clean hat—a baseball cap will do the job.

Preparing poultry

At its most straightforward, plucking poultry involves pulling out all the feathers until there are none left. Pull the feathers downward and go over the carcass with tweezers to remove the pin feathers or singe them off. You can dry or wet pluck: wet plucking is where the bird is plunged into hot water for a few minutes, which some people do to loosen the feathers.

Wear plastic gloves because your hands will get sore. It is possible to buy plucking machines, but these are really only cost effective if you are dealing with large numbers of birds.

When the bird has been plucked, it must be drawn (the innards removed), before it is trussed to hold it together while it is cooked.

Cuts

Basic cuts of beef

1 chuck;
2 rib;
3 loin;
4 sirloin;
5 round;
6 flank;
7 plate;
8 brisket;
9 shank.

Basic cuts of lamb

1 neck;
2 rib;
3 shoulder;
4 loin;
5 sirloin;
6 leg;
7 breast.

Basic cuts of pork

1 arm shoulder;
2 loin;
3 leg;
4 side;
5 whole shoulder.

Smoking, curing, and salting

Today most people eat preserved meat because they like the taste, such as bacon or slices of ham. Smoked chicken or fish is a delicacy, and salt beef is a distinctive dish. But the original purpose of smoking and curing was to halt the processes of decomposition and allow the meat to be kept for a longer time when there were no freezers.

Even today, preserving parts of a pig by curing remains one of the most economical ways of processing the meat, and the resulting bacon or ham is delicious. You can preserve part of your pig carcass this way—while freezing the rest. Even if you don't have home-produced meat, you could buy part of a free-range or organic pig and still experiment with curing.

You will need

As with the butchery, you will need a clean and washable area in which to work. Because you are working on a raw product, the expectation is that it will decompose. By curing it, you will stop or inhibit this process, but what you don't want are any outside contaminants from a dirty working area, fly strike, or even strong taints, such as perfume. The meat must be good to eat before you begin the process; if it is not, the curing won't make it safe and you run the risk of it making you ill. The curing process is a race against bacteria and it is one you have to be sure you will win.

One of the most important ingredients in curing is salt. There is considerable controversy surrounding the use of nitrate, and it is worth taking time to look at the pros and cons of its use. Saltpeter or potassium nitrate has been a traditional ingredient of the curing process, and

it features in all the old recipe books in various quantities. Confusingly, older recipes also call for *sal prunella*, another form of saltpetre, in which the saltpetre is fused into balls, which allow the curing process to start more quickly.

In recent times, there has been some reluctance to use nitrate for reasons linked to potential health problems, and obtaining it has become increasingly difficult because it is one of the constituents of explosives. However, nitrate arguably does have a place in curing, as it is a traditional, not a new, ingredient. Its main value is the ability to control harmful micro-organisms, which greatly reduces the risk of contamination during curing, helping remove the possibility of botulism. Incidentally, it is responsible for the pleasant pink color of cured meat.

It is possible to cure using salt only, and although the color will be grayer, if the curing process is carefully monitored and hygienically followed, the risk that harmful micro-organisms will develop is much reduced. The other possible effect is that the resultant product may be too salty and will need soaking before cooking.

Curing

There are two main ways of curing meat: the dry cure and the "pickling" or brine or wet cure. You will probably find it easiest to buy a cure and follow the instructions provided with it.

Dry curing This type of curing is done by mixing together salt and sugar, rubbing the mixture all over the meat and repeating several times. The mixture

can be combined with spices to give a distinctive taste. You can use brown sugar, but you must make sure that the salt crystals are fine so that they penetrate every area of the meat. Don't use iodized table salt because you don't want the iodine in it.

When you are doing this, you must make sure that the salt reaches every little crevice and that you plug each gap in the carcass with the mixture. When you have covered every surface with the mixture, allow the meat to cure, rubbing more salt in every few days. You will find that the salt draws out some liquid from the meat, so put a tray underneath to catch it. If you are curing a small amount, which is a good idea if it is your first attempt, you can leave it in the refrigerator to cure. Check the meat carefully to make sure that it is not decomposing—if it is, you did not make sure that sufficient salt reached every area—and after two or three weeks the bacon or ham should be ready to rinse off and hang in a cold place. The meat can be smoked at this point if you like (see below).

Wet cure, pickling, or brine cure The meat is covered in the liquid cure. Follow a standard recipe for your first attempt and use a small quantity of meat. As your confidence grows, you will be able to experiment with cures that include such ingredients as beer, honey, different kinds of sugar, and molasses.

A plastic bucket with a lid makes a good "curing" vessel, but make sure it is not tainted with anything. The ham can then be cooked by boiling or roasting when you are ready.

Corned beef
Corned beef is beef brisket with the fat trimmed from it. It is rubbed with salt (curing salt is best) and left in a covered, nonmetallic container for 24 hours. The salt will draw out the liquid, so you will have to pat it dry from time to time. It is then rubbed with a mixture of brown sugar and herbs and spices, such as black peppercorns, crushed bay leaves, cloves, coriander, ginger, or cloves. It's then put back into the refrigerator or cold area in a clean, covered container and turned once a day for 7–10 days. It is then simmered in water for 3–4 hours. It can be eaten hot or cold.

Smoking
Originally, smoking was the final step to curing. The curing process was used to control harmful

micro-organisms within a piece of meat, while smoking was the final fail-safe: it could not make badly cured meat safe to eat, but it could keep the outer area of well-cured meat free from bacteria. There are two main methods: cold smoking and hot smoking.

In cold smoking, the smoke is diverted from the source of the heat; it isn't exactly cold, more warm, but it is the traditional way of drying food while at the same time giving it a distinctive flavor. Cheese must be cold smoked, and other foods will need to have been cured or salted first to preserve it. If it is not, you will simply be providing the ideal conditions for bacteria to flourish. Hot smoking actually cooks the food and imparts a smoky flavor.

You can buy smokers in a variety of different sizes. They range from simple lidded trays in which the food is placed under a flat grill with the smoking medium set under that, to large, refrigerator-like machines that will hold a multitude of foods. You can make a smoker once you understand the principle behind the process, but as with anything involving fire, never leave it unattended, and always have plenty of water on hand in case of emergencies.

The wood you use for smoking will affect the flavor of the food. You can buy briquettes, but if you decide to make your own, choose fruit wood, such as apple, pear, or cherry, if you can. Green wood is best because it needs to smolder rather than flare. The wood should be chipped into small pieces, and you will have to keep adding to them to keep the smoke going.

ABOVE Originally smoking was the final method of ensuring cured meat was safe to eat but today it is done for its distinctive flavor.

Making sausages and burgers

Making sausages and burgers is one of the simplest yet most effective things you can do, and it offers plenty of scope for individual tastes and textures. If you raise your own livestock, it is a great way to use the meat, but even if you don't have your own source, you can still go to a good butcher and buy the meat of your choice to make flavorsome and wholesome sausages.

Sausages have a long history, and have undergone almost every possible incarnation, from feast foods to everyday pork sausages, while smoked, cured sausages have emerged as salamis. Recently, the sausage has experienced something of a "sizzle," as home producers and cooks have experimented with all sorts of ingredients, from mixing the traditional pork with a variety of ingredients to producing vegetarian sausages.

It's also easy to make burgers at home, and you can use many different flavors and types of meat, from chicken to traditional beef.

You will need

You will not need a large **kitchen**, but it must be perfectly clean. Raw ground meat is the perfect environment for bacteria to breed, so observe strict hygiene at all times, and as with any other meat processing, wear clean overalls and keep your hair out of the way.

As well as several sharp **knives**, you will also need a **mincer/grinder** and a **stuffer**. If you don't

want to invest in these straight away, use a hand mincer and a piping bag for stuffing. You will also need a **sausage funnel**. You will also need some **metal trays**, but you can use large, clean baking or roasting pans instead.

Basic ingredients

Casings The casing is the outer case of the sausage. They are normally natural hog or sheep casings, which are considered superior to artificial casings, but if you are making vegetarian sausages, you should use artificial casings.

Rusk or bread crumbs Many people think that top-quality sausages should not contain any "filler," but the rusk is an important part of a sausage because it mixes with the meat to provide texture and it helps to absorb the fat during cooking. You can buy plain rusks, to which you can add your own flavors, or you can buy flavored ones, such as hot and spicy, apple, or even beer. You need about 15 percent rusk in a sausage, although you can add more if you wish.

If you prefer, you can use bread crumbs instead of rusk, but they don't have the same consistency in your sausage.

Meat Use the best-quality meat for the best-quality sausages. Pork shoulder is ideal, but any good-quality meat cut into chunks will work well. It's also possible to combine meats, such as chicken and ham or pork and beef. You can also include extra fat if you like, adding about 10 percent in the form of natural meat fat or suet or pork belly. If you are making vegetarian sausages, add olive oil or they will be too dry.

Liquid Depending on the amount of fat you have added, you will need ½–¾ cup of liquid for every 2 pounds of meat, but you will be able to judge the amount by the consistency of the mixture after you have followed a few recipes. The liquid does not have to be just water; you can add a fruit juice, such as pear juice, beer, or even some diluted alcohol, such as whiskey. Think about the sort of flavorings that would go well with the meat you are using.

Seasoning This is where you can let your imagination run wild. Salt is usual (but don't make them too salty), as are pepper and herbs, but you

BELOW Burgers are so easy to make and you can experiment with ingredients and different flavors.

can add almost anything, from apple, leek, and garlic to cranberries at Christmas and blackberries in the fall. Use your fresh herbs and vegetables when they are in season—the options are almost endless.

Beef burgers

Burgers are even easier to make than sausages. Simply take a good cut of beef (or lamb, pork, venison, chicken, or turkey) and grind it to your required consistency. Although you can make burgers without bread crumbs, they do improve the consistency of the finished burger. Mix bread crumbs with the meat and add an egg. At this stage you can add whatever flavorings you like, from salt and pepper to chili or cheese, or pineapple in pork or cranberries in turkey.

You can buy reasonably priced burger makers, which are simply steel molds with a press. You can form burgers without one of these, but if you are making a large quantity, a machine will be quicker and turn out consistent sizes. You can freeze uncooked burgers.

Making the sausages

Method

1 First, you must prepare the casings by soaking them. Don't worry if they smell a bit; this is quite normal. Thoroughly wash them and allow them to soak for at least 30 minutes, changing the water once. They are slippery and surprisingly delicate to handle.

2 Grind the meat to the required texture, putting it through twice if you want a fine, smooth texture. Mix together the dry ingredients—the rusk and flavoring—and combine them with the meat. Add sufficient liquid to give the mixture a wet but not sloppy consistency.

3 Whichever method of stuffing you have chosen, whether it is a piping bag or a machine, you will have to attach the casings to the stuffer. Stuff the casing and twist at intervals to get the size you require. This is easier than it sounds. You can simply put them in the freezer at this stage, but sausage experts tie them in a special plait.

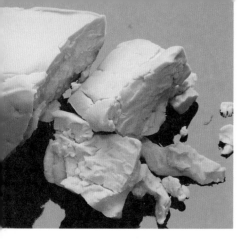

Home brewing

At times when clean water was not available at the turn of a faucet, home-brewed ales and homemade wines were vital elements in a healthy diet. Brewing was an important part of the household economy, and it was usually done by women.

The type of beverage common to an area depended on the ingredients available. Although there were vineyards in Britain at the time of the Romans, they gradually died out, and by the Middle Ages, beer, cider, and other beverages had become traditional. Mead was made from honey in many countries, while cider was popular in apple-growing areas. Wines and cordials were made of ingredients that were in season, such as blackberries, elderberries, and even pea pods. In the USA there are records of the Virginia colonists brewing ale as early as the 16th century.

Using alcohol

Alcoholic drinks were important because they could make water safe to drink. The beer was probably quite weak compared with today's alcohol content, and it was even served at breakfast. Another use for alcohol and one that is still employed, although to a lesser extent, was as a preservative, to keep foodstuffs through the winter. Today we enjoy the luxury of plums bottled in vodka or peaches preserved in brandy, but once it was an important and widely practiced method of preservation.

Although the popularity of brewed drinks did not wane, many small breweries and wine makers struggled in competition with the industrially produced drinks of the mid-20th century. Recently, however, an interest in locally produced wine and micro-breweries has coincided with a widespread desire for "real" ale and cider and brought about a resurgence in the making and drinking of brewed drinks.

Brewing your own

There are so many ways to make cider, beer, and wines, and so many variations on possible

RIGHT Who first discovered that fermented fruit and grain turn into a lovely-tasting liquid?

ingredients—especially for wine—that it is almost impossible to recommend one recipe rather than another. Every time you brew, you should keep a note of what you have used and how you did it, so that you can try and replicate it if it is particularly good.

Exactly who it was that first discovered that fruit and grain, if fermented, produced a sort of yeast that would produce a delicious-tasting alcohol is not recorded, but it must have been quite a startling discovery. There are different types of yeast, and it is the brewer's task to encourage the ones that will produce the desired result, at the same time as discouraging those that will do harm.

The basic principles of making alcohol are that an ingredient is fermented, and the result of fermentation is alcohol. The ingredients tend to define the drink—apples become cider, grain becomes beer and fruit and vegetables become wine. When yeast is added, it eats up the natural sugars to facilitate the production of alcohol, but there has to be a balance between the yeast, the sugars, and even the alcohol—and that's the art (or science) of brewing.

The enormous range of home-brewing equipment that is available might make you think that it is a complicated process, but it is not, and if you start on a small scale and with straightforward recipes, you will soon gain confidence and be able to move on to more demanding drinks. There are many wine and beer circles, and joining one of these can be a great source of help and practical advice, and members will be able to recommend both equipment and ingredients.

As with any foodstuff, if the final brew looks moldy, smells bad, or tastes disgusting, do not consume it. Don't take any risks. Look back through your notes to see what could have gone wrong. The final product should smell appetizing, should not contain mold spores, and should have a clean, pleasing appearance. You should expect to see sediment in some brews, but it's not usually present throughout the brew and certainly not as a noxious taste.

You will need

Making beer, cider, wines, and cordials requires different equipment, but whatever you use must be sterilized. You can do this with boiling water

ABOVE Clean bottles are essential to the process of making any kind of alcohol.

or just thoroughly wash the items in hot water and detergent before rinsing them in cold water. You can also buy sterilization tablets, made specially for the purpose.

You will need clean, food-standard, plastic **buckets** that can be sterilized, **funnels**, plastic **siphon tubing**, **cheesecloth**, and a room **thermometer**. You will find that a **hydrometer** is especially useful for beer making. A hydrometer measures the specific gravity (sometimes known as the original gravity) of a liquid, which shows the approximate sugar content and the alcohol level that will result if it is all converted.

You will also need somewhere for the fermentation to take place with a temperature of about 59°F. It's important that the area is not subject to sudden fluctuations in temperature because fermentation is a natural process and is affected by external conditions. The fermenting liquid must be left undisturbed and be kept uncontaminated by insects, dust, dirt, or even strong taint. It must also be kept out of the reach of children.

Home cider making

There are many recipes for both cider, which is made from apples, and for perry, which is made from pears. Opinions differ over whether the apples should be washed and whether yeast should be added, but the basic principle is to crush and press the apples to extract the juice, then to allow it to ferment at room temperature. When the fermentation has exhausted itself, the cider is siphoned out.

The apples

The great advantage of homemade cider is that it can be produced from almost any type of apple, and ripe windfalls are ideal. You can include bruised apples, but avoid bad apples, those that are already fermenting, and rotten apples. Be careful that you do not use maggoty fruit, and when you are collecting them, watch out for early-autumn wasps, which love to burrow into apples through existing holes.

Mixing some dessert and cooking apples will give a dryer taste, and a few crab apples will make it even drier, but don't worry if you have only one variety or if you're not certain what they are. The fruit does need to be ripe to extract the juice, and the sugar level in ripe fruit will be high, which is what will make the alcohol. You will need 11–13 pounds of apples to make about 4 quarts of cider, and this quantity of apples takes quite a lot of preparation.

RIGHT Cider can be made from any type of apple, including windfalls, although specialized makers learn which types of apples make the best cider.

If you are washing the apples, you should put them in cold water after collecting them. The apples should come into contact only with food-grade plastic, wood, or stainless steel; avoid all other metals. Change the water a couple of times or refresh it with a hose. If grazing animals, including poultry, have access to your orchards or if the area in which they fall is at all muddy, washing is essential. If they have fallen on long, clean grass, it might not be necessary.

Crushing and pressing

Before they are pressed, the apples have to be crushed, which can be difficult. It can be done by hand, but if you have a large quantity of fruit, you might need to use a hand-operated or mechanical crusher. Follow the safety instructions and be careful not to get your fingers in it. Always use the guard. Other methods include bashing the apples with a clean, thick pole in the bottom of a bucket, chopping, slicing, or mincing them (which is rather slow), or putting them in a mangle and grinding them.

After crushing the apples, you have to press them, and there are many excellent small-scale pressers available. If you are a member of a smallholding group, you might want to consider buying one that you can share at harvest time.

What is left over from pressing is called pulp, and you can feed it to your pigs or, in small quantities, to other livestock. Do not make your animals ill by giving them large amounts of a feed they don't usually get and remember that it ferments quickly, so after only a few hours on a warm day it could be lethal for ponies. Another excellent use for it is in your compost heap.

The other method of obtaining apple juice is to put the crushed apples into a cheesecloth bag, squeeze it, and allow the juice to drip out. It's important to keep insects away while this happens, and it's almost impossible to achieve this because cider flies get into unbelievably small spaces. If they get into your apple juice, they will cause a taint in the cider.

Fermentation

When you have obtained the apple juice, pour it into food-grade plastic buckets, filling them three-quarters full to allow for the lively fermentation. Cover each bucket with cheesecloth and tie it in place with string so that the cider flies cannot get in. Place the lids on top loosely, but don't seal them at this point. Keep them in a temperature of 59°F.

At this point cider makers differ. Traditional cider was made using only apples because they do have enough natural yeast to ferment, but many modern makers and some older recipes call for the addition of a cultured wine yeast. Some makers also add sulfur dioxide (in the form of Campden tablets) to control wild yeasts and bacteria, and to attempt to prevent any possible bad fermentation processes. Some makers like to add sugar to increase the strength of the cider; if you do this, you should use about 2 cups to 1 gallon. You can also use a hydrometer to see what the likely alcohol content of the finished cider might be.

The apple juice will now ferment in a lively way, possibly even leaking over the top of the container for a few days. After the initial activity, you can put the lids down firmly and leave the cider until the fermentation has exhausted the sugars or (if you have a hydrometer) the alcohol has risen to the level where the yeast is no longer able to interact with the sugar. Alternatively, if you have used demijohns, you can fit a fermentation lock, which is obtainable from brewing suppliers. It's difficult to say how long the total fermentation will take because it will depend on the apples, the warmth of the storage, and the sugar level—it can be anything from a few weeks to months. The liquid will stop bubbling, start to clear, and it should taste clean and not too sweet. A hydrometer should give a reading of 1005 or below.

Bottling

When it is ready you can rack off the cider. Do this in a cool place and allow it to settle so that the sediment settles, making racking off easier. Siphon off the cider into plastic containers or bottles; if you are using glass bottles, make sure that the cider has finished fermenting so that there is no risk of exploding bottles. Don't fill the bottles to the top. Some secondary fermentation will usually take place, and cider usually tastes better after a few months' storage.

Some makers prefer to rack off after the first fermentation and leave the cider to ferment in barrels or containers. Others prefer to rack off twice, adding sugar when they do so.

Cottage cider

An alternative recipe involves collecting apples, which are then bruised and covered in water. You should allow them to stand, protected from insects, for 10 days. Stir the apples every day, then strain and add 3 cups of sugar to each gallon of liquid. Make sure the sugar is thoroughly dissolved. Pour the cider into uncorked bottles and then cover the tops with cheesecloth to prevent flies. The author of this ancient recipe adds that the color can be improved by adding a slice of beet to the apples during fermentation.

Perry

Perry is made of pears, and you should try and use perry pears for making this drink because dessert pears will usually give disappointing results. The basic method is similar to making cider, but because pears have a different makeup, they require additional sulfur dioxide. It's worth trying to make perry with windfall fruit that would otherwise be discarded as long as the pears are clean and not rotten.

Gather the pears, allow them to stand for a week, then crush and juice them. Add yeast and Campden tablets together with some extra pectolase because pears don't contain the same amounts of pectin as apples. The juice will ferment and can be racked after a few weeks. Allow it to continue to ferment to produce a clear, sparkling perry. It is best to use a hydrometer to check the specific gravity before racking.

ABOVE Crushing apples by hand is easy for small quantities but you might want to invest in a crusher if you have a large amount of apples.

Making beer

Beer is a popular drink that has been in existence for thousands of years. It is an alcoholic drink fermented from malted grain with added hops, but it can also be made from roots, such as ginger.

Beer is well known throughout the world, and it is usually subdivided into lager beer, pale ales, regionally distinct ales (such as "real" ales), stouts, and brown ales, with variants between these. The alcohol is between 3 and 6 percent, but beer can be stronger or even alcohol free. Other flavors can be added to beer, and honey in particular seems to go well with the sweetness of the malt and the pleasant bitterness of the hops.

What is malt?

Malted grain is grain that is partially germinated and then dried in a kiln. The length of time that the grain is dried, the heat used, and the type of grain chosen will all affect the character of the beer. Most home brewers buy malt as an extract or as whole malt, and it's probably sensible to start in this way while you study the art of brewing. It would be annoying to put lots of work into growing your own grain and malting it and then not be able to produce the perfect beer.

What are hops?

Hops—or, to be more accurate, the flowers of hops—are used to balance the sweetness of the malt with some bitterness. But they also contribute other flavors, such as herbal, citrus, and even, some say, the taste of warm summer days, to the beer. The hops also interact with yeast to promote the "good" micro-organisms over the "bad" and help to maintain the foamy head that characterizes many beers. They are also acid, so helping to preserve the beer.

Hops were probably not used widely until the 13th century. Before then other herbs, such as wormwood, would be included, and beer was known as ale.

Hops are relatively easy to grow as long as your land is not wet. They like a rich soil and grow upwards, so you will need to provide strings to support them. You can pick the flowers and dry them for use in your beer making.

Hops can also make attractive decorations and they are quite salable if you have a market.

Water

The type of water used is important to beer making. Soft water tends to be better for brown ales, mild ales, and stout (the sweeter beers), whereas hard water is good for bitters, pale ales, and light ales (the more bitter, hoppy beers).

Basic beer making

There are many different recipes and variations, and there is plenty of equipment available, but

RIGHT Hops can be relatively easy to grow and use for your own homemade beer.

basically beer is made by taking malt, water, and flavorings, bringing the mixture to a boil and cooling it. At this stage it is known as a wort. An appropriate yeast is added, and controlled fermentation is allowed to develop. The brewer can either wait until fermentation has finished or the process is halted and the beer is racked off—that is, the clear liquid is taken from the sediment.

If you have not made beer before, you should consider buying a home-brewing kit and simply following the instructions. This might seem an odd suggestion for someone who is attempting to pursue a self-sufficient lifestyle, but it will give you an invaluable insight into the process for your next attempt. Most beer-making kits are simply wort in a can, to which you add water and, possibly, sugar and yeast, depending on what is in the can. You can also buy organic kits.

For your next attempt you could think about buying the raw ingredients, and after that you could consider growing the hops and thinking about other flavorings as you gain experience and confidence.

You will need

If you are making 1–2½ gallons of beer, you will need a large **pan**, ideally stainless steel, a food-grade, plastic **bucket**, a **funnel** and a **siphon**, an **airlock**, a beer **barrel**, preferably food-grade, and a **fermentation vessel**, usually a bottle. You will also need **sterilization tablets** and a **hydrometer** (see page 253).

You must sterilize all the equipment. Failure to do so can result in a bad-tasting brew or, even worse, one that will make you ill.

Basic beer

Boil the malt and water together. If you are using whole malt, stir the mixture to press the grains. Add the hops, which should be inside a cheesecloth bag or similar (like a giant bouquet garni), and allow to simmer for an hour. Allow the mixture to cool, then pour it into the fermentation vessel. If you are using whole malt, you will need to strain the mixture—you can give the spent malt to ruminants, but not to horses or ponies.

You can add more cold water at this point if you want to dilute the brew. Pour the water over the hops or malt grains to get the maximum from them. Add yeast. The first fermentation will take

around five days, after which you can siphon off the liquid into a plastic barrel. It is important that you don't disturb the sediment. Try to leave the sediment in the fermentation vessel so that you can dispose of it before you sterilize it for the next batch. Leave the beer for a few weeks before you drink it, although most beers will benefit from being left even longer.

As with all foodstuffs, if the beer smells acidic or looks moldy, do not drink it. Keeping records of the exact ingredients and process you have used will help you track where you went wrong but also, if you produce a particularly pleasant brew, what you did right.

ABOVE The first stage in beer making is to boil the water and the malt together before adding the hops.

Making wine and cordials

Wine is certainly an old drink, with a history that goes back thousands of years—there is evidence that it was being produced as early as 5000 BC. It has always been associated with ceremonial occasions, and we know that it was important in ancient Egypt and, of course, hugely significant in the civilizations of Greece and Rome.

Over the centuries the production of wine from grapes developed into an industry, and wine became a valuable commodity that was traded between countries and used for barter. It also gained a reputation among the relatively well off for being pleasant to drink, and this perception became more ingrained over the next few centuries. During the 1980s there was a rise in consumption, wines from the USA, South Africa, Australia, South America, and the Balkan countries providing strong competition for the more established European wine producers.

Nevertheless, against this commercial background, country folk were always making their own wine from surplus produce and from hedgerow fruits. It was something that could be easily made and offered some pleasure, and in some cases it was believed to have some medicinal uses. There has since been a recent resurgence in making homemade wine, and the remarkable variations in taste, color, and fragrance make it one of the most fascinating things to produce. When it is made commercially, wine making is a highly scientific process, but many self-supporters obtain excellent results from simple recipes that have underpinned country wine through the ages.

You will need

As with all brewing, it's essential that all your equipment is sterilized and that at all stages you protect the wine from contamination by foreign bodies and, above all, from the dirty feet of small flying insects. Contamination will almost certainly cause bacteria to take hold, and the result will be sour wine that is no good to drink.

Your basic wine-making equipment should include at least two food-grade, plastic, fermenting **buckets** with lids, **cheesecloth** or a **dish cloth** to cover the buckets and prevent insects from entering, two large demijohn glass **jars** or **bottles**, **airlocks**, large plastic **funnels**, a **siphon**, and **tubing**. You will also need **bottles** and **caps** or **corks**, and a **thermometer** and **hydrometer** (see page 253) will also be useful.

You will also need a clean kitchen or wine-making area away from insects, somewhere at room temperature where the wine can ferment, and a cool storage area.

Making wine

There are plenty of wine-making kits available and, as with beer making, a kit might be a good way to start making wine because they give full instructions, including an idea of what to expect at the various stages. Kits also give consistent results and are an ideal way of flexing your latent wine-making talents.

The main ingredient of wine is some plant material, such as fruit, flowers, herbs, or vegetables, but it helps if that material is sugary and juicy. Although it's possible to make wine from almost anything, you should start with something that not only consistently makes excellent wine but is something you have on hand and that is free or cheap. Obviously grapes make good wine, but so do blackberries, plums, damsons, rhubarb, and gooseberries. Elderberries and rosehips make superb-tasting wine, and these are also claimed to have medicinal properties. Parsley and parsnip (together with oranges and lemons) make unusual wines, as do potatoes and nettles. Making mead from honey is also reasonably straightforward. However, for your first attempt, it's best to start with a fruit wine.

RIGHT Grapes are becoming more widely grown in countries not previously noted for their vineyards.

Basic wine

The fruit should be in good condition, and it should be ripe so that it has a good sugar content. It must also be clean and not rotten in any way. To make even a small quantity of homemade wine, you will need a surprising amount of fruit—for example, you need 6½ pounds of elderberries to 1 gallon of water.

Method

1 The basic method is to crush or cut and pit the fruit (bruise it if you are using stone fruit), pour boiling water over it, and add the sugar. Allow the mixture to cool, then add the appropriate wine yeast; your home-brewing supplier will be able to advise you about this. At this point some recipes call for orange and/or lemon juice and rind and some for citric acid—lemon juice is a natural source. Not all wines need this, however.

2 You must cover the mixture with cheesecloth or a dish cloth to keep out insects and leave it for 12–24 hours. You then strain it into the fermentation jar (demijohn). Do not press, squeeze, or hurry the straining process, which can be done through a sieve or cheesecloth, or through both for a clearer end result. Haste now will result in a cloudy wine. Fit a fermentation lock to the jar, which will allow the lively gases to escape safely. Alternatively, you can let the wine have its initial fermentation in the buckets, then siphon it into the fermentation vessels and fit the airlocks. This will take two or three weeks. Some wine makers siphon off the wine two or three times at monthly or bi-monthly intervals until it is totally clear. You must avoid bottling it too early, because the secondary fermentation can cause the bottles to explode, which can be extremely dangerous.

RIGHT Homemade wine smells and tastes delicious and you can use your own home-grown fruit as a base.

Other ways of wine making, based on recipes from earlier times, are even more straightforward. You can, for example, make blackberry wine by alternating layers of ripe blackberries and sugar in wide-mouthed jars and leaving them for three or four weeks. After this time you should strain off the liquid and bottle it, adding a few raisins to each bottle. Lightly cork or cap the bottles to allow for further fermentation and for gases to escape, then seal tightly.

A typical country wine could be made by mashing any ripe fruit, covering it with boiling water, and leaving it for two weeks. The more water that was used, the weaker the wine would be. The liquid was then strained and sweetened with sugar or honeycomb mixed with water.

You can try these less usual ways of making wine yourself if you have excess produce to experiment with, but do remember that if it looks moldy, smells bad, or is excessively cloudy, don't drink it. Just learn from the experience.

ELDERBERRY WINE

You can add raisins, ground or grated ginger, cloves, or cinnamon, or all of these, for a more distinctive flavor. The lemon juice provides the necessary citric acid. The quantity of yeast will vary according to whether you use dried or fresh; check the package.

6½ lbs elderberries
1 gallon boiling water
6 cups sugar
juice of 1 lemon
1 envelope yeast

1 Strip the elderberries from the stalks and crush them lightly. Add them to the boiling water and stir in the sugar. Add the lemon juice.

2 Leave for 24 hours, then add the yeast. Allow it to ferment, then siphon away from the sediment into a fermenting vessel with an airlock. Rack the wine into bottles as it clears.

SLOE GIN

You can use more or less sugar in the recipe, depending on how sweet you want it to be. Some people freeze the sloes before using them because they soften as they defrost and are easier to prick. The hard part of the recipe is leaving the sloes in the gin for six months, because Christmas normally follows the sloe season after only about three months.

4 cups gin
1 lb sloes
2 cups sugar

1 Pick the sloes, but don't wash them because they have a natural bloom. Remove any debris. Prick the sloes and put them in a bottle with the sugar. Pour over the gin.

2 Shake the bottle every day until the sugar has dissolved. Leave for 6 months before straining and drinking.

Cordials

Defining what is meant by the word cordial really depends on where you live. The only common agreement is that it is a sweet liquid, but in Britain it is usually taken to mean a non-alcoholic drink, whereas in the USA it tends to mean a syrupy, sweet alcoholic drink. One definition says that a cordial is made from herbs and spices blended together with brandy. Cordials are also said to have medicinal properties—elderberry cordial, for example, is said to prevent colds and coughs. Whether you are making an alcoholic or non-alcoholic cordial, once you understand the basic principle, you can adapt the recipes according to what ingredients you have on hand and your tastes.

Alcoholic cordials These are usually an infusion of ingredients in an alcohol base, so the British favorite sloe gin would fall into this category. You could take any strong-tasting fruit and a clear alcohol, such as gin or vodka, to make a similar delicious drink. If you use a base such as brandy, which has a more distinctive taste, you should match the fruit or herbs more closely to the spirit's flavor—cherries and plums go particularly well with brandy.

One of the great advantages of these alcoholic cordials is that you can use an inexpensive base spirit. There is no need to buy the best-quality gin or vodka because the blending of the ingredients will smooth it and make it into a delicious drink. Do be aware that these cordials can be very strong.

Non-alcoholic cordials When you make non-alcoholic cordials, bear in mind that when you open the bottles to use the contents they will not keep for long, and you should store opened bottles in the refrigerator. If you can, keep the cordials in smallish bottles that you will be able to use up within a week or so of opening.

ELDERFLOWER CORDIAL

You can make a stronger cordial by increasing the proportion of flowers to water. The smell as the mixture comes to a boil is heavenly; it's a shame that it can't be bottled.

20 elderflower heads
3 lemons or lemons and limes
6-8 cups sugar
4 cups water
2 teaspoons citric acid

1 Carefully remove any insects from the elderflower heads.

2 Slice the lemons or lemons and limes and put them in a large saucepan with the elderflowers. Dissolve the sugar in the water and then pour over the elderflowers. Slowly bring to a boil. Add the citric acid, cover with cheesecloth or plastic wrap to keep out the insects and put in a cool place or the refrigerator, once cool, to steep.

3 Strain into sterilized bottles and seal. Store in a cool place and use within a few weeks.

ROSEHIP CORDIAL

This cordial should usually be diluted, unless you are drinking it for medicinal reasons—it contains a lot of vitamin C and is a traditional cold preventative.

1½ lb ripe red rosehips
4 cups boiling water
1¾ cups water
sugar, to taste

1 Top and tail the rosehips and chop them roughly.

2 Add the hips to the boiling water in a saucepan and boil for 5-10 minutes. Allow to cool and then strain through cheesecloth or a fine sieve, twice if possible.

3 Add the remaining water to the pulp and boil again. Strain as before. Return the liquid to the saucepan and boil until reduced to 4 cups. Stir in sugar to taste and make sure that it is dissolved.

4 Allow to cool before transferring to sterilized bottles. Store in a cool place.

Self-sufficiency in the home

Becoming self-sufficient

Self-sufficiency also covers many other areas of our lives. This chapter sets out practical steps to help you become self-sufficient in areas other than food production.

The self-sufficient house

In addition to having land that will allow you to produce the maximum amount of food, your ideal house should provide you with as much of its heating, lighting, and water as possible. If you have a new building or one that is being refurbished or extended, you should seek to maximize the amount of reused or recycled materials and look for new materials with the lowest environmental and carbon footprints.

The traditional self-sufficiency approach was to be independent of main heating, gas, electric, and water systems, which makes environmental and financial sense when a property is located far from the nearest utility services.

Electricity

Because most of us are already connected to a domestic electrical supply, the challenge is not how to cut yourself off completely from a utility supplier but how far you can reduce your need for energy. There is an increasing trend in many countries of allowing householders to export any excess electricity produced by renewable electricity to utility companies and be paid for it. These payments are known as performance-based incentives, and in countries such as Germany and Spain electricity companies are required to pay a premium on such exports, helping to cut the householder's capital payback period.

Households that minimize their electricity consumption could become net exporters, not only becoming self-sufficient in electricity but also helping the wider community cut its dependence on fossil fuel- or nuclear-produced electricity. The carbon credits accrued from such exports can be set against other carbon consumption by the household—such as for cooking—and so it may be possible to achieve net carbon negativity.

Gas

Finding self-sufficient alternatives to using utility-supplied natural gas for heating and hot water are also important if you want to cut your carbon footprint, but if you are already connected to a supplier it is sensible to remain connected while you seek to reduce or eliminate your dependence. For example, even if you decide to replace your gas-powered central heating and hot-water systems with wood-powered and solar hot-water systems, it makes sense to retain your gas system if it is still working as a backup in case your new systems break down or if you are unable to chop wood for your boiler.

It can be the case that taking the final steps to full energy independence might make no economic or environmental sense. You might, for example, achieve almost complete self-sufficiency for heating, hot water, and electricity, but still use utility-supplied gas for cooking. The minuscule annual cost of this gas, even though you cook every day, might mean that the expense of a wood-fired stove would make no financial or environmental sense, when the cost not only of acquisition and installation but also of the energy expended in the manufacture of a solid-iron stove would vastly exceed the tiny amount of energy you will be saving.

The aim of self-sufficient micro-generation is to be a net contributor to utility suppliers rather than be completely free from those suppliers.

Water

A similar approach is true for water. If you are already connected to a supplier, it is best to remain connected but aim to reduce your dependence on that supply as far as possible. Using aerated shower-heads, spray taps, flow regulators, dual- and low-flush toilets, and water-efficient washing machines and dishwashers will help to reduce consumption. Capture as much rain as you can, but allow the excess to flow into the communal system so that in periods of drought you can take back modest amounts.

Reducing waste

There is now a welter of reduce, reuse, and recycling schemes facilitating the modern self-sufficiency agenda. Farmers' markets encourage customers to bring back bags, jars, and egg boxes to be used again and again. Websites enable us to give second-hand objects a new home, and regulations, such as the European Union's WEEE (Waste Electric and Electronic Equipment) directive, mean that electronic waste is now recycled. Millions of people all over the world are reducing their waste, making themselves less dependent on expensive corporate and municipal waste streams and slashing the energy wasted in constantly making products for the discredited throw-away society.

Striking a balance

This approach encapsulates many self-supporters' philosophy of seeking to provide as much of their own needs as they feasibly can and to contribute to the wider community. But when they are in need, they want to be able to take something back. Today's self-sufficient pioneer is not seeking to create a selfish island behind ramparts, separate from the wider world, but is demonstrating to the rest of the community how to stand on their own feet as much as possible, recognizing that we have a crucial role in achieving the wider goal of self-sufficient communities.

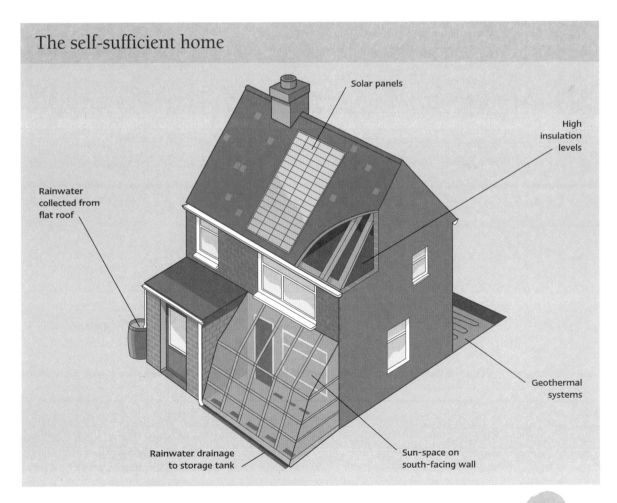

The self-sufficient home

Solar panels

High insulation levels

Rainwater collected from flat roof

Geothermal systems

Rainwater drainage to storage tank

Sun-space on south-facing wall

Reducing energy consumption

When it comes to electricity and heating self-sufficiency, the best place to start is efficiency. If you need less, you will have to do less work and spend less money providing those needs.

Saving electricity

Many renewable systems for producing electricity have been falling in cost, but such systems are still up to a hundred times more expensive for each kilowatt saved than some simple energy-efficiency steps, such as using energy-efficient light bulbs. Cutting down on waste and installing only the most efficient electrical equipment will reduce the huge capital investment needed to make your property self-sufficient in electricity.

Heating space and water

It is usually best to avoid using electricity for hot water and space heating, which will require a large capital investment in either wind or solar equipment. Ideally, in the self-sufficient property water would be heated by solar hot-water panels in summer, and in winter rooms and water would be heated by wood-burning boilers.

Narrow-based electric kettles help you to boil only the amount of water you actually need, or you could get an instant water boiler, which uses up to 60 percent less energy.

Electric immersion heaters are inherently inefficient, but if you have one, make sure it is well insulated, has an accurate thermostat set at 140°F and a 7-day timer.

Refrigerators and freezers

Refrigerators are one of the home's biggest consumers of electricity.

If you are buying a new refrigerator, choose a model that is energy efficient. Buy the smallest refrigerator suitable for your needs, because if the refrigerator is too big, you will be paying to cool empty shelves for the rest of its life.

Think carefully about whether you need a deep freeze at all. The energy you save in producing your own food could be lost if you preserve it in a deep freeze. Most traditional methods of preserving food, such as drying (see pages 206–7) and bottling (see pages 222–3), will waste less energy.

Make sure that the refrigerator is set at 41°F and the freezer compartment is not below 0°F.

Large home appliances

Only buy the most energy-efficient models. Some countries have a colored energy efficiency rating on the machine: green is the best; red is the least efficient. The water efficiency of models is also important because up to 90 percent of the energy used by a washing machine is for heating water.

Only use your washing machine when it is fully loaded and set it at the correct temperature for each load. The Australian government recommends using cold water for non-soiled clothes, and even setting your machine to wash at 86°F would help cut up to 45 percent of your washing energy costs.

Clothes driers

The electricity consumed by electric tumble-driers is so enormous that unless you have masses of spare renewable electricity capacity, such a machine has no place in the sustainable home. Dry your clothes outside in summer and by radiators in winter.

Lighting

Modern light-emitting diode bulbs (LEDs) can light an entire average house using as little as 100–150 watts—the equivalent of a single incandescent bulb. Although they can be expensive, these bulbs are a solution to low-energy lighting. They do not have the drawbacks of some energy-saving bulbs, such as long warm-up times, and they do not contain mercury. They are also flicker-free, which is useful for the small number of people who may be affected by CFL (compact fluorescent lamp) energy-saving bulbs. Energy-saving bulbs use a fifth less energy than halogen or traditional tungsten bulbs.

Avoid all halogen bulbs and dimmer switches, which are extremely inefficient.

Electronic goods

While they are left on standby, electronic goods are estimated to waste up to 10 percent of America's residential electricity consumption. Turn all electronic equipment off at the wall when it is not in use.

If you are replacing your computer, choose a laptop, which will use up to a third less energy than a PC. For electronic goods, check how many kilowatts the equipment uses and compare it with other brands. Remember that the smaller your TV, the less electricity it will consume, and bear in mind that plasma TVs are the most wasteful of all.

Heating your home

The options for self-sufficiency in heating space and water and installing insulation are covered elsewhere in this chapter, but bear the following points on heating efficiency in mind.

Temperature

A temperature of 66°F is usually recommended as a comfortable level for sedentary activities in the home or office, although a higher temperature is appropriate for the elderly or infirm. Try to maintain the recommended temperature because every degree above it will add more than 10 percent to your heating bills. A building heated to 80°F requires 80 percent more energy to heat than one maintained at 66°F. If you have to chop wood or pay for wood pellets, you will probably be more than happy to put on an extra sweater and be comfortable at 61–64°F.

Timing

Whether you have an automatic wood-pellet or gas-fired central-heating boiler, it is crucial that you set the timings accurately for when you need heat. In a properly insulated home, it should not be necessary for the heating to be on for more than 30 minutes before people get up. Similarly, if no one is in the house during the day, the timer should go off at least 30 minutes before the last person leaves the building and come on for a similar time before they come back. The heating should go off an hour before you go to bed.

Unoccupied rooms

Until the 1970s, when central heating became common, people normally heated the rooms they were occupying rather than the whole building. Heating the entire house significantly increases the energy used. You will substantially reduce your heating bills by closing doors and turning down the heating to frost protection in unoccupied rooms.

Boiler renewal and maintenance

If you have a gas boiler make sure it is serviced annually to maintain optimum efficiency. If you have an old oil or gas boiler, you should make an effort to find out its efficiency rating, because older models can have ratings as low as 65 percent, compared with modern condensing boilers, which have a rating of over 92 percent. It could be that you are losing up to 27 percent of the gas or oil being burned. If you check your annual heating fuel bill, you will be able to calculate the payback period for a new boiler.

LEFT Controls: correct temperature and timings will help slash heating and hot-water costs.

Buildings and insulation

We all need to reduce the energy required to run our homes. The more efficient our buildings are, the less capital we will have to spend on installing self-sufficient energy systems.

Making your house airtight

Reducing air loss is one of the most cost-effective ways of reducing building energy losses.

Windows, doors, and floors

Check that all windows and doors are draft-proofed with strip insulation, which is not expensive. Make sure that keyholes, openings, and cracks in outside doors are made airtight, and install door brushes at the bottom of external doors. Seal the ground-floor floorboards and also the gap between the baseboard and floor. If there is a cold cellar beneath the ground floor, fix insulation to its ceiling and make sure the cellar door is draftproofed.

BELOW Passive solar heating can be achieved by including a sun-space on a south-facing wall, reducing winter heating costs by up to 30 percent.

Open fireplaces

As much as 15 percent of the heating in a room can be lost through an open fireplace. If the fireplace is never used, the best thing you can do is seal it up. If it's used rarely, install a chimney balloon, which is made from industrial-strength plastic and blown up through a tube when it is placed in the chimney.

Coal-effect gas fires

These are extremely inefficient. They lose heat from your central heating through the chimney, even when the fire is off. Replacing one with a wood burner would prevent air loss.

Other gaps

Make sure that the loft hatch and any pipes leading to the outside are sealed. Broken air-extractors and window-trickle vents are frequent sources of air loss in existing buildings, and some older buildings from which gas fittings have been removed still have gas safety vents. Seal them off.

Do **not** seal up any safety air vents if there are gas appliances in a room. They are there to save lives if there is an undetected gas leak.

Porches

An airtight porch on both the main and rear entrance doors will provide an air lock between the outside and inside of the building. Make sure there is enough space for one door to close before the second is opened, otherwise heat will be lost. Check that both doors are draftproofed.

Insulating your home

Another cost-effective way to reduce building energy losses is to make sure the building is properly insulated.

Roof space

About 25 percent of energy is lost through the roof, so lay insulation to a depth of at least 12 inches in the roof space, including any hatches. Do not block the ventilation to the internal roof surface because it has a waterproof membrane.

There are a number of new materials that can be used. A material called Warmcel is made from fire-proofed mineralized recycled newsprint. There are also effective products made from sheep's wool and from flax, and easily installed rolls of insulation are made from recycled plastic. The payback period for installing roof insulation is usually less than two years.

Walls

It has been estimated that 50 percent of a building's heat energy can be lost through the walls. Cavity walls can be easily and cheaply insulated by contractors. This is effective and has a short payback time. In many countries you can obtain grants toward the cost of this work.

Older buildings with solid walls lose far more energy than cavity-built walls, but insulating them can be expensive and difficult, with long payback periods. You can attach an insulated shell to the external walls, although this may mean that you will lose any architectural stone or brickwork features. External insulation means that it is easier to avoid condensation problems, and you retain the positive mediating role of the thermal mass of the building that you often lose with internal wall insulation.

Internal insulation usually involves fixing battens to the walls, attaching the insulation and placing plasterboard over this. You will then have to redecorate the rooms and redo any window- and door frames, electric sockets, and lighting fixtures to fit with the new inner walls. It also means the loss of room space, which may be an issue in smaller properties.

You should consider such radical wall insulation when you are refurbishing a building, rather than it being an early item on your list of investments. Take expert advice for your particular circumstances.

Windows

About 15 percent of energy is lost through windows, and in many countries all new windows must be at least double-glazed. Replacing the windows need not be the most urgent task, if you have good-quality, airtight, single-glazed windows, as the payback period could be up to 80 years. You could simply purchase the double-glazed unit from a manufacturer and install it yourself in the existing wooden frame, which will be far cheaper. The ultimate windows use state-of-the-art triple-glazed, low-emissivity glass filled with argon gas.

New buildings

Self-sufficiency in the home should also extend to the materials you use for any new building because a significant proportion of a building's lifetime carbon emissions will be used in the building of it.

Today's self-sufficiency visionaries prefer to use a range of low-impact materials, including straw bales, reclaimed wood, and cob. There are even the so-called earth-sheltered buildings made with mud-packed waste car tires.

Even a simple detail like making sure that a house in the northern hemisphere faces south rather than east–west will reduce the amount of energy needed to heat it in winter, especially if you build a sun-space along the full south-facing front to take advantage of passive solar gain. The sun-space will not only prevent heat loss from the main building but the heat trapped during the day in winter can be circulated into the house.

It is also important to protect the house from excessive solar gain in summer by making sure that south-facing windows are overshadowed and that windows at the top of the sun-space or sun-porch can be left open during the summer months, although this may require special security installations.

Eco-glasshouses

You can eliminate the need to heat glasshouses in winter by ingeniously laying a layer of polished glass balls under the floor. You place a small fan (which might be powered by a mini solar panel) at the top of the inside of the glasshouse. This blows the rising hot air during sunny winter days down a tube to heat the glass balls beneath the floor. They release their heat during the night, almost entirely overcoming the need for extra heating.

Solar power

The power of the sun can be harnessed to provide hot water, electricity, and space heating, helping you to achieve self-sufficiency. In recent years solar panels have become less expensive and more efficient, making them a popular choice.

How it works

Solar power works in three ways:

- Solar electric or photovoltaic (PV) energy produces electricity
- Solar thermal or solar hot-water energy produces hot water
- Passive solar is the capture of the heat of the sun by south-facing glass walls during winter daylight hours for space heating (see page 267).

Solar electricity

Solar electric (PV) panels are formed of solar cells made from silicon and rare metals, and when sunlight hits the solar cells, they produce an electric current. This electricity is direct current (DC)—that is, the type used in batteries—and in order for it to be useful in most domestic environments, which are fitted with wiring designed for alternating current (AC), it needs to be converted using an inverter.

Solar electricity is most often installed with the solar cells placed on metal panels mounted on the roof. They can also be installed on trailer or houseboat roofs, fields, or just about anywhere you can mount a frame where the panels face south (in the northern hemisphere) and are not overshadowed.

Panels have halved in price in the last decade or so, and at the same time they have doubled in efficiency—that is, the amount of electricity produced for each square yard. The usual panel size for domestic installations is about 5 x 26 feet, and the installation will generally consist of between 8 and 12 panels. However, they do come in a range of sizes, right down to mini panels that can be used to power radios and mobile phones.

The capital cost of installing solar panels is large, but they are virtually maintenance free because they have few moving parts. If you are not connected to an electricity supply, you will need batteries to store the electricity produced during the day for use at night. If your wiring and household electronic equipment is designed for AC, you will need the inverter to be attached to the outgoing wiring from the battery system.

If you reduce your consumption of electricity by 75–80 percent through lifestyle changes and by installing energy-efficient electronic equipment, a 2–3 kW-rated system could provide all your net family needs over the course of a year. If you are connected to a utility company's grid, you will export far more than you consume in summer, but in winter the opposite will be true.

In sunny, cloud-free areas such as the Sahara, PV systems are, of course, far more effective, producing up to 8 kWh (kilowatt hour) per square yard each day, whereas in northern regions such systems produce about 1 kWh a day for every square yard installed. However, this is still sufficient to justify installation.

Solar electric systems are easy to integrate into any home's existing AC electrical systems.

Grid-connected solar electricity

Most homes are connected to an electricity company's supply network, so it makes sense to use the utility's grid as your battery system. In many developed countries, utility companies allow householders to export excess solar electricity produced during the day into the grid and then import it at night or when the on-site system is not producing enough. This is controlled automatically, so there is no need for messing around with switches. Many countries are following Germany's example by requiring utility companies to pay a premium for this home-produced solar electricity, which reduces the payback period for the capital investment, since your own electricity is free and you are also being paid for what you are producing.

Some schemes even pay for the electricity that you produce and consume on site, making them even more economically attractive. The system also eliminates the capital and environmental costs of battery systems, which is desirable because batteries, although nearly fully recyclable, contain a number of toxic acids.

Solar thermal or solar hot-water systems

Solar hot-water systems produce hot water when the heat of the sun hits a liquid, and they vary widely in design and sophistication. The most basic consist simply of placing water in a black plastic bag, which absorbs the sun's heat, and then suspending it outside and attaching it to a shower-head. The next option, which many DIY enthusiasts are implementing, is to pass water through an old, black-painted central heating radiator set on the roof. Modern high-tech systems involve using electric pumps and evacuated tubes.

Solar hot-water systems in hot climates generally differ from those in colder climates in that they circulate the water to be used directly through a metal and glass panel, fitted with black metal tubes, that is placed on the roof of the building. The water is usually stored on the roof and is used when necessary.

In areas that have frequent frosts, such systems can cause problems because the water might freeze and burst the pipes, and to overcome this a heat-exchange system has been developed whereby the liquid that is passed through the solar panel is treated with antifreeze. This is piped down into, and passes through, a highly insulated hot-water tank before being pumped back up through the panel on the roof again. As the antifreeze-containing metal tube passes through the solar panel, it picks up the heat from the sun, and as it then passes through the hot-water tank, it heats the water. This system requires an electric pump, which can be operated off domestic power, or you can choose

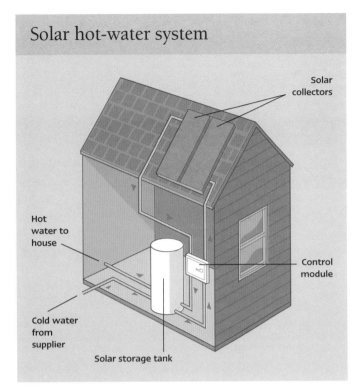

Solar hot-water system

Solar collectors

Hot water to house

Control module

Cold water from supplier

Solar storage tank

to be even more self-sufficient by having a DC pump operated by a small extra solar PV panel charging a car battery.

A properly sized solar hot-water system will supply nearly all your hot water needs between late spring and mid-autumn in northern temperate climates—that is, 60 percent over the entire year. A single 5 x 26 feet panel is plenty bi enough for most households of one or two people. Larger households will probably require a second panel.

As with any new industry, the solar water industry has attracted cowboys. Check that your installers are registered with your national solar trade standards organization and choose a company with a good maintenance record, because unlike solar electric systems, these are plumbing systems, which can break down and require maintenance.

Unlike solar electric systems, solar hot-water systems are more difficult to integrate into a home's existing system. A wide range of factors will influence your decision about the feasibility of the system and the type of backup system you will need in winter. Ask an expert to carry out a feasibility survey.

Wind turbines

There are few things more inspiring to a self-supporter than the sight of a wind turbine in full flow on a windy day. They are environmentally friendly and could help provide some of your energy needs.

Long payback, low output

For centuries, wind has provided useful energy for numerous people, from outback farmers in the US to traditional European flour mills. Large offshore and onshore commercial wind farms are already providing large amounts of energy in some countries and smaller turbines can provide useful amounts of energy for self-sufficiency pioneers as long as they are in the right location.

However, the technology is really not yet ready for small wind turbines attached to urban buildings. For example, a 400 watt turbine, producing 30 kWh in the first three years, would represent a payback period of over 2,000 years, and even though small turbines are moderately quiet and may not raise objections from the neighbors once installed, they might still create some vibration problems inside the house.

Some installers claim that low outputs are the result of the existing built-in drawbacks of grid-connected inverters, which need 3 minutes of constant electrical current before they activate.

Other suppliers say that in order to maximize wind turbine output, the roof needs to be professionally aerodynamically designed. However, many independent observers doubt that the technical problems for domestic building-attached turbines can be overcome.

The overall advice for people considering installing a small turbine at the moment is that they are just not feasible for the majority of existing homes. If your home is on the windy side of a hill or exposed to onshore winds and you have the space to erect a pole of reasonable height, wind is an option. In such cases, it really is important to make sure that you have checked your local wind speeds and possible payback time. This is crucial because it is also important to remember that many manufacturers will quote the amount of energy produced by a wind speed and at a height that may bear no relation whatsoever to your home's location.

Power Predictor

The Power Predictor, a small device that recently came on the market, collects wind speed, wind direction, and solar energy data from your site. This data can be uploaded to a website that will provide you with a full report on your location.

The report will enable you to compare your potential annual energy generation, payback times, and annual bill and CO_2 savings for the main turbines and solar panels on the market, and indicate whether it makes sense for you to go ahead. These devices must be mounted on a high pole, which the manufacturer can also supply.

You should remember that the amount of energy harvested from the wind speeds at your location is exponential to the height of the turbine. Therefore, every yard you can raise the

Relying on wind power

The factors that will affect the amount of energy your wind turbine will produce include:

- The height of the pole
- The height above sea level of the turbine location
- The size of the wind turbine

- The average wind speed at the height and location of the turbine on the pole
- The presence or absence of nearby obstructions, such as buildings or trees
- The direction of the prevailing wind at the site of the location turbine
- The efficiency of the inverter

turbine is crucial to maximizing the amount of energy that can be harvested. A 50 percent increase in pole height could give you eight times more energy.

Choosing a turbine

There are two main types of wind turbine: the horizontal axis and the vertical axis.

Horizontal-axis turbines are more effective in exposed places with high winds as long as the sites are free from local turbulence caused by nearby buildings or trees. Vertical-axis turbines have the advantage for urban situations of being less susceptible to the turbulence caused by adjacent rooftops. They will also cut in at a much lower wind speed, but they can be less effective at high speeds.

Batteries or on-grid

If you are already on the grid and live in a country where performance-based incentives are in place, it makes no sense to invest in an expensive and temperamental battery system. A feed-in tariff means that the utility company will pay you for the electricity exported to the grid from your wind turbine. This means that during windy periods, if the turbine is producing more than your household is consuming, the excess electricity is exported to the utility's grid. A normal electricity meter will measure the amount, and the utility company will pay you for it. In some countries, such as Britain, the feed-in tariff will be paid for all the energy produced by the wind turbine, even the electricity consumed on the premises. In the course of a year, such a grid-connected system will be exporting during windy periods and importing during calm periods (unless you have other renewables, such as solar and hydro, to cover windless days). You will, in effect, be using the utility's grid as a zero-cost battery store that can actually pay you substantial amounts of money, depending on the output of the turbine, so helping to cut the payback period for your investment.

Many farmers who have a good wind source on their land are already finding that wind energy is a useful source of income.

Wind cowls

Wind cowls are an alternative way of utilizing the wind's energy if you do not want to install a turbine. They are used to power zero-energy passive ventilation and heat-recovery systems. A heat-recovery system is one that uses the heat from the air being extracted from a building to heat the air being drawn into the building. Traditionally, these have been mechanically operated, and because the electrical energy being used can be up to, usually, three times more intensive than the fossil fuel heat energy being saved, the investment often makes no sense in CO_2 terms. However, using a wind cowl can replace this electrical energy and, combined with the natural stack effect, will provide effective ventilation over most of the year and so reduce heating costs in winter and cooling in summer.

BELOW Vertical-axis wind turbines are useful in urban situations as they are less susceptible to turbulence.

Hydro-power

If you are lucky enough to have access to a river or stream with a good head of water, you might be able to install a micro-hydro turbine providing a regular, steady, 24-hour-a-day supply of electricity.

Using water

The key questions to ask yourself if you are thinking of trying to derive energy from a stream on your land are: what is the hourly flow of water and what is the drop? The larger of either of these, the more energy you will be able to harvest from the water.

If, instead of a stream that can easily be diverted into a downpipe to power a hydro-turbine, you have a spring on the side of a hill, you can try to generate power by diverting the water into a reservoir and then releasing it when you need the electricity. The water from the holding tank flows downhill through a pipe, within which the turbine is situated at the bottom of the fall, and the power of the water turns the turbine and so creates the electricity.

Considerations

Regulations differ from country to country about your rights to use streams or rivers for energy extraction, so it is vital that you consult the relevant local authorities before you begin to install or use a hydro-turbine or watermill. It is also advisable to commission a feasibility study before you make any serious investment into the project.

Don't forget that you will need to provide for the safe passage of fish and wildlife if you are diverting a stream or river into your turbine.

Seasonality

Your stream may be seasonal—that is, it is likely that it will have a greater flow of water in winter than in summer because there is more rainfall—but because you are more likely to have greater energy needs in winter, this may not be a major problem for you.

Unless you are already off-grid, it is best to use the utility company's grid as your energy store instead of relying on a battery system. Remember that if batteries are overcharged, they will get damaged. Similarly, if they are left uncharged or half-charged for long periods, they will be damaged. Lithium ion batteries are more robust, but they can be quite expensive.

Results

With a reasonable year-round flow you will be able to generate substantial excess electricity, which, if you live in a country that pays a premium feed-in tariff for renewable electricity, can be a source of extra income to help pay off the initial capital costs.

Many self-sufficiency aficionados are already searching out old watermill races across Europe and installing medium-size hydro-electric turbines. These will generally not only supply in a zero carbon manner all of their heating and electricity needs but depending on the flow of water, will provide a healthy and profitable surplus to sell to the grid.

As much of the original major land and water-works may often remain in situ, this will significantly reduce initial capital costs. Also as it is likely the original builders chose an advantageous spot for water energy, it is probable that there will be an excellent year-round supply of free water-power.

Transport

The amount of cars on the road, number miles driven, and amount of fuel used continues to rise throughout the world. If you really want to be self-sufficient, therefore, transport is a crucial area.

The usual mantra of reduction first applies here, too. You must see how you can reduce your need for transport in the first place. Working from home or walking or cycling to work and the local stores will be helpful. You could also see if there is a local car club or car-sharing scheme, which might mean that you don't need your own car at all. However, many of us have jobs or live in areas where public transport or cycling will not always be practicable and a mechanically propelled vehicle will be necessary. If this is the case, make sure the car you buy is the smallest that is compatible with your needs and that its engine has the lowest CO_2 emissions in its class.

Renewable electricity and bio-fuels are the two main routes to self-sufficiency here.

Electric vehicles

If you have a surplus of renewable electricity produced by one of the methods outlined elsewhere in this chapter, you can use this to power a plug-in electric car or scooter. You can even buy electric bicycles now. Susan Roaf, the pioneer eco-house builder who taught at Oxford Brookes University, was the first person in Britain to start doing this in the early 1990s, using the electricity produced by the solar electric panels on her beautifully designed eco-house in Oxford. The range, speed, and efficiency of such electric vehicles are improving every year, and they now constitute a viable option for the regular urban commuter.

Bio-fuels

A bio-fuel is made from organic materials. Like gasoline and diesel, which are manufactured from oil, they normally also come in two main types: bio-diesel is an oil like diesel, and bio-

ethanol is an alcohol like gasoline. Bio-diesels are usually made from plant oils, such as soya or sunflower oil. Bio-ethanols are usually made from grains, such as corn or wheat.

The original diesel engine was designed to run on peanut oil, and many diesel engines will, without any adaptation, be able to take up to a 30 percent mix of straight vegetable oil and run perfectly well. However, it is always best to check with the manufacturer first.

If you want to use 100 percent vegetable oil, you will need to have the engine specially adapted, and there are now special kits on the market to do this. This is necessary because in colder temperatures the oil can congeal, causing havoc with your engine. You will need to find out from your local tax authorities if there are any taxes to be paid if you do use vegetable oil. Different countries have different tax regimes to encourage the use of bio-fuels.

It is important that you do not use palm oil, as the clearance of rainforest and peat land for this crop is leading to a massive release of greenhouse gases and the destruction of biodiversity and homes of indigenous people. It is also important to realize that ethanol varies widely in the amount of greenhouse gases its use displaces, depending on its source. Brazilian ethanol made from sugarcane is up to eight times more efficient than the equivalent produced from US corn, which has a low—if any—climate-change benefit because of the energy required to produce it and the carbon released from the soil if it is converted to produce it.

Even if you avoid palm oil, there are concerns that using food crops for transport is not a sustainable approach. However, using treated recycled vegetable oil avoids this problem.

Heat pumps

Providing heat is one of the biggest challenges for self-supporters after food and shelter. Heat pumps, a common solution in some countries, work using pressure to harvest and upgrade the passive heat in the soil, air, or water.

Ground-source heat pumps

About 3 feet under the surface of temperate soils, the temperature is a fairly constant 50°F. By pumping a liquid through pipes laid under the soil and then through the ground-source heat pump (GSHP) heat exchanger, this heat is captured and ratcheted up to the temperature required for central heating or hot water. On paper it looks like free heating from the earth. Sadly, there is a catch: electricity is needed to pump the liquid through the series of pipes laid underground.

The manufacturers claim that for each unit of electricity used to power a heat pump, you get three or four units of heat into the building. However, in practice heat pumps do not always achieve the manufacturer's performance claims. One group reported that the system they had installed was delivering only 2.3 units of heat per unit of electricity, and other users have reported even worse performances. This means that these users were actually producing more CO_2 emissions than a modern condensing gas boiler.

Warning

In temperate countries, some advertisements claim that a heat pump will dramatically lower your heating bills and carbon footprint. However, the fine print states that this is possible only when the pump is combined with underfloor heating and a green electricity tariff. This is because underfloor heating, which requires the water to be only 104°F, is significantly more efficient than radiator systems, which require the water to be at 140°F. But the gain in efficiency has nothing to do with the source of heating the water—that is, the heat pump. The reason the claim about reducing carbon footprint is true is that all electricity sourced from a reputable green tariff is zero-carbon rated, and this has nothing to do with the heat pump.

Ground-source heat pump

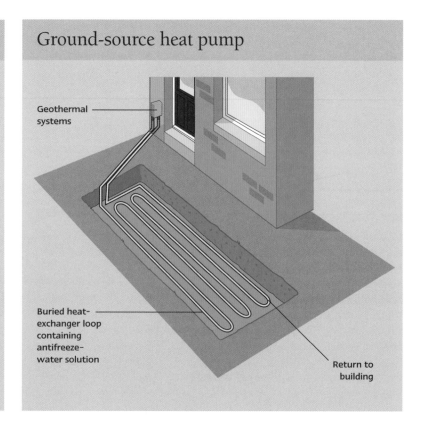

Geothermal systems

Buried heat-exchanger loop containing antifreeze-water solution

Return to building

The important factor is to determine the carbon dioxide coefficient of your country's electricity production (see right). This figure will change from year to year depending on the mix of fuels being used to produce electricity. The more coal or other fossil fuels used, the higher it will be. The more renewable energy used, such as hydro, wind or solar electricity, the lower it will be. Some Scandinavian countries already source a large proportion of their energy from renewable sources, such as hydro or wood, and they will have a lower carbon coefficient. In such countries heat pumps can play a useful role.

If you have access to a large surplus of renewable electricity from a medium-size wind turbine or a micro-hydro system, or a huge array of solar electric panels, a GSHP could make sense in terms of CO_2 emissions, but it would require an additional large capital investment. The bottom line is that in many circumstances GSHPs at present are not the perfect solution for our climate crisis or self-sufficiency.

GSHP pipe installations

There are two types of pipe installation for GSHPs. One is a large network of pipes installed parallel to the surface about 3 feet under the soil. You will need a large garden to have room for such a system.

The second type uses a bore hole drill to install the piping directly downward for about 330 feet into the ground. Although they are more expensive, they can be installed where space is limited.

Air-source heat pumps

An air-source heat pump (ASHP) works on a similar principle to a ground-source heat pump except that it pumps air from outside the building through the heat exchanger to extract and upgrade the latent heat in the air. The same issues apply to these pumps as to ground-source heat pumps. Their usefulness will depend on the carbon intensity of the electricity used to power the pump and the real—as opposed to the claimed—coefficient of performance (COP) of the heat pump. They have the added drawback that in very cold weather, when the ASHP is actually required, more electricity is needed to achieve the desired temperature.

National electricity coefficient

The national electricity coefficient is the number of grams of CO_2 released on average to produce 1 kilowatt of electricity (g per CO_2 per kWh), taking into account the mix of fuels used to produce a country's total electricity production in the last financial year. They vary from year to year as the mix of fuels changes.

Country	NEC	Country	NEC
Brazil	68	Japan	389
Canada	224	Russia	522
China	795	South Africa	890
France	57	Sweden	212
Germany	567	United Kingdom	520
Italy	509	United States	594

Water-source heat pump

The third type of heat pump uses the latent heat in the water from a lake or river, which is pumped through the heat pump's heat exchanger.

Coefficient of performance

The coefficient of performance (COP) of a heat pump is the amount of heat (expressed in kilowatts) produced from the inputted electricity (also expressed in kilowatts). For example, if a system produces 3 kilowatts of heat per kilowatt of electricity consumed, its COP is 3. Because it takes up to 3 units of fossil fuel to produce 1 unit of electricity in Britain, this means in carbon terms that if your heat pump had a COP of 3 you would only be breaking even on carbon emissions, compared with modern gas-powered condensing central-heating systems, which have efficiencies of over 92 percent.

Do not take the COP provided by the manufacturer of your heat pump at face value. The COP depends not just on the equipment provided but also on how well the system was installed, on whether the correct-size system was chosen, and on the actual temperature of the ground, air, or water at time of use. Check with other owners of such systems to see if the advertised COP has any relation to their experiences. The internet makes it possible for people to contact others in similar situations.

Ranges and stoves

Humans have used wood to provide heat and for cooking for thousands of years, but since the Industrial Revolution we have come to depend on expensive, complex, and centralized corporate systems based on oil, coal, electricity, and gas.

Burning wood

The regulations covering wood burning vary from area to area and from city to city. New high-temperature wood burners have been licensed for use in many smoke-free zones, and even in large cities such as London it's possible to heat a house from waste wood. Try contacting a local tree surgeon, who might be glad of an outlet for offcuts. If you are taking wood from building sites, make sure it is not painted or treated with chemicals. Do not use laminates or plywood, which release poisonous chemicals as they burn.

Regulations covering the installation of wood burners are designed to avoid accidental fires, and they must be placed on a fireproof surface that extends in front of the stove. Make sure you do not sacrifice your home for the sake of self-sufficiency or saving the planet.

If you do not have a sound chimney, you will need to install a smoke flue. These normally go up an existing chimney, but they can also be installed in homes without a chimney. Check local building regulations before you proceed. Even if regulations do not require it, it is best to install the cleaner, high-temperature models that reduce soot emissions.

Carbon-neutral fuel

Burning wood is an almost carbon-neutral activity as long as the wood is sourced locally. This is because the carbon released is part of the natural carbon cycle—it releases the carbon absorbed from the atmosphere during the tree's growth. When you burn coal, oil, or natural gas, you release carbon stored as fossil fuel over millions of years. As long as trees are planted to replace those cut down to provide your fuel, the amount of carbon in the atmosphere remains the same. However, it is crucial that the wood does not come from the destruction of virgin or tropical forests.

Traditional coppicing is even more positive because only the branches of the trees are cut for fuel, with the trunk providing new growth and fuel for future years. An additional advantage is that carbon is stored in the tree trunk.

Fuel for wood burners

There are three types of fuel for wood burners:

• Wood pellets
• Logs
• Wood chips

RIGHT A wood burner can provide heating, hot water, and even some cooking.

Pellets are manufactured from highly compacted sawdust, and they can be easily pumped from the delivery truck into your storage area. They provide a constant heat and do not suffer from the potential problems caused by wood chips with a high moisture content or logs that are not dry enough to burn efficiently. They are automatically fed into the wood burner. The disadvantages are that you cannot use untreated waste wood or logs, and the pellets are more expensive.

Collecting fallen wood or waste building wood for winter use can be a year-round task. If you can, set aside regular times for sawing the wood throughout the year so that you do not have to spend long periods chopping wood just as winter closes in.

Wood-burning systems

For domestic homes there are three main types of wood-burning system:

• Room wood-burning stove
• Wood-burning range
• Wood-burning central-heating boiler

Wood-burning stoves

These are available in a variety of designs, with the flue coming either out of the top of the burner or out of the back. Flat-topped stoves can be also used for boiling water, toasting bread, brewing coffee, or even cooking. Some wood burners have a chamber directly above the stove that allows some limited baking and stewing.

A disadvantage of a wood burner is that the heat rises up rather than spreads laterally, but this can be remedied by using an eco-fan placed on the flat top, using the heat of the stove by means of a thermocouple to power the fan in order to blow the rising hot air around the room.

A stove with a back-boiler can provide hot water, and larger versions will run some radiators in adjacent rooms. These will reduce the available heat in the room in which the stove is sited, so it is important to purchase a stove of the correct size. Combined with a solar hot-water system, such a back-boiler can provide year-round self-sufficient hot water. Wood-burning stoves are up to five times more efficient than open wood-burning fires.

Wood-burning ranges

The traditional large, solid-iron ranges have to be fueled by oil, gas, or coal. Because they are always on permanently, they are one of the most wasteful forms of heating and cooking you can possibly imagine—the carbon emissions can be truly staggering. These are even worse if they are electrically powered. There are, however, wood-burning versions, which can also be used for hot water and central heating.

While potentially carbon neutral, they are wasteful of biomass because they are on round the clock, and the space heating is completely wasted in summer.

Wood-burning central heating

Modern electronically controlled, automatically fed systems are now available. They can be located in a cellar, garage, or in a special shed by the house, and they will often operate using a large heat store rather than providing the heat directly into the house. They are expensive to install, but have the advantage of being automatic.

Alternative cooking stoves

There have been numerous experiments with alternative cooking stoves over the last decades, including corn-pellet stoves, biogas stoves, and ethanol and solar stoves. Replacing the petroleum product kerosene, which is used in many developing countries for cooking and lighting, with locally produced plant ethanol is a positive step forward.

There are already over 2 million biogas stoves in use in rural India. These involve placing manure into an airtight, concrete container that is then buried in the ground. The container has a single exit pipe that takes the methane produced from anaerobic digestion to a gas stove installed in the kitchen.

Solar stoves use the heat of the sun to cook food slowly in open sunshine. It is easy to make a homemade version, but there are also commercial versions, such as the HotPot, now on the market.

Storm kettle

After an open wood fire, the next simplest form of self-sufficient heat is probably a storm kettle. This is an ingenious kettle inserted into a similarly shaped metal sleeve, into which you stuff a small amount of dry twigs. When lit, it produces boiling water in a matter of minutes to make you a conscience-free cup of tea.

Sewage

The taboos that surround the topic of human waste means that applying self-sufficiency to sewage can often represent the final frontier to being a self-supporter. However, there is a lot you can do to become self-sufficient in this area.

The mains sewage system, while effective at safely removing waste from millions of homes, has serious downsides. The average US family uses about 66,000 gallons of water each year flushing the toilet, and over 5 million tons of CO_2 are released every year by waste-water systems in the US.

We cannot reduce the amount of feces we produce, so the only way of reducing sewage is to reduce the amount of water we contaminate it with. This ranges from simply not flushing your toilet after urinating to elaborate, electrically heated automatic composting toilets and the latest ultra water-efficient dual-flush toilets.

Urine

Urine is an excellent self-sufficient source of nitrates for your garden.

If you have a garden, simply use a traditional potty and throw the contents on the compost heap. Alternatively, install a modern, waterless urinal that is plumbed either into the main sewage drain or into a container from which you can throw it on your compost. Many modern composting toilets have a built-in separator that captures the urine and directs it into a container that can be emptied on the compost.

Dry composting toilets

The advantages of a dry composting toilet are:

- It eliminates water consumption for sewage—toilet flushing in temperate climates uses about one-third of a family's water consumption.
- For a home off the mains sewage grid, it provides a cost-effective alternative to an expensive septic tank, which has to be emptied by a tanker.

- It provides a free source of nitrogen-rich fertilizer.
- It overcomes the need for contaminated black water (from the toilet) to be treated off site.

If you install a dry composting toilet, you will need two separate compost-containing chambers located beneath the toilet shed, which will have two toilet seats, each connected to one chamber. The urine is directed from the front of the toilet bowl to a container. After each use, you throw a handful of sawdust onto the solid waste in the chamber and close the lid.

After a year you stop using one chamber. You open the previous year's chamber and dig out beautifully decomposed humus, which can be spread on the soil, and the chamber is then refilled. Ideally, the containers are sited on sloping land so that you can get access to the compost chambers without having to elevate the shed over the chambers.

In-house composting toilets

You could make a composting toilet yourself if you are good at DIY, but there are now several companies supplying ready-made products for in-house installations.

The two main types are long-drop and self-contained composting toilets.

Long-drop composting toilets

These toilets require a basement or a room located immediately below the toilet to hold the composting containers, which are connected by a pipe to it. The Rotaloo, for example, which is made by an Australian company, has between six and eight containers located on a turntable, which is rotated as each container fills up. By the time it has gone full circle in just over a year, the waste has composted into pathogen-free humus, ready for emptying and digging into the soil.

Self-contained composting toilets

These toilets can be installed in a bathroom and there is no need for a basement beneath. The waste is captured in a container within the toilet bowl, and the urine is captured separately. Odors are channeled outside by way of a ventilation pipe.

There are electronic and non-electronic versions. Electronic models have fans to move odors through the ventilation pipe and a heating element to speed composting. They use between 55 and 110 watts a day of electricity. Some models have a solar-powered DC system, which is ideal for off-gridders and low-carbon homes, while others can be connected to the usual AC supply. They need a minimum room temperature of about 64°F to operate effectively. The container can be lined with a compostable bag, which can be removed after about six months to compost in the garden.

Most branded composting toilets come with a self-closing mechanism that covers the waste container within the bowl, which is automatically opened when someone sits on the toilet seat.

Reed beds

Through transpiration and evaporation, a reed bed will treat gray water on site in a natural and usually odorless process. A four-bedroom house requires about 270 square feet of reed bed, plus space for the holding tank, from which sludge is removed about every three years.

The beds should be located in a sunny position so that the reeds grow well, and you will have to cut back about a third of the bed each year. The bed itself, which is usually made of reinforced concrete or sealed brick, should be about three times longer than its width.

Septic tanks

Septic tanks are often used in rural areas that are not on the sewage mains. The sewage pipe is directed into a large holding tank, which is divided into two chambers. The solids sink to the bottom, where anaerobic digestion reduces the volume, while the liquid enters the second chamber. Here it is further purified before exiting

the tank through a pipe system into an adjacent field. The tank has to be emptied by a tanker when it is full, the frequency depending on the number of people using the system and the size of the tank. Factors such as the use of grease, tampons, and cotton buds, too little water, or tree and shrub roots can block or damage the system.

The main disadvantages are that because the system uses anaerobic digestion, it releases substantial amounts of CO_2 and methane (a powerful global-warming gas), and it uses the same amount of water as a AC-connected system. In addition, it does not remove nitrates from the waste water, which can cause algal blooms if they enter nearby watercourses.

The installation and operation of septic tanks is usually subject to local regulatory controls.

BELOW Reed beds provide a natural alternative for treating gray water.

Harvesting water

Self-supporters who care about the environment as well as being self-sufficient in as many ways as possible will not only try to limit the amount of water they use but also look for their own supply.

As well as the satisfaction of using your own water, if your property has a water meter, saving water will also save you money.

There are three main ways of supplying your own water:

• Harvesting rainwater
• Recycling gray water
• Using a well or bore hole

Harvesting rainwater

The capture of rain falling on the roof or other hard surfaces on your property can be achieved in several ways, from the traditional water barrel or butt plumbed into a downpipe from the roof to highly complex rain-harvesting systems that are buried in the ground outside or below a building.

Rain barrels or rain barrels are extremely simple to install, especially if you have easily cut PVC downpipes. A simple rain diverter channels the water into the barrel when it is raining, and when the barrel is full, the rain simply flows down the pipe into the storm drain as usual.

More sophisticated systems have a large holding tank under the ground outside the building or, as happened in some 19th-century buildings, placed under the house itself as the foundations are excavated. An electric pump in the bottom of the tank pumps water into a separate system of pipes installed in the house to supply the shower, toilet, and washing machine. This water is not usually used for drinking, although ultra-violet purifying equipment can be used to make it potable. These systems are expensive to retro-fit into existing homes, but they make sense if a new property is being built.

A simpler system that relies on gravity instead of an electric pump can be used if you are using the water immediately below the tank in which the rainwater is collected, usually a bathroom or utility room. The ease and practicality of retro-installation will depend on the layout of the building and the structural strength of where you want to place the tank—a tank full of water is enormously heavy. However, even if the system supplies only most of the water for the toilet, it would, in fact, represent nearly one-third of your household's water requirements, so would be worth considering.

Before you install a gravity-fed system, bear in mind that toilets are designed to take either mains pressure or overhead-tank pressure, which is a lot less. If your toilet is a mains-fed design, it will take ages to fill if you install a header rainwater system. If, on the other hand, you have a header-tank toilet design with a rainwater tank and you then move to mains-pressure backup, it will burst the toilet within a few weeks. Ideally, you want header mains and header rainwater systems complementing each other.

The regulations covering such systems invariably require the use of a nonreversible valve to separate the mains drinking water from the rainwater to remove any risk of contaminating the mains supply.

Gray-water systems

The term gray water is used to describe the water resulting from washing processes throughout the home—from dish and clothes washing and the sink and bath. Black water is the contaminated water from the use of the toilet. Like rainwater systems, gray-water systems vary from the free and simple to the expensive and complex.

At its most basic, you can simply reuse the water from washing the dishes for another purpose—for soaking pans or watering plants, for example. Water that contains dishwashing liquid is an effective spray for aphids. Another simple method is to place a trug in the shower unit. Trugs (large, flexible, two-handled, plastic containers) make perfect containers for catching the water used in the shower, which can then be used for flushing the toilet or washing the car.

Gray-water diverters

The next step up from using a trug is to install a gray-water diverter into the used-water downpipes from the bathroom or washing machines. The water can be used for watering the lawn or washing the car. Diverters work better if the waste water is coming from an upstairs room. Do not try to store this water, which may be contaminated, but aim to use it straight away.

Automated gray-water systems

There are some sophisticated automated systems on the market, which collect all the gray water from a house and remove the human hairs and soap from it so that the water can be reused for non-drinking purposes around the house. Like the sophisticated rain-harvesting systems, these systems need storage tanks, pumps, and a separate pipe system from that used for mains drinking water.

Like any complicated plumbing system, these systems require regular maintenance, especially as the water is contaminated with hair and soap. It will also be contaminated with human bacteria, which will multiply in lukewarm water, so the system has to flush itself out automatically every three days or so. They can also consume a considerable amount of electricity.

It makes better sense to install a rainwater system than such elaborate gray-water systems unless you are in an area with low rainfall, where even gray water is precious.

Natural springs or wells

Properties in rural areas may already have a natural spring or well on the site and you should take advantage of it. The water must be tested regularly to make sure that it is not contaminated, and you must take steps to protect its purity—by keeping animals away to prevent fecal contamination, and to avoid the use of fertilizers and pesticides around the water-catchment.

LEFT If you are lucky enough to have a well on your land then you should take advantage of it.

You can pump the water into a header tank in the house by gravity, if the source is located on a hillside above the house, or by using a small electric pump.

Bore holes

If there is land attached to your property but you do not have a well or spring, it would be worth investigating if it is possible to dig a bore hole.

The capital costs of bringing in a drilling rig and lining and installing an electric pump at the bottom of the hole will be high, so this would clearly not make sense for a small family already supplied with mains water. However, such an arrangement can make good economic sense for small industries, large farms, or a larger development, especially if the mains water is metered. Where there is some decent local wind, the pump could be powered with a small wind turbine or even with a solar PV array (see page 268). Similar health precautions apply as for wells, but if the bore hole has been properly sealed and is drawing water from an aquifer rather than relying on ground water, the danger of contamination is greatly reduced.

Making your own

When you tan your own hides, dye your own fabrics, spin your own yarns, weave your own cloth, or make your own candles, you are participating in activities that have been practiced by humans for thousands of years.

The green benefits

Although it can be fun to go shopping and bring home lots of bulging carrier bags, there is great satisfaction to be derived from whiling away long winter evenings by making your own clothes, especially if you've also dyed and spun the yarn from which they are made. What's more, if you create your own designs you will know that you are making something unique. There will be no danger of seeing anyone else in the same outfit.

Instead of buying mass-produced candles, you can create your own. Rather than having to make do with what's available commercially, you have the scope to choose the exact color, scent, and shape that appeal to you. You can make candles for special occasions and as gifts. If you tan your own hides, you'll be able to use the resulting leather in a range of ways, many of which will dovetail with the other crafts in this section.

As well as having the enjoyment of working on your own projects, you will also have the satisfaction of knowing that you are saving money and helping the environment. We often hear of food miles, but there are clothing miles to consider, too, and if you make your own you will be dramatically reducing the mileage involved in their manufacture. If you spin yarn from your own animals, dye it using plants that you've grown yourself, and then either knit or weave it into an item of clothing, the clothing miles involved will be almost nonexistent.

There are other environmental advantages, too, because it's much more sustainable to reuse items that you own than to buy something new. You are recycling something and you are also avoiding the environmental and transportation costs involved in the manufacture and retailing of objects that are sold commercially. Instead of throwing out old clothes so that they end up in a landfill site, cut the fabric into strips that you can then use in weaving projects to make anything from book covers to table runners. This is an especially good way to use up favorite clothes that you're reluctant to say goodbye to. Offcuts of fabrics made from animal or vegetable fibers can be cut into small pieces and put on the compost heap where they'll rot down to provide nutrients for your vegetable plot. Hand-knitted clothes that you no longer want can be unpicked and the yarn wound into balls ready to be used for a new project. Not only will you be reducing the amount of household waste, but you will also be adding to your wardrobe at little or no cost to you and the environment.

Finding what's right for you

It's always fun to experiment, so there is plenty of enjoyment to be had in trying out some of the techniques in this section. Some, such as knitting, are easy once you get the hang of them, yet they open the door to all manner of interesting projects, from the small to the wildly ambitious. What is more, knitting requires little specialized equipment. You may already have everything at home or know someone who can lend you a pair of needles.

Some of the other techniques in this section, such as weaving and spinning, involve using specialized equipment. If you would like to experiment with a particular craft but want to be certain that you have an aptitude for it before buying the necessary items, you could enroll in a local class or workshop where you can learn the basics. You can then decide if it's a skill that you want to develop or if you would prefer to branch out in a different direction.

Taking it gently

Even though it's tempting to jump right in, you will get better results if you begin modestly and don't tackle anything beyond your capabilities. Once you've made sure that you're familiar with the techniques and feel comfortable with them, you can begin to stretch yourself. What starts as a hobby may grow to become a passion.

Financial incentives

Although you may decide to learn these crafts because they appeal to your creativity, they're a good way to save money, too. You may not even have to buy brand-new equipment if you can find a second-hand version of exactly what you want locally or on the internet. You will soon recoup your initial outlay in buying specialized equipment when you begin to make lots of items, because the cost of your projects will be much lower than anything you could buy in a store. If you discover a particular talent, you might even be able to turn it into an income by selling your projects at craft fairs, in a local store, or over the internet, or by swapping them for something that you need. What's more, you'll be able to make wonderful presents to give friends and family for Christmas and birthdays.

Many of us accumulate a treasure trove of oddments that we don't know what to do with but are reluctant to throw away. Our grandmothers often had boxes of buttons that they carefully collected over the years and used and reused when they made clothes. We can do the same, either by sewing reused buttons on the garments we make or by creating special projects that are designed to showcase the buttons themselves. All sorts of other items can be squirreled away, too, ready to be used in your projects. Ribbons, braid, wrapping paper, beads, shells, feathers, and other oddments that might otherwise be thrown away will all make your projects more decorative and more interesting.

LEFT Dyeing your own yarns and fabrics gives you an almost infinite palette of colors with which to experiment. You can also make your own natural dyes.

The naturally clean home

Before you reach for your chemical-laden products, take a few practical steps to minimize dirt and then find a few natural ingredients to keep your home sparkling.

How clean is clean?

There is an argument being made now for living in a less sterile environment, that exposing the body to low levels of bacteria results in the body developing a resistance. So perhaps the first concept to consider is how clean you want your home to be. Healthily clean or sterile clean?

The next thing to consider is how you can take a few easy steps to avoid potential dangers and minimize unnecessary dirt. For example, you should make sure you don't store raw meat on top of cooked meat so that the raw juices leak into them and that you don't put raw meat straight on a draining board, which is harder to clean than a smooth cutting board. An old-fashioned pantry, with a door that closes, will not only keep food and vegetables cool but will also mean that foodstuffs and pans or crockery will not be exposed to the cooking residues and dust in the kitchen. Remember to take off your shoes at the door so that you don't traipse mud through the house—you could have a crossover point between the muddy outside and your cleaner house, such as a porch or conservatory. A curtain of strips or beads will help to keep out flies and dust when you have the back door open.

Using nature to help

There is no need to buy air fresheners: open a window and let in the fresh air. In summer grow cut flowers, such as sweet-smelling stocks, sweet peas, and freesias, and bring them into the house to act as natural air fresheners. Put arrangements of hedgerow berries and fresh-smelling leaves and a homemade pot-pourri using cinnamon sticks and dried citrus to impart a winter freshness on your windowsills and still open the windows for a short time each day.

Elbow grease

Many chemical products make the actual job of cleaning easier by "cutting through grease" and "dissolving grime." But they still need someone to wield the cloth or scrubbing brush. So why not change to a more natural cleaner and scrub a bit harder? There are several old-fashioned agents that still work well.

Baking soda

Also known as sodium bicarbonate, baking soda is an effective and nontoxic all-rounder. It will remove stains in washing and can be used for washing dishes, cleaning a wide range of items, from aluminum to porcelain and even silver.

RIGHT Fresh flowers are nature's air fresheners—choose strong-smelling blooms such as freesias or stocks or even fresh herbs. Best of all, grow your own for the house.

Washing soda

Sodium carbonate decahydrate or washing soda is used to soak grubby washing and it also softens hard water. It's a great general cleaner all round the house because it acts on grease, but be careful to wear gloves when you use it because it can irritate the skin. It cleans and deodorizes the bathroom and kitchen and is good for really stubborn dishwashing, but not for aluminum.

Salt

Salt not only has cleaning properties but also has an abrading action as well.

Soap

A good commercial soap or a homemade version has a range of uses, from cleaning surfaces to direct application to stubborn laundry stains.

Lemon juice

Because it contains naturally occurring citric acid, lemon juice is a friend to the cleaner. It acts on grease, so is ideal for dishwashing, and it's also good for cleaning brass and copper. You can extract the juice or cut a lemon in half and use it like that. Lime juice has similar properties.

Vinegar

Vinegar contains acetic acid. It has been shown to act as a disinfectant, and, like lemon and lime juices it acts efficiently on grease. It also deodorizes. It can be used neat or diluted. White wine vinegar offers similar benefits, but is also good for carpet and fabric stains.

Tea tree oil

There are several sources of tea tree oil, but the Australian plant *Melaleuca alternifolia* is the usual one. The oil is an antibacterial and acts as a fungicide, and because you can put most forms directly on your skin, it is safe to use within the home. It will kill mold, so is great for shower and bathroom areas, and has a lovely sharp smell.

Beeswax

The basis of all the best furniture polishes, beeswax has been used in home cleaning for centuries. It can be used alone, not only for shining but protecting. If you are following a recipe in which you melt beeswax, take great care because it is highly flammable.

Herbs

Many of the herbs already growing in your garden have a place in your cleaning cabinet. They will need to be prepared by infusing. Place the freshly picked herbs in a heat-resistant glass container or bottle and pour on boiling water—the proportion of herbs to water will depend on how strong you want the infusion to be. Allow the mixture to stand uncovered and then keep in the refrigerator. Use within two weeks, including as a spray. Bay (*Laurus nobilis*), basil (*Ocimum*), sage (*Salvia*), lavender (*Lavandula*), thyme (*Thymus*), lemon balm (*Melissa officinalis*), peppermint (*Mentha x piperita*), spearmint (*M. spicata*), and rosemary (*Rosmarinus*) are some of the herbs that are antibacterial and antiseptic. Basil, lavender, peppermint, and thyme also act as disinfectants and fungicides, and as insect repellents.

Getting results

The basis of natural cleaning is to understand what you want to achieve: identifying the problem and understanding the properties of the various agents available to you.

Soaking using the appropriate natural cleaning agent and then scrubbing and rinsing will shift all but the most stubborn cleaning problems, but you have to understand whether to soak hot or cold. Very hot water will work for greasy stains, but not for things like egg and other cooking ingredients, which will simply "cook" onto the surface of the fabric, making it harder to remove. Cold or lukewarm water would then work better.

Using natural agents is a long way from simply spraying a chemical spray as an all-purpose solution, but it is not only eco-friendly but will reduce your costs, as many of the agents can be grown or produced at home.

BELOW Lemon is a very versatile cleaner—extract the juice or use the whole lemon. It's the perfect way to use up leftover half-squeezed citrus fruit from cooking.

Making candles and soap

There are many candle-making methods, some of which have been practiced for hundreds of years, but people are still developing ways to make, scent, and mold candles.

Candle making

The earliest candles were simply rushes or, to be more precise, the pith in the center of rushes, which was dipped in some kind of fat and lit at the top. They must have ranged in smell from pleasant to greasy depending on the type of fat that was used. Today we are more used to candles formed with a wick through the center of a cylinder or other shape of wax.

You will need

So that you can melt the wax safely you will need a **double boiler** (water bath) in which you have hot or boiling water in the saucepan that is in contact with the heat source, while the top saucepan stands in the water but doesn't directly touch the heat source. Make sure the upper saucepan has a thick base. You will also need candle **wicks**, which you can buy from craft shops or online, a sharp **knife** or craft knife, **scissors**, and possibly **long-nosed pliers**. A flat, heat-resistant **cutting board** and a selection of **wooden spoons** will also be useful.

You will also, of course, need **wax**. You can recycle the ends of old candles, molding the wax around new wicks or perhaps in more imaginative molds, but if you are buying wax, bear in mind that there are various types, from paraffin wax, beeswax, to soy wax. Each has a different melting and burning point, so be sure to read the instructions on the package. If you are

BELOW A double boiler or water bath is a useful piece of equipment to ensure that wax is melted easily and safely.

recycling old candles or using beeswax, make sure it does not get overheated.

Because this procedure involves heat and hot wax, you must work in an area from which children and animals have been excluded, and take care that you do not allow spots of hot wax to fall on your skin.

Basic candle making

There are two basic methods. You can roll a wick in prepared beeswax sheets (which gives a lovely smell) or you can dip the wicks.

Rolling If you are using sheets of beeswax you can prime the wick (dip it in melted wax), cut the sheets into strips, and roll them round the wick. Alternatively, you can take a sheet and warm it, usually with a hair dryer; the wax should be warm, not melted. Cut the wick to fit the short side of the sheet. Cut a narrow triangle from the longest side of the wax and roll the wick along the shorter side. This is harder than it sounds, and it may take a few attempts before you can make a tight, tidy candle.

Dipping Carefully melt the wax, stirring to avoid bubbles. Beeswax melts at a lower temperature than most other waxes. Stir in coloring if you like. You can also add fragrances at this point, but be careful because some can make the wax more flammable. Read the instructions if you are using bought fragrance and take special care if you are using any form of oil.

Prime the wick and seal it. You then need to let it cool, and the best way to do this is to fold the wick in half and hold it at the top so that you are dipping two wicks at once. This has the advantage of keeping your fingers well away from the hot wax. You can then use this wax-free loop to hang up the candle at any point in the making. Take the primed wick and dip it between 20 and 30 times. Allow the wax to cool and set before you trim the bases.

Home soap making

The basis of many soaps is sodium hydroxide ($NaOH$), also known as lye or caustic soda, mixed with water, and during the 1940s a recipe for a basic scrubbing soap featured clarified waste fat, caustic soda, water, and just a teaspoon of olive oil or what you had on hand. Hand soap was similar, but included coconut oil, glycerin and "nine pennyworth perfume oil." The ingredients reflect the chemical reaction that occurs when the fats and oils (traditionally animal fats) meet sodium hydroxide, with the addition of heat, to produce soap. It is possible to make vegetarian soaps using variations on hard vegetable fat, coco butter, olive oil, beeswax, and coconut oil.

If you keep dairy animals, you will find that milk is a great ingredient for soap. You can also include honey, and herbs from the garden, such as lavender and rosemary, will add fragrance.

You will need

Because you will be working with caustic soda, you must wear **protective clothing**, including goggles to protect your eyes from splashes and gloves. Make sure there are no children or animals around when you are working, and don't leave any hot saucepans unattended.

You will need a **thermometer** to check the temperature, which for most recipes is 80–100°F, and a **stainless steel saucepan**, large enough to allow the mixture to be stirred (do not overfill it). Caustic soda reacts with many metals and surfaces, including Teflon and aluminum, and it will cause iron saucepans to discolor. A rubber or silicone **spatula** will last longer than a wooden one, which might disintegrate. You will also need a heat-resistant glass **pitcher**, **cutting board**, and a **mold**, which can be simply a tray lined with plastic, although a wet cloth can also be used. If you are making lots of soap, you can buy special molds.

Basic soap making

There are so many recipes and variations that it is worth doing some research first to find the one that suits your ingredients, your lifestyle, and your tastes. The basic ingredients are usually 2 pounds fat to 2½–3½ ounces caustic soda and 1¾–2 cups water.

Slowly melt the fat in the pan up to a maximum of 100°F. Switch off the heat. Meanwhile, blend the water and caustic soda in a pitcher (taking great care to avoid spills) and then carefully add this mixture to the saucepan, stirring it in thoroughly. It will saponify—that is, turn into soap—gradually changing from a watery consistency to a thicker, more uniform texture. You may have to stir it at regular intervals until it is thick enough; it should hold a trace of the mixture falling from the spoon for a moment when it is ready. Pour it into blocks to harden and cut it into smaller pieces a day or so later.

The exact recipe you follow will depend on which fat or oils you choose to use—there is more available liquid in some fats, so you will need less water, for example. As with all new recipes, make a note of what you have used so that you can improve or change the formula as necessary.

BELOW Use home-grown herbs to add fragrance and decoration to your homemade soaps.

Spinning

People have been spinning threads into yarn for thousands of years, and hand-spinning is still a popular pastime. If you keep your own goats, sheep, or rabbits, you can spin their fleeces into yarn, then dye and knit or weave into clothes.

Knowing how to spin yarn will enable you to create your own clothes out of all manner of unspun fibers, so you will be wearing clothes that are unique and a demonstration of your own creativity. If you take things a step further and spin fleece that you've collected yourself, you will have the satisfaction of knowing that you have created these clothes completely from scratch, making this part of your life self-sufficient.

It takes practice to learn how to spin properly. There are two main spinning methods: **long**

BELOW Spinning fleece into yarn is immensely satisfying and is an age-old craft.

draw spinning, which uses short fibers that are carded, and the **worsted technique**, which uses long fibers that are combed. The length of the fibers is known as the staple length.

You will need

Spinning requires little specialized equipment.

Drop spindle This is a simple and inexpensive form of spinning wheel, consisting of a long shaft inserted through a wheel. It is a good option if you've never tried spinning before.

Spinning wheel This is a costly alternative. There are several types of spinning wheel operated by a foot treadle, including fly and bobbin wheels, which twist the yarn and wind it onto a bobbin at the same time, double- and single-drive wheels, or Scotch tension wheels.

Niddy-noddy You will need a niddy-noddy to wind skeins of spun wool.

Lazy Kate This is a stand on which you store bobbins, and it's helpful when you are plying yarns together.

Leader This is a length of spun yarn to which you attach the leading end of the fibers that you are working.

Comb You will need this when combing fibers before spinning with the worsted method. You can use an ordinary dog comb for this.

Carders You will need a pair of carders, which are flat or curved paddles of wood covered with wire teeth that prepare loose fibers for spinning.

Buckets You will need a couple for washing the fleeces and for finishing the spun yarn.

Detergent Fleeces must be washed before spinning. You can either use dishwashing liquid or a gentle shampoo.

Fibers

You can spin with a wide selection of fibers that are sold as "tops"—commercially prepared yarn that has been washed and combed, ready for spinning. In addition to wool, other animal hair yarns include mohair, cashmere, alpaca, camel, rabbit, and goat fibers. You can also buy silk tops.

Cotton is excellent for spinning. Short cotton fibers, called noils, are quite coarse. The longer fibers are finer and are sold as combed tops.

Other vegetable fibers suitable for spinning include soy, bamboo, flax, and ramie.

Preparing a fleece

If you rear your own sheep or have access to fleeces, you will have to prepare the fleece ready for spinning.

You will find it easiest if you divide the fleece into segments, otherwise it may become too large and unwieldy to control when it's wet. First, you must remove all soiled areas. Then separate the fleece into different qualities, keeping the worn areas away from those that are perfect. Shake the fleece well to remove any loose material.

Put the first piece of fleece in a bowl of hot, soapy water. Gently submerge it, but don't rub it. Leave the fleece to soak for a few minutes, then lift it out and put it in a bowl of clean water the same temperature as the soapy water. Continue to rinse the fleece until the water runs clear.

Put the fleece in a clean pillowcase and spin on a gentle cycle in the washing machine to remove excess water. Remove the fleece from the pillowcase and lay it flat to air-dry.

ABOVE AND RIGHT
Instead of having to be satisfied with the colorways of commercial yarns, you can spin your own combinations to create the effect you want.

Combing

If you are working with locks of wool fleece, you might want to comb them to separate the individual fibers. This gives you more control when you are working with them. Traditional combs are expensive, but an ordinary dog comb will be perfectly adequate for most purposes. Combed fibers, which are spun using the worsted technique, produce tight, durable yarns that can take a lot of wear.

1 Firmly grasp a lock of fleece near the butt (sheared) end. Place the dog comb near the tips of the fleece and comb it through. Work backward toward the butt end, then repeat until you have removed all the tangles. Turn the lock round so that you are holding the tip and repeat the process at the butt end until the fibers lie smooth. Put the short hairs caught in the comb to one side so that they can be carded for long draw spinning.

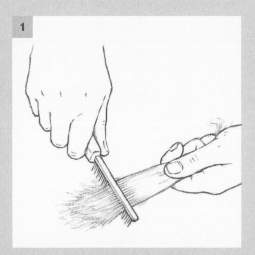

Carding

Carding enables you to turn short hairs into light, lofty yarns that are suitable for knitwear and other delicate items. Work with small amounts of wool at a time.

1 Open out the wool and place it on the wire teeth of one of your carders. Use the other carder to pull the fibers lightly across the teeth—this is called a pass. Repeat the process, then hold the empty carder against the base of its mate and catch the fibers in its teeth as you lift it up toward its handle. This will transfer the fibers to the empty carder. Repeat until the fibers are smooth and straight.

2 Now transfer the fibers to the other carder so that they sit on top of the teeth. Fold the fibers back on themselves with the wooden edge of the empty carder, then use it to push the fibers into a long roll, known as a rolag. Lift the rolag off the carder. Turn the carder over and place the rolag on its wooden back. Cover it with the wooden back of the other carder and roll it between them to create a long sausage of wool.

Using a lazy Kate

Lazy Kates are designed to store bobbins of yarn when they are not in use. Make sure that the ends of the yarns are securely fastened to prevent them tangling in the yarns you are using.

Working with a drop spindle

A simple drop spindle is extremely versatile and, despite its modest size, gives a better result for some yarns than a full-size spinning wheel.

1 Tie one end of the leader to the point where the base of the spindle shaft meets the top of the whorl. Wrap the leader several times around the base.

2 Wrap the leader around the lower end of the shaft so that it sits under the whorl, then take it back up to the top of the spindle.

3 Tie the leader to the top of the shaft with a simple knot in the notch.

4 Hold the fibers that are ready to be spun in your right hand, with the spindle in your left. Twist the spindle clockwise, then hold the leader with your right hand as it spins. Tease some fibers of yarn with your left hand and hold them against the leader. They will twist against the leader and become joined to it.

5 The rotating spindle will pull the yarn downward. Pinch this yarn between your finger and thumb to stop the twist running up into the unspun yarn. Release more fibers by pulling your right hand upward, controlling the twist with the fingers of your left hand. When the spindle reaches the floor, stop spinning. Undo the knot in the leader, release the yarn from below the whorl, and wind most of the spun yarn around the base of the shaft. Wrap the remaining yarn around the lower end of the shaft, as in steps 2 and 3. When you've finished the yarn or the spindle is full, wind the yarn onto a bobbin or into a ball. Pull the end of the yarn free of the leader.

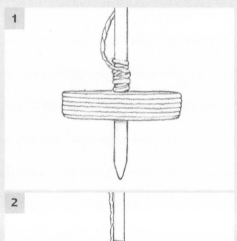

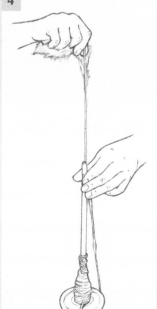

Working with a spinning wheel

It will take time to get used to working the treadle with your foot while you feed through the yarn with your hands, so keep practicing. Before you start working with the yarn, it will help if you practice operating the treadle first, to make sure that the wheel runs smoothly.

1 Twist the leader round the bobbin, through the nearest guide hook to the bobbin and through the orifice at the front of the flyer.

2 Slowly treadle the wheel. Pull a few fibers from the unspun yarn and hold them against the leader until they have twisted together.

3 Let the twist run up the fibers as they wind onto the bobbin. When you've finished spinning, release the tension from the wheel. The bobbin will now run freely. Take the yarn back through the orifice and wind it into a ball or a skein.

Long draw spinning

This technique uses rolags that are prepared by carding (see page 290). It produces light, soft yarns that are ideal for hand-knitting. You can use a drop spindle for long draw spinning or use a spinning wheel, as described here.

1 Allow the rolag to twist onto the leader. With your left finger and thumb, hold the yarn near the orifice, while keeping the rolag in your right hand. Pinch the yarn passing through your left hand, then release a short length of it and pull the rolag away from the wheel. Control the yarn with your left hand so that it has a little twist as it runs onto the bobbin.

2 Continue to pull the rolag away from the wheel, allowing some twist into the yarn, until your arm is fully extended. If the yarn needs more twist, hold it still while treadling the wheel a couple of times, then let it wind quickly onto the bobbin. Begin to draw out the next section of rolag.

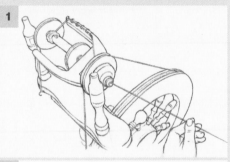

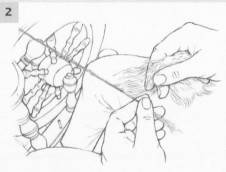

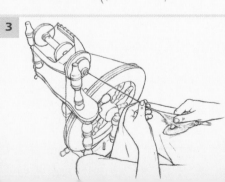

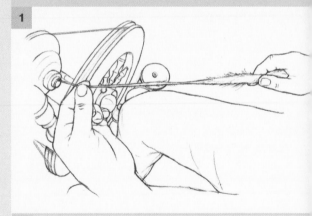

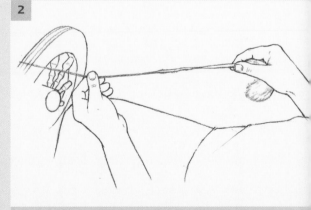

Worsted spinning

This technique creates a hard-wearing, tightly spun yarn, and it uses fibers that have been prepared by combing (see page 290). You can use a drop spindle for worsted spinning or a spinning wheel, as described here.

1 Draw out the combed fibers by hand until you have the amount needed for the width of singles yarn that you want to spin. This length of selected fibers is called a roving.

2 Prepare the rest of the fibers. Store them for safe keeping by wrapping them around your hand in a slight twist and tucking the ends inside the middle of the loose ball.

3 When you start to spin the rovings, let the first one run onto the leader. Let the twist run up into the yarn fibers.

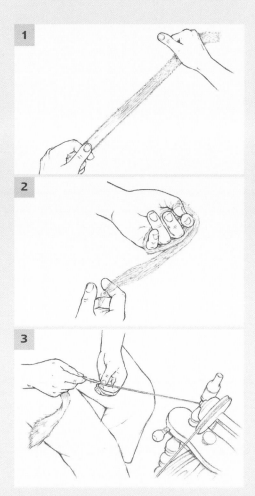

Plying

When you spin yarn on a drop spindle or spinning wheel, you will create single-ply yarn. This has a lot of twist, making it difficult to work. Plying two or more single-ply yarns will create what is known as balanced yarn, which means that it hangs down in an untwisted loop from the orifice.

Twists

There are two types of twist. A Z twist, which gets its name because the angle of twist in the yarn is Z-shaped, is created by turning the spinning wheel in a clockwise direction. An S twist, so named because the angle of twist is S-shaped, is created by turning the spinning wheel in a counterclockwise direction. These twists are important if you want to ply two single yarns together.

Two-ply yarn

Spin two bobbins of Z singles yarn and place them on the lazy Kate. Put a new bobbin on the spinning wheel, ready to spin the two single yarns together using a leader.

1 Turn the spinning wheel in a counterclockwise direction while holding the two Z singles yarns parallel to each other.

2 Let the twist run down the two singles so that they twist around each other. Let the two-ply yarn run onto the bobbin.

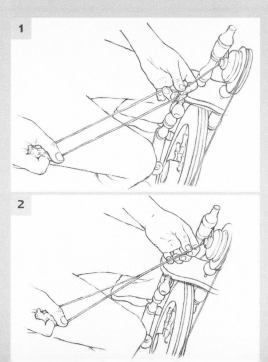

Dyeing

Dyeing fabric and yarn at home is a highly creative activity. You can make the dyes from plants that you've grown yourself, such as onions (for yellows and oranges), rhubarb (yellows and coppers), or red cabbage (greens and mauves).

Any yarn from an animal or vegetable source is suitable for dyeing, although the most commonly dyed fabrics are made from wool, cotton, and silk. Silk absorbs color more quickly than wool, which absorbs it more quickly than cotton. As well as dyeing clothes that you already own, you can also dye lengths of fabric and skeins of yarn before transforming them into garments. In addition, you can dye unspun wool.

No two batches of fabrics and fibers will take up dye in exactly the same way, so always make sure that you dye enough material for a project in one batch to avoid inconsistencies in the shades you produce.

You will need

Many household items can be turned into dyeing equipment. However, dyes can be toxic, so you must keep the equipment you use for dyeing well away from everything else. It is also imperative that you only use this equipment for dyeing.

BELOW You need a large bowl for soaking and rinsing yarns. You will also need something to stir the yarn in the bowl, an old knitting needle is ideal.

Dye bath A large, clean aluminum or stainless steel saucepan is ideal. It will be extremely heavy when it's full of water and fabric, so make sure it's easy to carry.

Large bowl Try to find as large a bowl as possible.

Stirrer You will need a chrome knitting needle or a steel rod to stir the contents of your dyeing pan.

Tongs These are essential when you are moving wet fabric and yarns in and out of hot liquids.

Set of scales Choose an accurate set of scales so that you can weigh out the different dyes and mordants that you'll be using.

Glass jars You'll need a collection of clean glass jars in which to dissolve the ingredients before you add them to the dye baths.

Heat source Although you could use an ordinary stove to heat the dyes, you may prefer to use a separate, portable heat source, such as a camping stove or an electric ring.

Dust mask This is essential to make sure that you don't inhale powdered dyes and mordants.

Protective clothing Dyes do exactly what their name implies, so it's a wise precaution to wear plastic gloves, a waterproof apron, and old clothes when you are dyeing. You might also want to use plastic sheeting to protect the surfaces and floor where you're working.

Other possible equipment Depending on the dyeing process you're using, you may also need:

• Thermometer
• Sieve
• Jelly bags or coffee filters
• Measuring cups
• Color-run remover

Cleaning the raw material

All the yarn and fabric you intend to dye must be completely clean because grease and dirt will interfere with the dyeing process. Even if you are using brand-new commercial fabric or yarn, you must remove its dressing before you begin.

Whether you're washing cotton, wool, or silk, try to handle it as little as possible to avoid damaging the fibers. Use hand-hot washing water and use the same temperature for the rinsing water to avoid shrinkage and other problems. Be prepared to rinse the fabric or yarn several times to remove all traces of soap. When you've finished, you can either leave the raw material to dry naturally or you can move on to the next stage in the dyeing process and apply a mordant.

Mordants

Mordants are minerals that ensure that the chemicals in the dye bind with the fabric or yarn and prevent it from fading. They include copper (copper sulfate), iron (ferrous sulfate), chrome (potassium dichromate), alum (potassium aluminum sulfate), and tin (stannous chloride). Sometimes you have to add what are known as assistants—extra ingredients such as cream of tartar, vinegar, washing soda, and tannic acid—when you use particular mordants on specific types of fabric. Each combination of mordant and an assistant will create a different shade. Alum works particularly well with animal fibers, giving clear, bright colors when the dyes are applied.

Mordants are always applied to wet fabric and yarn, otherwise the takeup of the chemicals will be patchy and give an uneven result. After use, dispose of the mordants on waste ground, away from pets and watercourses.

Using mordants with cotton

Cotton absorbs dyes best when mordanted with tannic acid, alum, and washing soda. Before you dye it, steep the wet cotton in a solution of water and tannic acid for 24 hours. Rinse the cotton several times in clear water to remove all trace of the tannic acid.

Put the alum and washing soda in a glass jar and add boiling water. Stir until dissolved, then stir into a pan of hot water. Add the wet, clean cotton and soak for 24 hours. Remove and rinse thoroughly in cool water. You can either leave the cotton to dry or you can immediately move on to the dyeing stage (see right).

Using mordants with wool

Wool and other animal fibers work with alum. You don't need to add an assistant if you use chrome or iron. Soak the wool in warm water.

Place the mordant in a glass jar and dissolve it in a little boiling water. Fill the dye bath with warm water, then pour in the mordanted water and stir well.

Submerge the soaked wool in the water. Bring the water to a simmer and simmer for 1 hour, stirring occasionally. Turn off the heat and leave the wool to steep in the mordant overnight. Remove the wool and rinse thoroughly in clean water the same temperature as the mordanted water. When the wool is clean, you can either allow it to dry or move on to the dyeing stage (see below).

Using mordants with silk

Silk is an animal fiber, so you use the same mordants as you do for wool. However, alum gives the best results. Be careful when using iron because too much of it will weaken the fibers. Soak the silk in warm water. Place the mordant in a glass jar and dissolve it in a little boiling water. Fill the dye bath with warm water, then pour in the mordanted water and stir well.

Submerge the soaked silk in the water. Bring the water to a gentle simmer and immediately remove from the heat. Allow to steep overnight. Remove the silk and rinse thoroughly in clean water that's the same temperature as the mordanted water. When the silk is clean, either leave it to dry or move on to the dyeing stage.

Using dyes

Always make sure that the fabric or yarn you want to dye is thoroughly wet. You can never get exactly the same results twice, so always dye everything that you need for a project in one batch. You don't need to separate yarn and fabric that has been treated with different mordants.

When you are using commercial dyes, always follow the instructions. If you're using natural, plant-based dyes that you've prepared yourself, the weight of the dye must at least equal that of whatever you will be dyeing.

ABOVE An ordinary stainless steel or aluminum saucepan makes an excellent dye bath, but it can't be used again for cooking because many dyes are toxic.

Hot-water dyeing

This is the most suitable method for wool and cotton. Be careful when you are simmering the water that it doesn't boil, because this will cause felting of the yarn or fabric that you're dyeing. When you've dyed your first batch, you can reuse the liquid in the dye bath, although you'll get a paler color each time you do this. If the material to be dyed isn't still wet from being mordanted, you must soak it in water before dyeing it.

1 Chop up the plant material and put it in the dye bath. Cover it with boiling water. If you are using powdered concentrated extract, tip it into a glass jar, mix to a paste with a little warm water, and pour this into the water in the dye bath. Bring to a simmer and allow to simmer for 1 hour. Top up with extra water if necessary.

2 Remove the dye pan from the heat and let steep for another hour. Strain or filter the liquid into a clean bowl. Pour the strained liquid back into the dye pan and add the wet mordanted fabric or yarn. If necessary, add a little warm water to make sure that the fabric or yarn is completely submerged. Stir well.

3 Place the dye bath on the heat and bring to a simmer, then simmer for 1 hour. Remove from the heat and allow to cool. Remove the yarn or fabric as soon as it's reached the desired color. Rinse thoroughly in water that's the same temperature as that of the dye bath. Squeeze out the excess water and hang up to dry.

Cool-water dyeing

This is the method to use for dyeing silk, as hot water will spoil its natural sheen and create wrinkles in the fabric that are difficult to remove. If the material to be dyed isn't still wet from being mordanted, you must soak it in water before dyeing it.

1 Chop up the plant material and put it in the dye bath. Cover it with boiling water. If you are using powdered concentrated extract, tip it into a glass jar, mix to a paste with a little warm water, and pour this into the water in the dye bath. Bring to a simmer and allow to simmer for 1 hour. Top up with extra water if necessary.

2 Remove the dye pan from the heat and let steep for another hour. Strain or filter the liquid into a clean bowl. Pour the strained liquid back into the dye bath.

3 Add the wet mordanted fabric. If necessary, add a little warm water to make sure that the fabric is completely submerged, and stir well. Place the dye bath on the heat and bring to just below simmering point. Immediately remove from the heat and allow to cool. Remove the fabric as soon as it's attained the desired color. Rinse in water of the same temperature as that of the dye bath. Squeeze out the excess water and hang up to dry.

Vat dyeing

This is the method for dyeing with indigo because it produces good, clear blues. Washing soda acts as the assistant. Take care not to let the water get too hot or the dyeing process won't work. As always, the depth of color will vary according to the length of time the fabric or yarn is left in the dye bath, but bear in mind that exposure to the air will deepen the color of the wet fabric or yarn.

1 Put the indigo powder in a glass measuring cup and slowly add a trickle of warm water, stirring all the time, until it forms a paste. Stir in about 1 cup warm water. Place some washing soda in a glass jar and dissolve it in a small amount of boiling water. Fill the dye bath with clean water, add the dissolved washing soda, and heat to 122°F. Stir in the indigo dye liquid. Remove from the heat and allow to stand for 30 minutes. Return the dye bath to the heat until the liquid once again

reaches 122°F. Remove from the heat and sprinkle on some color-run remover, but don't stir it in. Let stand for 40 minutes.

2 Submerge the fabric or yarn in the dye bath and allow to stand until it becomes the desired color. Soaking it for 20 minutes will give a dark shade of blue. Don't stir it because getting air into the dye will eventually destroy its dyeing properties. Carefully remove the dyed material without letting any drips fall back into the dye bath, as these will aerate the dye.

3 The blue of the fabric or yarn will deepen as soon as it's removed from the dye bath. Allow it to dry in the air, then rinse thoroughly in clean water. Wash it, rinse it again, and hang up to dry.

Keeping note

Whenever you use dyes it's a good idea to write down the exact ingredients and method so that you can either use them in the same combination again or alter them for a different effect.

Weaving

Weaving is an ancient method of creating fabric from interlocking threads that run at right angles to each other. You can make anything from quite small projects to large pieces of fabric, depending on the size of the loom you use.

BELOW This is a rigid heddle loom; a simple, portable loom that will produce a wide variety of projects, from the simple to the more complicated.

You can make a simple loom yourself, on which you can create small pieces of weaving, or you can invest in a manufactured loom that will last for years and give you much greater scope, not only in the size of the projects you are able to produce but also their complexity.

If you know someone who owns a loom, you could ask them to show you how to weave. Alternatively, you might be able to attend weaving classes or a workshop so that you can find out if you have a talent for weaving before spending a lot of money on the equipment.

Looms

Choose a loom that will be suitable for the type of weaving you enjoy and for your level of skill. If you buy a loom that is too complicated to use for your first attempts at weaving, you may quickly be deterred from continuing with it.

If you fall in love with weaving, you will want to buy a proper loom, such as a rigid heddle. Before that happens, you might like to experiment with a loom that you make yourself from cardboard or from a few wooden pegs.

Rigid heddle loom

This is a versatile, wooden-framed loom, which will produce everything from tightly woven fabrics to those that are much looser. It is a good starting point because it will teach you all the techniques you need if you eventually graduate to a much larger and more expensive loom. You can use it to make a good range of items, from scarves and clothing fabric to cushion covers, shawls, and throws, depending on its size.

The heddle is the vertical device in the middle of the loom that raises and lowers alternate strands of the warp threads so that a shuttle of yarn can be passed through the space, known as the shed, between them. It contains the reed through which the warp yarns are threaded.

Heddles are available in different sizes and are graded according to the number of dents (warp spacings) per inch.

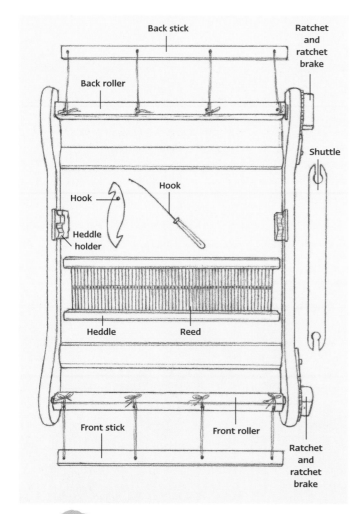

Back stick

Ratchet and ratchet brake

Back roller

Shuttle

Hook

Hook

Heddle holder

Heddle

Reed

Front stick

Front roller

Ratchet and ratchet brake

Table loom

This is a small loom. It is suitable for small pieces of weaving and also for beginners.

Floor loom

This is a larger and faster loom than a table loom and provides much more scope for projects, including rugs. Some types of floor loom can be folded away when not in use.

You will need

Some of the equipment you need for weaving must be bought specially for the purpose, but you might be able to improvise other items from articles that you already own.

Warping board or posts If you intend to weave long pieces of fabric with a rigid heddle loom, table loom, or floor loom, you will need either a warping board or warping posts around which you can wind the warp threads before securing them to the front and back rollers of the loom. Some types of loom incorporate a warping board or post so that you won't have to buy one.

Shuttle The shuttle holds the yarn that forms the weft threads. You will need one shuttle for each yarn when you are working with more than one color in a single piece.

Threading hook You will find a threading hook useful when you are working with thin yarns because it will help you thread them through the reed's holes in a rigid heddle loom.

Sheets of newspaper You should wrap sheets of newspaper around the back roller when you are weaving long lengths of fabric on a rigid heddle loom.

Yarn

Weaving gives you enormous scope when you are choosing the yarns you want to work with. For a truly self-sufficient project, you can weave yarns that you've dyed and spun yourself. Alternatively, you can buy many different yarns made from animal and vegetable sources, as well as synthetic yarns, including acrylic and nylon.

Choose yarns that are suitable for the project you have in mind, not only in terms of the feel of the finished article but their elasticity and whether they are easy to wash. Yarns from animal sources, such as wool, alpaca, cashmere, and mohair, are soft and warm, have good elasticity but require careful washing. Silk is beautiful, but not very elastic. Yarns from vegetable sources, such as cotton and hemp, are cool and durable and are easily cared for. There is also a range of fancy yarns to add extra interest to your weaving.

The thickness of the yarn will determine the size of the heddle you will need when you are using a rigid loom and will, therefore, dictate the finish and texture of the woven item. Thin yarn will create cloth with a good drape, whereas thick yarn will make chunky fabrics.

Don't be afraid to experiment. In addition to using conventional yarns, whether they're from animal, vegetable, or synthetic sources, you can also weave with many other items. Instead of throwing away old dresses or shirts, you can recycle them by cutting them into long, narrow strips and incorporating them in your weaving. Old T-shirts, socks, and colored tights can be given the same treatment. If you have a collection of beautiful ribbons but don't know what to do with them, try weaving them into a special piece of fabric. Bright craft cottons and raffia add color and texture, but your options don't stop there. Get into the habit of saving interesting wrapping papers, gift ribbons, shiny metallic candy wrappers, strips of colored cellophane, colored string, and even colored plastic bags, all of which can feature in your weaving.

BELOW This plain cushion was made with cotten, linen, and silk yarns, while the multicolored cushion was made from a mixture of chunky natural wool and a rainbow-colored sheep's fleece.

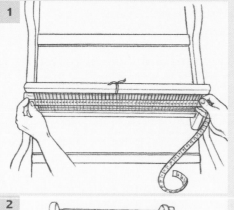

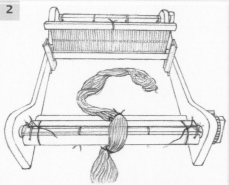

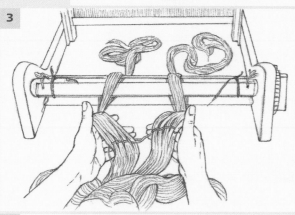

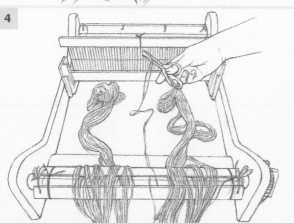

Setting up the loom

There are four distinct processes when setting up the rigid heddle loom: threading the heddle (steps 1–5), tying the warp to the back stick (step 6), winding onto the back roller (steps 7–10), and tying the warp onto the front stick.

Threading up

1 Make sure the warp is spread evenly across the heddle by finding the center point of the heddle using a measuring tape. Mark this point with a strand of thread in a different color.

2 Tie the cross-sticks to both ends of the front roller with a strand of yarn—this will keep the warp secure while you thread up. Make sure the warp chain is supported on the table.

3 Using the counting thread as a guide, find the center of your warp and part it from the counting thread through to the end of the unchained section of your warp.

4 Keeping the center of your warp clearly visible, spread the warp ends along the cross-sticks across the width of the loom. Each pair of warp ends should be visible. Then, working from the center outward, take each pair of warp ends in order and cut the loop to make two separate warp ends.

5 Working from the center of the heddle outward, use your threading hook to thread the warp through the holes and slots of the reed. Take each warp end from the cross-sticks in consecutive order, the over thread, then the under thread. All over threads go through the holes and all under

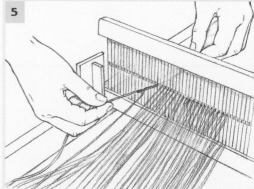

threads go through the slots. To create a balanced plain weave, each slot and hole should be used. Finish with a pair of warp ends in the last hole or slot, to help form a firm edge (selvage). Repeat the process across the other half of the heddle, working from the center to the edge of the loom.

Tying to the back stick

6 Now tie the warp ends to the back stick. Starting at the center of the warp and working outward, divide the ends into small bunches of 6, 8, or 10 threads. Wrap each bunch of ends around the back stick, then as you bring the threads up, split them into two groups on either side of the warp and tie them in a double knot over the top of the warp ends. Once all the ends are tied to the back stick, turn the ratchet until the back stick sits on top of the back roller.

Winding onto the back roller

7 Before you begin to wind the warp onto the back roller, untie the cross-sticks from the front roller and remove them from the warp. Take a piece of newspaper and make sure it is wider than the width of the warp but not as wide as the loom. Slip the edge of the newspaper under the back roller, then up between the back roller and the warp ends.

8 Now start to wind the warp onto the back roller by turning the ratchet. Undo the warp chain, removing any ties and the counting thread as you go, making sure that the warp remains smooth and untangled. Roll the newspaper on at the same time, adding a new piece as required.

9 As you wind on, smooth the warp ends from the front of the heddle with your other hand. Every few turns, check that there is no snagging in the heddle and the tension is even.

10 Carry on winding until most of the warp is on the back roller, leaving approximately 15 inches at the front of the heddle to tie securely to the front stick.

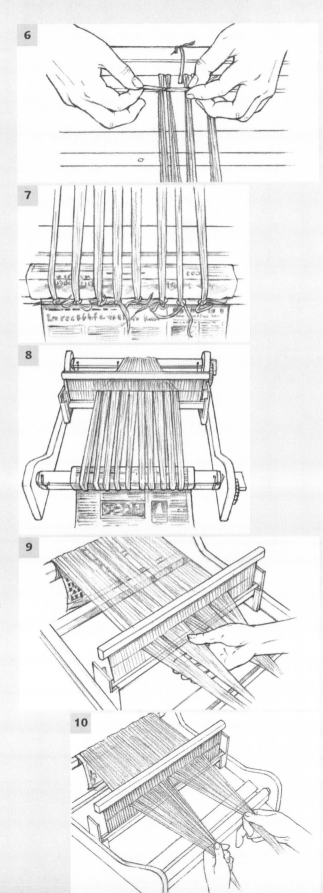

Tying to the front stick

11 Next, tie the warp ends to the front stick. Working from the center of the warp, take bunches of 6–10 warp ends and take them over and around the front stick.

12 Begin to knot the bunches to the front stick as you did on the back stick, but use a single knot only. Work from side to side to maintain an even tension.

13 When all the threads have been tied, return to the center knot and begin again. Check each bunch, retightening by lifting and pulling the knot toward the heddle to take up any slack. Then secure with a double knot. Test for even tension by gently patting the warp ends with the palm of your hand.

Plain weaving

Once you have learned the basic plain weaving technique, you can go on to add embellishments and patterns to your projects. As you become more experienced, you will find the separate stages of plain weaving become one continuous movement and your weaving will get much quicker. When you start off your weaving project, the first thing you do is to make the header out of a thick yarn in a contrasting color. The header is also woven using plain weaving.

1 Wind the weft evenly around your shuttle. Avoid overloading it as the shuttle must pass easily through the shed—the space created when you raise and lower the heddle. If you want to experiment with different weft yarn combinations, you will need to wind a separate shuttle for each weft.

2 Take the heddle out of the heddle shafts (rest position) and lower it into the down position to create a shed between the warp ends. As you lower the heddle, the warp ends threaded through

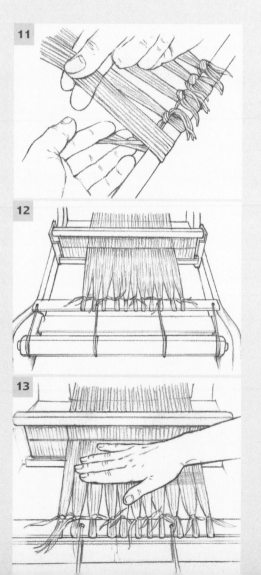

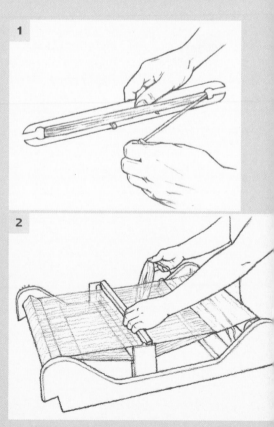

the slots in the reed will move up to the top of the heddle. Slide the shuttle through to the other side, leaving the loose end to be trimmed later.

3 Ensure you don't pull the weft too tight by making an arc shape with your weft yarn before pulling the shuttle gently out on the other side.

4 Put the shuttle down, hold the weft with both hands, and pull it toward you. Check that the edges (selvages) are even and not pulling in or forming straggly loops.

5 Remove the heddle from its resting position, holding it from the top with one hand at either end. Bring it toward you and push the weft evenly into place. Now repeat steps 2–5 with the heddle raised in the up position. The warp ends threaded through the slots in the reed will now move down to the bottom of the heddle.

6 Continue with steps 2–5 until you no longer have a wide enough shed to pass the shuttle through.

To wind on, put the heddle in the rest position and release the ratchet brakes. Turn the ratchet brake on the front roller and roll on the woven fabric until its edge is 2 inches from the front roller. Secure both ratchet brakes and adjust the tension, which should be firm. When the weft yarn runs out, wind the shuttle as before (see step 1 opposite). Join in the new weft thread and continue weaving.

7 Continue weaving and rolling on until all the warp has been used. When you have finished weaving, place the heddle in the rest position and release the ratchet brakes on the front and back rollers. Cut the warp off the back stick and pull the warp ends through the heddle. Unroll your weaving from the front roller and cut the warp from the front stick. Remove the header one row at a time. You can now secure the raw edges with a sewing machine stitch sewn alongside the first and last rows of weaving.

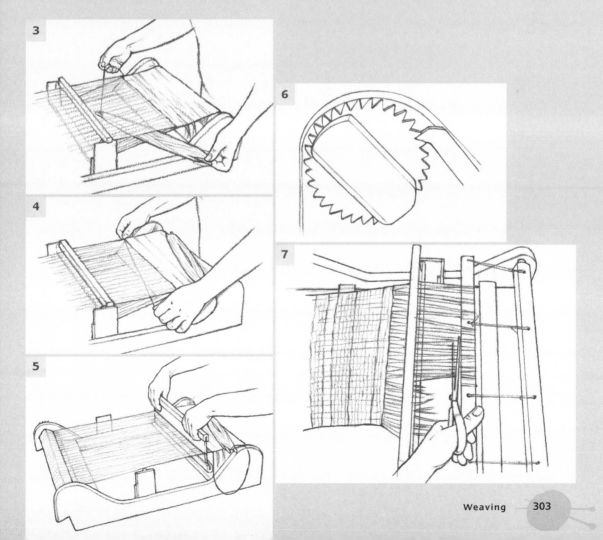

Working with a peg loom

This is a simple form of loom, consisting of a row of removable wooden pegs, each with a hole at the base, that sit in a flat strip of wood.

1 Clamp the loom to your working surface. Calculate the finished length of the piece you intend to make, then make each warp end at least twice this length, plus a little extra for finishing. Cut one warp end for each peg. Working on each peg in turn, lift it out of the base and thread a warp end through the threading hole, then pull this through until each end is the same length. Arrange the warp ends on the working surface and loosely tie the ends into small bundles. Prepare the weft yarn by winding it into balls.

2 With a ball of weft yarn and beginning with the furthest peg on the left, start to weave it in and out of each peg. Wind it around the first peg a

couple of times to secure it. When you reach the end of the row of pegs, take it round the end peg and start weaving from right to left. Keep the tension even by pressing down firmly on the weft, but avoid making it too tight.

3 Continue until the rows of weft have almost reached the top of the pegs. Pull the center peg out of its hole, then ease the weaving off the peg and on to the warp end. Repeat with every peg.

4 Replace each peg in its hole, with the top edge of the weaving near the base of the pegs. Continue to weave the weft yarn through the pegs until they are nearly full again, then repeat step 3. Work like this until your weaving has covered all the warp threads. Repeat step 3 again so that the weaving has been pushed onto the warp.

5 Beginning at the center, pull the peg out of its hole and pull through enough of the warp to be able to tie the two ends in a knot. Don't knot it at this stage. Cut the warp close to the peg. Repeat with the next peg, then tie the four ends together in a knot close to the end of the weaving. Continue like this, tying ends together in bunches of four. When you've finished, pull up the warp ends equally from each end of the completed work and push the weaving into the center of the warp. Finish each end of the warp neatly.

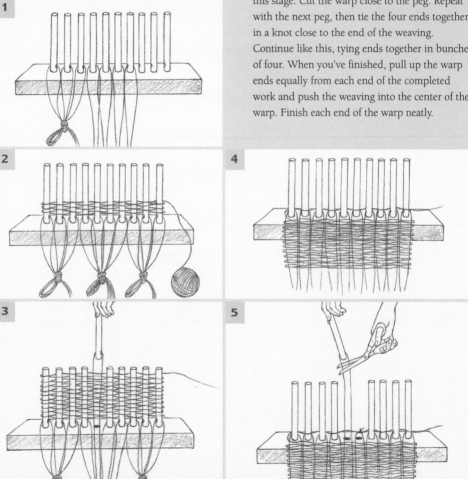

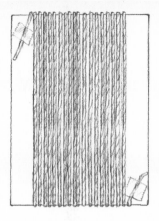

1

2

Working with a card loom

It's simple to make a card loom yourself: all you need is a large sheet of stiff cardboard. The weaving will be slightly smaller than the sheet of card, which makes it ideal for small items such as placemats, book covers, and bookmarks. This is a good method when you are working with unusual weft threads, such as fancy yarns, strips of fabric, and strips of plastic bags.

1 Choose the right size of card for the project you want to work. Beginning at one edge of the card, wind a continuous warp thread around the back and front of the card. Keep the spacing even and the tension fairly firm. Tape the two ends of the warp thread to the back of the card.

2 You can either weave the weft threads through the warp with your fingers or with a blunt, large-eyed wool needle. Each time you finish a row, push the weft down with your fingers. When you've finished your weaving, turn over the card and cut across the center of the warp threads. Knot the warp ends neatly. You can either trim the ends or keep them as fringing.

Weaving techniques

A few techniques will help you to improve your weaving results.

Selvages

Selvages are the two side edges of the weaving. You need to keep these edges neat, without letting any of the weft protrude in loops. You must also avoid pulling the weft too tightly, which will make the selvages pucker.

Combining threads at the selvage

If you want to weave with more than one weft thread, you must carry the thread not being used up the side of the selvage. To avoid long threads that will look ugly, you must interlock the spare weft with the one you're using by twisting them around each other. As always, keep the selvages straight by making sure that they are neither too tight nor too loose.

Introducing a new weft thread

The best way to join the new weft thread with the old one is to overlap them by at least 2 inches. Push them down with your fingers so that they lie smoothly. They will be held in place by the rows of weaving either side of them and won't be noticeable in the finished work.

Finishing off the warp

You can give your weaving some attractive finishing touches, according to the style of the weaving and what you want to do with the end result.

Overhand knots

Divide the warp fringing at each end of the weaving into groups of two or three strands. Tie each group in an overhand knot and pull it gently up to the edge of the weaving.

Braids

Divide the warp fringing into groups of three strands. Braid them by bringing each outside strand over the central one in a continuous sequence. Finish with an overhand knot.

Tip

Don't expect perfect weaving at your first attempt. In order to achieve the best results, practice until you develop a regular, smooth rhythm.

Knitting

Hand-knitting is one of the simplest yarn-based crafts and one of the most versatile. If you're working with yarn that you've spun yourself, you will be able to create knits designed to complement the color, texture, and quality of your wool.

Knitted clothes and blankets have been keeping us warm for hundreds of years. The techniques described here are for hand-knitting. Knitting with a machine is a more complicated process. Hand-knitting is a skill that's easy to learn, and it will provide hours of pleasure and relaxation as well as useful or decorative finished products.

Getting started

Most knitters begin with simple projects, such as scarves, so that they can learn the basics of holding the knitting needles, controlling the yarn, keeping the edges straight, coping with dropped stitches, and other techniques. Once you know what you're doing, you can branch out into more complicated projects.

You will need
The basic hand-knitting equipment required is simple and inexpensive.

Knitting needles These come in three styles. Single-ended needles are sold in pairs and are used for most general projects. Double-ended needles, which are sold in fours, are used for more intricate work such as socks, but also when making cable patterns. Circular needles are double-ended with a long nylon middle. They are used for wide pieces of knitting as well as seamless garments. All are sold in specific sizes.

Spare needles These look rather like enormous safety pins and are used to hold stitches that will be knitted later, such as when making pockets.

Row counter If you are unsure of your ability to count the number of rows you are working, you can attach a row counter to one of your needles.

Safety pins These are useful when you need to isolate small numbers of stitches.

Tape measure This is essential for measuring your knitting.

Tapestry needles You will need these to sew the seams when you make up your knitting.

Yarn
Knitting yarn consists of sheep's wool or some other natural fiber, such as angora or goats' wool, cotton, man-made fibers, or a mixture of these. It is sold by weight, either in ready-wound balls or as long skeins that you must wind into balls yourself. In addition to using wool that you have

spun yourself, you can either buy your yarn from a commercial source or unpick old hand-knitted garments and reuse their yarn. Many knitters accumulate half-used balls of yarn that can be knitted into projects that lend themselves to a variety of colors, thicknesses, and types of yarn.

Knitting yarn is graded according to its weight. The thinnest yarn is extremely fine and is generally worked with thin needles to create delicate, subtle work, while the thickest is extremely chunky and is worked with fat needles so that the stitches stand out.

Patterns

When you're an accomplished knitter you might enjoy creating your own designs, but at first you will find it easier to follow a knitting pattern. You can buy these singly or in collections printed in books and magazines. Many local libraries stock good selections of knitting books, offering a wide range of patterns. In addition, you will find many free patterns on the internet. Rummage sales and charity shops may also yield collections of knitting patterns. Another option is to join a knitting group so that you can share both your patterns and your expertise.

Whenever you follow a pattern, you must knit a sample piece first so that you can check the tension of your knitting—that is, knitting a given number of stitches, both vertically and horizontally, within a set measurement—in case it is too tight or too loose. If you don't check the tension, you might create something that's too small or too big.

Special effects

You can combine knit and purl stitches in different ways to create a variety of effects.

Ribbing

Ribbing is used to create an elastic edge at the top or bottom of the piece you are knitting. It is usually knitted with needles that are one or two sizes smaller than those used for the main body of the knitting. Single ribbing consists of alternate knit and purl stitches, usually knitted on an even number of stitches that always start with a knit stitch and end with a purl. Double ribbing alternates two knit and two purl stitches, and treble ribbing alternates three knit and three purl stitches.

Moss stitch

Moss stitch creates raised stitches that are particularly attractive for welts, cuffs, pocket flaps, collars, scarves, and cushions. When it takes the place of ribbing, it is knitted with needles that are one or two sizes smaller than those used for the main body of the knitting. Moss stitch consists of alternate knit and purl stitches, usually knitted on an odd number of stitches that start with a knit stitch. It differs from ribbing because you work a knit stitch on top of what was a purl stitch in the previous row, and a purl stitch on top of what was previously a knit stitch.

Stocking stitch

Stocking (stockinette) stitch is one of the most popular knitting techniques, often used for socks, jackets, and sweaters. It consists of alternate rows of knit and purl stitches. When viewed from the front (the knit side), it has a smooth surface. When viewed from the back (the purl side), it has an interesting, ridged surface. Some patterns use the purl side as the front, when it's called reversed stocking stitch.

Garter stitch

Garter stitch is a good technique for beginners because it consists entirely of rows of knit stitches. It has a similar appearance to reversed stocking stitch, but the rows are further apart. It's particularly effective for scarves, children's clothes and toys, and simple blankets.

Shaping

You can shape your knitting by increasing or decreasing the number of stitches you are working, whether at the start or end of a row or in the middle of it.

Decreasing

To narrow the outline of your knitting, knit two stitches together at the beginning and/or the end of a row, for as many rows as necessary. Decreasing on alternate rows gives a more gradual narrowing than decreasing on every row.

Increasing

To widen the outline of your knitting, you knit twice into one stitch, known as increasing a stitch, at the beginning and/or the end of a row, for as many rows as necessary.

Casting on

A piece of knitting must have a neat start, otherwise it will have an uneven lower edge and you might find it difficult to knit the first row. When you are working, try to keep the knitting as even and tidy as possible.

1 Creating the foundation row is called casting on. This method uses one needle and creates a neat edge. Pull out a long length of yarn with the end on the left. It should be at least twice the length of the finished width of knitting. Always keep this piece of yarn on your left.

2 Make a loop with your left thumb and hook the long end of the yarn through it with the needle, which you hold in your right hand. Pull the yarn firm but not taut. This is the first stitch.

3 Hook the long length of yarn round your left thumb and insert the needle through the right-hand side of the loop. With your right hand, bring the wool round the back of the needle and drop the left-hand loop over the back of the needle. Pull the yarn firm. This is the second stitch.

4 Continue until you have cast on the required number of stitches. Turn the needle round so its end is pointing to the right, ready to start the next row. You will now need the second needle.

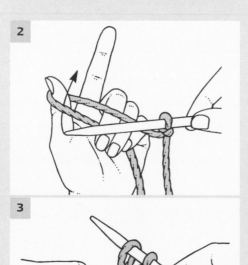

Knit stitch

Most knitting is based on combinations of just two basic stitches: the knit stitch and the purl stitch. Once you have mastered these two stitches, you can work many different stitch patterns.

1 Hold the needle with the stitches to be knitted in the left hand with the yarn behind.

2 Insert the right-hand needle into a stitch from front to back. Take the yarn over it, forming a loop.

3 Bring the needle and the new loop to the front of the work, and slide the original stitch off the left-hand needle.

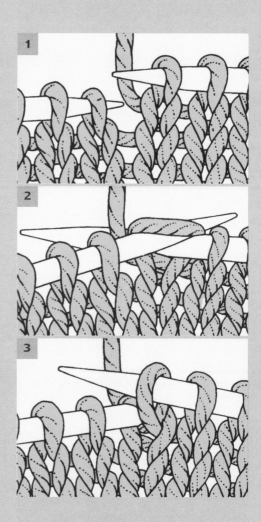

Purl stitch

Begin by casting on about 25 or 30 stitches, using a double-knitting yarn in a light color, preferably all wool or a wool mix for its resilience. Make sure you have practiced the knit stitch until you can work it fairly smoothly. Now move on to the purl stitch.

1 Hold the stitches to be purled in the left hand, with the yarn at the front of the work.

2 Insert the right-hand needle through the front of the stitch, from back to front. Take the yarn over and under, forming a loop.

3 Take the needle and the new loop through to the back; slide the stitch off the left-hand needle.

Casting off

Finishing your knitting tidily is as important as giving it a neat start. The process is called casting off. Always keep to the designated pattern when you are casting off, especially when you are working ribbing or moss stitch, otherwise you will spoil the effect.

1 Work the first two stitches as usual, then hook the left-hand needle into the front of the first stitch on the right-hand needle.

2 Slip the first stitch over the second. Now work another stitch and slip the second stitch on the right-hand needle over the third. Continue in this way until you've cast off the designated number of stitches. When you are finishing off the piece completely, cast off until you reach the final stitch. Work this stitch, turn your knitting and work it again, then cut the yarn and pull it through the loop of the stitch to fasten it.

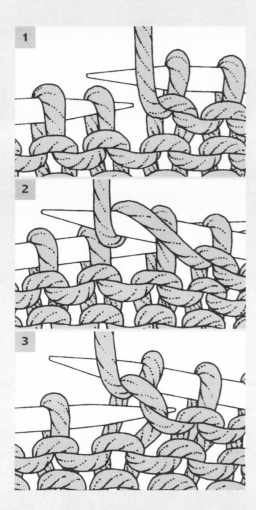

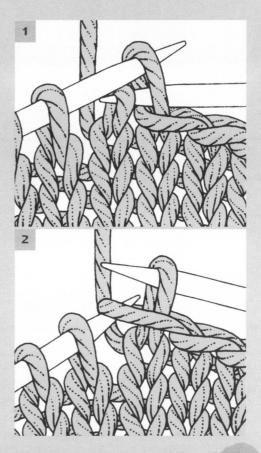

Tanning

Tanning animal skins produces a wide range of products, from leather to hides with the hair on, such as sheep skins, or small animal hides, such as rabbit skins. The idea behind tanning is to keep the skin supple.

Most self-sufficient households who are interested in tanning will probably want to finish some of their sheep skins for cosy mats, especially if the sheep breed has a very beautiful colored or patterned fleece.

If you have to skin an animal, bear in mind that it is easier to do this while it is still warm from slaughter rather than when rigor mortis has set in. It's more likely, however, that you will send your animal away to be slaughtered and that the hide will be removed at the slaughterhouse. Often, if you want to get your hide back from the slaughterhouse, you need to agree this with the slaughterhouse before you send the animal. Don't assume that the sheep or goat skins will automatically return with the meat.

Rawhide and buckskin

There are several tanning methods, but the most usual are rawhide and buckskin. They are the tanning methods most used by indigenous people because they don't require any inputs except tools and a lot of work. Rawhide normally leaves the leather quite stiff, unless it's wet. Buckskin is traditionally produced by continuously pulling and stretching the fibers while they dry, and finally smoking them.

Tanning uses chemicals, including the "tannin" in the name, which often originated from oak trees. This still lingers on in the phrase seen on high-quality leather—oak-bark tanned.

Salting

Rawhide and buckskin hides are not salted because the curing process for these skins needs to start soon after slaughter.

For many people, the most practical thing is to send the skins to a tannery to be finished into

sheep or goat skins because it is a complicated process. Because skins start to rot almost from the moment of skinning, they must be preserved by curing, and you need to do two things. First, you must make sure that you have plenty of fine salt (not granular), which you can buy in large sacks from agricultural merchants. You will, in any case, need the salt even if you are not going to be able to start the tanning process immediately. Second, you must get the skins back from the slaughterhouse within a few hours of slaughter.

You will need a clean, flat surface that can be hosed down. Alternatively, cover the area with clean paper or a plastic sheet. Lay out the skin, fleece down, and inspect it. The skin should be white. It should not smell putrid, and there should definitely be no maggots. If you notice any maggots, the skin has probably gone too far to be tanned. If it is in good condition, use a sharp knife to trim it, removing any blood-stained edges.

Apply salt liberally over the skin, making sure that all the surface area is covered right up to the edges. You shouldn't be able to see the skin through the salt. You may see water puddles forming. If this happens, shake the skin to remove any water and resalt. Leave the skin in a covered place, making sure that it can't come into contact with metal, or it will cause staining rust.

The idea is to get the salt to penetrate into the skin, which won't happen if the skin is hung up vertically or laid in sunlight. The salt must be in contact with the skin at all times until it is cured.

When the skin feels firm but flexible, it is cured. Carefully fold the skin, sides to the center and roll it tightly from the head end down. Don't do this if the skin feels wet, because it will deteriorate in travel. If you have done it properly, the skin will keep like this for weeks until you can attend to it yourself or until you can get it to the tannery.

If you are sending skins to a tannery, make sure that you have made the arrangements before you send the animal for slaughter. Label each skin with the breed, age, date of slaughter and curing, and any other information needs. Make sure that the skins are well packed for transport.

Tanning

There are several ways to tan your own sheep or goat skins. The process involves a certain amount of trial and error, so for your first attempt, do as much research as possible and don't try to do too much. If there is a fleece that is particularly precious to you, either send it away to be tanned or attempt something less special first.

First, soak the skin in cold water to get rid of the blood. Then wash it in a mild detergent to break down the grease. Deflesh the skin by taking a sharp knife—you can buy fleshing knives—and dragging it across the skin until all the flesh is removed. Take care that you do not cut into the skin. Defleshing a medium-size skin is likely to take a relatively fit person an hour or more.

Next, soak the skin. There are various solutions you can use, and it's best to get advice from your local tanning supplier about the ones that are best for your type of skin. They all include dangerous chemicals, so be careful when you are using them. Read the instructions carefully, especially about concentrations and timing, but most involve soaking the skin in the solution for several days.

Then, wash the skin again in a mild detergent and rinse it thoroughly in cold water. You need to dry it now. Some people prefer to dry skins while they are semi-flat, but others hang them to dry. The argument against hanging a skin is that it dries out too quickly, which can make it less flexible. Opinions also differ over when to apply oil to dress the skin. Some people like to oil the skin when the excess water has been removed, but others wait until after drying. Neat's-foot oil, which is made from the boiled feet of cows, is usually used. You will need to apply a few coats of oil and then continue to work the skin to keep it flexible, hanging it over a bar and pulling it backward and forward. Continue to rub in oil and pull the skin about until it is flexible. This can take several days.

The method for producing rawhide is similar, except that you omit the chemical tanning. Dry the stretched skin in a shady area, then apply oil while you work the hide.

If you have access to a supply of oak leaves or oak chippings, you can also try mixing these with tea leaves (strain the mixture) or tea bags plus vinegar and water. Simmer these together and then apply the mixture to smaller skins, such as rabbit. The mixture contains tannin, but take care that you do not stain white fur.

LEFT Skins can be dried flat but many people prefer to hang them out. Do be careful that they don't dry out too quickly.

Index

Page numbers in *italic* refer to the illustrations

samphire, marsh 197
sandy soils 32, 65
sauerkraut 221
sausages 248–9, *249*
savory 127
saws 80
scallions 104
scarecrows *48*, 51
sciarid fly 89
sea fish 201
seakale 114
seashore, wild food 193
seasons, working with 39
seaweed 67, 77
seedlings: hardening off 72–3
   pricking out 72
   thinning 73
   transplanting 73, *73*
seeds: reseeding grassland 34
   saving 84–5
   sowing 70–2, *70–2*, 129
self-sufficiency: first steps 28–31
   full-time vs part-time 22–3
   micro-self-sufficiency 17
   preparing for 14–15
   preparing plot 64–5
   reasons for becoming 10–11
   what is self-sufficiency 12–13
septic tanks 279
sewage 278–9
shade 40
shaggy ink caps 198
shallots 104–5
sheep 168–71, *168–70*
   boundaries 46
   breeding 170–1, 186–7
   breeds 168–9
   butchery 244, *245*
   clearing ground 64
   feeding 170
   fencing 169–70
   health 171
   part-time work and 23
   rare breeds 184, 185, *185*
   shearing 171
   shelters 40, 43, 170
   tanning hides 310–11
sheep netting 45, 46, 169
shellfish 201
shelters 43
shooting 51, 200–1
shredders 79
shrubs, wild food 196–7

silage 34–5
silk 289, 294, 295
silty soil 65
silver leaf 91
skills 31
skinning animals 310
slaughter 15, 242–3
   chickens 141
   geese 145
   pigs 163
   rabbits 159
slaughterhouses 163, 243
sloe gin 258
slugs 89, 93
small farms 25
small gardens 18, 56–61
smallholdings 22, 23–4, 28–31, 36, 37
smoking meat 246, 247, *247*
snails 89, 93
soap 285, 287
soft fruit 82, 83, *83*
soil 32–3
   compaction 33, 56
   container gardening 57, 58
   digging 65
   drainage 33
   fertility 34
   grassland 32
   ground-source heat pumps 274–5, *274*
   improving 66–7
   mulching 78–9
   pH values 65, 66
   preparing plot 64–5
   preparing seedbeds 72, *72*
   productivity 32–3
   raised beds 56
   soil management 33
   types of 32, 65
solar power 38, *39*, 268–9, *268–9*
soot, improving soil 67
sowing seeds 70–2, *70–2*, 129
spades 65
spinach 101
spinach beet 100, *100*
spinning 288–93, *290–3*
spinning wheels 292, *292–3*
springs 281
sprinklers 76
squashes 85, 107
stables 179
staking: fruit trees 82

vegetables 82–3, *82*
Steiner, Rudolf 55
Stilton knot *240*
stinging nettles 197
stings, bees 154
stock-proof boundaries 44–5
stocking rates, on grassland 34
stone walls 46, *46*
storage 40–1, 204–5
storm kettles 277
stoves 276–7
strawberries 73, *73*, 119
   wild strawberries 197, *197*
streams 46, *47*, 272
stress, intensive farming 13
sugar 214, 227
supporting plants 82–3, *82*
swarming, bees 155–6
sweet peas 83
sweet potatoes 101–2, *101*
Swiss chard 84, 101

T

tanning leather 310–11, *311*
tarragon 124
tea tree oil 285
temperature, heating houses 265
tethering goats 166
thinning seedlings 73
thistles 34
threshing wheat 129
thyme 127
time constraints 14, 132–3
toads 93
toilets 278–9, 280
tomatoes 102, *102*
   container gardening 59, 60, *61*
   green tomato chutney 217
   saving seeds 85
   supports 82, 83
tools *see* equipment
topping grassland 34
traceability, food 36
training fruit trees 81, *81*
transplanting seedlings 73, *73*
transport 43, 273
tree loppers 80
trees: wild food 196–7
   wildlife in *48*, 49
   woodland 36–8
   see also fruit
trout *191*, 201

Acknowledgments

The author would like to send thanks to *Smallholder Magazine*, past and present, the Donkey Sanctuary, Miriam Parker, Christine Westrop, the Federation of City Farms and Gardens, Joan Lee Smith for her inspirational account of country life, and Bessie the Jersey cow from the USA. Thanks go to Jessica Cowie, Ruth Wiseall, and Sandra Rigby of Gaia for their patience and encouragement.

Executive Editor Jessica Cowie and Sandra Rigby
Editor Ruth Wiseall
Deputy Creative Director Karen Sawyer
Designer Sally Bond
Illustrator kja-artists.com
Production Controller Linda Parry
Picture Researcher Giulia Hetherington

Picture credits

Key: a above; b below; c center; l left; r right